Macworld Guide To
(First

■ "Contains a very visual, right-brain approach to learning System 7, so most Mac-o-philes will find it very intuitive."

— *California Computer News*

■ "The Mac Bible is the Old Testament — this book is the new Testament!"

— Leonard H. Pinaud, System 7 User
Needham, MA

■ "This probably could be an example of how all Apple manuals should be written — thanks!"

— Robert Peloquin, Mac fanatic
Portland, ME

■ "Everything about System 7 is covered including one of the most detailed explanations of publish and subscribe and networking...."

— Cheryl Kirk *Anchorage Daily News*,
Anchorage, Alaska

■ "Clear, well organized, easy reference."

— Bill Bogusky
Maimi, Florida

■ "Well organized and painless transition for System 6 users."

— Shing Chi Poon
Taipei, Taiwan

■ "Even better than the book supplied with my System 7 upgrade from Apple."

— Paul B. Elwell
San Antonio, Texas

■ "All computer books should be as well written as this one is."

— Steven Fink
Farmington Hills, Mississippi

■ "Seems clearer than the other three books I have seen on the topic."

— Stefan Andrew
Menlo Park, California

■ "Starting out the book discussing the trendy 3-D graphics was reason alone to buy this over similar books. Grayscale photos were excellent also."

— Kevin Crossman
Mountain View, California

■ "Balanced — easy to understand — very complete."

— Dan A. Townsend
Memphis, Tennessee

■ "Every chapter was worth reading."

> — Matthew T. Miles
> Sacramento, California

■ "Outstanding book — goes far beyond Apple's own System 7 manuals."

> — Karl F. Kontyko
> East Amherst, New York

■ "Cut through the techno-talk and got me up and going — fast. Thanks!"

> — Charlie Moger
> Houston, Texas

■ "The only book which even mentioned the four fonts installed in the system."

> — Jeffrey Norwood
> Chico, California

■ "Just when I thought System 7 was just another system, this book shows me I bought more than I thought I had paid for."

> — Andrew Pepper
> Northridge, California

About *Macworld Guide To...* Books

Macworld Guide To System 7.1, 2nd Edition is part of the *Macworld Guide To* . . . series of books, brought to you by IDG, the leading publisher of computer information worldwide. This is a new kind of book designed to meet your growing need to quickly find what you want to do and learn how to do it.

These books work the way you do: They focus on accomplishing specific tasks — not learning random functions. *Macworld Guide To* . . . books are not long-winded tomes, manuals, or even quick reference guides, but are the result of drawing from the best elements of these three types of publications.

The designers of the *Macworld Guide To* . . . series use the following visual elements to make it easy to find the information you need:

Troubleshooting sections provide workaround solutions to possible traps and pifalls you may encounter while using System 7.

Undocumented icons include any concept or idea not found in Apple's documentation for System 7 users.

Quick Tip sections include tips and insights contained on the material in each chapter which enable you to get the most out of your application or operating system no matter what level user you are.

The authors of the *Macworld Guide To* . . . books are leading Macworld columnists, technology champions, and Mac gurus, who are uniquely qualified to provide you with expert advice and insightful tips and techniques not found anywhere else. We're sure you'll agree that the *Macworld Guide To* . . . approach is the best.

— David Solomon
Vice President and Publisher

MACWORLD
GUIDE TO
SYSTEM 7.1 2nd Edition

MACWORLD
GUIDE TO
SYSTEM 7.1 2nd Edition

By Lon Poole
Macworld "Quick Tips" columnist

Foreword by Jerry Borrell
President, Sumeria and former Editor-in-Chief, *Macworld* magazine

IDG Books Worldwide, Inc.
An International Data Group Company

CALIFORNIA ♦ INDIANA ♦ MASSACHUSETTS

Macworld Guide To System 7.1, 2nd Edition

Published by
IDG Books Worldwide, Inc.
An International Data Group Company
155 Bovet Road, Suite 610
San Mateo, CA 94402
(415) 312-0650

Copyright © 1993 by IDG Books Worldwide, Inc. All rights reserved. No part of this book, including interior design, cover design, and icons, may be reproduced or transmitted in any form, by any means (electronic, photocopying, recording, or otherwise) without the prior written permission of the publisher.

Library of Congress Catalog Card No.: 92-74303

ISBN 1-878058-65-7

Printed in the United States of America

10 9 8 7 6 5 4 3 2 1

Distributed in the United States by IDG Books Worldwide, Inc.

Distributed in Canada by Macmillan of Canada, a Division of Canada Publishing Corporation; by Woodslane Pty. Ltd. in Australia and New Zealand; and by Computer Bookshops in the U.K. and Ireland.

For information on translations and availability in other countries, contact Marc Jeffrey Mikulich, Foreign Rights Manager, at IDG Books Worldwide. Fax: (415) 358-1260.

For sales inquiries and special prices for bulk quantities, write to the address above or call IDG Books Worldwide at (415) 312-0650.

Trademarks: Apple is a registered trademark of Apple Computer, Inc. All other brand names and product names used in this book are trademarks, registered trademarks, or trade names of their respective holders. IDG Books Worldwide and Macworld are not associated with Apple or any other product or vendor mentioned in this book. Macworld is a registered trademark of IDG Communications, Inc.

Limits of Liability/Disclaimer of Warranty: The author and publisher of this book have used their best efforts in preparing this book IDG Books Worldwide, Inc., International Data Group, Inc., Macworld Communications, Inc., and the author make no representation or warranties with respect to the accuracy or completeness of the contents of this book, and specifically disclaim any implied warranties or merchantability or fitness for any particular purpose, and shall in no event be liable for any loss of profit or any other commercial damage, including but not limited to special, incidental, consequential, or other damages.

Acknowledgments

At the top of my list of people to thank is my wife. Thanks, Karin, for enduring my slavish attention to scribbling again and yet again. You'll always be number one in my book.

David Angell and Brent Heslop untied me from the log that was hurtling toward the spinning saw blade by stepping in at the last minute to research and write the initial draft of chapters 6, 8, and 9. They deserve credit for those three chapters, and I most gratefully acknowledge their contribution.

Rita Lewis took a bare idea, pored through many disks from BMUG and BCS•Mac, and came up with Chapter 13 for the second edition in record time. She also wrote the installation instructions in Appendix C. I greatly appreciate her assistance.

Dorothy Aylward wore her fingers to the bone dialing software publishers to update Appendix A with the latest compatibility information. Many thanks for a lot of hard work.

Finally, I must thank Jeremy Judson for suffering good-naturedly through the tribulations of the second edition. If you want to know how touchy telecommunications can get, ask Jeremy about all the ways you can't send files by modem from Mexico (where I prepared the second edition). Thanks, Jeremy, for not getting all over me like a preying mantis.

(The publisher would like to give special thanks to Patrick J. McGovern, without whom this book would not have been possible.)

About IDG Books Worldwide

Welcome to the world of IDG Books Worldwide.

IDG Books Worldwide, Inc., is a division of International Data Group (IDG), the world's largest publisher of computer-related information and the leading global provider of information services on information technology. IDG publishes over 185 computer publications in 60 countries. Thirty million people read one or more IDG publications each month.

If you use personal computers, IDG Books is committed to publishing quality books that meet your needs. We rely on our extensive network of publications, including such leading periodicals as *Macworld, InfoWorld, PC World, Computerworld, Publish, Network World,* and *SunWorld,* to help us make informed and timely decisions in creating useful computer books that meet your needs.

Every IDG book strives to bring extra value and skill-building instruction to the reader. Our books are written by experts, with the backing of IDG periodicals, and with careful thought devoted to issues such as audience, interior design, use of icons, and illustrations. Our editorial staff is a careful mix of high-tech journalists and experienced book people. Our close contact with the makers of computer products helps ensure accuracy and thorough coverage. Our heavy use of personal computers at every step in production means we can deliver books in the most timely manner.

We are delivering books of high quality at competitive prices on topics customers want. At IDG, we believe in quality, and we have been delivering quality for over 25 years. You'll find no better book on a subject than an IDG book.

John Kilcullen
President and C.E.O.
IDG Books Worldwide, Inc.

IDG Books Worldwide, Inc. is a division of International Data Group. The officers are Patrick J. McGovern, Founder and Board Chairman; Walter Boyd, President; Robert A. Farmer, Vice Chairman. International Data Group's publications include: **ARGENTINA's** Computerworld Argentina, InfoWorld Argentina; **ASIA's** Computerworld Hong Kong, PC World Hong Kong, Computerworld Southeast Asia, PC World Singapore, Computerworld Malaysia, PC World Malaysia; **AUSTRALIA's** Computerworld Australia, Australian PC World, Australian Macworld; **AUSTRIA's** Computerwelt Oesterreich, PC Test; **BRAZIL's** DataNews, Mundo IBM, Mundo Unix, PC World, Publish; **BULGARIA's** Computerworld Bulgaria, Ediworld, PC World Express; **CANADA's** ComputerData, Direct Access, Graduate Computerworld, InfoCanada, Network World Canada; **CHILE's** Computerworld, Informatica; **COLUMBIA's** Computerworld Columbia; **CZECHOSLOVAKIA's** Computerworld Czechoslovakia, PC World Czechoslovakia; **DENMARK's** CAD/CAM WORLD, Communications World, Computerworld Danmark, Computerworld Focus, Computerworld Uddannelse, LAN World, Lotus World, Macintosh Produktkatalog, Macworld Danmark, PC World Danmark, PC World Produktguide, Windows World; **EQUADOR's** PC World; **EGYPT's** PC World Middle East; **FINLAND's** Mikro PC, Tietoviikko, Tietoverkko; **FRANCE's** Distributique, GOLDEN MAC, InfoPC, Languages & Systems, Le Guide du Monde Informatique, Le Monde Informatique, Telecoms & Reseaux; **GERMANY's** Computerwoche, Computerwoche Focus, Computerwoche Extra, Computerwoche Karriere, edv aspekte, Information Management, Macwelt, Netzwelt, PC Welt, PC Woche, Publish, Unit; **HUNGARY's** Computerworld SZT, PC World; **INDIA's** Computers & Communications; **ISRAEL's** Computerworld Israel, PC World Israel; **ITALY's** Computerworld Italia, Lotus Magazine, Macworld Italia, Networking Italia, PC World Italia; **JAPAN's** Computerworld Japan, Macworld Japan, SunWorld Japan; **KOREA's** Computerworld Korea, Macworld Korea, PC World Korea; **MEXICO's** Compu Edicion, Compu Manufactura, Computacion/Punto de Venta, Computerworld Mexico, MacWorld, Mundo Unix, PC World, Windows; **THE NETHERLANDS'** Computer! Totaal, LAN Magazine, Lotus World, MacWorld Magazine; **NEW ZEALAND's** Computerworld New Zealand, New Zealand PC World; **NIGERIA's** PC World Africa; **NORWAY's** Computerworld Norge, C/world, Lotusworld Norge, Macworld Norge, Networld, PC World Ekspress, PC World Norge, PC World's Product Guide, Publish World, Student Guiden, Unix World, Windowsworld, IDG Direct Response; **PERU's** PC World; **PEOPLES REPUBLIC OF CHINA's** China Computerworld, PC World China, Electronics International; **IDG HIGH TECH** Newproductworld, Consumer Electronics New Product World; **PHILLIPPINES'** Computerworld, PC World; **POLAND's** Computerworld Poland, PC World/Komputer; **ROMANIA's** InfoClub Magazine; **RUSSIA's** Computerworld-Moscow, Networks, PC World; **SOUTH AFRICA's** Computing S.A.; **SPAIN's** Amiga World, Autoedicion, Communicaciones World, Computerworld Espana, Macworld Espana, Network World, PC World Espana, Publish, Sunworld; **SWEDEN's** Attack, CAD/CAM World, ComputerSweden, Corporate Computing, Lokala Natverk/LAN, Lotus World, MAC&PC, Macworld, Mikrodatorn, PC World, Publishing & Design (CAP), Datalngenjoren, Maxi Data, Windows World; **SWITZERLAND's** Computerworld Schweiz, Corporate Computing, Macworld Schweiz, PC & Workstation; **TAIWAN's** Computerworld Taiwan, Global Computer Express, PC World Taiwan; **THAILAND's** Thai Computerworld; **TURKEY's** Computerworld Monitor, Macworld Turkiye, PC World Turkiye; **UNITED KINGDOM's** Lotus Magazine, Macworld, Sunworld; **UNITED STATES'** AmigaWorld, Cable in the Classroom, CIO, Computerworld, DOS Resource Guide, Electronic News, Federal Computer Week, GamePro, inCider/A+, IDG Books, InfoWorld, InfoWorld Direct, Macworld, Multimedia World, Network World, NeXTWORLD, PC Games, PC World, PC Letter, Publish, RUN, SunWorld, SWATPro; **VENEZUELA's** Computerworld Venezuela, MicroComputerworld Venezuela; **YUGOSLAVIA's** Moj Mikro.

 The text in this book is printed on recycled paper.

About the Author

Lon Poole, a *Macworld* magazine contributing editor, answers readers' questions every month in his column "Quick Tips." He also writes feature articles regularly, including "Installing Memory," which won a 1988 Maggie award for Best How-To Article in a Consumer Publication. His feature article "Here Comes System 7" was a finalist in the 1990 Excellence in Technology Communications competition. He helped found *Macworld* in 1983, and every issue ever published has carried at least one of his columns and articles.

In addition, Lon Poole has authored four other Mac books. He also wrote the now-classic *Apple II User's Guide,* which sold over half a million copies worldwide. He has been writing books about personal computers and their practical applications since 1976 and has a BA in Computer Science from the University of California, Berkeley.

Credits

President and C.E.O.
John J. Kilcullen

Vice President and Publisher
David Solomon

Managing Editor
Mary Bednarek

Acquisitions Editor
Terrie Lynn Solomon

Project Editor
Jeremy Judson

Technical Reviewer
Dennis Cohen

Production Director
Lana J. Olson

Editorial Assistant
Megg Bonar

Text Preparation
Mary Ann Cordova
Dana Bryant Sadoff

Proofreader
Shirley Coe

Indexer
Anne Leach

Book Design and Production
Peppy White
Francette M. Ytsma
(University Graphics, Palo Alto, California)

Contents at a Glance

Introduction 1

PART I

Quick Start 5

Chapter 1: The Essence of System 7 7

PART II

System 7 in Detail 53

Chapter 2: The New Look 55
Chapter 3: Finder Improvements 81
Chapter 4: Organized at Last 115
Chapter 5: Tailored to Fit 131
Chapter 6: Fast Access with Aliases 161
Chapter 7: Smooth Text Everywhere 173
Chapter 8: File Sharing for the Rest of Us 189
Chapter 9: Creating Living Documents 217
Chapter 10: QuickTime 229
Chapter 11: Advanced Capabilities 243

PART III

Customizing System 7 255

Chapter 12: Tips and Secrets 257
Chapter 13: Utilities and Enhancements 289

PART IV

Appendixes 309

Appendix A: Product Compatibility Table 311
Appendix B: Glossary 339
Appendix C: Moving To System7 347
Index 361

Table of Contents

Acknowledgments xi

Contents at a Glance xx

Foreword xxxi

Introduction 1

PART I Quick Start 7

Chapter 1: The Essence of System 7 7

Color Windows 8
Color Icons 9
Custom Icons 10
Editing Icon Names 11
Aliases 11
    Making an alias 12
    Using aliases 12
Outlining Folder Structure 13
Custom Views 14
Item Labels 15
    Using labels 15
    Changing label names and colors 17
Smart Finder Windows 17
Fast File Finding 18
Directory Dialog Improvements 19
    The desktop 19
    Navigating by keyboard 20
    Opening and creating folders 21

System Folder Organization	21
Divided Control Panel	22
Desk Accessories	23
Apple Menu	24
Installing Fonts, Sounds, and More	25
Variable-Size Fonts	26
Multitasking	27
Hiding Window Clutter	29
Extending Memory	29
32-Bit Addressing	29
Virtual memory	29
Controlling virtual memory	31
Disk Cache	31
Chooser Changes	31
File Sharing	32
Sharing someone else's folders	32
Sharing your folders with others	34
Interactive Help	36
Stationery Pads	37
Folder Nesting Revealed	38
Smart Drag	39
Keyboard Shortcuts	40
A New Opening	40
Naming Duplicates	41
Background Copying	41
Trash Behavior	42
Live Copy/Paste	43
Accessing Data	44
Linking Programs	46
At Ease	47
QuickTime Movies	48
WorldScript	49
Determining What You Need	50
Exploring Is the Key	50

PART II System 7 in Detail 53

 Chapter 2: The New Look 55

    Desktop 56
        Creating a custom desktop pattern 57
        Desktop pattern alternatives 57
    Windows 58
        3-D window controls 58
        3-D motion 59
        Inactive windows pale 59
        Dialog box shading 60
        Choosing a window color 60
    Icons 62
        Icon colors 62
        Icon sizes 63
        Icon highlighting 63
        Old icons 63
    Menus 64
    Directory Dialog Boxes 65
        The desktop 66
        Navigating by keyboard 67
        Naming the item you're saving 69
        Creating a new folder 69
        Opening an item 69
    Balloon Help 70
        Turning balloon help on and off 70
        Working with balloon help on 71
        What balloon help knows 72
        Other help 73
    Opening Multiple Programs 73
        Switching programs 74
        Reducing window clutter 75
        Memory partitions 75
        Background operations 75

New Error Messages 77
    Emergency quit 79
    Bomb recovery 79
Big Changes 80

Chapter 3: Finder Improvements 81

Outlining Folder Structure 81
    Collapsing folders 82
    Expanding folders 82
    Selecting from multiple folders 82
Smart Zooming 84
Finding Items 85
Opening an Enclosing Folder 86
Custom Views 87
    Setting the text font and size 88
    Setting icon alignment 88
    Determining list view contents 89
Changing List Views 89
Horizontal Scrolling 90
Auto Scrolling 90
Selecting by Dragging 92
Renaming Items 92
Naming Duplicates 94
Labeling Items 94
    Using labels 95
    Changing label names and colors 96
Polite Drag 96
Desktop Database 97
Background Work 98
Smarter Copying 99
Stationery Pads 100
    Making stationery pads 100
    Using stationery pads 100
Custom Icons 102
    Making a custom icon 102
    Reverting to a standard icon 104

Removing Disk Icons 104
Trash Disposal 105
    Trash warnings 105
    Trash retrieval 106
    Trash contents 106
    Drag open 107
Cleaning Up Options 107
Finder Power 108
At Ease 109

Chapter 4: Organized at Last 115

System File 116
    Seeing System file contents 116
    Working with System file contents 117
    Multiple languages 117
Fonts Folder 118
    Viewing font samples 119
    Exchanging fonts with older systems 119
Apple Menu Items Folder 120
Startup Items Folder 120
Control Panels Folder 121
Extensions Folder 122
Preferences Folder 123
More Special Folders Outside 124
Adding to the System Folder 125
Fooling the Finder 126
Removing from the System Folder 127
Troubleshooting a Conflict 127

Chapter 5: Tailored to Fit 131

Desk Accessories 131
    Opening desk accessories 132
    Using desk accessories 132
    Alarm Clock 133

    Calculator 134
    Chooser 134
    Key Caps 134
    Note Pad 136
    Puzzle 136
    Scrapbook 137
Your Own Apple Menu 138
    Adding and removing items 138
    Apple menu organization 138
    Making your own arrangements 139
    Grouping and separating items 139
    Hierarchical Apple menu 140
Control Panels 141
    Standard control panels 142
    Brightness 143
    CloseView 143
    Date & Time 143
    Easy Access 144
    General Controls 145
    Keyboard 145
    Map 145
    Monitors 147
    Mouse 149
    Numbers 149
    Portable and PowerBook 149
    Sound 149
    Startup Disk 150
    Text 150
Memory Management Tactics 151
    Analyzing memory use 152
    System memory size 152
    Program memory size 153
    Memory fragmentation 154
    Disk Cache 155
    32-Bit Addressing 156
    Virtual memory 157
Old Drivers Cause Trouble 159

Chapter 6: Fast Access with Aliases 161

Understanding Aliases 161
Making an Alias 162
Changing an Alias 163
Changing an Original Item 164
Finding an Original Item 165
Using Aliases 166
    Aliases in the Apple menu 166
    Universal Show Clipboard 166
    Aliases as startup items 167
    Aliases on the desktop 167
    Aliases in directory dialog boxes 168
    Abridged System Folder 168
    Aliases for favorite folders 169
    Aliases of items on floppy disks 169
    Aliases and CD-ROM 170
    Aliases of shared items 170
    Aliases keep shared documents current 170
    Your office on a disk 171

Chapter 7: Smooth Text Everywhere 173

Three Font Technologies 173
    About fixed-size fonts 173
    About TrueType fonts 174
    About PostScript fonts 175
    Recognizing best font sizes 176
    About font styles 176
Seeing Font Samples 177
Adding and Removing Fonts 179
Combining Fixed-Size and TrueType Fonts 181
Printing with TrueType 182
    TrueType alone 182
    TrueType and fixed-size 182
    TrueType and PostScript 182

Understanding TrueType Fonts 184
TrueType Font Availability 186

 Chapter 8: File Sharing for the Rest of Us **189**

System 7's Distributed File Sharing 189
    AppleShare 3.0 dedicated file server 190
Connecting Your Network 191
Selecting Your Network 192
    Turning AppleTalk on and off 193
Identifying Your Macintosh 194
Starting File Sharing 195
Sharing Your Folders and Hard Disks 196
    Guidelines for sharing folders and disks 198
Who Can Access Your Shared Items 198
    The Owner 199
    Guests 200
    Registered users 200
    AppleTalk Remote Access privileges 201
    Groups of users 202
Controlling Access to Shared Items 204
    Setting access privileges 204
    Specifying who has access privileges 205
    Icon indicators for access privileges 208
Access Privilege Scenarios 208
    Universal access 208
    Restricted access 209
    Private access 210
    A private in-box folder 210
    A user or group bulletin board 210
Monitoring File Sharing Activity 211
    Temporarily disconnecting users 212
Sharing Someone Else's Folders and Disks 212
    Connecting as a registered user or guest 213
    Selecting shared disks and folders 213
    Automatically sharing items from another Macintosh 214

Working with items shared from another Macintosh 214
Transferring items between computers 215
Disconnecting from another Macintosh 215
Network Insecurity 216

Chapter 9: Creating Living Documents 217

About Publishers, Editions, and Subscribers 217
Creating a Publisher 219
Subscribing to an Edition 221
Publisher and Subscriber Borders 222
Publisher and Subscriber Options 223
    Adorning a subscriber 224
    Opening a subscriber's publisher 225
    Making changes to a publisher 225
Updating Editions 226

Chapter 10: QuickTime 229

The Magic Behind QuickTime 230
QuickTime Technology 230
System Software 231
    Movie Toolbox 231
    Image Compression Manager 232
    Component Manager 232
What's in a MooV 233
PICT Extensions 234
User Interface 235
Image Compression 236
    Compression ratio 236
    Compression fidelity 236
    Compression speed 236
    Compressors 237
Content, Content, Content 238
Movie Makers 238
QuickTime in Your Life 240

Chapter 11: Advanced Capabilities 243

Program Linking 243
    Using program linking 245
    Program linking example 247
    The promise of program linking 250
System-Wide Scripting 251
Data Access 251
    Using data access 252
    About query documents 253

PART III
Customizing System 7 255

Chapter 12: Tips and Secrets 257

Icons 257
    Spotting a name selected for editing 257
    Edit, don't open 258
    Undoing accidental name change 258
    Copy/Paste icon names 258
    Removing "alias" 259
    Permanently removing "alias" 259
    Desktop aliases 260
    Trash everywhere 260
    Express access to CD-ROM 260
    Cataloging items on floppy disks 260
    Making many aliases 260
    Duplicating fonts 261
    Making a font suitcase 261
    Stationery workaround 261
    Icon updating 262
    Fixing blank icons 262
    Problems with custom color icons 263
    Revert to standard icon 266
Folders and Windows 266
    Finder power 266
    Special folder replacement 266

- Special folder mistakes 267
  - Abridged System Folder 267
  - Removing from the System Folder 267
  - Easy startup items 267
  - Seeing desktop items 267
  - Narrow Finder windows 267
  - Viewing by size 268
  - Folder size slowdown 268
  - Find in next window 268
  - Drag to scroll 268
- Trash 268
  - Skip the Trash warning 268
  - Discarding locked items 269
  - Trash retrieval 269
  - Discarding items from one disk 269
  - Rescued items 269
- Directory Dialog Boxes 269
  - Directory dialog keystrokes 269
  - Find an alias's original item 269
  - Folder switching 269
  - Aliases for favorite folders 270
  - Copy and Paste 270
  - Double-click sidestep 270
  - Double-click cancel 270
- Desk Accessories 270
  - Puzzle pictures 270
  - Scripted calculator 270
  - Printed key caps 271
  - Alternate scrapbooks 271
- Control Panels 271
  - Revert to standard gray desktop 271
  - Revert to standard labels 271
  - Easy Access shortcuts 271
  - Big map 271
  - Color map 272
  - Hidden free beep 272
- Apple and Application Menus 272
  - Hiding windows while switching 272
  - Hide windows to boost performance 272

- Apple menu organization 272
- Apple menu separators 273
- Fast Apple menu changes 273
- Too-full Apple menu 273
- Universal Show Clipboard 273

File Sharing 273
- Reducing network cabling costs 273
- Picking a secure password 274
- Allow saving, not trashing 274
- Share disks or outer folders 274
- Improving file sharing performance 274
- Cutting file sharing red tape 274
- Office on a disk 275
- The latest shared document 275
- What people have trashed 275

Memory and Performance 276
- Disk Cache performance boost 276
- Finder out of memory 276
- Quitting startup programs 276
- Paring memory to the bone 277
- Reducing system memory size 277
- Fragmented memory 277

Troubleshooting 278
- Printed font doesn't match display 278
- Can't put away hard disk icon 278
- Can't switch cartridges 278
- Can't share a disk 278
- Blank icons 279
- Program unexpectedly quits 279
- Bomb message causes 279
- Emergency quit 280
- Bomb recovery 280
- System extension conflicts 280

Other 281
- Desktop by Name 281
- LaserWriter test page 282
- Easter egg hunt 282
- More Chicago symbols 283
- Desktop pattern 283

Cancel startup items 285
Keyboard changes 285

Chapter 13: Utilities and Enhancements 289

What is Shareware or Freeware? 289
Using Shareware and Freeware 290
    Alias assistance 291
    Disk and file utilities 292
    Finder helpers 294
    System Management 298
    Windows and dialog boxes 300
    Sounds 301
    Menus, folders, and icons 302
    Network enhancements 305
    Summary of network enhancing software 306
    PowerBook enhancements 306

PART IV Appendixes 309

Appendix A: Product Compatibility Table 311

Compatibility Checker 311
Judge Compatibility Yourself 337

Appendix B: Glossary 339

Appendix C: Moving To System 7 347

Equipment Requirements 347
    Memory requirements 347
    Disk requirements 349
Which System Version to Use 349
    Who should use System 6 350
    Who should use System 7 350
    Who should use System 7 Tune-Up 350

Mixing Systems 352
    Mixed networks 352
    Extra folders and missing items 353
    Desk accessories and fonts 353
    Automatic rebuilding 353
Switching Systems 353
Where To Get System 7 353
How To Install System 7 355
    Preparing your Macintosh 356
    Installing System 7 357
    If your Macintosh will not restart 360
    Recovering disk space 360
    Using desk accessories 360

Index 361

Reader Response Survey .... Back of Book

Foreword

Do you understand the Macintosh operating system; its system software? Do you ever wonder what impact the Mac's OS has on your computer and its software applications? Or wonder whether you are getting the most out of your Macintosh; whether you really understand all of its capabilities? Then buy this book and keep it near your computer.

Lon Poole's *Macworld Guide to System 7.1, 2nd Edition* is your non-technical guide to the universe of Macintosh technology. A Macintosh Baedeker for everyone using the Mac's new system software; from the technically inept to the most gnarly nerd out there. Lon was one of the founding editors of *Macworld*. After his last seven years of writing about the Macintosh for *Macworld*, I can confidently write that Lon knows more about the Mac than any single person outside of the engineering groups at Apple. In fact *Macworld* almost lost Lon to Apple two years ago — but that's another story. Happily he continues to write for *Macworld*, and also found time to write this book to help us all get through our confusion about Apple's system software.

Jerry Borrell
President, Sumeria and former
Editor-in-Chief, *Macworld* magazine

Introduction

System 7 changes everything. After you install this new system software, your Apple Macintosh computer looks and feels different. On the surface it's almost as easy to use as the Macintosh you now know. But at another level, System 7 makes your Macintosh more sophisticated, complicated, powerful, and fun than before. This book helps you take full advantage of System 7's power.

You can use this book to learn just the basics that apply to all versions of System 7. When you're ready to go beyond the basics, you can read about the details that unlock the power of the original 7.0 version, the 7.0.1 update, the System 7 Tune-Up, and the latest 7.1 version. You can also learn what you gain by using related Apple software such as At Ease, AppleTalk Remote Access, AppleShare 3.0, and QuickTime.

Who Can Use This Book

This book is aimed at people who already know Macintosh basics such as choosing commands from menus, opening programs and documents, rearranging the contents of folders and disks, and copying information from one place and pasting it to another. About 95 percent of what you already know how to do transfers directly to System 7. Mastering the new system software means acquiring new skills, not learning new methods for old skills.

If you do need to learn Macintosh fundamentals, look at the documentation that came with your Macintosh. In particular, study the introductory written material and the program *Macintosh Basics*.

Macintosh veterans can also benefit from this book. If you are one, get started quickly with System 7 by reading the condensed coverage of it in the first section of this book. Once you're comfortable with the new system software, increase the depth of your knowledge by reading the details in the second section.

If you're looking for tips, secrets, and ways to improve the standard System 7, browse the third part of this book.

What's in This Book

Macworld Guide To System 7.1, 2nd Edition, is really many books in one. First, a quick summary of System 7 contains just what you need to know to begin using System 7 immediately (Part I). Second, a complete reference covers the new system software in detail (Part II: Chapters 2 through 11). Third, a customization part lists lots of ideas for getting the most from System 7, and a compendium of useful software describes ways you can enhance System 7 (Part III: Chapters 12 and 13). Also included are three appendixes, which deal with compatibility, terminology, upgrading, and installation.

Chapter 1 concisely describes the many important new capabilities System 7 brings to the Macintosh. It also illustrates them and gives you condensed how-to instructions.

Chapter 2 shows how different System 7 looks compared to older system software. It also explains how interactive on-screen help works and how to have multiple programs open at once.

Chapter 3 details the myriad improvements in the Finder that help you organize your disks more effectively and find items in them more quickly than older Finders.

Chapter 4 covers the special folders that organize the System Folder. It also describes the direct methods for installing fonts and other items in your System Folder.

Chapter 5 deals with changes that make desk accessories and control panels more versatile. It also tackles memory management, which gains new importance with System 7.

Chapter 6 gives you ideas for using aliases to better organize the contents of your disks and to streamline access to items you use frequently.

Chapter 7 examines Apple's TrueType font technology, which gives you smooth text at any size on screen and on any printer. It also correlates new fonts with old Macintosh fonts and PostScript fonts.

Chapter 8 explains how to share your files with other people whose computers are connected to yours, and how to share their files.

Chapter 9 explores the capability of automatically updating copied material when the original material changes by using the Publish and Subscribe commands.

Chapter 10 describes Apple's QuickTime technology, and how you can use it to include movies and compressed still images in your everyday documents.

Chapter 11 investigates how programs can work together. One program can use the commands and tools of other programs made by different program developers. Also covered is Apple's Data Access Manager (DAM), which provides a common, simple method for getting data from a variety of large databases resident on host computers of all brands and sizes.

Chapter 12 contains a collection of tips and tricks for getting extra power, performance, and flexibility from System 7.

Chapter 13 categorizes and describes over 70 software utilities and enhancements for System 7, all of them available on a five-disk set from the Berkeley Macintosh User Group (BMUG) by returning the order card in the back of this book.

Appendix A contains compatibility information, including a listing of specific version numbers for hundreds of third-party products and a checklist for evaluating just how System 7-savvy your own software is.

Appendix B contains a glossary of terms commonly associated with System 7 and with QuickTime.

Appendix C discusses the issues you face when you upgrade your Macintosh to System 7: equipment requirements, whether to upgrade, where to get System 7, and installation instructions.

Conventions Used in This Book

You can get more out of this book if you understand the conventions used in its writing and publication. Each chapter begins with a list of the chapter's main topics and ends with a summary of the chapter's contents. Certain types of information — warnings, tips, undocumented facts, and troubleshooting techniques — appear throughout the book. Icons in the margin alert you to each type of information.

Warning icons alert you to possible problems or special exceptions you might encounter while operating System 7.

Quick Tips icons are how-to shortcuts that will save you time and trouble when working with System 7.

Undocumented icons include any concept or idea not found in Apple's documentation for System 7 users.

Troubleshooting icons provide workaround solutions to possible traps and pitfalls you may encounter while using System 7.

How This Book Can Help You

Conventional wisdom says the Macintosh is so easy to use you don't need to read books about it. In fact, discovering all the power System 7 gives your Macintosh would take months of exploring and experimenting. Reading this book shortcuts that process so you can put the full power of the new system software to work for you weeks earlier.

Macworld Guide To System 7.1, 2nd Edition, complements Apple's System 7 manuals. It contains lots of useful information you won't find in the manuals. It also provides a different perspective on any subjects you don't quite understand in the manuals. And because this book describes System 7 completely, you can use it instead of the reference manuals if you don't happen to have them.

To help make future editions of this book better, I would appreciate getting your feedback. Please send your comments or questions to me, Lon Poole, in care of IDG Books Worldwide.

And now... let's get started!

Part I:
Quick Start

Chapter 1 7
The Essence of System 7

Chapter 1
The Essence of System 7

In This Chapter

- Coloring windows and icons on a color Mac under System 7.
- The new Finder: making it easier to access and organize information.
- How TrueType fonts improve the quality of on-screen text and printing devices.
- A look at file sharing under System 7.
- Multitasking: having as many programs open as will fit in your computer's memory.
- Virtual memory: increasing your Mac's memory without installing more RAM.
- A look at how balloon help makes learning new programs easier.
- Sharing information on documents dynamically by publishing and subscribing.
- IAC: giving programs the ability to collaborate and you the ability to control them with scripts.
- Simplifying the desktop with At Ease.
- QuickTime: putting movies on your Macintosh.

If you want to grasp the essence of System 7 and you only have a couple of hours, read this chapter. Here you'll learn about the new features you can use as soon as you install System 7 as well as features that lay a foundation for future improvements in application programs.

As you read this chapter, you'll see three special symbols imbedded at the beginning of some paragraphs:

- ✓ Tells you which Macintosh models and what types of software can use the System 7 capabilities under discussion.

- ✗ Tells you about Macintosh models and software that can't use a particular System 7 capability.

- ☛ Refers you to another part of the book where you will find more information about the System 7 capability just discussed.

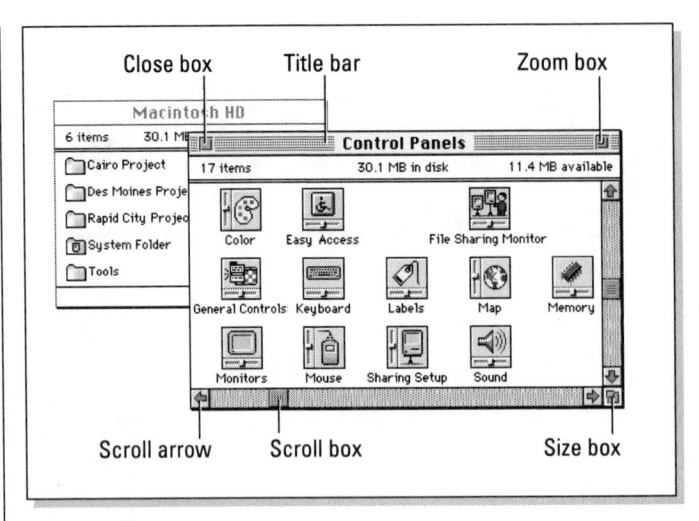

Figure 1-1: Shaded window controls.

Color Windows

Trendy three-dimensional shading modernizes all System 7 window frames on monitors displaying 16 colors or gray shades. Muted colors and shades of gray accent the window components under your control: title bar, close box, zoom box, size box, and scroll bars, as shown in Figure 1-1. Some of the colorized components even look like they work in three dimensions when you use them. For example, clicking the close box makes it look pressed down.

Only the active window has 3-D shading. It stands out from inactive windows behind it because System 7 displays inactive windows with gray borders and a gray title. Of course the contents of inactive windows are never dimmed so you can see the contents easily. Also, System 7 does not stray from white window backgrounds, a cornerstone of the Macintosh interface.

You choose one shading tint for all windows from nine tints listed in a pop-up menu in the Color control panel, as shown in Figure 1-2. The window tint you choose will not apply to tool palettes and special-purpose windows created by some application programs unless the programs have been upgraded for System 7. You cannot create your own window-shading color using the Color control panel.

✗   You see traditional black-and-white windows unless your Macintosh is displaying at least 16 grays or 256 colors.

☞   For more information, see "Windows" in Chapter 2.

Figure 1-2: The Color control panel.

Color Icons

Color icons spruce up the System 7 desktop on systems displaying colors or grays. Apple has taken the same low-key approach with its icons as it has taken with windows, using gray shades and subdued colors to make them look three-dimensional, as shown in Figure 1-3. Bright colors are used mainly for highlights.

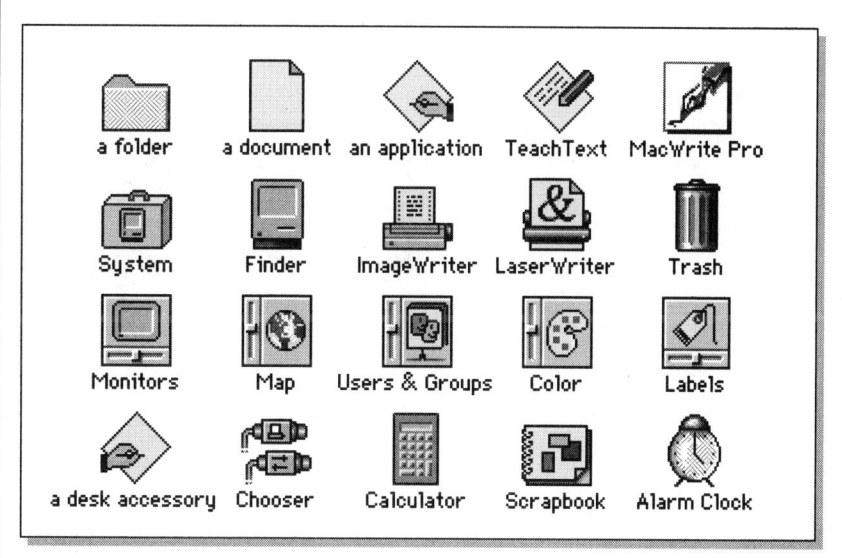

Figure 1-3: Some standard-size color icons.

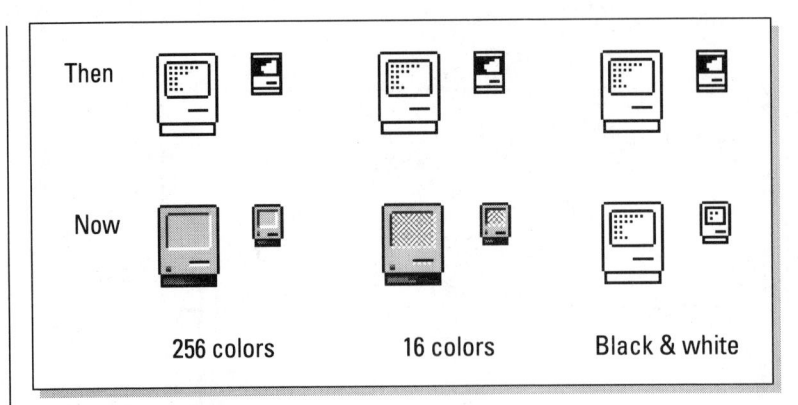

Figure 1-4: Large and small icons.

Prior to System 7, the small icons used in menus and Finder windows were mechanically shrunken from full-size icons. Now any program developer can design separate, better looking small icons, as shown in Figure 1-4.

✘ You see the old-style black-and-white icons and shrunken icons for programs and documents until you upgrade those programs with versions having color icons and small icons.

☞ For more information, see "Icons" in Chapter 2.

Custom Icons

Tired of the same old icons? Now you can replace individual full-size icons with your own designs, as shown in Figure 1-5. First you create a new icon design in color, grayscale, or black-and-white with a paint program. Copy the new icon to the Clipboard. In the Finder, select the icon you want to customize, choose Get Info from the File menu, select the icon in the Get Info window, and paste. The painting you copied replaces the current icon. If your painting is bigger than a standard icon (32 × 32 dots), it is scaled down to fit the icon space.

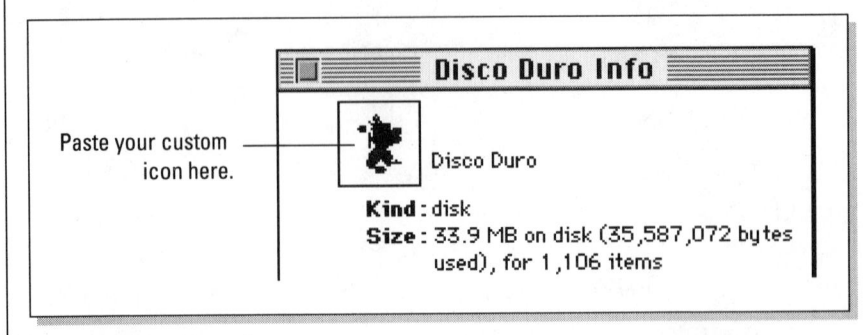

Figure 1-5: Customizing an icon.

✔ You can replace the icon of any unlocked file, folder, or disk. You cannot replace any system software icons such as the System Folder, Finder, Control Panels folder, and Trash.

☞ For more information, see "Custom Icons" in Chapter 3.

Editing Icon Names

Before you can edit the name of a disk, folder, program, document, or other item in Finder 7, you must carefully select the name. When the name is selected for editing, it has a box around it in addition to being highlighted, as shown in Figure 1-6. Clicking an icon itself (not its name) does not select the name for editing as it does with older versions of system software. The good news is you can no longer accidentally and perhaps unknowingly rename a selected document or folder by bumping the keyboard; the bad news is if you are accustomed to an old version of system software, you have to relearn how to change icon names.

Figure 1-6: An icon name selected for editing.

To select the name of an icon, you either click the icon and then press Return or Enter, or you click the name itself. After selecting the name, wait until the box appears around the name. You won't have to wait long if you move the mouse slightly after clicking the name, or if you move the insertion point by pressing the arrow keys. Pressing up arrow moves the insertion point to the beginning of the name, Down arrow moves it to the end, left arrow moves it left, and right arrow moves it right. Then you can click again to select an insertion point, double-click to select a word, or drag to select a range of text. If you click again before a box appears around the name, the Finder thinks you're double-clicking the icon and opens it.

✘ Experienced Macintosh users will probably find the new method of editing icon names one of the toughest changes to get used to because old editing habits suddenly cause unexpected behavior.

☞ For more information, see Chapter 3.

Aliases

Stop digging for documents, programs, folders, and other items buried deep within nested folders on who-knows-which disk. Instead, make aliases of the items you use frequently and put the aliases on the desktop, in the Apple menu, or in other accessible places. Aliases act like real items when you open them or drag items to them, but they are only small (1K to 3K, depending on total disk capacity) stand-ins. An alias looks exactly like the original item except its name is in italics and initially has the word *alias* as a suffix, as shown in Figure 1-7.

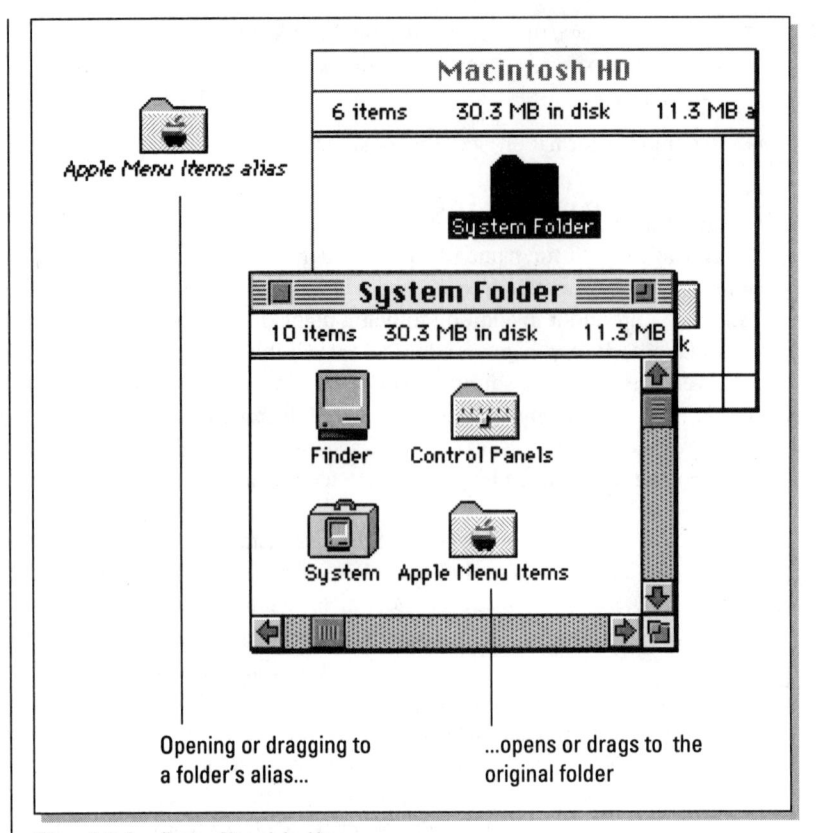

Figure 1-7: An alias and its original item.

Making an alias
You make an alias by selecting an item and choosing Make Alias from the Finder's File menu. You can move the alias, change its name, set options using the Get Info command, or classify it using the Label menu, all independently of the original item.

Using aliases
Aliases have a variety of uses, as shown in Figure 1-8, some of which include the following:

✦ Opening frequently used programs, documents, and folders from the desktop while the real items remain buried in nested folders.

✦ Adding items to the Apple menu without moving them from the folders they are in.

✦ Organizing documents and folders according to multiple filing schemes without duplicating items. For example, you could file documents by project, addressee, date, and topic.

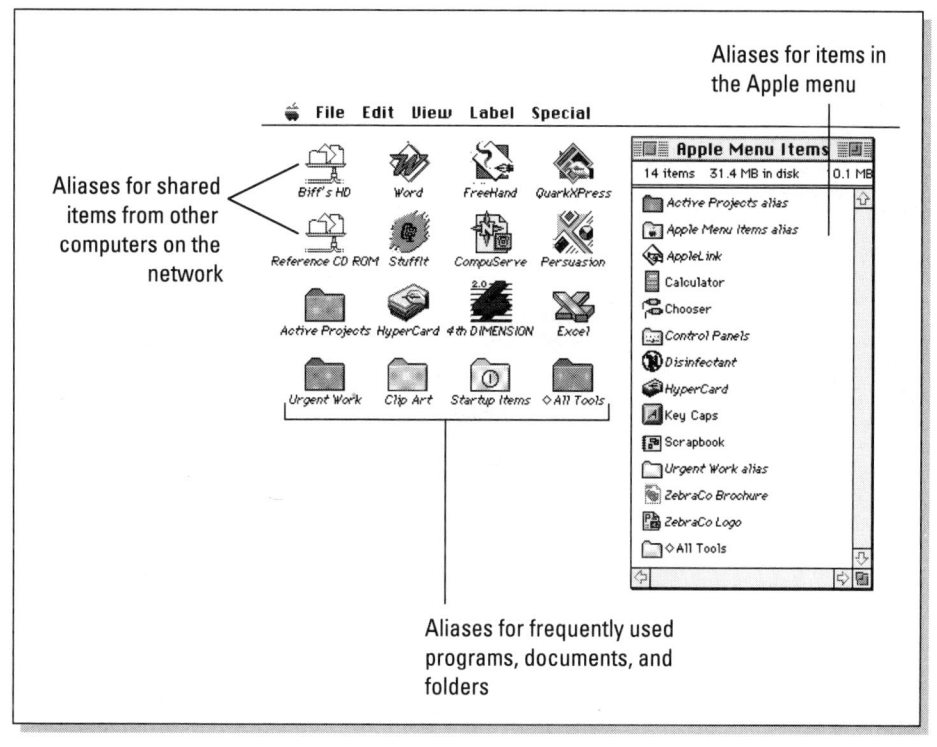

Figure 1-8: Some uses of aliases.

- ✦ Simplifying access to file servers and individual items on servers. Opening an alias of an item on a server makes automatic connection with the server (except for providing the password, which you must type unless you got access to the original item as a guest).
- ✦ Getting nearly automatic access to your Mac's hard disks using a floppy disk in any other Mac on the same network.

✔ Aliases work with all software and on all Macintosh models that can use System 7.

☞ For more information, see Chapter 6.

Outlining Folder Structure

One of Finder 7's myriad improvements enables you to see, select, and reorganize items from different folders in the same window. Views that list items by name, size, kind, and so on (not by icon or small icon) display folders and their contents in an indented outline format. The levels of indentation in the outline clearly diagram the structure of your

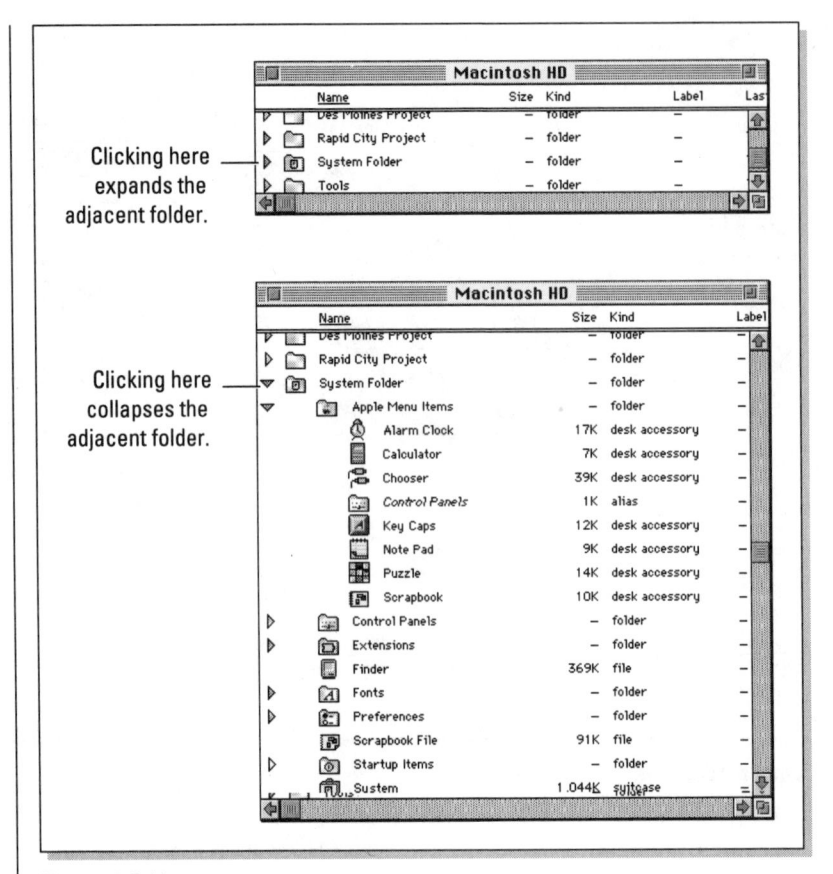

Figure 1-9: Folder structure.

nested folders. You can expand or collapse any level in the outline to show or hide the corresponding folder's contents by clicking a triangle next to the folder's icon, as shown in Figure 1-9.

✓ Indented outlining works on all Macintosh models that can use System 7.

☞ For more information, see "Outlining Folder Structure" in Chapter 3.

Custom Views

The new Finder gives you control over the format and content of its windows. You select options using the Views control panel (see Figure 1-10), and your settings immediately affect all windows. You can set the following:

- ✦ Font and size of text used for item names and window headings in all views
- ✦ Alignment method in icon and small icon views
- ✦ Content of and icon size in list views

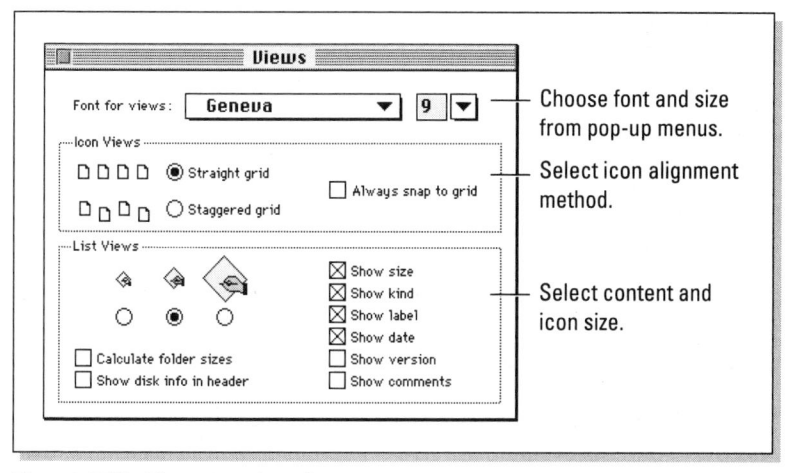

Figure 1-10: The Views control panel.

List views (name, size, kind, and so on) always include an icon and a name for every item. You select which of six other columns of information to include: size, kind, label, date, version, and comments. The last two are new in list views with System 7. You cannot change the order of the columns, only whether each appears or not.

The Views control panel also enables you to decide whether list views show folder sizes and whether the disk information that formerly appeared only in icon views also appears at the top of list views.

✔ Custom views work on all Macintosh models that can use System 7.

☞ For more information, see "Custom Views" in Chapter 3.

Item Labels

The Finder now enables you to classify folders, programs, and documents by labeling them with a word or phrase. On systems capable of displaying color, labeling an item also colorizes it. This capability is an extension of an older Finder's capability to colorize items.

Using labels

To label an item, select it and choose a label from the Finder's Label menu, as shown in Figure 1-11. After labeling items, you can view Finder window contents arranged by label, as shown in Figure 1-12. You can also search for items by label using the Finder's Find command, as shown in Figure 1-13.

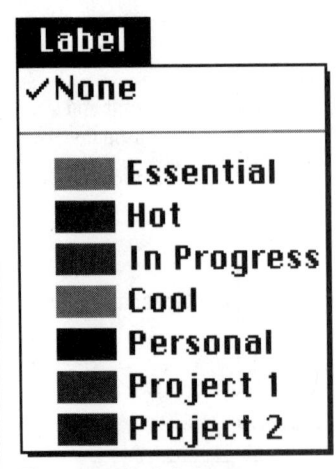

Figure 1-11: The Label menu.

Figure 1-12: Viewing by label.

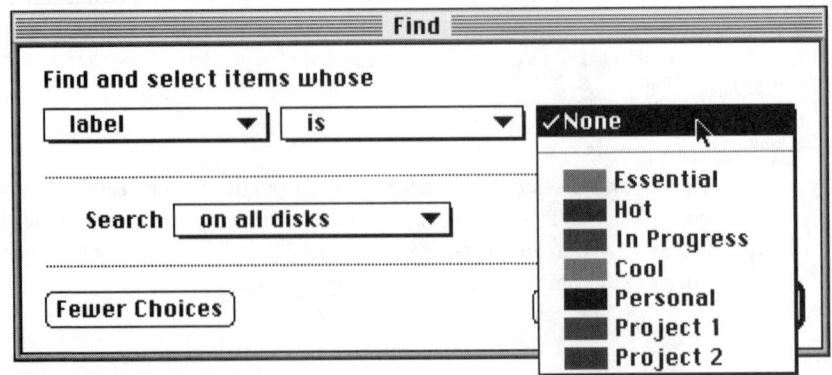

Figure 1-13: Finding by label.

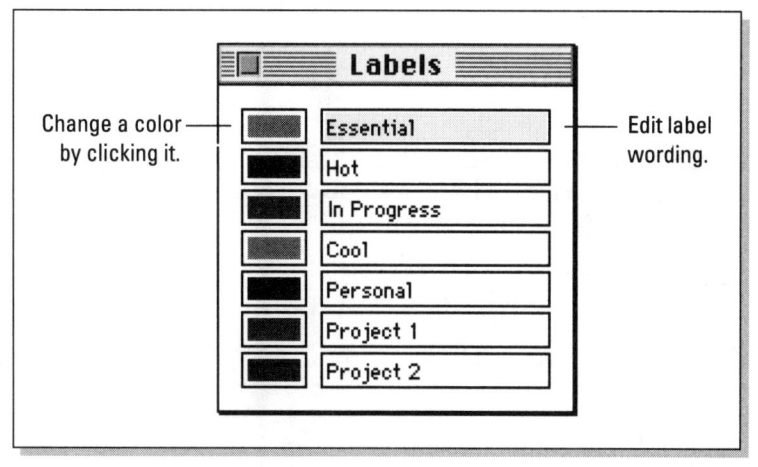

[Figure: The Labels control panel, showing labels "Essential", "Hot", "In Progress", "Cool", "Personal", "Project 1", "Project 2" with color swatches. Annotations: "Change a color by clicking it." and "Edit label wording."]

Figure 1-14: The Labels control panel.

Changing label names and colors

You change the standard label names and colors using the Labels control panel, as shown in Figure 1-14.

✔ Icon labels work on all Macintosh models that can use System 7. You can see the standard seven label colors only on a monitor displaying at least 16 colors.

☞ For more information, see "Labeling Items" in Chapter 3.

Smart Finder Windows

A number of improvements to the Finder give you more control over its windows, as shown in Figure 1-15. These improvements enable you to do the following:

✦ Change the order of items in a list view by clicking a column heading. You can tell the current order by looking for the underlined column heading.

✦ Scroll automatically by dragging an item or a group of selected items past the active area of the window. Dragging into a window corner scrolls diagonally.

✦ Zoom a window just enough to show all items in it by clicking the zoom box. The window only covers the whole screen if it contains enough items to fill a screen-size window.

✦ Select multiple items by dragging over them in any view (not just icon and small icon views). Items are highlighted one-by-one as you drag over them, not en masse when you stop dragging.

✔ View switching, auto-scrolling, precise zooming, and drag-selecting in any view work on all Macintosh models that can use System 7.

☞ For more information, see "Smart Zooming," "Auto Scrolling," "Selecting by Dragging," and "Changing List Views" in Chapter 3.

[Figure 1-15 illustration with callouts:]
- Selected items are highlighted as you drag.
- Zoom just enough to show all contents.
- Scroll automatically by dragging past a window edge.

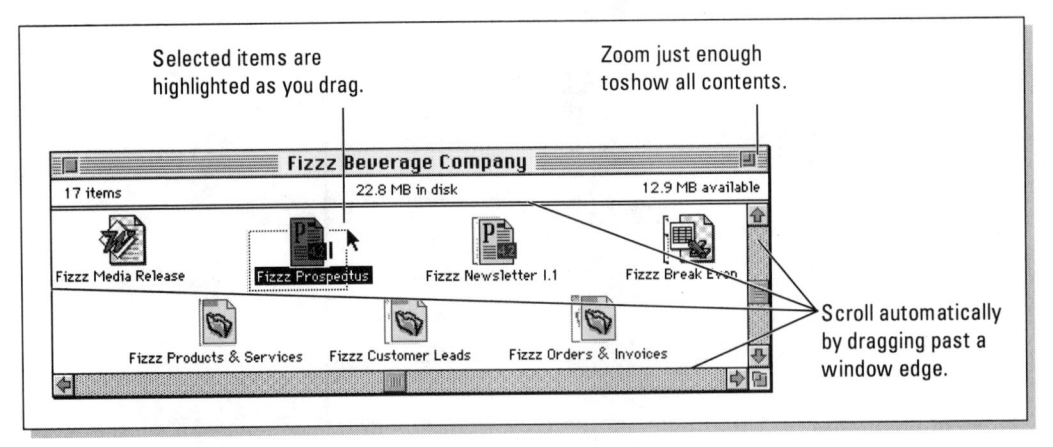

Figure 1-15: Finder window improvements.

Fast File Finding

No more hunting through folders and disks for lost items — a chore even with the new outline views — nor waiting for the old slow Find File desk accessory to turn them up. Finder 7's Find command (File menu) finds and fetches lost items for you quickly. In its simplest form, the Find command looks through all disks whose icons are on the desktop for an item whose name contains the text you specify, as shown in Figure 1-16. It displays the first item it finds, opening the folder that contains the item to show the item in its native surroundings. You can find additional matching items with the Find Again command.

The Find command has an exotic form as well, as shown in Figure 1-17. Clicking the More Choices button enables you to specify the type of search: by name, size, kind, label, date created, date modified, version, comments, or lock status. You also specify exactly what you want matched (for example, you enter a date) and how you want it matched (for example, look for items modified before the date you specify).

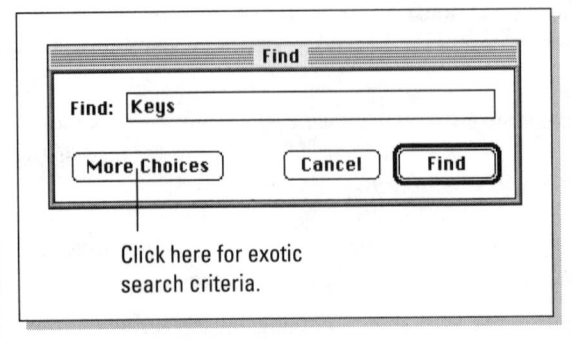

[Figure 1-16 illustration: Find dialog with "Keys" entered, More Choices / Cancel / Find buttons. Callout: Click here for exotic search criteria.]

Figure 1-16: A simple find.

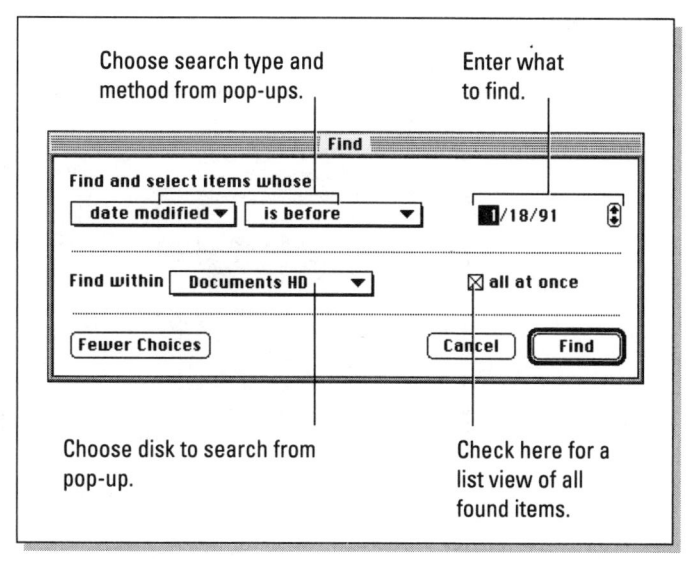

```
                  Choose search type and              Enter what
                  method from pop-ups.                to find.
          ┌─────────────────────────────────────────────────────┐
          │                        Find                          │
          │  Find and select items whose                         │
          │   ┌─date modified ▼─┐ ┌─is before ▼─┐   │1/18/91│ ⬔  │
          │                                                      │
          │  Find within │ Documents HD  ▼│   ☒ all at once      │
          │                                                      │
          │   ( Fewer Choices )              ( Cancel ) ( Find ) │
          └─────────────────────────────────────────────────────┘
                  │                              │
                  Choose disk to search from     Check here for a
                  pop-up.                        list view of all
                                                 found items.
```

Figure 1-17: An exotic find.

You can restrict the search to a single disk, to the active window, or to a group of items you selected in the active window before choosing the Find command. The Find command can also select all the items it finds at once in an outline view.

- ✔ The Find and Find Next commands work on all Macintosh models that can use System 7.

- ☞ For more information, see "Finding Items" in Chapter 3.

Directory Dialog Improvements

The directory dialog boxes you get when you use Open and Save As commands work like a one-window Finder. As with earlier versions of system software, a single directory window lists the contents of one folder or disk at a time, alphabetically by name. The System 7 directory window uses compressed-style text for names longer than 25 characters.

The desktop

Directory dialog boxes in System 7 provide a view of the desktop and enable you to open disks and other items on it. In fact, opening a disk at the desktop level is how you switch disk drives, as shown in Figure 1-18. The old Drive button has been replaced by a Desktop button, which takes you to the desktop when you click it. You can also get to the desktop by choosing it from the pop-up menu above the directory window.

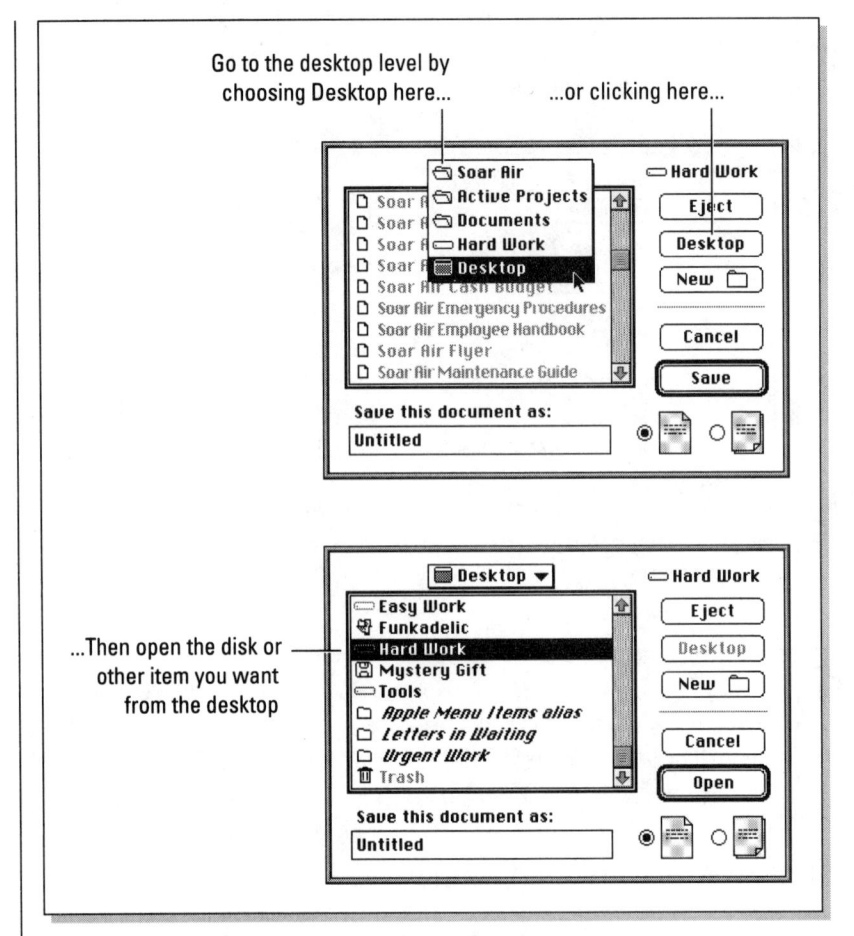

Figure 1-18: At the desktop.

Navigating by keyboard

You can open items and move through folders in any directory dialog box using the keyboard as well as the mouse. For example, typing *k* selects the first item that begins with the letter *K* or *k*. Older system software doesn't allow this keyboard navigation in Save or Save As dialog boxes, where you must use the keyboard to edit the name of the item you're saving. In System 7, a heavy black border around a Save or Save As dialog's directory window tells you that your typing will select an item in the window, as shown in Figure 1-19. You can alternate between the save dialog box's filename entry area and the list by using the Tab key. System 7's many other keyboard shortcuts are covered in Chapter 2.

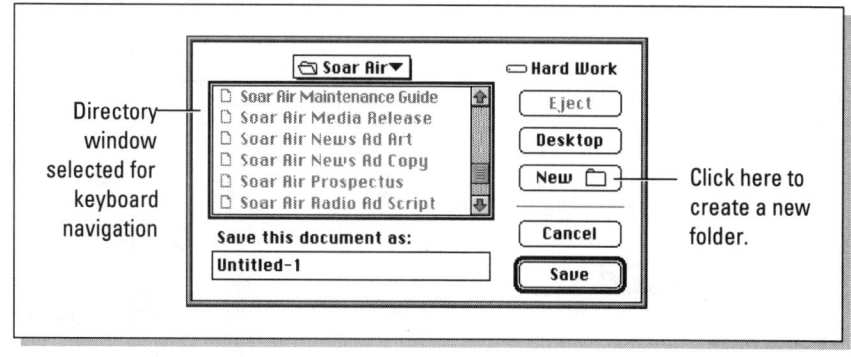

Figure 1-19: Moving around by keyboard.

Opening and creating folders

An even more subtle change in Save and Save As dialog boxes further reduces confusion when moving through folders. When you select a folder in the directory window, the Save button becomes an Open button. Clicking it opens the selected folder. In older system software, the button works the same way, but it's always named Save (even when clicking it opens a selected folder).

The Save or Save As dialog boxes of some programs also include a new button you can click to create a new folder. In addition, you can use the Edit menu to cut, copy, and paste while editing the name of an item you're saving.

✘   The New Folder button is missing from the Save and Save As dialog boxes of most programs that have not been updated for System 7.

☛   For more information, see "Directory Dialog Boxes" in Chapter 2.

System Folder Organization

What a mess the System Folder had become! Control panel documents here, startup documents there, preference files everywhere — Finder 7 keeps such items in special new folders inside the System Folder. Other new folders provide new features. All the new folders have distinctive folder icons, as shown in Figure 1-20. Moreover, Finder 7 puts many items in their proper places when you drag them to the System Folder icon. The inner folders relieve much of the clutter that plagues System Folders of older system software.

✘   Some items from old System Folders don't work right when they're put in the new Extensions, Control Panels, Fonts, or Preferences folders. You have to put stubborn old preference files, control panels, fonts, and system extensions loose in the System Folder by dragging them to the System Folder window (not to the System Folder icon).

☛   For more information, see Chapter 4.

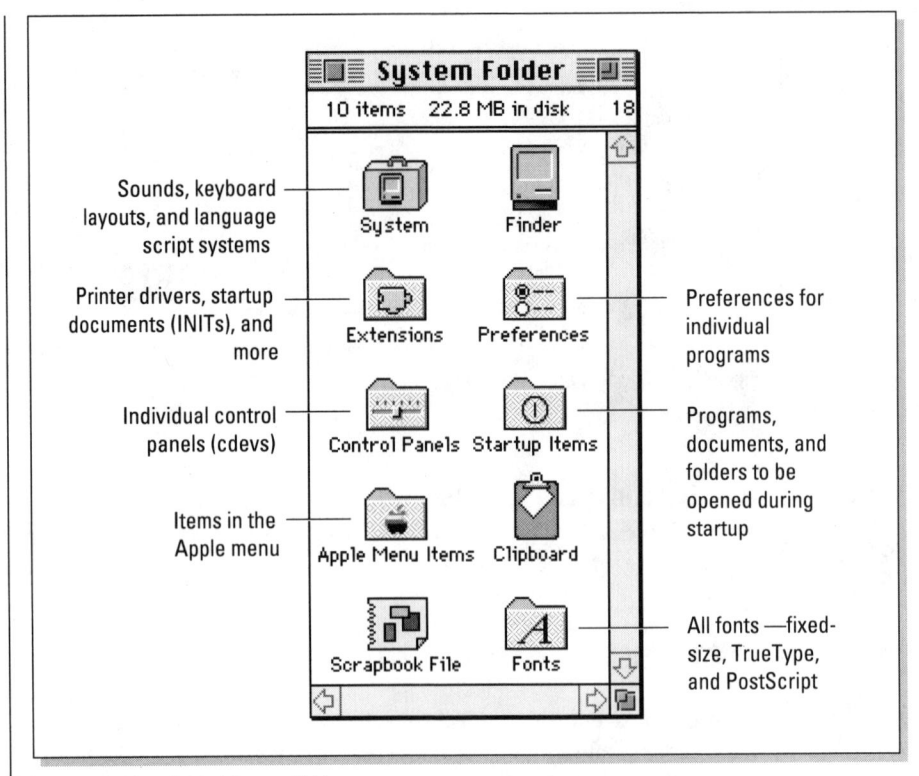

Figure 1-20: Subdivided System Folder.

Divided Control Panel

The Control Panel desk accessory, like the System Folder, easily becomes overcrowded and hard to use in older system software. System 7 doesn't use a Control Panel desk accessory; instead it has a special Control Panels folder full of individual control panels, each of which you open like an ordinary document, as shown in Figure 1-21. Each open control panel appears in its own window.

Control panel documents are kept in a special Control Panels folder within the System Folder. For convenience, the Control Panels folder appears in the Apple menu so you can open the folder easily. With the Control Panels folder open, you can rearrange the individual control panels in it by using the View menu or by dragging icons.

✘ Some old control panel documents (also called cdevs) work properly only if you put them in the System Folder itself, not in the Control Panels folder.

☞ For more information, see "Control Panels Folder" in Chapter 4 and "Control Panels" in Chapter 5.

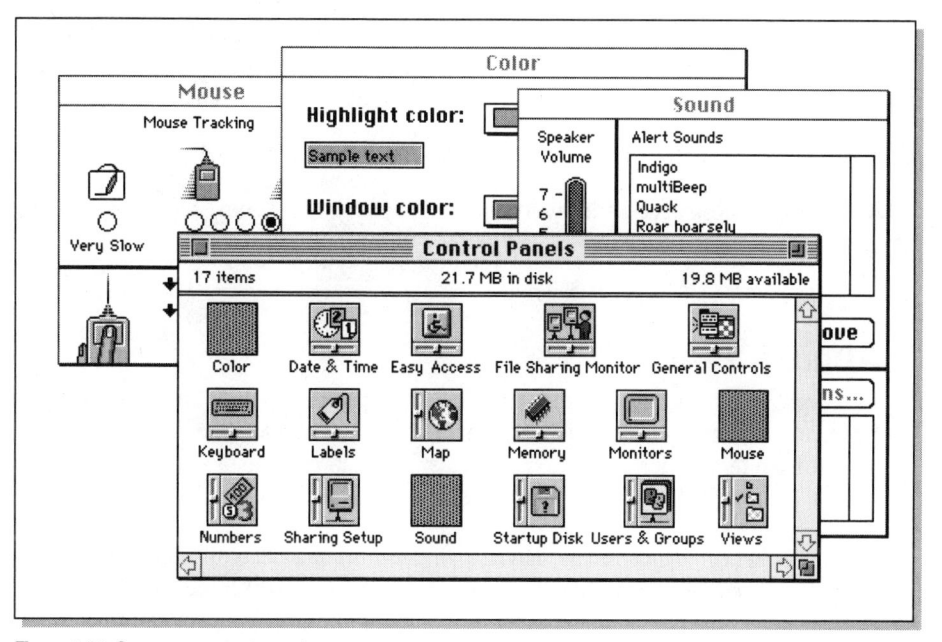

Figure 1-21: Separate control panels.

Desk Accessories

Desk accessories in System 7 do not have to be in the Apple menu. Each desk accessory has its own icon, as shown in Figure 1-22, which you can put in any folder or on the desktop. You open desk accessories like regular application programs, for example, by double-clicking their icons. You have the option of installing desk accessories in the Apple menu by dragging their icons or aliases of them to the Apple Menu Items folder within the System Folder.

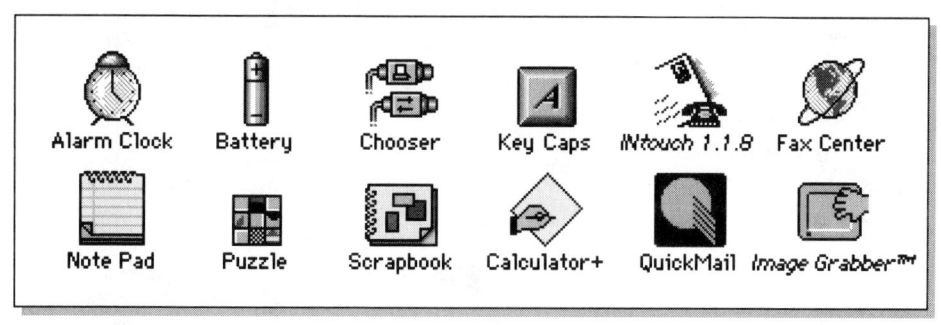

Figure 1-22: Some desk accessory icons.

You move and copy desk accessories by dragging their icons in the Finder. You do not use the Font/DA Mover utility program. For compatibility with earlier system software versions, desk accessories can exist in suitcase files, which the Font/DA Mover program creates. You must drag desk accessories out of suitcase files before you can open them in System 7, however.

✗ Most old desk accessories work fine with System 7, but some require updating.

☞ For more information, see "Software Compatibility" in Chapter 13 and "Desk Accessories" in Chapter 5.

Apple Menu

The Apple menu has a new role. In System 7, it expedites opening anything you use frequently. Any item you can open using the Finder you can put in the Apple menu and open it from there. This includes documents, application programs, desk accessories, folders, control panels, and even fonts and sounds.

You put an item in the Apple menu by dragging its icon or an alias of its icon into the Apple Menu Items folder, as shown in Figure 1-23, which is in the System Folder. The item becomes instantly available in the Apple menu (no need to restart your Macintosh).

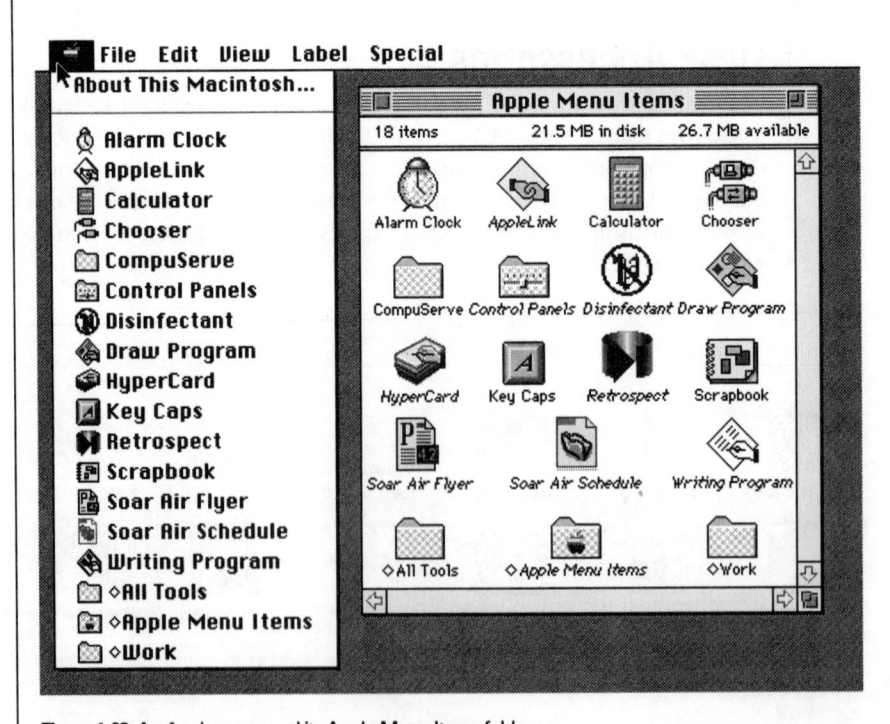

Figure 1-23: An Apple menu and its Apple Menu Items folder.

To remove an item from the Apple menu, drag its icon or alias out of the Apple Menu Items folder.

- ✔ The Apple Menu Items folder works with all software and on all Macintosh models that can use System 7.
- ☞ For more information, see "Apple Menu Items Folder" in Chapter 4 and "Your Own Apple Menu" in Chapter 5.

Installing Fonts, Sounds, and More

Installing fonts and sounds is now simply a matter of dragging their icons to the System Folder icon. You don't use the Font/DA Mover utility program, as you must in earlier versions of system software. Installing fonts makes them available in programs that enable you to pick fonts. Installing sounds makes them available as system alert sounds selectable in the Sound control panel. (As an option, you can also install sounds by pasting them into the Sound control panel.) You also install script systems for foreign languages by dragging their icons to the System Folder icon.

Starting with System 7.1, all fonts go in a special Fonts folder inside the System Folder. Finder 7.1 knows to put fonts in the Fonts folder when you drag them to the System Folder icon. With System 7.0 and System 7.0.1, all fonts except PostScript fonts go in the System file, which is inside the System Folder, and PostScript fonts go in the Extensions folder (or in the System Folder itself).

You can open the System file as if it were a folder to inspect or remove items in it, as shown in Figure 1-24. Each installed item — sound, keyboard layout, language script system, and in System 7.0 and System 7.0.1, font — is represented by an icon in the System file window.

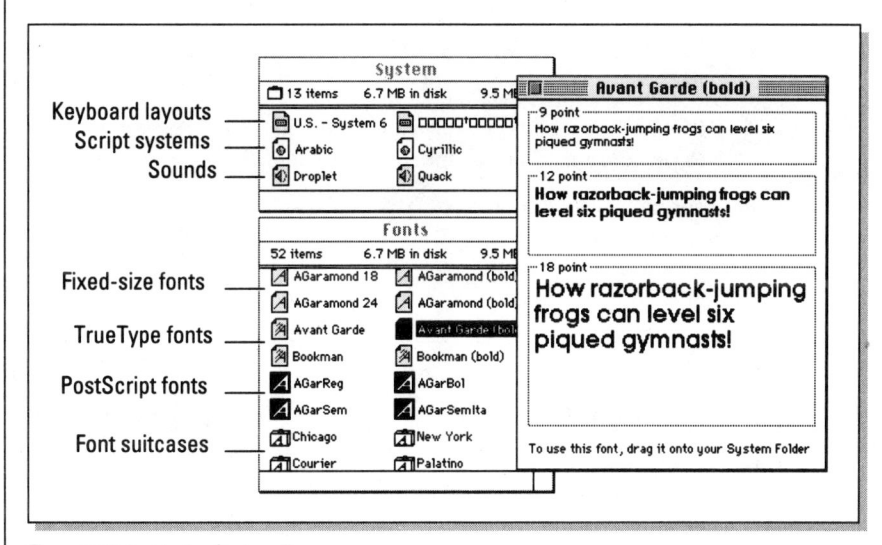

Figure 1-24: Inside the System file.

Opening a font icon from the Fonts folder (System 7.1) or the System file (Systems 7.0 and 7.0.1) displays some sample text using that font. Opening a sound icon plays the sound. To remove a font or sound, you drag its icon to an ordinary folder or to the desktop.

- ✔ All old screen fonts (not PostScript printer fonts) can be installed or removed by dragging to or from the Fonts folder (System 7.1) or the System file (Systems 7.0 and 7.0.1).
- ✘ The sounds used in HyperCard are a special format that don't work properly as system alert sounds.
- ☞ For more information, see "System File" and "Fonts Folder" in Chapter 4.

Variable-Size Fonts

Text looks smooth at any size on any screen or printing device thanks to the TrueType font technology built into System 7. TrueType fonts are variable-size outline fonts similar to the PostScript fonts that look so sharp on LaserWriters. System 7 smoothly scales TrueType fonts to any size, as shown in Figure 1-25. Old-style fonts still work; they look good at their fixed sizes and look lumpy when scaled to other sizes.

You install a variable-size font by dragging it to the System Folder icon. A typical variable-size TrueType font takes up 10K to 20K more disk space than a set of corresponding fixed-size fonts in sizes 9, 10, 12, 14, 18, and 24. However, TrueType fonts save disk space if you use large sizes or if you have a printing device that uses screen fonts. With TrueType, ImageWriters, fax modems, ink-jet printers, and laser printers without PostScript don't need the double, triple, or quadruple fixed sizes that take up a lot of disk space.

LaserWriters and other PostScript devices use PostScript fonts instead of equivalent TrueType fonts. If a document contains a TrueType font that has no PostScript equivalent, System 7 scales the TrueType font to the resolution of the output device.

- ✔ Variable-size fonts work on all Macintosh models, all printing devices, and with the programs you already have.
- ✘ Some old programs only provide a fixed list of font sizes and must be upgraded to provide a method for specifying any font size.
- ☞ For more information, see Chapter 7.

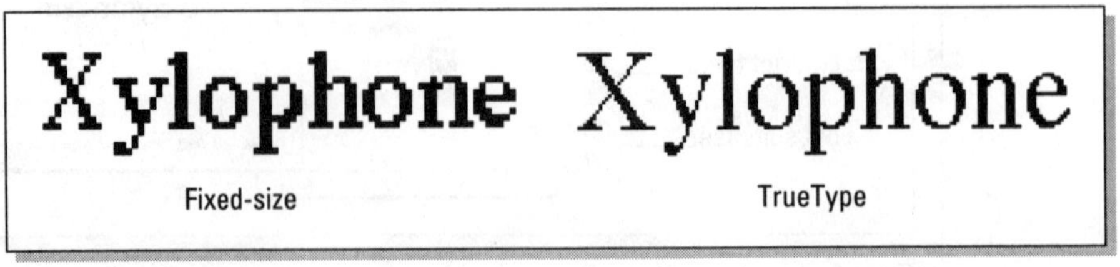

Xylophone   Xylophone

Fixed-size   TrueType

Figure 1-25: 36-point Times.

Multitasking

You will need your wits about you to get used to System 7's multitasking capabilities unless you already use the optional MultiFinder with System 6. With System 7, multitasking is not optional. Multitasking means you can have as many programs open simultaneously as will fit in your computer's memory, as shown in Figure 1-26. You can copy and paste among documents of open programs without closing documents and quitting programs. Also, you can switch to the Finder without quitting programs, and there open other programs, find documents, organize folders and disks, and so on.

Multitasking's valuable benefits have disorienting side effects. For instance, you may think the program you're using has unexpectedly quit when actually you switched to another open program. You must condition yourself to look at the menu bar when you need to know which open program is currently active.

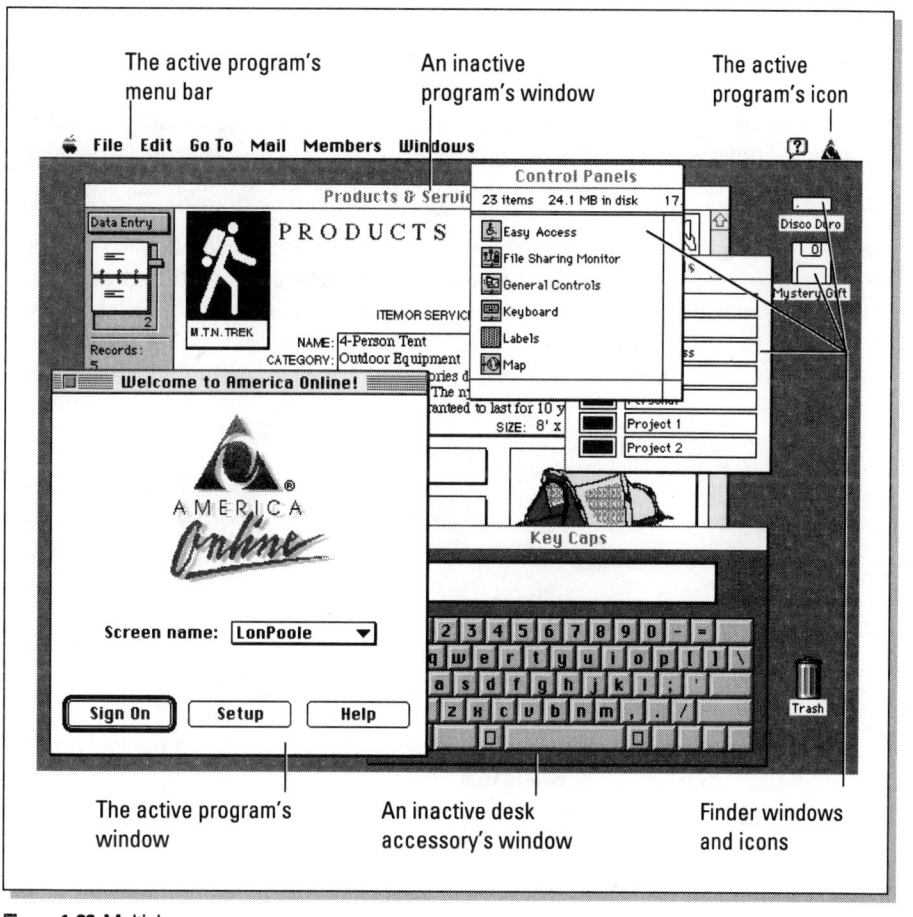

Figure 1-26: Multiple programs open.

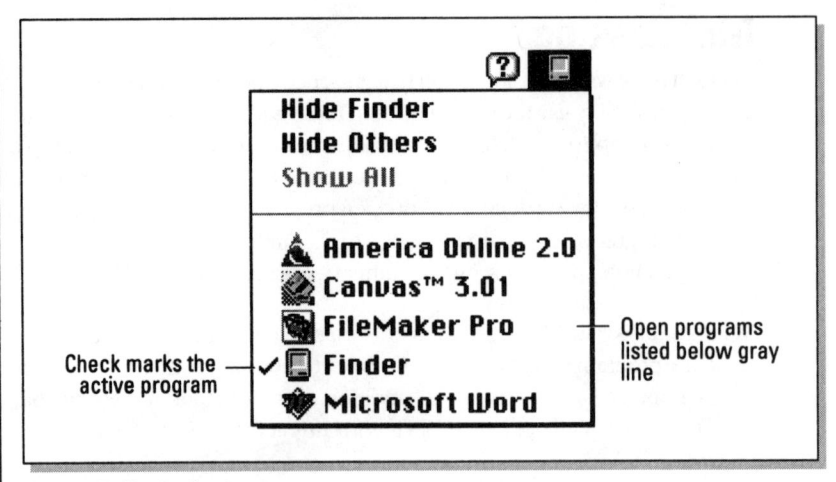

```
                    ┌─────────────────────────┐
                    │                  ? □   │
                    │    Hide Finder          │
                    │    Hide Others          │
                    │    Show All             │
                    │                         │
                    │   △ America Online 2.0  │
                    │   ◊ Canvas™ 3.01        │
                    │   ▨ FileMaker Pro       │ ── Open programs
Check marks the ──  │ ✓ □ Finder              │    listed below gray
  active program    │   ▨ Microsoft Word      │    line
                    └─────────────────────────┘
```

Figure 1-27: The Application menu.

The active program's icon appears at the right end of the menu bar. Clicking that icon reveals the Application menu, which lists the programs that are open, as shown in Figure 1-27. Choosing a listed program makes it the active program. You can also make a program the active program by clicking in any of its windows or by opening (double-clicking) its icon or any of its documents' icons in the Finder.

Programs that know how can operate in the background (while you work with another program) by using System 7's multitasking capabilities. Background programs operate during the intervals — only split seconds long — when the active program isn't using the computer. Background programs can't use the menu bar or interact directly with you in any way. They can, however, perform the following tasks:

♦ Recalculate spreadsheets

♦ Make backup copies of disks

♦ Print documents

♦ Sort databases

♦ Copy items in the Finder

♦ Send and receive electronic mail

✔ System 7's multitasking works with most software and on all Macintosh models that can use System 7. However, you can't use any program with System 7 that doesn't work when MultiFinder is active in older system software.

☞ For more information, see "Opening Multiple Programs" in Chapter 2.

Hiding Window Clutter

Having multiple programs open leads to a confusion of windows. You can eliminate window clutter by using Application menu commands to temporarily hide windows, as shown in Figure 1-28.

✔ Window hiding works with all software and on all Macintosh models that can use System 7.

☞ For more information, see "Opening Multiple Programs" in Chapter 2.

Figure 1-28: Window management.

Extending Memory

Application programs are becoming more memory-hungry all the time, and System 7 has a large appetite itself. Seems like a computer can never have too much memory.

32-Bit Addressing

Some Macintosh models can access more RAM (random-access memory) by using System 7's 32-Bit Addressing capability. Older system software does not have this capability and cannot access more than 8MB of RAM regardless of the amount installed. To turn 32-Bit Addressing on and off, you use the Memory control panel, as shown in Figure 1-29. With 4MB RAM SIMMs installed, for example, turning on 32-Bit Addressing enables you to use 10MB of RAM on a Mac LC, LC II, Classic II, Performa 200, or Performa 400; 17MB on a IIsi; 20MB on a Performa 600, IIvx, IIvi, or Quadra 700; 32MB on a IIci or IIfx; and 64MB on a Quadra 900 or Quadra 950. If 32-Bit Addressing is off, you can only use 8MB of RAM regardless of the amount installed.

Virtual memory

You may be able to increase the amount of memory available on your Macintosh without installing more RAM. System 7 can transparently use part of a hard disk as additional memory. This extra memory, called *virtual memory,* enables you to open more programs at once and increase the amount of memory each program gets when you open it, as shown in Figure 1-30. Given more memory, many programs

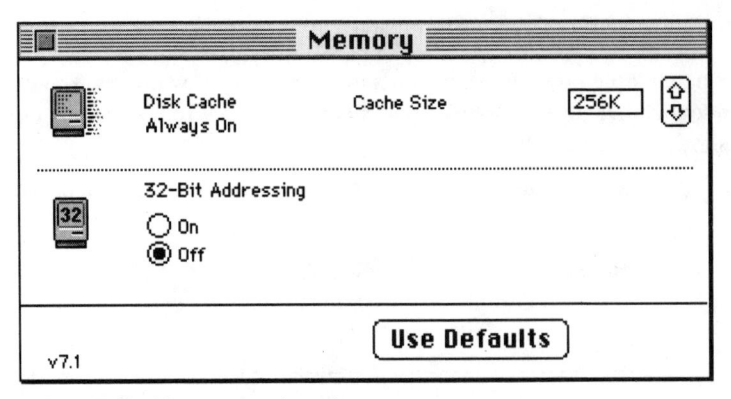

Figure 1-29: The Memory control panel.

enable you to open additional documents or larger documents. Virtual memory enables you to get by with less RAM. You buy only as much as you need for average use, not for peak use.

Virtual memory only works on a Macintosh equipped with a *paged memory management unit* (PMMU). The Classic II, LC II, SE/30, IIcx, IIx, IIsi, IIci, IIvx, IIvi, and IIfx models all have PMMUs, and so do all Performas, all Quadras, and all PowerBooks except the 100. A Mac II can be retrofitted with a PMMU, and an LC can be upgraded with an accelerator card containing a PMMU. However, a Mac Plus, SE, Classic, or Portable cannot use System 7's virtual memory even if it has such an accelerator, because the ROMs in those models are missing some information System 7 needs to implement virtual memory.

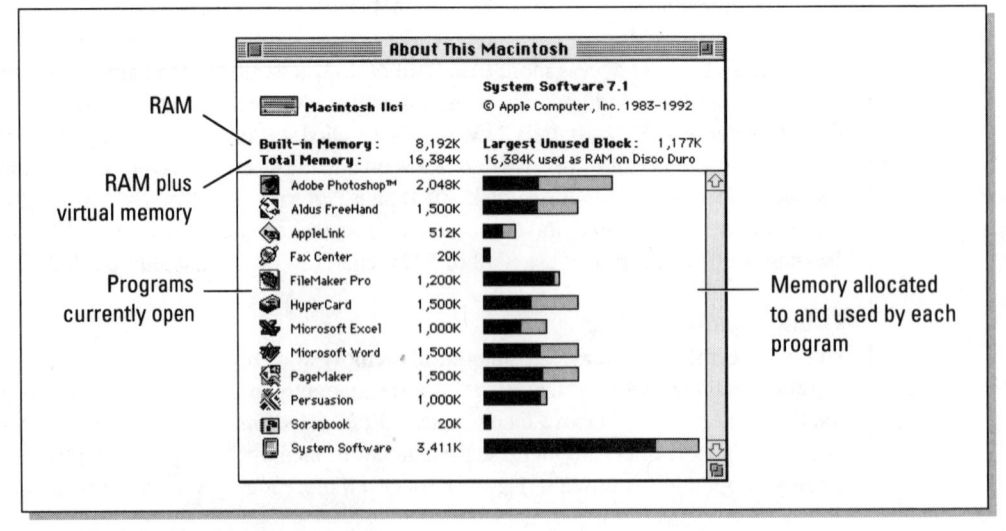

Figure 1-30: Using virtual memory.

[Figure showing Memory control panel with Disk Cache Always On, Cache Size 256K, Virtual Memory On/Off, Select Hard Disk: Disco Duro, Available on disk: 26M, Total memory: 12M]

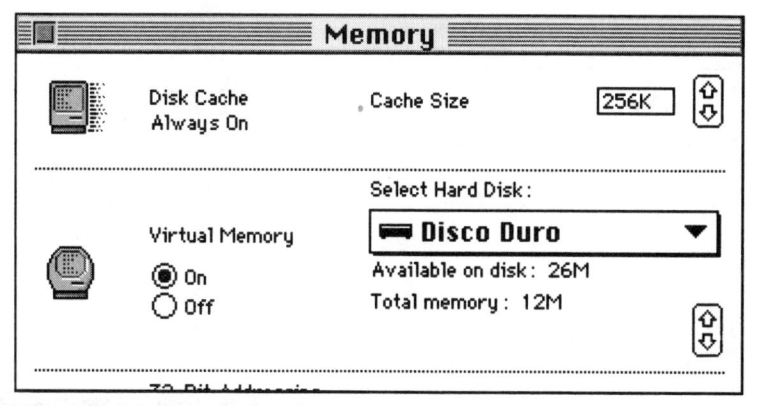

Figure 1-31: Virtual memory settings.

Controlling virtual memory

To turn virtual memory on and off, you use the Memory control panel, as shown in Figure 1-31. You also set the size of total memory and select a hard disk that has a block of space as large as the total amount of memory you want available (RAM plus virtual memory). These controls are not available on computers that cannot use virtual memory.

Disk Cache

You also use the Memory control panel to adjust the amount of RAM allocated for the Disk Cache, which improves disk performance. You cannot turn off the Disk Cache as you can its equivalent in older system software, the RAM Cache control in the General section of the Control Panel.

- ✔ The Disk Cache works on all Macintosh models that can use System 7.

- ✘ Virtual memory doesn't work on a Mac Plus, SE, Classic, or Portable, and a Mac LC or II must be upgraded to use it. The 32-Bit Addressing capability doesn't work on a Mac Plus, SE, or Portable. To use 32-Bit Addressing on a Mac IIcx, IIx, II, or SE/30, you must install the MODE32 system extension, which Apple distributes free through dealers, user groups, and on-line information services. Also, your old application programs, desk accessories, system extensions, control panels, and hard disk software may not work when 32-Bit Addressing is on.

- ☞ For more information, see "Memory Management Tactics" in Chapter 5.

Chooser Changes

In older system software you specified your network name in the Chooser desk accessory. System 7 has you enter it along with your network password and a name for your Macintosh in the Sharing Setup control panel (described in the next section). In addition, Chooser 7 can show more devices and zones than older versions, as shown in Figure 1-32.

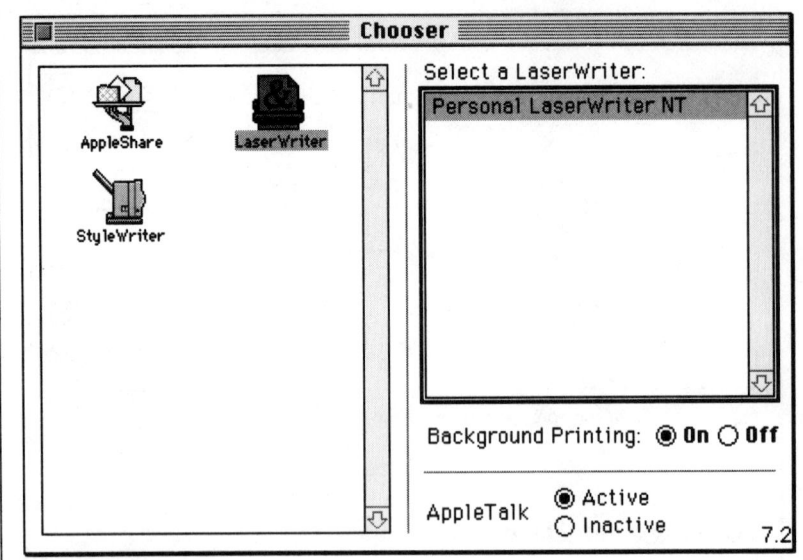

Figure 1-32: The Chooser.

File Sharing

If your Macintosh is connected to others in a network, System 7 enables you to share hard disks, folders, and the files in them with other network users. You can access folders and disks others have made available to you. You can also make your folders and disks available to others on the network (including those using System 6.x with AppleShare client software).

Sharing someone else's folders

To share another Mac's folder or disk, you use the Chooser desk accessory. It lists as AppleShare file servers the names of all computers that are sharing their folders and disks. After you choose one, the Chooser asks you to connect as a guest or a registered user and then presents a list of items you may share, as shown in Figure 1-33.

Accessing someone else's folders or disks is considerably slower than accessing your own. Also, your computer's performance degrades markedly while others share your folders or disks. For better performance, especially in networks with more than ten active users, everyone can put folders to be shared on the hard disk of a Macintosh dedicated to sharing its files (a dedicated file server). For best performance in large networks, you need a dedicated file server such as Apple's AppleShare 3.0.

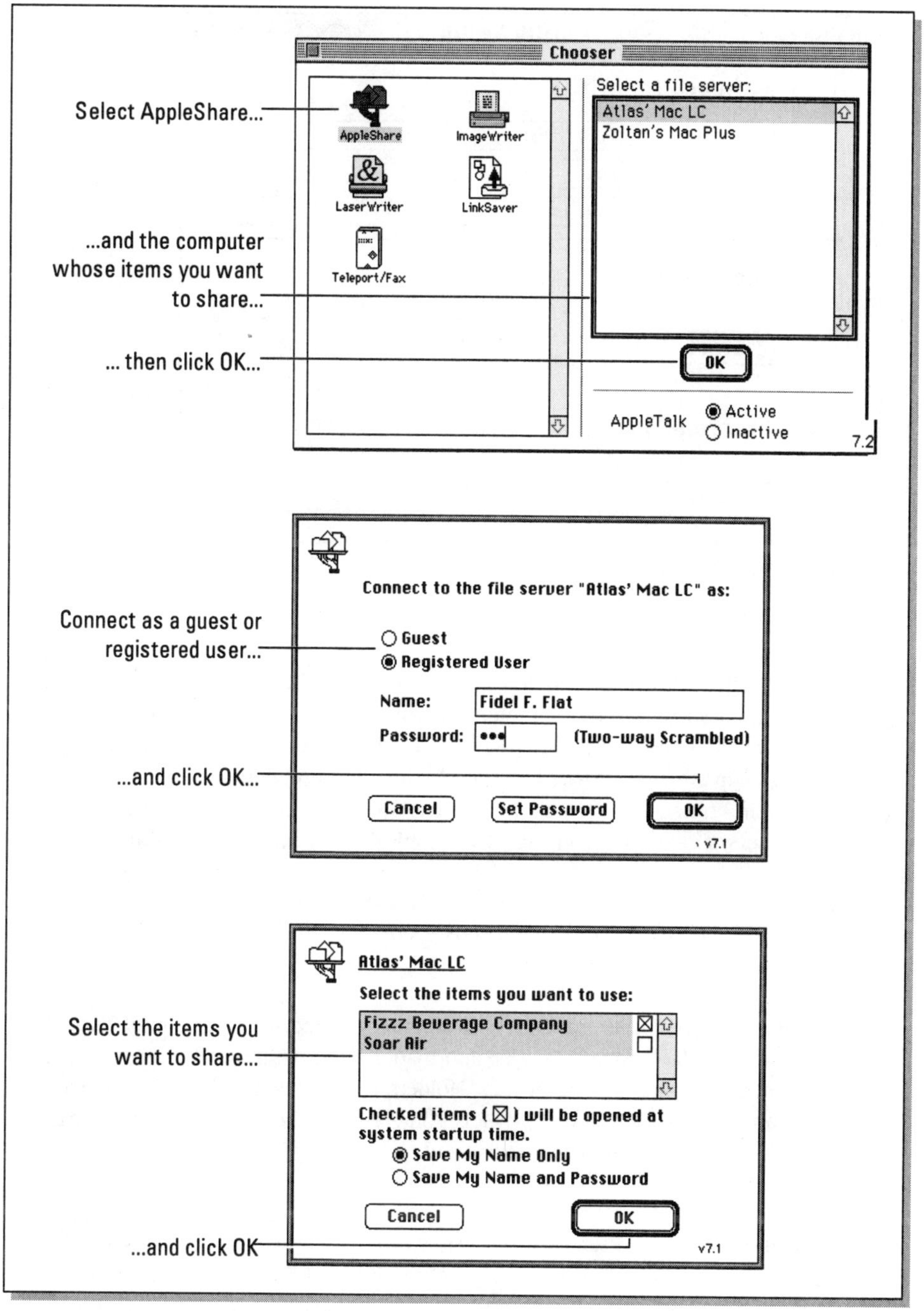

Figure 1-33: Selecting folders to share.

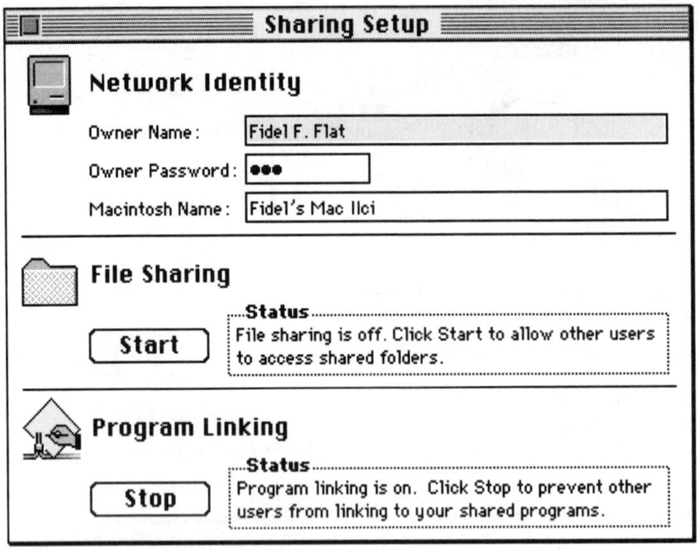

Figure 1-34: The Sharing Setup control panel.

Sharing your folders with others

Before you can share your disks or folders, you must configure your Macintosh as an AppleShare file server with the Sharing Setup control panel, as shown in Figure 1-34. It then shows up as an AppleShare file server in the Choosers of other network users who have System 7 file sharing software installed. It also shows up as an AppleShare server in the Choosers of System 6.*x* users who have AppleShare client software installed.

Sharing your disks or folders with others increases your system memory usage by 250K to 300K. That leaves only about 600K for opening programs on a 2MB Macintosh.

To share one of your disks or folders with others, you select it and use Finder 7's Sharing command to display the item's sharing information window, as shown in Figure 1-35. There you specify who can see the item's folders, see its files, and make changes to them. You can grant these access privileges differently to the owner of the item (usually you), to one other registered user or group of registered users you designate, and to everyone else.

You identify registered users, set their passwords, and create groups of users with the Users & Groups control panel, as shown in Figure 1-36. Another control panel, File Sharing Monitor, enables you to see who is sharing what and how busy they're keeping your Macintosh. You can also use that control panel to disconnect individual users who are sharing your folders and disks.

Figure 1-35: Sharing information (access privileges).

✘   File sharing works on all Macintosh models that can use System 7. However, your Macintosh should have at least 2.5MB of RAM if you want to open more than a single mid-size program while sharing your folders or disks.

☞   For more information, see Chapter 8.

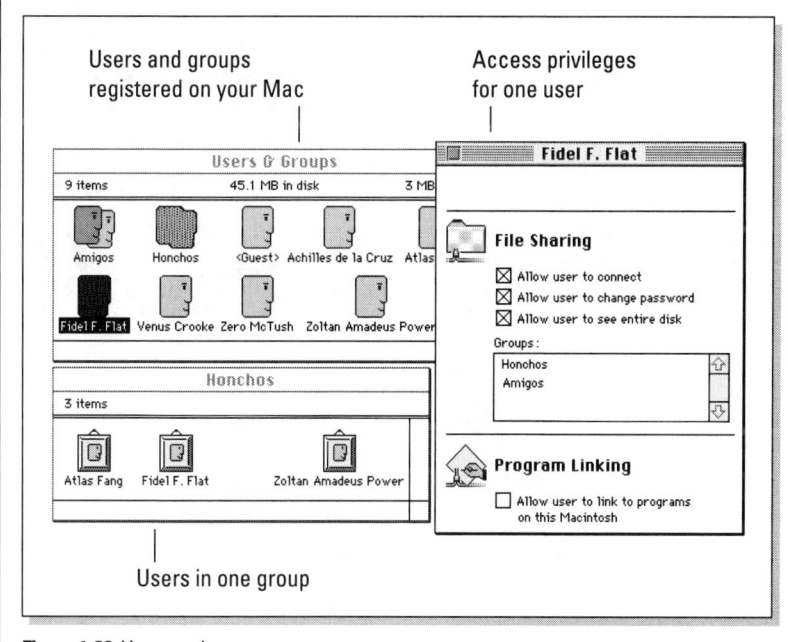

Figure 1-36: Users and groups.

Interactive Help

At last the Macintosh can explain itself. You can get a description of objects you see on screen by turning on System 7's optional balloon help. With balloon help on, you place the pointer over an object and a concise description of it appears in a cartoon-style balloon, as shown in Figure 1-37. Aside from balloons appearing and disappearing, everything works normally when balloon help is on. You may perceive a slight delay as help balloons come and go, especially if you use a slower Macintosh.

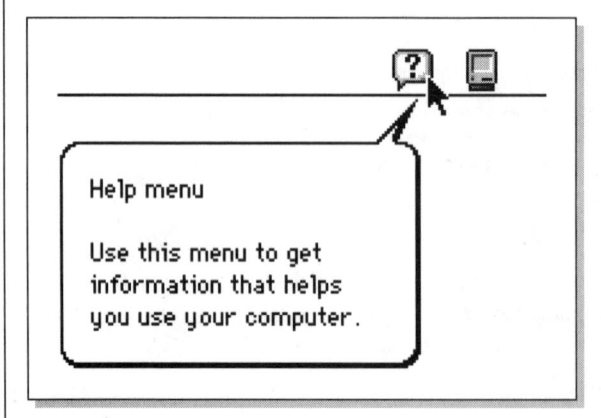

Figure 1-37: A help balloon.

To turn on balloon help, choose Show Balloons from the new Help menu, which is always near the right end of the menu bar, as shown in Figure 1-38. That command then changes to Hide Balloons, and choosing it turns off balloon help.

Each program can add items to the Help menu for accessing other types of help, such as how-to help. For example, the Finder adds a Finder Shortcuts item that displays a list of tricks for using the Finder.

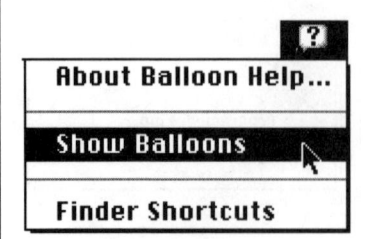

Figure 1-38: The Help menu.

✗ Balloon help knows about all standard objects in the Macintosh interface. However, it cannot describe a specific program's menu commands, window contents, dialog boxes, and so on unless the program has been revised to include the necessary help balloons.

☞ For more information, see "Balloon Help" in Chapter 2.

Stationery Pads

Stationery pads save time if you regularly create new documents with common formatting, contents, and so on. Opening a stationery pad is like tearing a page from a pad of preprinted forms. You get a new document with all the common elements preset. Stationery pads have a distinctive icon that looks like a stack of document icons, as shown in Figure 1-39. The Finder uses a generic stationery pad icon if the program that handles that type of document doesn't know about System 7's stationery.

You can make any document a stationery pad by setting the Stationery Pad option in its info window, as shown in Figure 1-40. To see an item's info window, select the item and choose Get Info from the Finder's File menu. Some programs enable you to directly save a document as a stationery pad by setting a Stationery Pad option of their Save and Save As commands, as shown in Figure 1-41. These programs have been upgraded specifically to work with System 7's stationery pads.

Programs that know about stationery pads open an untitled document identical to the stationery pad. For programs that don't know about stationery pads, the Finder automatically creates a new document by making a copy of the stationery pad, asking you to name it, and having the program open the copy.

✔ Stationery pads work with most software, but work best with software that has been updated to take advantage of them.

☞ For more information, see "Stationery Pads" in Chapter 3.

Figure 1-39: Stationery pad icons and ordinary icons.

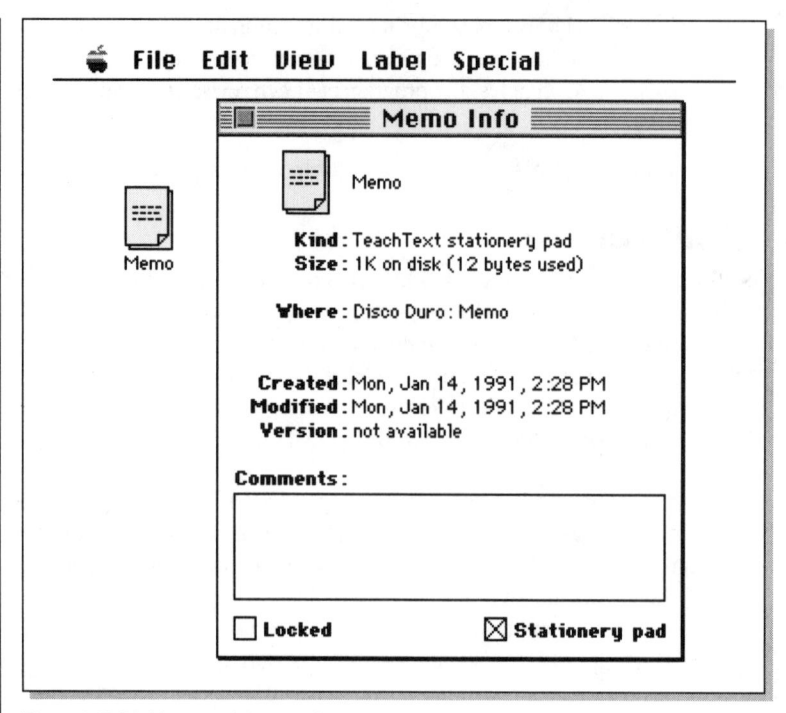

Figure 1-40: Making a stationery pad.

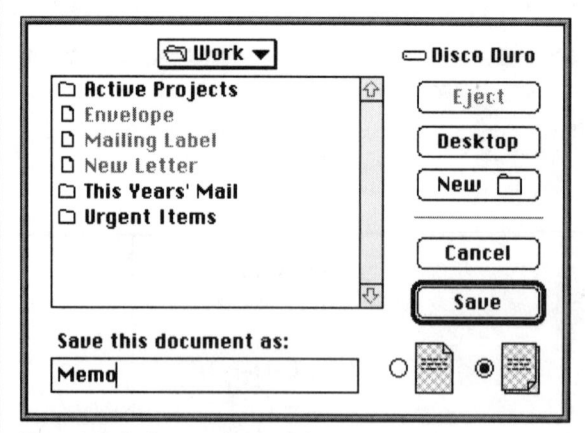

Figure 1-41: Saving a stationery pad.

Folder Nesting Revealed

A pop-up menu in the title bar of the active Finder window reveals the path through your folder structure from the active window to the disk containing it. The menu pops up when you press Command while clicking the window title, as shown in Figure 1-42.

Figure 1-42: Folder path pop-up menu.

You can open any folder along the path by choosing the folder from the pop-up menu. To close the active window while opening a folder along the path, press Option while choosing the folder from the pop-up menu.

✔ All folder windows have a pop-up menu in the title bar.

Smart Drag

When you drag an item from one window to a folder in an overlapping window, Finder 7 keeps the destination folder in view, as shown in Figure 1-43. Older Finders bring the source window in front of an overlapping target window as soon as you begin dragging, possibly covering the destination folder.

✔ Dragging from an inactive window works on all Macintosh models that can use System 7.

☛ For more information, see "Polite Drag" in Chapter 3.

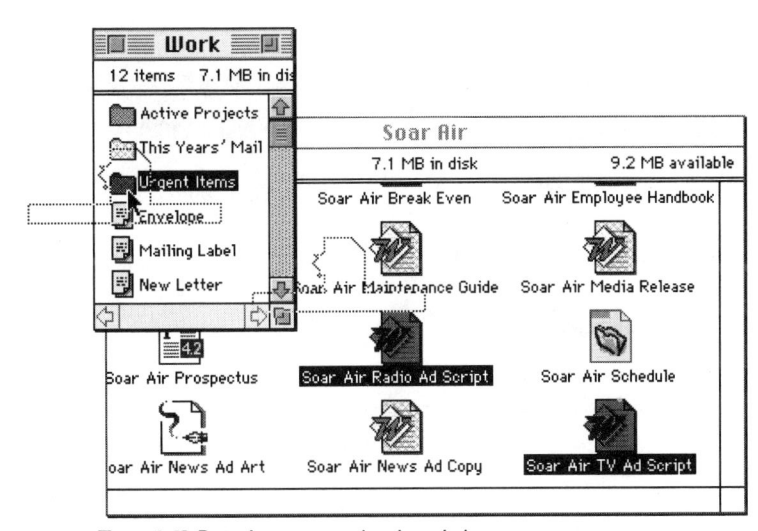

Figure 1-43: Dragging to an overlapping window.

Keyboard Shortcuts

You can select an item in the active Finder window (or the desktop, if no window is active) without using the mouse. Typing an item's name or the first part of it selects the item. Other keystrokes select an item near the currently selected item, open the item, and more. Table 1-1 has the details.

- The keyboard shortcuts work on all Macintosh models that can use System 7.
- For more Finder shortcuts, see "Finder Power" in Chapter 3.

Table 1-1:	Finder keyboard shortcuts
Objective	**Action**
Select an item by name	Type the item's full or partial name
Select the next item alphabetically	Tab
Select the previous item alphabetically	Shift-Tab
Select next item up, down, left, or right	Up Arrow, Down Arrow, Left Arrow, or Right Arrow
Select the item nearest the upper-right corner of the desktop	Command-Shift-Up Arrow
Open the selected item	Command-O or Command-Down Arrow
Open the selected item and close the active window	Command-Option-O or Command-Option-Down Arrow
Open the parent folder, disk, or volume	Command-Up Arrow
Open the parent folder, disk, or volume, and close the active window	Command-Option-Up Arrow
Make the desktop active	Command-Shift-Up Arrow
Begin editing the selected item's name	Return or Enter
Expand the selected folder	Command-Right Arrow
Expand the selected folder and its nested folders	Command-Option-Right Arrow
Collapse the selected folder	Command-Left Arrow
Collapse the selected folder and its nested folders	Command-Option-Left Arrow
Skip installing all system extensions during one startup	Hold down Shift during startup

A New Opening

You can open a document from Finder 7 by dragging the document icon to the icon of any application program that can open it, as shown in Figure 1-44. The program need not have created the document but must be compatible with it. When you drag a document to a compatible program, the program's icon becomes highlighted.

- This new method of opening documents works with all programs, including those that haven't been updated for System 7.

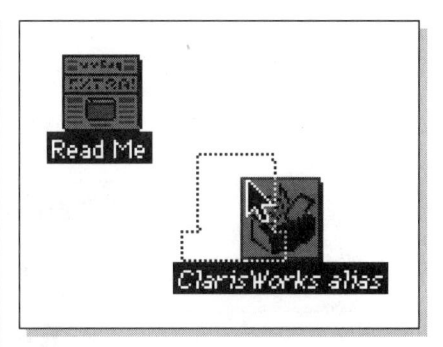

Figure 1-44: Dragging a document to open it.

Naming Duplicates

The Finder constructs names of duplicate items more economically than it used to. Instead of prefixing the name with the words Copy of, it now simply suffixes the name with the word *copy*, as shown in Figure 1-45. Additional copies of the same item also have a serial number suffixed.

- The new method of naming duplicate items works on all Macintosh models that can use System 7.

- For more information, see "Naming Duplicates" in Chapter 3.

Figure 1-45: Names of duplicate items.

Background Copying

You can work with any application program or desk accessory while the Finder copies items in the background, as shown in Figure 1-46. This capability is especially useful when copying from or to a shared folder or disk. To switch to another program, click in any of its windows or choose it from the Application menu any time after starting the copy process. You can't open a program or a document by double-clicking its icon or by using the Finder's Open command (File menu), but you can open application programs, desk accessories, and documents by choosing them from the Apple menu while the Finder is copying files. Control panels are considered part of the Finder, so you can't use them while copying.

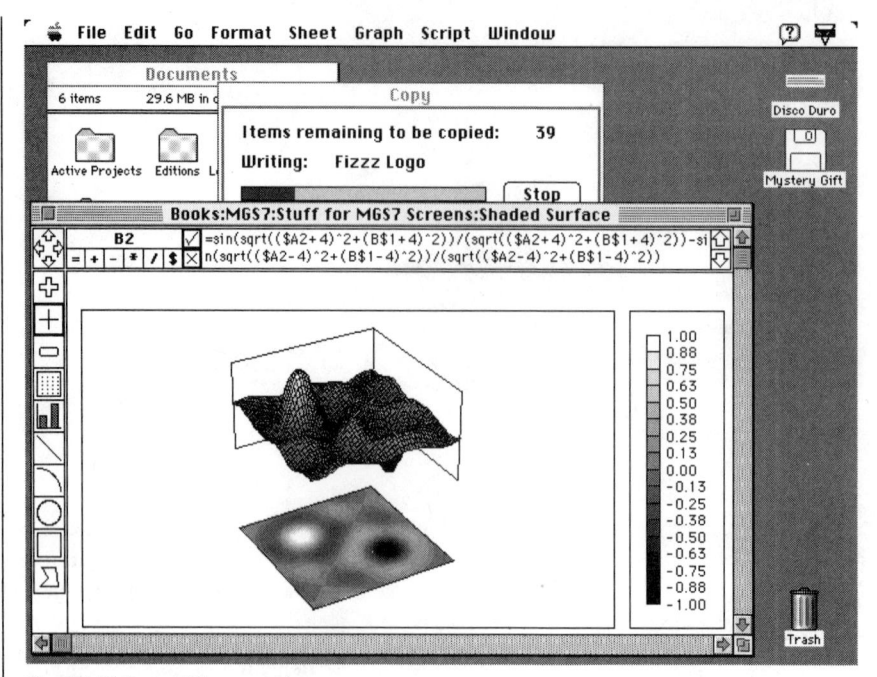

Figure 1-46: Copy while you work.

✔ Background copying works on all Macintosh models that can use System 7.

☞ For more information, see "Background Work" in Chapter 3.

Trash Behavior

Items you drag to the Trash now remain there indefinitely. You must empty the Trash manually using the Finder's Empty Trash command (Special menu). When you do, Finder 7 tells you how many items the Trash contains and how much disk space they occupy, as shown in Figure 1-47. You decide whether to discard them all or cancel. To bypass this notice, press Option while choosing the Empty Trash command.

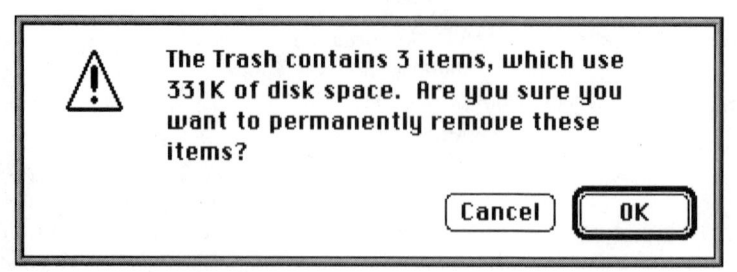

Figure 1-47: The Trash warning.

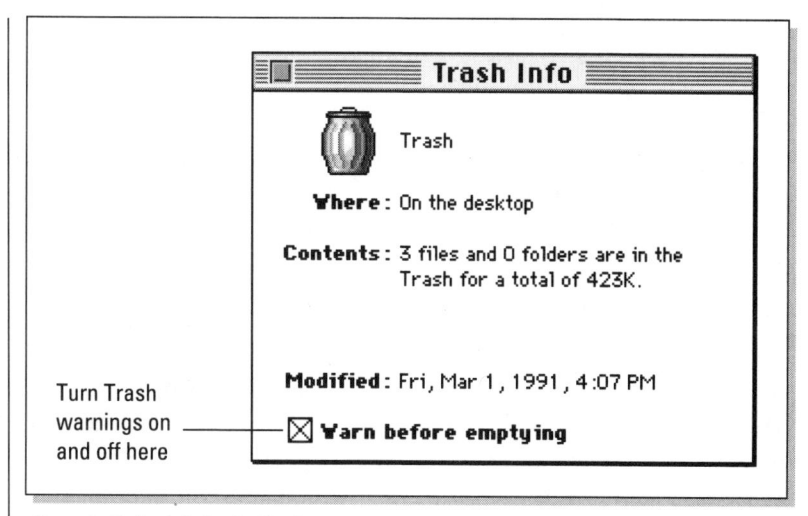

```
                 ┌─────────────────────────────────────┐
                 │ ▀▀▀□▀▀▀▀▀▀▀▀▀   Trash Info   ▀▀▀▀▀▀ │
                 │                                     │
                 │           ▆  Trash                  │
                 │                                     │
                 │    Where: On the desktop            │
                 │                                     │
                 │    Contents: 3 files and 0 folders  │
                 │              are in the             │
                 │              Trash for a total of   │
                 │              423K.                  │
                 │                                     │
Turn Trash       │    Modified: Fri, Mar 1, 1991, 4:07 PM │
warnings on ─────│    ☒ Warn before emptying           │
and off here     │                                     │
                 └─────────────────────────────────────┘
```

Figure 1-48: Get Info for the Trash.

You can disable the Trash warning by selecting the Trash, using the Get Info command, and turning off the appropriate option, as shown in Figure 1-48.

When you drag locked items to the Trash, Finder 7 does not display a warning as older Finders do. Instead, the warning appears when you choose the Empty Trash command with any of the locked items in the Trash. And unlike older Finders, Finder 7 does not confirm whether you want to discard application programs and system files when you drag them to the Trash.

- ✔ The Trash exhibits its new behavior on all Macintosh models that can use System 7.

- ☞ For more information, see "Trash Disposal" in Chapter 3.

Live Copy/Paste

Some programs use System 7 to enable you to share information dynamically from one document with other documents. Because the sharing is dynamic, changing the original information automatically updates copies of it wherever they are. Think of it as live copy-and-paste. The automatic updating extends to computers interconnected on a network, so a document on your computer can dynamically share information from a document on another networked Macintosh. By contrast, copying and pasting shares information statically and on one Macintosh only.

You make a live copy of information by *publishing* an *edition* of it. You include copies of the information in a document by *subscribing* to the edition, as shown in Figure 1-49. Publishing material from a document creates a live copy of the material in an edition file on disk. Any number of other documents (on your Mac or others

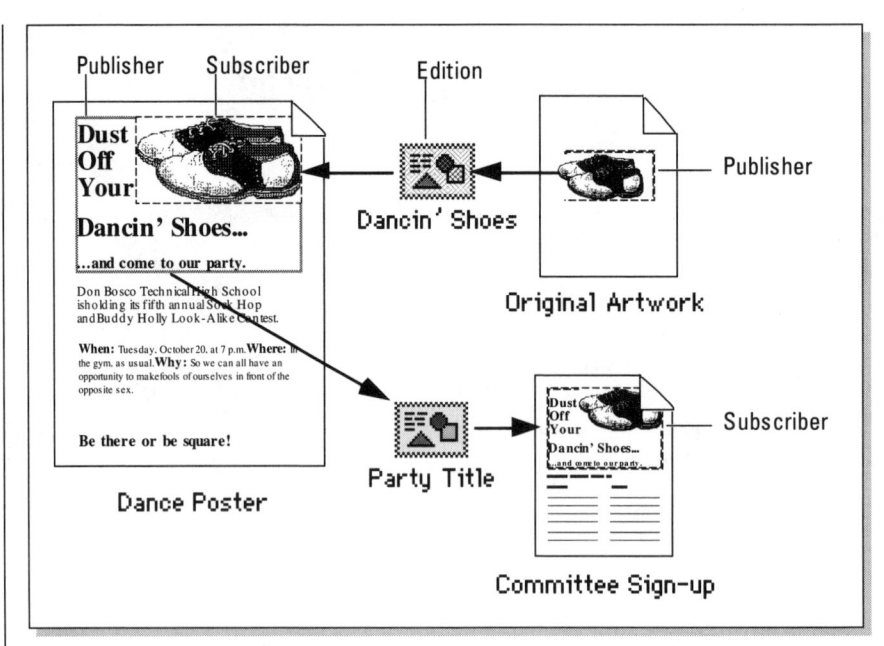

Figure 1-49: Publishing and subscribing.

networked to yours) include live copies of the material by subscribing to the edition. When you change the original material and save the document it's in, the edition is automatically updated. Every subscribing document learns of the update the next time it is opened.

Information can only be shared dynamically among documents created by programs that include Edit menu commands for publishing and subscribing, as shown in Figure 1-50. You won't find these commands in your old programs because developers must upgrade their programs to include publishing and subscribing commands.

✘ Old programs require modification to publish and subscribe information.

☞ For more information, see Chapter 9.

Accessing Data

Some programs now enable you to use System 7's Data Access Manager (DAM). It provides a common, simple method for getting data from a variety of large databases resident on host computers of all brands and sizes. You can usually recognize one of these programs by the Open Query command in its File menu.

To get data, you use the Open Query command to open a query document that describes the type of data you want. A dialog box describes what you get if you enter the information it requests and click a button to start the query, as shown in Figure 1-51.

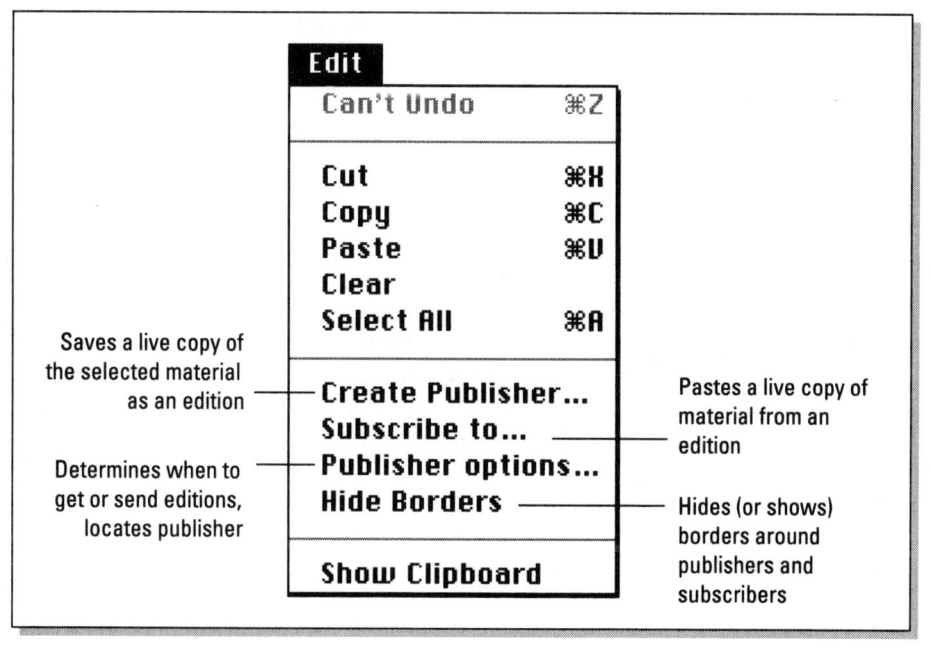

```
                    ┌─────────────────────┐
                    │ Edit                │
                    │ Can't Undo      ⌘Z  │
                    │                     │
                    │ Cut             ⌘X  │
                    │ Copy            ⌘C  │
                    │ Paste           ⌘V  │
                    │ Clear               │
                    │ Select All      ⌘A  │
Saves a live copy of│                     │
the selected material│Create Publisher... │ Pastes a live copy of
    as an edition ──│ Subscribe to...     │ material from an
                    │ Publisher options...│ edition
Determines when to  │ Hide Borders        │
get or send editions│                     │ Hides (or shows)
    locates publisher                     │ borders around
                    │ Show Clipboard      │ publishers and
                    └─────────────────────┘ subscribers
```

Figure 1-50: Commands for publishing and subscribing.

Behind the scenes the query document and DAM connect to the host computer, request the information using the arcane commands of the host database, obtain the information, and paste it into your document.

```
┌─────────────────────────────────────────────┐
│              Financial Reports              │
│ ........................................... │
│   This query document retrieves corporate   │
│   financial reports from the accounting     │
│   department mainframe computer. The reports│
│   are current as of the latest postings.    │
│                                             │
│      Your Name: [Zero McTush            ]   │
│                                             │
│   Your Password: [•••••                 ]   │
│                                             │
│   Type of Report:  ● Trial Balance          │
│                    ○ Net Worth              │
│                    ○ Profit and Loss        │
│                                             │
│                    ( Cancel )  (( Start ))  │
└─────────────────────────────────────────────┘
```

Figure 1-51: A query dialog box.

✘ Old programs require modification to use System 7's simplified data accessing capabilities. System 7.1 does not include data accessing; you must obtain it separately from Apple.

☞ For more information, see "Data Access" in Chapter 10.

Linking Programs

System 7 paves the way for programs to work together. While you work in one program, you can use the commands and tools of other programs made by different software vendors. For example, an Aldus page layout program could use the functions of a Microsoft word processing program when you wanted to edit a story; a Deneba proofreading program when you wanted to check spelling; an Adobe image editing program when you wanted to edit a photo; a Claris drawing program when you wanted to change a graphic; and so on, as shown in Figure 1-52.

Software developers can create specialized program modules that you combine to obtain the set of features and functions best for you. Developers can concentrate on their specialties instead of all trying to create competing monoliths.

Program collaboration relies on System 7's framework for information interchange, called Apple events. It enables any program to send messages to other programs. System 7 stores Apple events messages sent to a closed program and forwards the messages when the program is next opened. It also dispatches messages across a network to programs on another Macintosh.

In addition, Apple events is the basis for system-wide user scripting. With products such as UserLand Frontier and AppleScript (due from Apple sometime in 1993), users can write scripts (sets of instructions) that carry out sequences of tasks unattended to in one

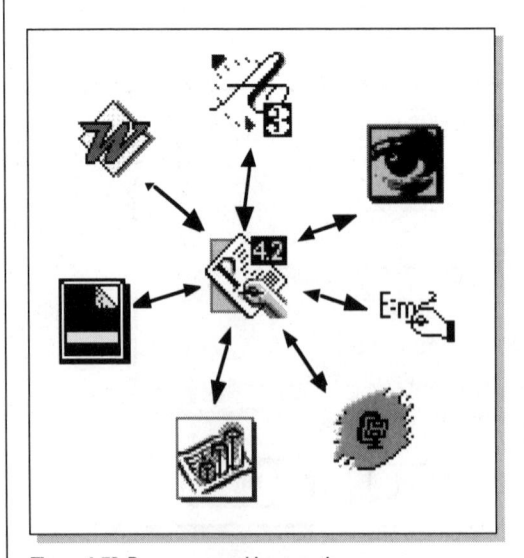

Figure 1-52: Programs working together.

program or many programs. For example, a script could correct the spelling of a name in the text of several documents created by a number of application programs.

✗ Old programs require modification to use System 7's program linking capabilities and to respond to user scripting.

☞ For more information, see "Program Linking" in Chapter 10.

At Ease

As an alternative to the Finder's standard desktop, Apple's At Ease software provides a simplified view of the Macintosh environment, as shown in Figure 1-53. A system administrator installs At Ease on a Macintosh and determines which programs and documents the users of the Macintosh can access. Each available program and document has a large button on the At Ease desktop, and clicking a button once opens the item (unlike Finder icons, which require double-clicking to open). The administrator can also prevent users from saving documents on the hard disk, and can set a password to restrict access to items not on the At Ease desktop or in the Apple menu. At Ease is not included with System 7; it must be purchased and installed separately.

✔ At Ease works on any Macintosh with System 7.0 or later installed.

☞ For more information, see "At Ease" in Chapter 3.

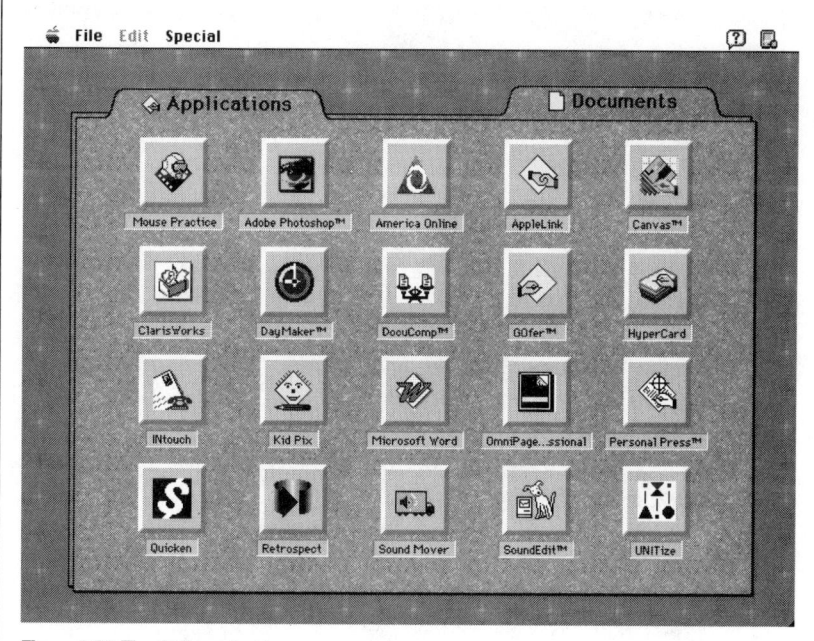

Figure 1-53: The At Ease desktop.

QuickTime Movies

A system extension called QuickTime, introduced in 1992, extends the standard Macintosh system software so you can incorporate movies into documents you create with mainstream application programs. After installing QuickTime, you can copy and paste movies as easily as you copy and paste individual graphics. QuickTime can also compress individual graphics, and when you open a compressed graphic, QuickTime automatically decompresses it.

Applications may use two methods for controlling movie playback. They may display a standard VCR-like controller just below the movie, as shown in Figure 1-54. You use this playbar to play, stop, browse, or step through the movie and adjust its sound level.

Applications may also display movies without controllers. In this case, a badge in the lower-left corner of the movie distinguishes it from a still graphic. To play a movie that has a badge and no controller, you double-click the movie. Clicking a playing movie stops it.

QuickTime is not included with System 7; you must obtain it and install it separately. Apple sells a QuickTime Starter Kit through retail channels, and QuickTime comes with many related products.

✔ QuickTime works on any Macintosh with a 68020, 68030, or 68040 main processor that has System 6.0.7, System 7.0, or later system software installed.

☞ For more information, see Chapter 12.

Figure 1-54: A QuickTime movie with playback controller.

WorldScript

System 7.1 is the first Macintosh system software capable of handling multiple languages without modification. You can install resources called script systems in the System file for languages that do not use the Roman alphabet. Each script system supplies fonts, keyboard layouts, rules for text sorting and word breaks, and rules for formatting dates, times, and numbers. Some script systems handle very large character sets and bidirectional or contextual text. Two system extensions included with System 7.1, WorldScript I and WorldScript II, process language script systems.

With multiple script systems installed in your System file, a Keyboard menu appears between the Help menu and the Application menu (see Figure 1-55) and you can use it to switch languages and keyboards.

✔ WorldScript I and WorldScript II work on any Macintosh with System 7.1 installed. Many programs require no modification to work with simple alphabets (Roman and Cyrillic) and with bidirectional and contextual languages (Hebrew, Arabic, Greek, and Thai).

✘ Old programs require updating to use languages with large alphabets such as Chinese and Japanese, and to take full advantage of WorldScript capabilities.

☞ For more information, see "Multiple Languages" in Chapter 4 and "Control Panels" in Chapter 5.

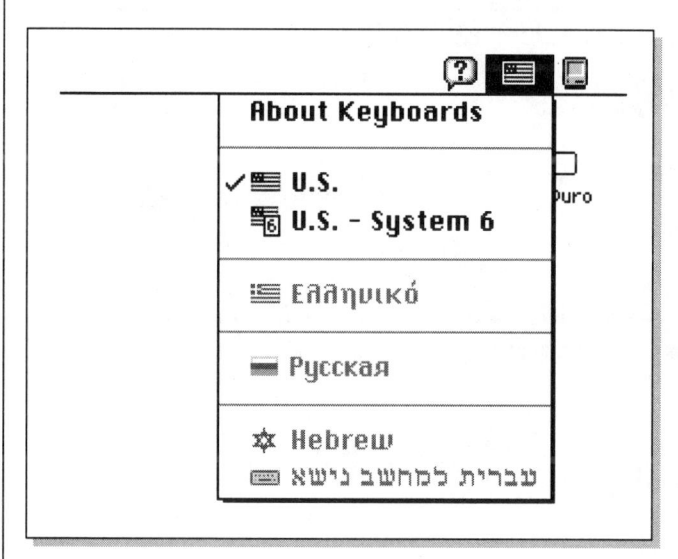

Figure 1-55: The Keyboard menu.

Determining What You Need

My how the system software has grown! The About This Macintosh command (which replaces About the Finder) in the Apple menu shows System 7 and Finder 7 together need two to three times as much memory as their immediate predecessors (Figure 1-56). To use the new system software, your Macintosh must have at least 2MB of RAM (random-access memory) and a hard disk.

You'll need more than the minimum 2MB if you use large or complex application programs; if you want to open several programs at once; or if you want to use the new file sharing capability and open any but the smallest program as well. As a rule of thumb, figure you'll need 1MB more than you use with older system software. You'll enjoy System 7 more if your Macintosh has at least 4MB of RAM.

To see colorized windows on your Macintosh, it must be displaying at least 256 colors or 16 grays. If it's set at a lower number — or if your Mac has only a black-and-white monitor — your windows and dialog boxes will look like they always have.

Most of System 7 works on all Macintosh models: the Plus, SE, Classic, and up. Only the three oldest models — the 128K, 512K, and XL — can't use System 7.

☛ For more information, see Appendix C.

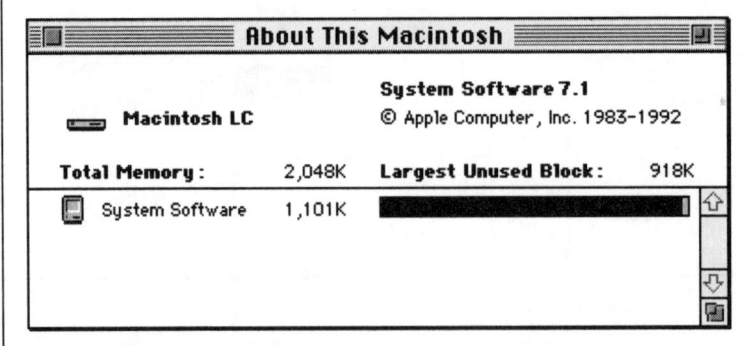

Figure 1-56: System 7 memory requirements.

Exploring Is the Key

So many features and capabilities may seem intimidating. Remember though, that you can learn how to use System 7 at your own pace. Take your time exploring the many Finder improvements. Wait on file sharing, virtual memory, and 32-Bit Addressing until you need them. Turn on balloon help only when you find it beneficial. Figure out publishing and subscribing (live copy/paste) and data access when you get programs that include them.

System 7 brings only a few changes you must face from the moment you begin using it. You can't dodge multitasking; you must get used to having multiple programs open at once. Also, you have to relearn a few basic skills like editing icon names and using the standard directory dialog boxes for opening and saving items.

You upgrade to System 7 not for the changes it forces on you immediately, but for the possibilities it offers. Take your time. Upgrade when you can afford to increase your Mac's memory (and get a hard disk, if you don't already have one), but do it. Apple has made it clear that System 7 is the standard system software for Macintosh computers. System 7 capabilities are Macintosh capabilities.

On the whole, Apple engineers have succeeded admirably in making System 7's new capabilities available but not intrusive. The system software's look and feel has changed amazingly little considering all it enables you to do.

Summary

- You can access and organize files and folders on your disks faster and easier with a greatly improved and omnipresent Finder.
- For a simplified alternative to the regular Finder, you can install At Ease (not included with System 7).
- System 7's multitasking allows several programs to be open concurrently (memory permitting) and have unattended tasks done in the background while you continue working.
- Virtual memory allows you to use disk space as if it were memory for opening programs and documents (though not on a Mac Plus, SE, Classic, standard LC, Portable, or PowerBook 100).
- File sharing provides the capability of sharing files with other computers networked to your Macintosh.
- Variable-size TrueType fonts are outline fonts similar to PostScript fonts that enable you to see sharp text at any size on any screen, printer, or other output device.
- The capability of using color windows and icons adds increased functionality and variety to the Mac interface (requires a color monitor).
- Installing the QuickTime system extension (not included with System 7) enables you to include movies in your documents (not on a Mac Plus, SE, Classic, Portable, or PowerBook 100).

Part II:
The Complete Reference

Chapter 2 .... **55**
The New Look

Chapter 3 .... **81**
Finder Improvements

Chapter 4 .... **115**
Organized at Last

Chapter 5 .... **131**
Tailored to Fit

Chapter 6 .... **161**
Fast Access with Aliases

Chapter 7 .... **173**
Smooth Text Everywhere

Chapter 8 .... **189**
File Sharing for the Rest of Us

Chapter 9 .... **217**
Creating Living Documents

Chapter 10 .... **229**
QuickTime

Chapter 11 .... **243**
Advanced Capabilities

Chapter 2
The New Look

In This Chapter
- How to select a desktop pattern as well as customize your own.
- A look into the windows of System 7.
- System 7 icons: restyled and redesigned for an improved Mac interface.
- Directory dialog boxes used as a one-window Finder.
- Balloon help: how the Mac can explain itself.
- Opening multiple programs using the Application menu.
- A summary of System 7's error messages.

Black and white gets the job done, but color makes the job fun. A colorized desktop is more than a frivolous fad, though. By making your environment more pleasant, color can make you more productive. In addition to this incidental benefit, color can also directly impart information. Traffic lights illustrate this principle. Even though they work for the color-blind, color makes the lights more effective.

On color Macintosh systems, System 7 subtly enhances the desktop with color and shades of gray. Some of the improvements are also visible on systems that display true grays but not color. On a basic black-and-white screen (no colors or gray shades), the desktop looks the same as it does with older system software.

Color isn't the only change System 7 brings to the Macintosh user interface. Two menus — one for program switching and the other for controlling on-screen help — have taken up permanent residence at the right end of the menu bar. Like the Apple menu, the Help and Application menus have small icons instead of words as titles in the menu bar. Those small icons and other small icons no longer look like mutated standard-size icons. In the File menu, the Open, Save, and Save As commands have improved dialog boxes. Also, most of the system dialog boxes contain more detailed information than the messages they replace.

This chapter describes and illustrates all these ubiquitous changes in detail. Be sure to see the remaining chapters for detailed information on other new aspects of system software, such as the Finder and the System Folder.

Desktop

Look closely at the standard gray desktop prior to System 7 and you see a checkerboard pattern of little black and white dots, as shown in Figure 2-1. You see the same thing on a basic black-and-white screen (no colors or gray shades) with System 7.

On a Mac that displays colors or gray shades, however, the standard desktop pattern is made up of two gray shades, as shown in Figure 2-2. The overall effect is a smooth, continuous tone.

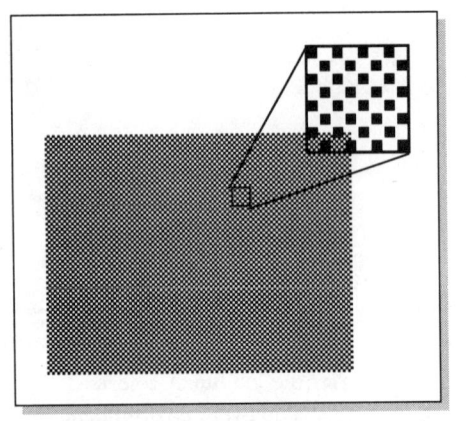

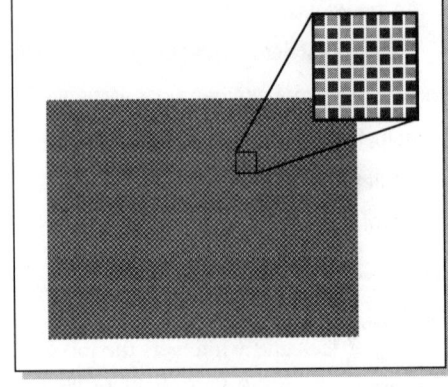

Figure 2-1: Gray desktop (black-and-white screen).

Figure 2-2: Gray desktop (256-color screen).

Selecting a desktop pattern

As always, you can select a different desktop pattern, or create your own pattern, using the General Controls control panel, as shown in Figure 2-3. It looks and works the same as the General section of the Control Panel desk accessory in older system software.

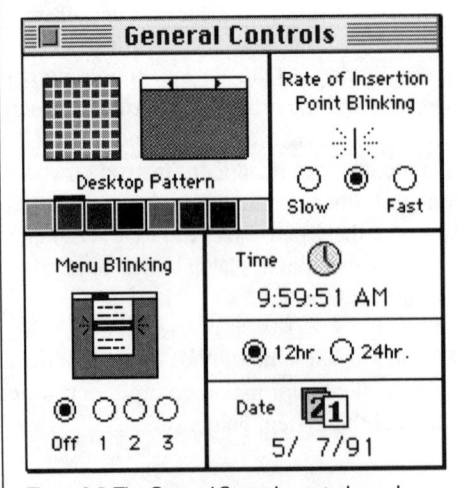

Figure 2-3: The General Controls control panel.

To scroll through the available standard patterns, click the miniature menu bar in the Desktop Pattern section of the General Controls control pattern. As you scroll, the pattern below the miniature menu bar changes. System 7 comes with five new color desktop patterns, plus the three of old and the standard gray, as shown in Figure 2-4. When you see a pattern you like, click it to make it the desktop pattern.

Your Mac will not have the standard patterns if you install System 7 on a disk that has custom desktop patterns (created as described in the next section).

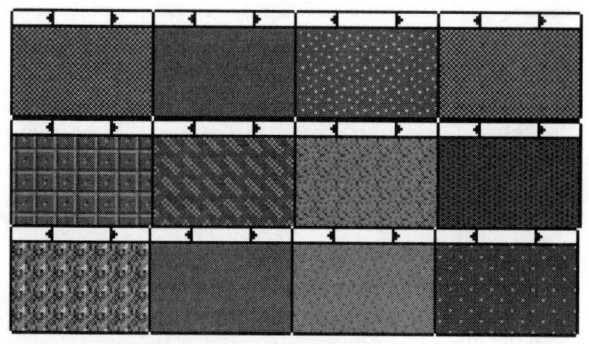

Figure 2-4: All the standard desktop patterns.

You can get the new patterns by dragging the System file outside the System Folder before installing System 7. If you do this, any other nonstandard resources that have been installed, such as extra fonts, will not be included automatically when you install System 7.

Creating a custom desktop pattern

You create a custom pattern by changing the magnified view of a standard pattern in the General Controls control panel. Select a color from the eight-color palette in the Desktop Pattern section of the control panel and click a square in the magnified view, as shown in Figure 2-5.

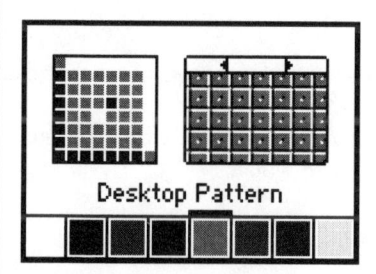

Figure 2-5: Editing a desktop pattern.

To change a color in the palette, double-click it. A dialog box opens in which you can pick another color by clicking a color wheel or by typing values for red, green, and blue or for hue, saturation, and brightness, as shown in Figure 2-6. When you've created the pattern you want, click below the miniature menu bar to make it the desktop pattern.

Changes you make to a desktop pattern persist until you select a different pattern. To make a custom pattern revert to its standard configuration, scroll through all available patterns in the General Controls control panel until you see the standard pattern you want and then select it.

Desktop pattern alternatives

Ordinarily the desktop pattern is made from tiles measuring 8 pixels (dots) square, but you can decorate your desktop with a custom pattern made from much larger tiles. Instead of a desktop pattern, you can display a desktop picture. For complete details on how to get bigger desktop patterns or a desktop picture, see "Desktop pattern" in Chapter 12.

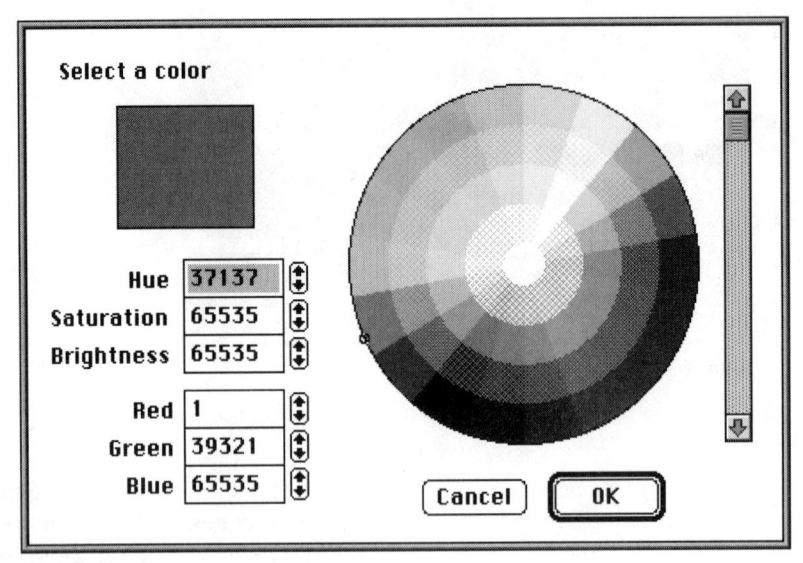

Figure 2-6: Picking a color for a desktop pattern.

Windows

The Macintosh windows that looked so avant-garde in 1984 now look dated. System 7 brings them up to date with trendy 3-D shading on monitors displaying colors or gray shades.

3-D window controls

Muted colors and shades of gray accent the window components you can manipulate, such as the title bar, scroll arrows, scroll boxes, close box, zoom box, and size box, as shown in Figure 2-7. Subtle colors emphasize the window controls without jerking your attention away from your work as bright colors would.

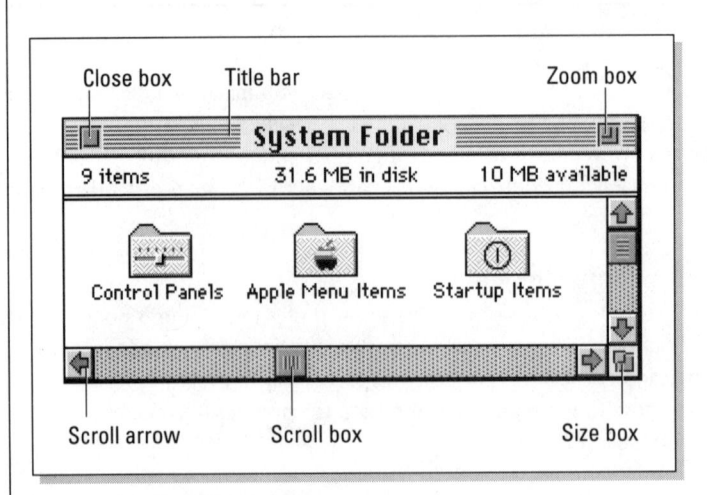

Figure 2-7: Window shades.

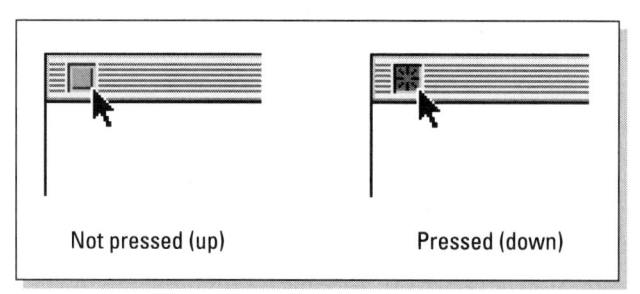

Figure 2-8: Simulated motion.

3-D motion

Shading tricks also make some of the colorized components seem to work in three dimensions when you use them. Clicking a close box or zoom box, for example, makes it look pressed down, as shown in Figure 2-8. (The close box and zoom box also flash as they always have.) The title bar, scroll arrows, and size box do not simulate 3-D motion.

Inactive windows pale

Only the active window has 3-D shading. It stands out from inactive windows behind it because System 7 displays inactive windows with gray borders and a gray title, as shown in Figure 2-9. Older system software displays black borders and titles for inactive windows.

Figure 2-9: The frontmost window stands out.

The contents of inactive windows are never dimmed, so you can see the contents easily. Also, window backgrounds are always white. White windows are a fundamental part of the Macintosh interface.

If the active window is large enough to show the full width or height of its contents without scrolling, System 7 shades its scroll bars a light gray.

Dialog box shading

Three-dimensional shading carries over to standard dialog boxes. System 7 replaces the double-line border of movable and fixed dialog boxes with a narrow half-round molding, as shown in Figure 2-10. (Movable dialog boxes have a title bar but no close box or size box.)

Choosing a window color

The standard color for shading window controls is light purple. You can select any of seven other colors or black-and-white as the shading color for window control areas using the Color control panel, as shown in Figure 2-11. Your choice of window tint affects all windows immediately, but the Color control panel doesn't save its settings to disk until you close it. The window tint you choose will not apply to tool palettes and special-purpose windows created by some application programs until the programs have been upgraded for System 7. You cannot create your own window-shading color using the Color control panel.

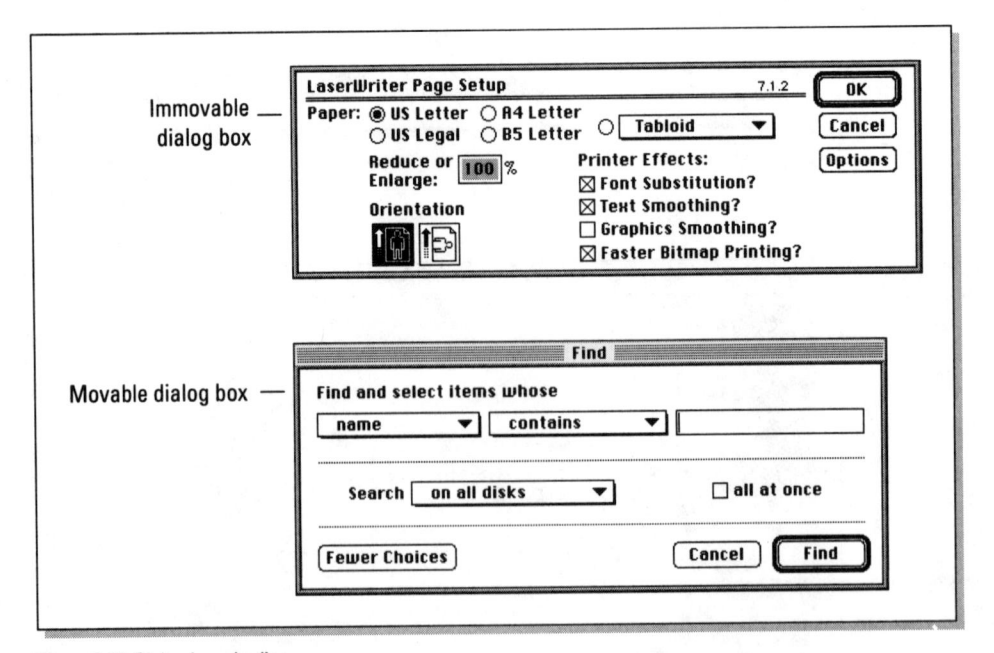

Figure 2-10: Dialog box shading.

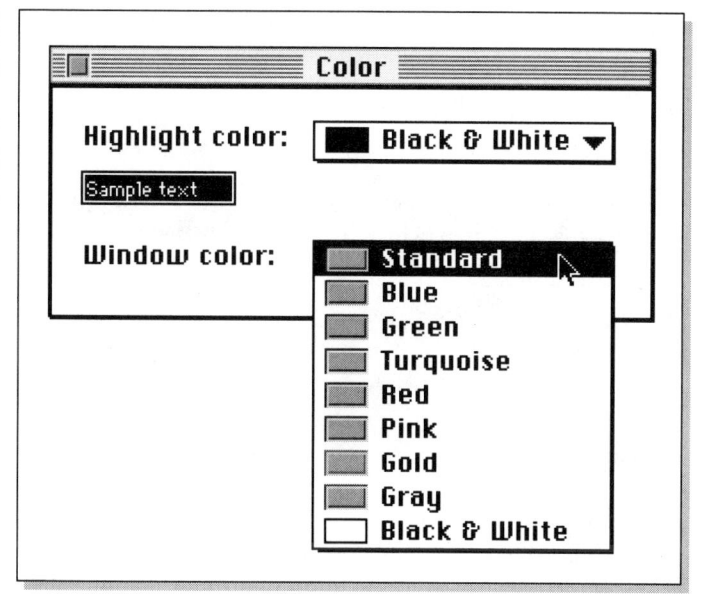

Figure 2-11: The window color pop-up menu.

To see colorized windows and shaded dialog boxes on your Macintosh, your Monitors control panel (formerly the Monitors section of the Control Panel desk accessory) must be set for at least 16 grays or 256 colors, as shown in Figure 2-12. If it's set at a lower number — or if your Mac has only a black-and-white monitor — your windows and dialog boxes will look like they always have.

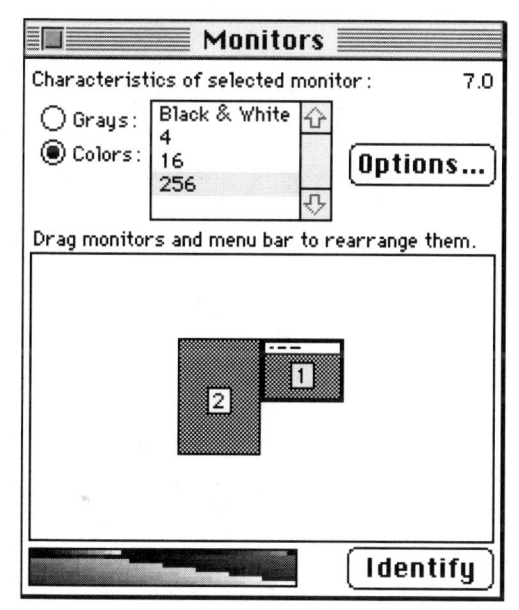

Figure 2-12: The Monitors control panel set for 256 colors.

Color windows have a disadvantage: They're slower than black-and-white windows. For best display speed, set the number of colors in the Monitors control panel to 16 or less.

Icons

Windows aren't the only colorful part of System 7. Apple has also restyled the icons for folders, the Finder, the System file, the items in the System Folder, Apple utility programs, other Apple software, and generic applications, desk accessories, and documents.

Icon colors

Most of the new icons are shaded using a color similar to the standard purple window color to achieve a 3-D effect. Bright colors are used mainly for highlights, as shown in Figure 2-13 (represented by shades of gray).

The new icons have three separate color schemes. One of the color schemes is optimized for monitors set to display 256 or more colors or grays. Another color scheme looks best on monitors set to display 16 colors or grays. The third color scheme is used on monitors that display black-and-white or four colors or grays, as shown in Figure 2-14.

You can alter an icon's natural color by selecting it and choosing a label from the Finder's Label menu. The Finder blends the label color with the icon colors. It looks like you

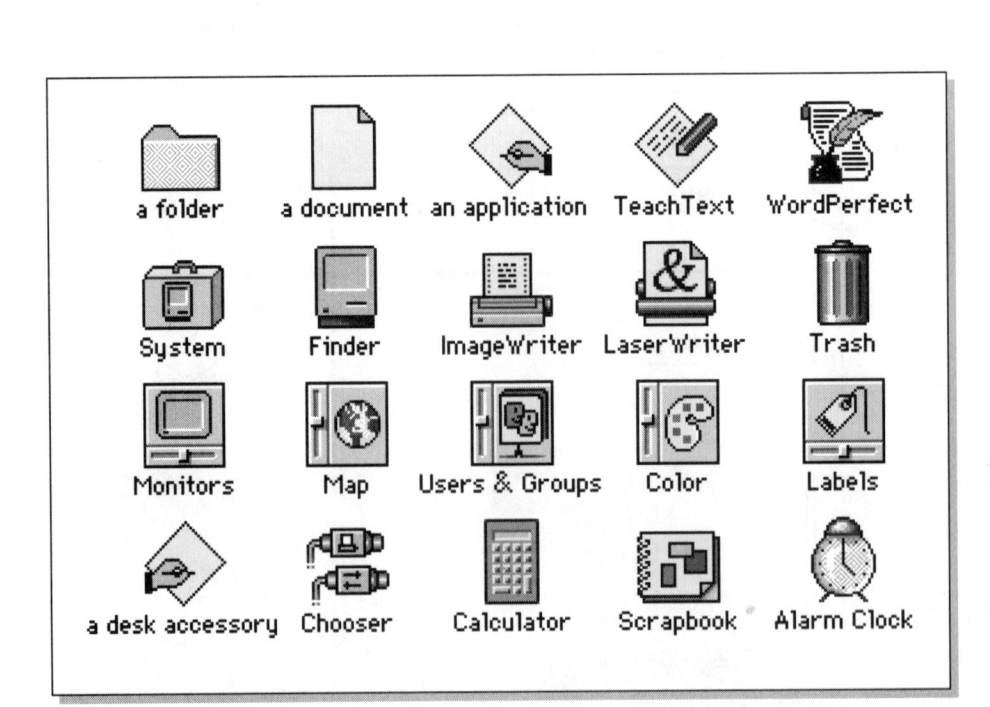

Figure 2-13: Some full-size color icons.

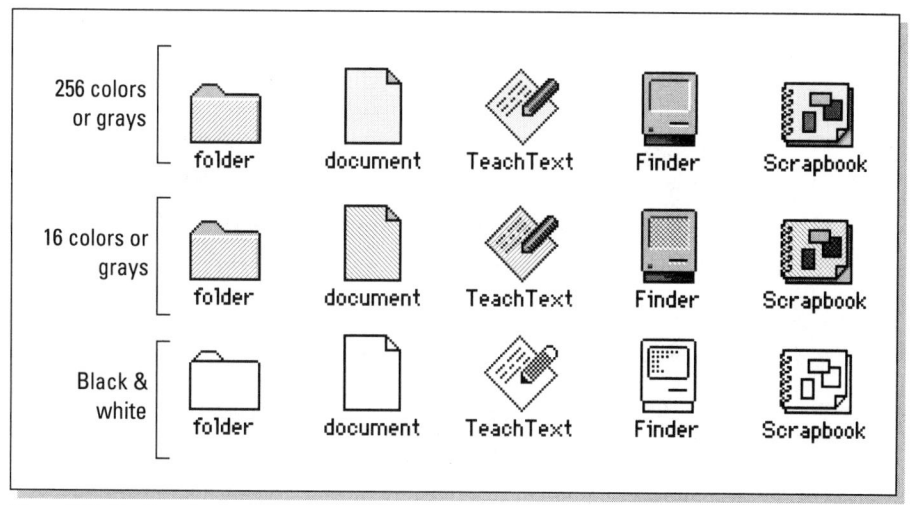

Figure 2-14: The three icon color schemes.

covered the icon with a piece of acetate the color of the label. Using the Color control panel to select an alternate window color does not affect the color of any icons.

Icon sizes
For each of the three color schemes there are two icon designs, one large and one small, as shown in Figure 2-15. Large icons appear on the desktop and in the Finder's By Icon view of disk and folder windows. Small icons appear in menus and in the Finder's Small Icon view of disk and folder windows.

Prior to System 7, the small icons were mechanically shrunken from full-size icons. Now any program developer can design separate, better looking small icons.

Icon highlighting
Regardless of icon size and color, System 7 highlights selected icons on monitors displaying 16 or more colors or grays by darkening the icons, as shown in Figure 2-16. On a monitor displaying fewer than 16 colors or grays, System 7 highlights selected icons by inverting the colors; white becomes black and black becomes white.

Old icons
Just as Apple had to redesign its icons for System 7, so must the developers and publishers of other programs. Until then, the old program and document icons will look like they always have. Many programs that have been revised for System 7 have only some of the possible combinations of icon colors and sizes. For example, some programs use the same icons with number of colors set to 256 or 16 in the Monitors control panel.

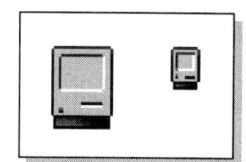

Figure 2-15: Large and small icons.

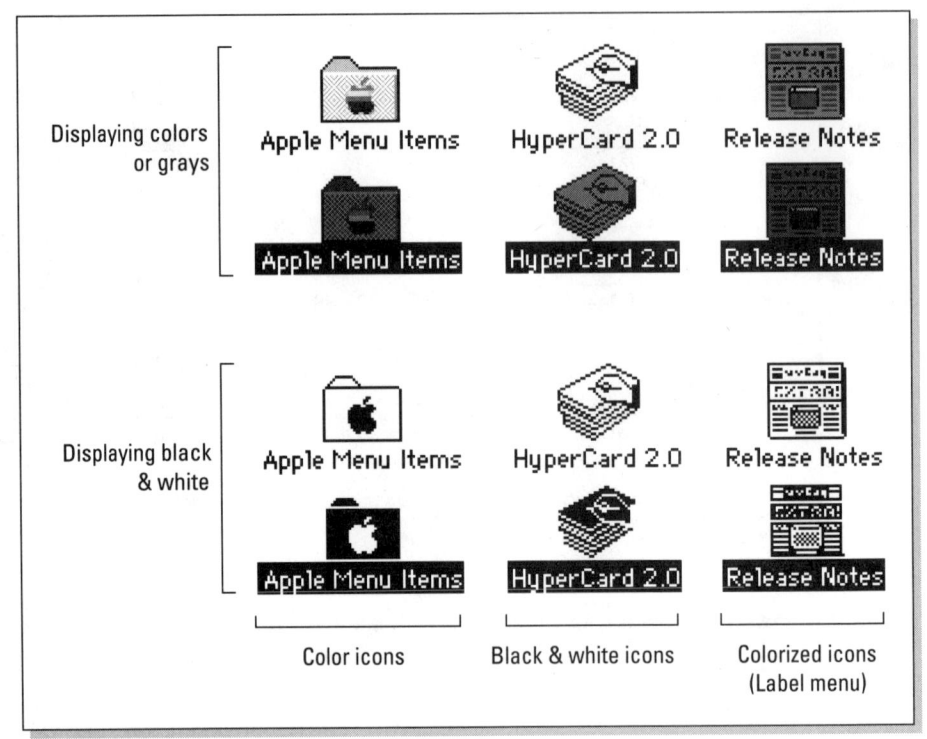

Figure 2-16: Icon highlighting.

When you install an updated program that includes redesigned icons on your disk, you usually have to rebuild the disk's desktop to see the new icons for that program and its documents. To rebuild the desktop of any disk whose icon normally appears on the desktop after startup, press Command-Option while starting your Macintosh. For each disk in turn, the Finder asks whether you want the disk's desktop rebuilt. To rebuild the desktop of a floppy disk or other removable disk whose icon is not on the desktop, press Command-Option while inserting the disk.

Warning: Rebuilding the desktop erases anything you have typed into the Comments box of an icon's info window (which you access with the Finder's Get Info command). See Chapter 13 for a description of utility software that preserves Get Info comments during desktop rebuilding.

Menus

System 7 enhances menu looks with true grays and colors on monitors that can display them, as shown in Figure 2-17. The small icons in the menu bar for the Help and Application menus appear in color or shades of gray on a monitor displaying at least 16 colors or gray shades. In addition, small icons in menus such as the Apple and Application menus appear in color or shades of gray.

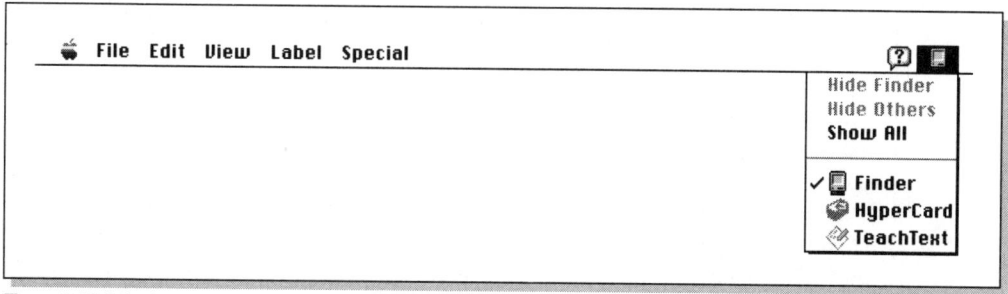

Figure 2-17: Color in menus.

On monitors displaying at least four grays or 16 colors, System 7 uses true gray text to display inactive menu titles, inactive menu items, and the gray lines that divide sections of menus. In a program with color menus, System 7 displays inactive items in a blend of the menu item color and the menu background color. On a monitor displaying less than 16 colors, System 7 simulates gray text by alternating black and white dots. Older system software simulates gray text at all color or gray levels and does not display color icons in menus or the menu bar (except for the Apple icon).

Menu enhancement works automatically for most existing application programs. However, programs that don't use standard menu management software will not display true gray text and dividing lines in menus until they are revised.

Directory Dialog Boxes

At first glance the new directory dialog boxes you get when you use Open, Save, Save As, and similar commands look little changed from the older ones. Using them dispels that notion quickly. In System 7, directory dialog boxes work more like a one-window Finder, as shown in Figure 2-18.

Figure 2-18: An Open command's dialog box.

All directory dialog boxes still have a single directory window, in which you locate an item you want opened or a folder where you want an item saved. The directory window lists the names of items from one folder or disk at a time, always alphabetically by name. System 7 displays longer names than its predecessors by using compressed-style text for names that exceed 25 characters.

The System 7 directory dialog boxes display icons in the seven colors assigned by the Finder's Label menu. Also, they show the names of items that can't be opened (such as the names of files in a Save dialog box) using true gray text. Your Monitors control panel must be set for at least 16 colors or four grays. Some programs must be upgraded to show icons in color and text in true gray.

The desktop

Directory dialog boxes now provide a view of the desktop and enable you to open disks and other items on it. No more switching disks using the Drive button. Instead, you go to the desktop level and open the disk whose contents you want to see, as shown in Figure 2-19. This new procedure makes switching among more than two disks easier. A

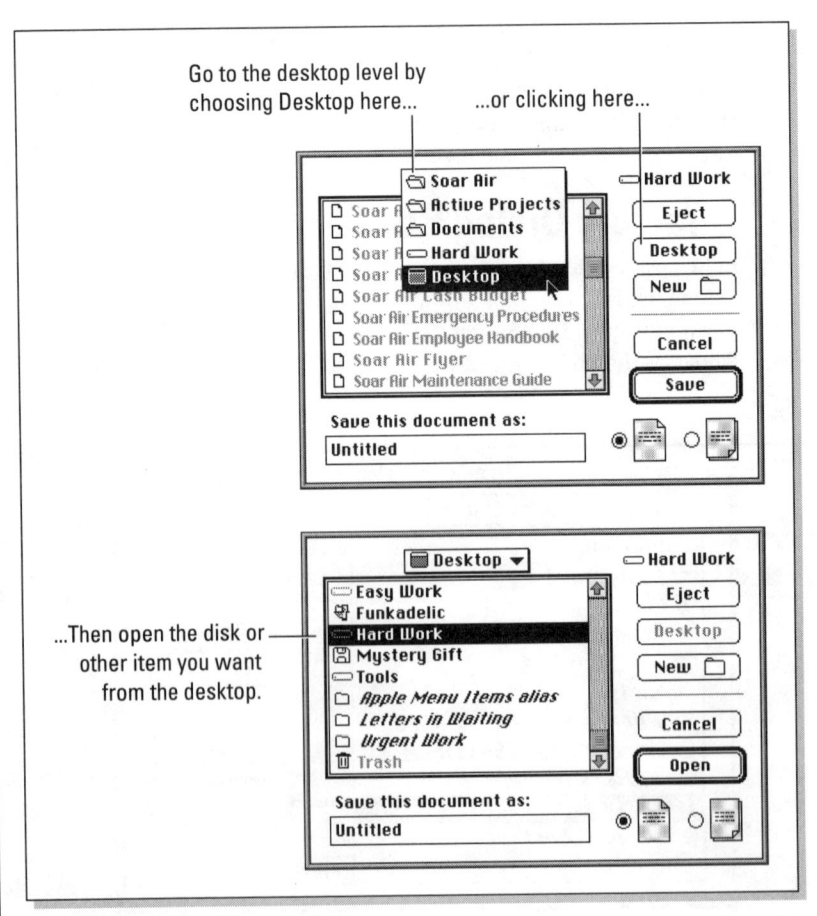

Figure 2-19: Switching disks at the desktop.

new Desktop button replaces the old Drive button and clicking it takes you to the desktop level. You can also go to the desktop by choosing it from the pop-up menu above the directory window.

Navigating by keyboard

Like older system software, System 7 enables you to move through folders and open items using the keyboard as well as the mouse. In an Open dialog box, typing an item's name or the first part of it selects the item in the directory window. For example, typing *m* selects the first item that begins with the letter *M* or *m*. Typing several letters quickly specifies a longer name to be selected in the directory window. Pausing while typing starts selecting all over. The Key Repeat Rate setting in the Keyboard control panel determines how long you must pause to make a fresh start. Once you have selected an item in a directory window (by any means), pressing Return or Enter opens the item.

System 7 makes this keyboard navigation available for the first time in Save and Save As dialog boxes. You also use the keyboard in these dialog boxes to enter a name for the item you're saving. System 7 lets you know when your typing affects a Save or Save As dialog box's directory window by outlining the window with a heavy black border. A flashing insertion point or highlighted text in the text entry box means your typing will go there, as shown in Figure 2-20.

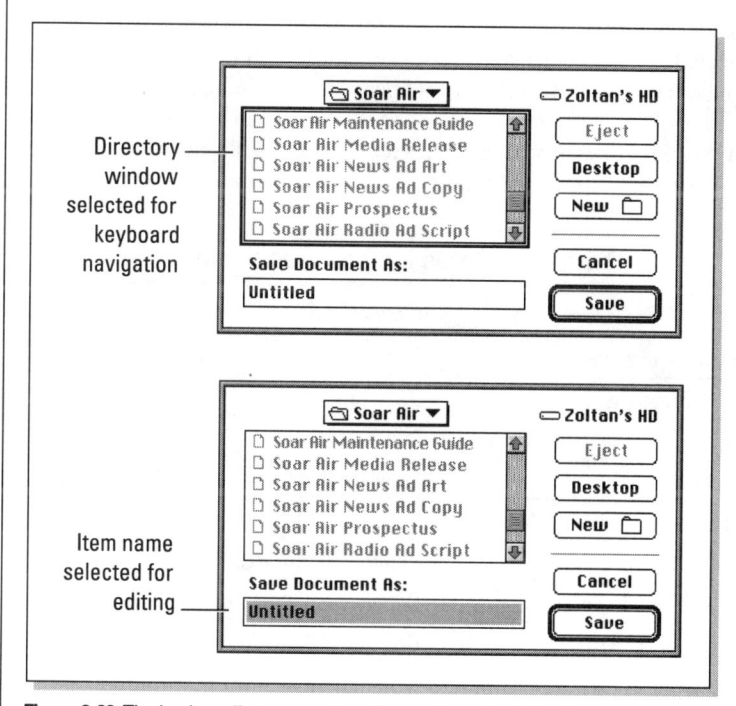

Figure 2-20: The keyboard's two uses in a Save or Save As dialog box.

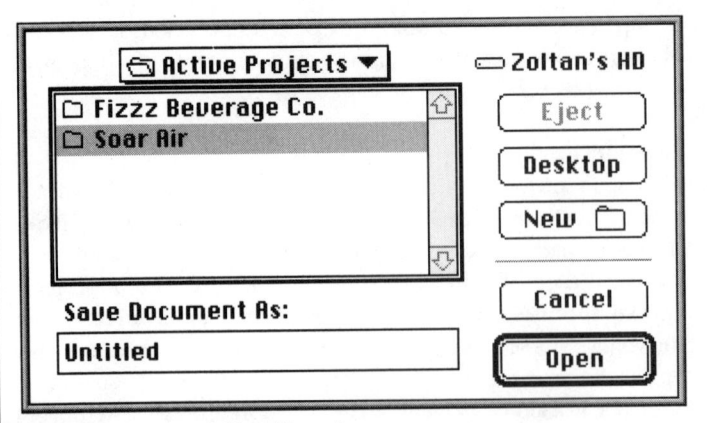

Figure 2-21: Opening a folder while saving.

You select the directory window or the text entry box by clicking or dragging in the one you want. You can also alternate between them by pressing Tab. Prior to System 7, pressing Tab in an Open, Save, or Save As dialog box switched to the next disk. (You can do that in System 7 by pressing Command-right arrow or Command-left arrow.)

An even more subtle change in Save and Save As dialog boxes further reduces confusion when moving through folders. When you select a folder in the directory window, the Save button becomes an Open button, as shown in Figure 2-21. Clicking it opens the selected folder. In older system software, the button works the same way, but it's always named Save (even when clicking it opens a selected folder).

The System 7 directory dialog boxes recognize more keyboard equivalents than older versions. Table 2-1 has the details.

Table 2-1:	Directory dialog keyboard equivalents
Objective	**Keystroke**
Select an item in the directory window	Type the item's full or partial name
Scroll up in the directory window	Up Arrow
Scroll down in the directory window	Down Arrow
Open the selected item	Command-Down Arrow or Command-O
Open the parent folder, disk, or volume	Command-Up Arrow
Go to the previous disk or volume	Command-Left Arrow
Go to the next disk or volume	Command-Right Arrow
Go to the desktop	Command-Shift-Up Arrow or Command-D
Eject the disk in drive 1	Command-Shift-1

continued

Table 2-1: Directory dialog keyboard equivalents *(continued)*

Objective	Keystroke
Eject the disk in drive 2	Command-Shift-2
Move to the next keyboard target	Tab
Click the default button (usually Open or Save)	Return, Enter
Cancel the directory dialog	Escape, Command-Period
Make a new folder (doesn't work with some older programs)	Command-N
Select the original of the selected alias (instead of opening it)	Option-Command-O, Option-double-click, or Option-Click Open

Naming the item you're saving

While you are editing the name of the item you're saving, the Cut, Copy, and Paste commands are available from the Edit menu. You can now cut and paste names. When pasting, only the first 31 characters are used; the rest are omitted. In some programs that haven't been revised for System 7, you must use the keyboard equivalents: Command-X, Command-C, and Command-V.

Creating a new folder

The System 7 Save and Save As dialog boxes include a button you can click to create a new folder, as shown in Figure 2-22. However, the button is missing from the Save and Save As dialog boxes of most programs that have not been updated for System 7, as well as from many programs that have been updated for System 7.

Opening an item

As usual, you can open an item in the directory window by double-clicking it. If you double-click the wrong item and realize it before you release the mouse button, continue pressing and drag the pointer to the item you want to open. When you release the mouse button, the currently selected item opens. In older system software, dragging on the second click of a double-click cancels the double-click and nothing is opened. To cancel a double-click in a System 7 directory dialog box, hold down the mouse button on the second click and drag the pointer outside the dialog box before releasing the mouse button.

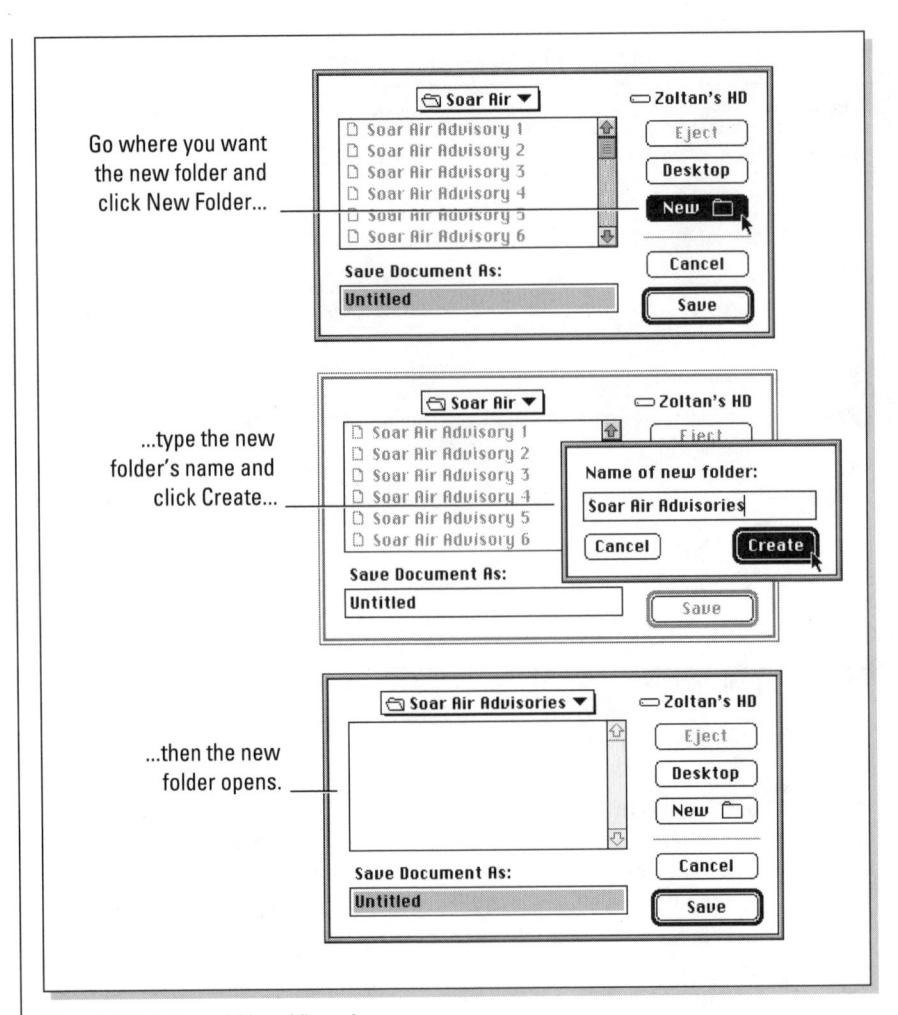

Figure 2-22: Making a folder while saving.

Balloon Help

When you need immediate information about objects you see on screen, you can turn on System 7's optional balloon help. With balloon help on, you place the pointer over an object and a concise description of it appears in a cartoon-style balloon, as shown in Figure 2-23. The balloon points to the object and tells you what the object is, what it does, what happens when you click it, or some portion of this information. You do not have to press any keys or click anything to make a help balloon appear.

Turning balloon help on and off

You turn on balloon help by choosing Show Balloons from the Help menu. That command then changes to Hide Balloons, and choosing it turns off balloon help. The Help menu is near the right end of the menu bar, as shown in Figure 2-24.

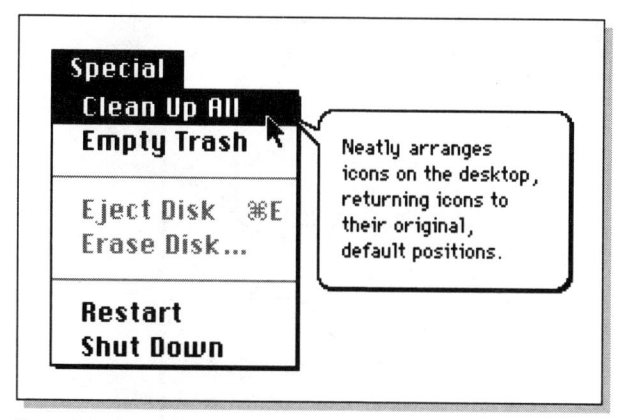

```
    ┌─────────────────────────────────────┐
    │  Special                            │
    │  Clean Up All                       │
    │  Empty Trash  ↖  ╭──────────────╮   │
    │               ╲  │Neatly arranges│  │
    │                  │icons on the desktop,│
    │  Eject Disk  ⌘E  │returning icons to│
    │  Erase Disk...   │their original,│  │
    │                  │default positions.│ │
    │                  ╰──────────────╯   │
    │  Restart                            │
    │  Shut Down                          │
    └─────────────────────────────────────┘
```

Figure 2-23: A help balloon.

The Help menu takes up little space on your menu bar because its title is an icon instead of a word. Moreover, Apple adjusted System 7's menu bar to use no more space with the Help menu than the older system software's menu bar without a Help menu.

Working with balloon help on

Everything works normally when balloon help is on. Using balloon help does not put the Macintosh into a help-only mode. Help balloons appear whether you are pressing the mouse button or not. You click, double-click, and otherwise use programs normally, except that you will probably perceive a slight delay as help balloons come and go when you move the pointer slowly across items that have balloon help descriptions. It's like someone is standing over your shoulder and describing objects on the screen to you.

The object a help balloon describes may be large or small and individual or collective, as shown in Figure 2-25. For example, the close box in the active window's title bar has its own help balloon. In contrast, an inactive window has one balloon for the whole window. Sometimes a help balloon describes a whole group, as in the Mouse control panel where one balloon tells you about the seven settings for the Mouse Tracking option.

UNDOCUMENTED

```
┌──────────────────────────────────────────────────────────────┐
│  🍎  File  Edit  View  Label  Special              ?  ▢     │
│                                          ┌──────────────────┐│
│                                          │ About Balloon Help...↖│
│                                          │ Show Balloons    ││
│                                          │ Finder Shortcuts ││
│                                          └──────────────────┘│
└──────────────────────────────────────────────────────────────┘
```

Figure 2-24: The Help menu.

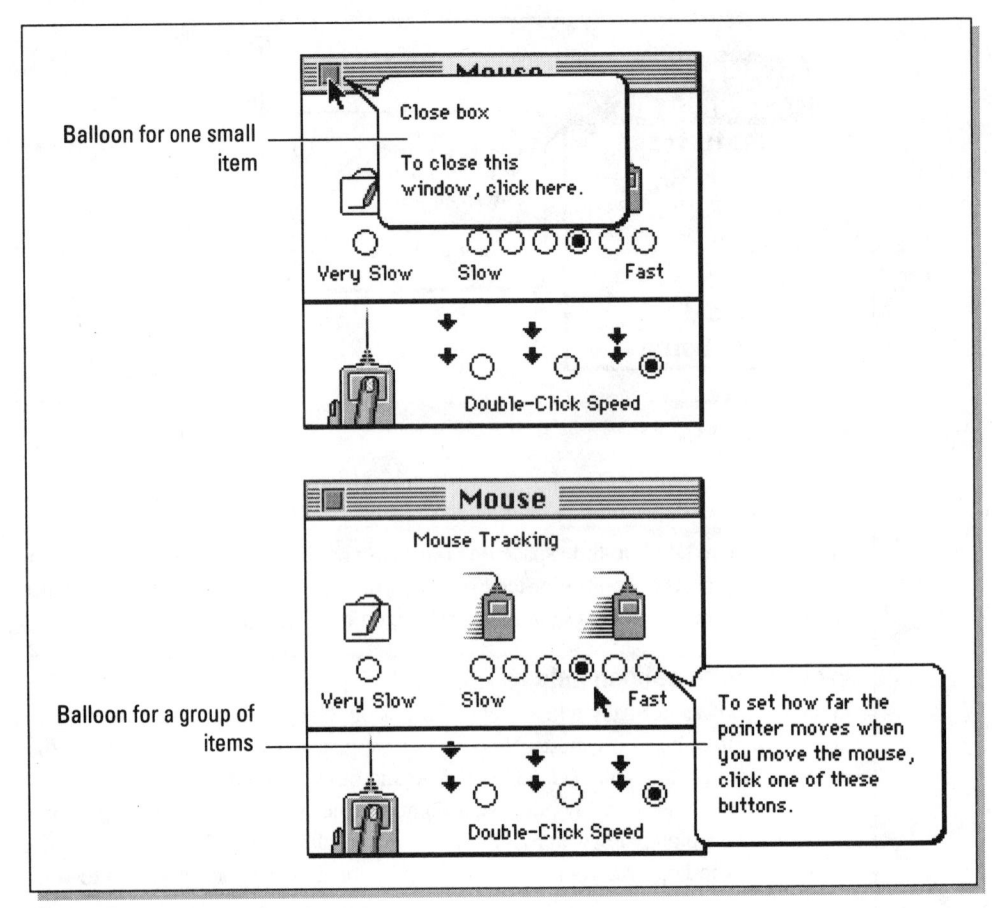

Figure 2-25: Help balloons vary in scope.

Moving the pointer slowly over several objects that have help balloons opens and closes balloons in sequence. To prevent excessive flashing of help balloons, they do not appear when you move the pointer quickly. For a help balloon to appear, the pointer must be in the same area for about one-tenth of a second or longer. You cannot change this timing.

What balloon help knows

Balloon help knows about all standard objects in the Macintosh interface. They include the Apple menu, the Help menu, the Application menu (described in the next section), windows in general, and standard parts of directory dialog boxes, the Page Setup dialog box, and the Print dialog box. Balloon help cannot describe a specific program's menu commands, window contents, dialog boxes, and so on unless its developer or publisher has revised it to include the necessary help balloons. For example, Apple has provided complete balloon help for the Finder, TeachText, standard control panels, and standard desk accessories.

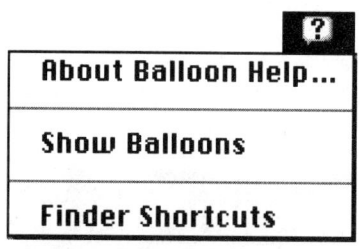

Figure 2-26: The Finder's Help menu.

Other help

Balloon help does not teach you how to combine features of a program to accomplish tasks. However, a program can add how-to help, an on-screen reference, or other items to the Help menu. The Finder, for example, has a Finder Shortcuts item (see Figure 2-26) that displays a dialog box containing tricks for using the Finder.

Opening Multiple Programs

Next to the Help menu is another new menu with System 7, the Application menu, as shown in Figure 2-27. It is represented in the menu bar by a small icon that tells you which application program or desk accessory is currently active. You can use the Application menu to switch to another open application program or desk accessory. To this extent the Application menu is like the MultiFinder icon (also called the application icon) of older system software.

MultiFinder's multitasking capabilities are built into System 7. The Finder is always available without quitting the program you're using and you can have as many programs open simultaneously as will fit in your computer's memory, as shown in Figure 2-28. You can copy and paste among documents of open programs without closing documents and quitting programs. Also, you can switch to the Finder without quitting programs, and there open other programs, find documents, organize folders and disks, and so on.

Regardless of how many programs you have open, only one can be working at a time. Programs that are open but not working are in a state of suspended animation. In older system software, MultiFinder, and consequently multitasking, can be on or off. System 7's multitasking is always on.

Multitasking's valuable benefits have disorienting side effects. For instance, you may think the program you're using has unexpectedly quit when actually you switched

Figure 2-27: The Application menu.

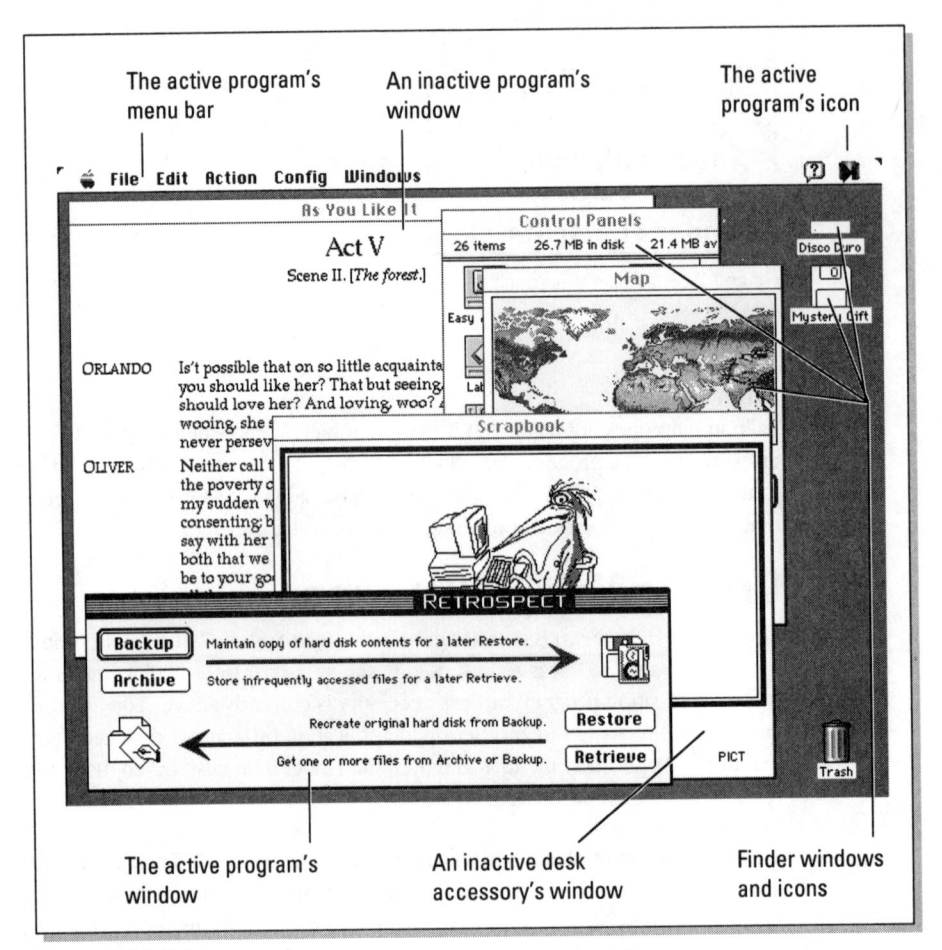

[Figure 2-28 shows a screenshot with the following labels:
- The active program's menu bar
- An inactive program's window
- The active program's icon
- The active program's window
- An inactive desk accessory's window
- Finder windows and icons]

Figure 2-28: Multiple programs open.

to another open program by clicking one of its windows. You must condition yourself to look at the menu bar when you need to know which open program is currently active. The active program's icon appears at the right end of the menu bar as the placeholder for the new Application menu.

Switching programs

You use the Application menu to switch from one open program to another. All open programs are listed in the Application menu by name and small icon. (With MultiFinder, open application programs are listed near the bottom of the Apple menu.)

To make a program listed in the Application menu the active program, you choose it from the menu. When you do, that program takes over the menu bar and the program's windows come to the front. The program that was active becomes inactive. Its windows drop back but remain visible except for the parts covered by other open programs' windows. You can also make another program the active program by opening its icon or any of its document icons in the Finder or by clicking in any of its windows. Clicking the desktop or a Finder icon makes the Finder active.

Reducing window clutter

With many programs open, the desktop quickly becomes a visual Tower of Babel. You can eliminate the clutter by choosing the Application menu's Hide Others command, as shown in Figure 2-29. It hides the windows of all programs except the currently active one. The command also dims the icons of open and hidden programs listed in the Application menu. To make the windows of all programs visible again, choose Show All from the Application menu.

You can hide the active program's windows and simultaneously switch to the most recently active program by choosing the first command from the Application menu. The command's name begins with the word Hide and ends with the name of the currently active program.

To hide the active program's windows as you switch to a particular program, press Option while choosing the other program from the Application menu. Or press Option while clicking another program's window. You hide windows and switch to the Finder by pressing Option while clicking the desktop, a Finder icon, or a Finder window.

Memory partitions

Every application program and desk accessory you open has its own memory partition in System 7. (Older system software lumps all open desk accessories together in a single partition if MultiFinder is active, or includes them with the open application program if MultiFinder is inactive.) You can see how your computer's memory is partitioned at any time by choosing About This Macintosh from the Apple menu when the Finder is active, as shown in Figure 2-30.

Background operations

Programs that know how can operate in the background by using System 7's multitasking capabilities. Background programs operate during the intervals, typically less than ⅛ of a second long, when the active program isn't using the computer. This usually happens while the active program waits for you to do something.

A background program can't use the menu bar or interact directly with you in any other way. It can, however, ask you to activate it by some or all of the following means:

- ✦ Display a diamond symbol next to its name in the Application menu
- ✦ Flash its icon on top of the Application menu's icon or the Apple menu's icon
- ✦ Play a sound (commonly a beep)
- ✦ Display a brief alert message which you must dismiss before continuing

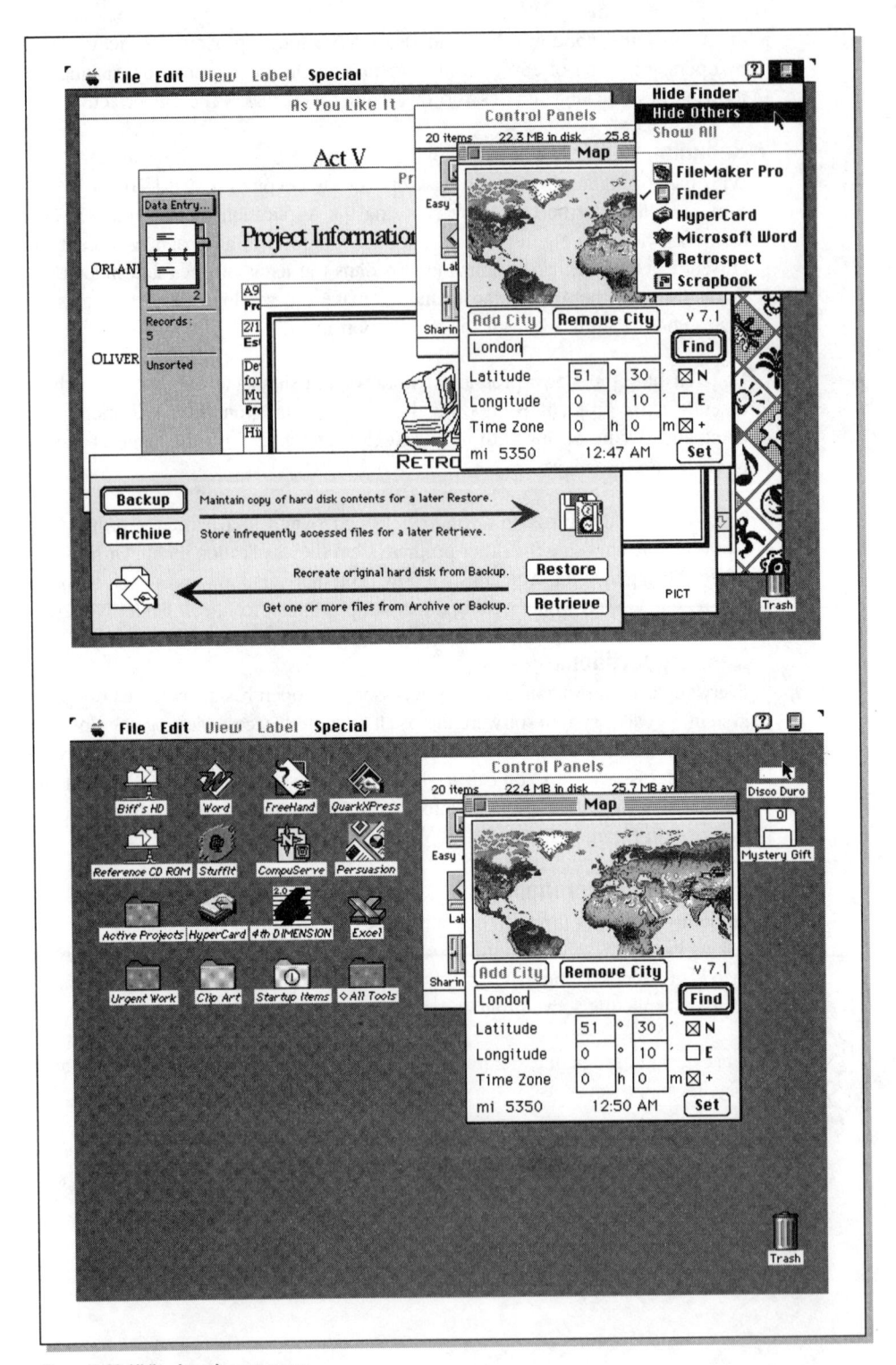

Figure 2-29: Hiding inactive programs.

```
┌─────────────────────────────────────────────────┐
│ ▭        About This Macintosh            ▭     │
├─────────────────────────────────────────────────┤
│                       System Software 7.1       │
│      PowerBook 140    © Apple Computer, Inc. 1983-1992 │
│                                                 │
│  Total Memory :   8,192K    Largest Unused Block :   919K │
│                                                 │
│   DayMaker™        750K   ▓▓░                   │
│   Fax Center        20K   ▓                     │
│   MacDraw Pro     2,000K  ▓▓▓▓░░                │
│   PrintMonitor     130K   ▓                     │
│   Quicken          750K   ▓▓░                   │
│   System Software 3,222K  ▓▓▓▓▓▓▓▓░             │
└─────────────────────────────────────────────────┘
```

Figure 2-30: Checking on memory use.

New Error Messages

System 7 is much more stable than earlier versions of system software, recovering fairly gracefully when an application program quits with a message advising that the application has quit unexpectedly instead of crashing to a halt. Although Apple hasn't yet managed to eliminate system errors and their dreaded bomb alert boxes (see Figure 2-31) from the Macintosh interface, System 7 does soften their blows a little. Whereas system software versions 6.0.5 and older report a cryptic error ID number in a bomb box, System 7 reports a brief message that's merely arcane.

Where you used to read "ID = 02," for example, you now read "address error." You still don't know what's going on, but at least you don't feel like a calculator. Table 2-2 lists the error messages that can appear in the system error alert box, their equivalent ID numbers, and likely causes.

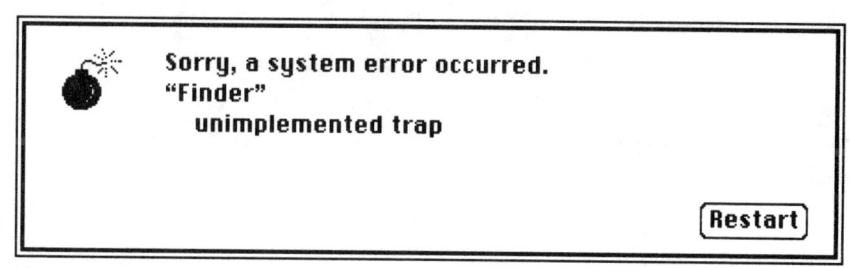

```
┌─────────────────────────────────────────────────┐
│   💣    Sorry, a system error occurred.         │
│        "Finder"                                 │
│        unimplemented trap                       │
│                                                 │
│                                      ┌────────┐ │
│                                      │Restart │ │
│                                      └────────┘ │
└─────────────────────────────────────────────────┘
```

Figure 2-31: The system error (bomb) alert box.

Table 2-2: Fatal error messages

Error message	ID	Likely cause
bus error	01	Software error or incompatibility
address error	02	Software error or incompatibility
illegal instruction	03	Software error or incompatibility
divide by zero	04	Software error
CHK error	05	Software error
numeric overflow	06	Software error or incompatibility
error type 7	07	Software error or incompatibility
error type 8	08	Hardware error or a programming tool had trouble
error type 9	09	Software error
bad F-line instruction	10	Software error
error type 11	11	Software error or incompatibility
unimplemented trap	12	Software error or incompatibility
unserviceable interrupt	13	Someone pressed the interrupt part of the programmer's switch, hardware malfunctioned, or a programming tool had trouble
Device Manager error	14	Hardware malfunctioned or a programming tool had trouble
Segment Loader error	15	System file probably damaged
SANE error	16	System file probably damaged
List Manager not present	17	System file probably damaged
BitEdit not present	18	System file probably damaged
Disk Initialization package not present	19	System file probably damaged
Standard File not present	20	System file probably damaged
SANE not present	21	System file probably damaged
SANE transcendental functions	22	System file probably damaged or not present
International Utilities not present	23	System file probably damaged
Binary-Decimal Conversion package not present	24	System file probably damaged
out of memory	25	A program unexpectedly ran out of memory
file system map inconsistent	27	System file probably damaged
stack collision with heap	28	A program unexpectedly ran out of memory or a conflict occurred among system extension software

continued

Table 2-2:   **Fatal error messages (continued)**

Error message	ID	Likely cause
Memory Manager error	33	A program unexpectedly ran out of memory
unserviceable slot interrupt	51	Macintosh malfunction or NuBus card error
bad SANE opcode	81	Software error
menu purged while in use	84	Software error
couldn't load MBDF	85	Software error
couldn't find hierarchical menu's parent	86	Software error
couldn't load WDEF	87	Software error
couldn't load CDEF	88	Software error
floating point coprocessor not installed	90	Software error

Emergency quit

Sometimes you can recover from a system error — or the related problem of a hung or frozen system — without restarting your Macintosh. Pressing Command-Option-Esc may bring up a dialog box asking whether you want to force the Finder (or some other program) to quit, as shown in Figure 2-32. If so, click the Force Quit button and cross your fingers. If you get to the Finder, immediately save all open documents and restart the computer.

Bomb recovery

If that trick doesn't work and the plastic programmer's switch is installed on your Macintosh, try pressing the Interrupt part of the switch (not the Restart part). On most Macintosh models, the Interrupt part is labeled with a tiny circle and the Restart part is labeled with a tiny arrow. Some Macs, such as the LC, LC II, and IIsi, have no programmer's switch; try pressing Command and Power-On. With luck, you'll see a dialog box containing a greater-than symbol in its upper-left corner, as shown in Figure 2-33. Type `G FINDER` and press Return. If you get to the Finder, immediately save all open documents and restart the computer.

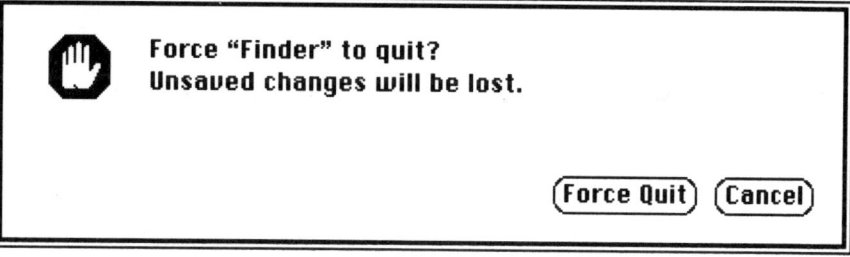

> Force "Finder" to quit?
> Unsaved changes will be lost.
>
> (Force Quit) (Cancel)

Figure 2-32: Forcing a program to quit.

```
>G FINDER
```

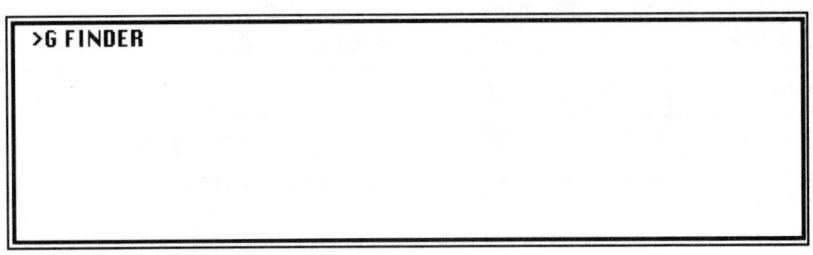

Figure 2-33: Recovering from a system error.

Big Changes

Overall, the changes to the Macintosh desktop interface are the most noticeable in its history, yet they don't disrupt the way you work. Compared to other graphical interfaces — Next's chiseled features and Microsoft Windows' colorful facade, for instance — System 7 looks quite conservative. While System 7 may not win a fashion award, you'll be able to wear it comfortably for a couple of years after neon colors fade from favor.

None of the cosmetic or functional changes to the Macintosh interface described in this chapter change the basic Macintosh experience. They refine it.

Summary

- ✔ System 7's cosmetic changes affecting the desktop, windows, icons, and menus only show up on a Macintosh with a color or grayscale monitor. You can see the functional changes on any Macintosh, however.
- ✔ On a Mac that displays colors or gray shades, the standard desktop pattern in System 7 is made up of two gray shades resulting in a smooth, continuous tone.
- ✔ The updated Mac windows in System 7 include 3-D motion and window controls, as well as the ability to select shading color for window control areas.
- ✔ System 7's icons have been shaded to achieve a 3-D effect and designed in two sizes to allow for better looking small icons.
- ✔ Directory dialog boxes in System 7 enable you to open disks from the desktop without having to use the Drive button as with the older versions; move through folders and open items using the keyboard; and edit the name of an item to be saved using the Cut, Copy, and Paste commands from the Edit menu.
- ✔ Balloon help consists of cartoon-like balloons that appear when the pointer is placed over any standard object in the Mac's interface. The balloons point to the object and tell what the object is, what it does, what happens when it is clicked, or some portion of this information.
- ✔ System 7 enables you to have multiple programs open simultaneously. You use the Application menu to switch from one program to another as well as to hide the windows of all programs except the active one.

Chapter 3
Finder Improvements

In This Chapter

- Zooming, scrolling, and selecting with smart windows.
- Finding and fetching items quickly by simple or complex search criteria.
- Methods for naming documents, folders, disks, and other desktop items.
- Classifying the contents of disks with text labels and colors.
- A look at copying multiple items quickly.
- Working with other programs while copying, duplicating, or finding in the background.
- Making and using stationery pads (template documents).
- Customizing, removing, and aligning icons in windows or on the desktop.
- A summary of shortcuts using the keyboard and mouse.
- Simplifying and controlling the desktop with At Ease.

Ask 100 Macintosh users to name the application program they use most often. Only a few would answer correctly, "the Finder." People don't think of it as a program they use or need to learn to use. In fact, the Finder is a very rich application program that is included with the system software for managing your disks and their contents.

The Finder that comes with System 7 has capabilities that help you organize your disks more effectively and find items in them more quickly than older Finders. You'll use all of Finder 7's capabilities more often because they're never more than a mouse click away. This chapter describes in detail the capabilities that set Finder 7 apart from its predecessors.

Aliases are covered in Chapter 6 and file sharing is covered in Chapter 8. For more information on the new System Folder organization, see the next chapter.

Outlining Folder Structure

Finder 7 displays list views (name, size, kind, and so on) in an indented outline format, as shown in Figure 3-1. The levels of indentation in the outline show how your folders are nested. The indented outline provides a graphical representation of a disk's organization. You can look through and reorganize folders without opening additional windows.

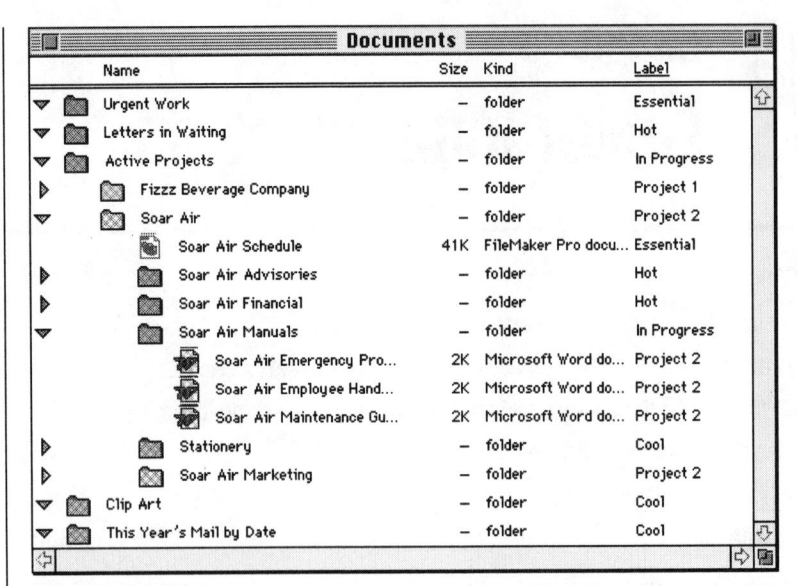

Name	Size	Kind	Label
▽ 📁 Urgent Work	—	folder	Essential
▽ 📁 Letters in Waiting	—	folder	Hot
▽ 📁 Active Projects	—	folder	In Progress
▷ 📁 Fizzz Beverage Company	—	folder	Project 1
▽ 📁 Soar Air	—	folder	Project 2
Soar Air Schedule	41K	FileMaker Pro docu...	Essential
▷ 📁 Soar Air Advisories	—	folder	Hot
▷ 📁 Soar Air Financial	—	folder	Hot
▽ 📁 Soar Air Manuals	—	folder	In Progress
Soar Air Emergency Pro...	2K	Microsoft Word do...	Project 2
Soar Air Employee Hand...	2K	Microsoft Word do...	Project 2
Soar Air Maintenance Gu...	2K	Microsoft Word do...	Project 2
▷ 📁 Stationery	—	folder	Cool
▷ 📁 Soar Air Marketing	—	folder	Project 2
▽ 📁 Clip Art	—	folder	Cool
▽ 📁 This Year's Mail by Date	—	folder	Cool

Figure 3-1: Expanded and collapsed folders.

Triangles next to folder names tell you whether the folders are expanded or collapsed. If a triangle points to the right, the folder next to it is collapsed and you cannot see its contents. If the triangle points down, the folder is expanded and you can see a list of the items in the folder indented below the folder name.

Collapsing folders

To collapse a folder, click once on the triangle to the left of the folder's icon, as shown in Figure 3-2. To collapse a folder and all the folders nested within it, press Option while clicking the triangle of the outer folder. Resist double-clicking, which causes the folder to expand and then immediately collapse most annoyingly.

Expanding folders

To expand a folder, click once on the triangle to the left of the folder's icon, as shown in Figure 3-3. To expand a folder and all the folders nested within it, press Option while you click.

When you expand a folder, the Finder remembers whether folders nested within it were previously expanded or collapsed and restores each to its former state.

Selecting from multiple folders

Finder 7's outline views enable you to select multiple items from any number of folders, as shown in Figure 3-4. All folders must be on one disk.

To select an additional item, expand the folder that contains it and press Shift while clicking the item. You can also select consecutive items by pressing Shift while dragging a selection rectangle around them. If you need to deselect a few items, Shift-click each item or Shift-drag across consecutive items.

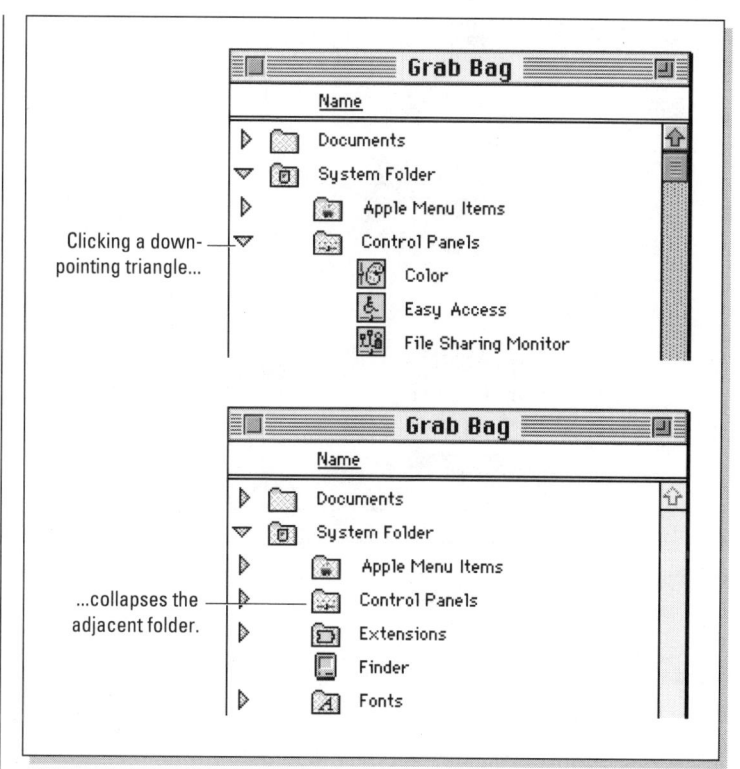

Figure 3-2: Collapsing a folder.

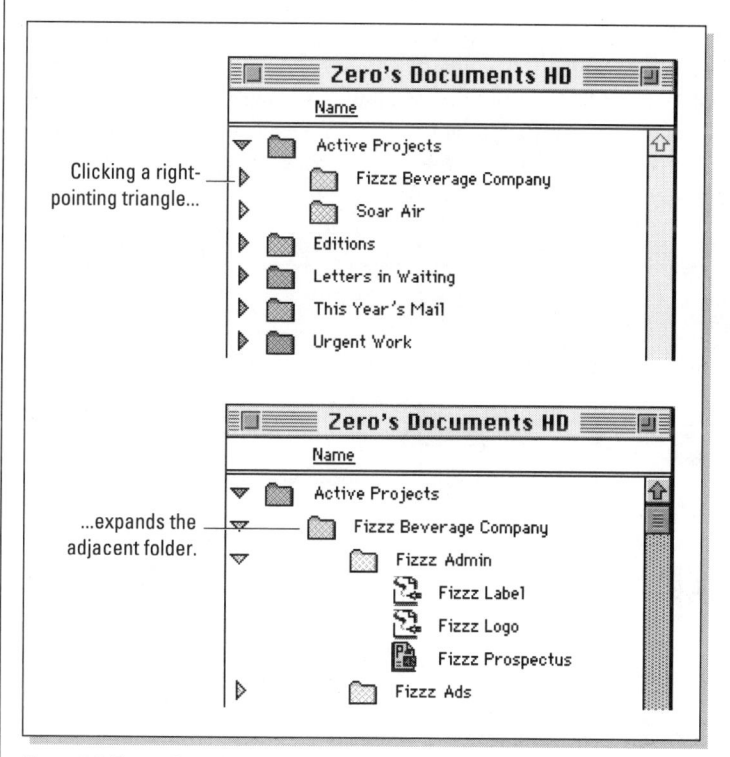

Figure 3-3: Expanding a folder.

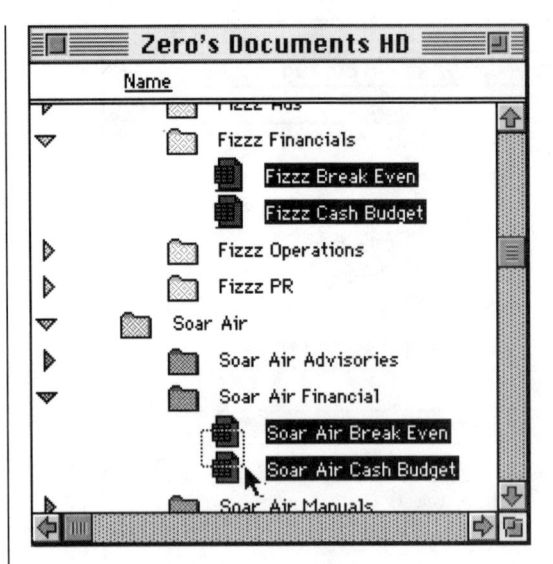

Figure 3-4: Items selected from multiple folders.

Smart Zooming

After expanding and collapsing folders in an outline view, you may want to make a window just large enough to show all the items currently listed in it. To do that, simply click the zoom box, as shown in Figure 3-5.

Older Finders always zoom up to full-screen size, but Finder 7 zooms up or down to fit a window's contents. The window only covers the whole screen if it contains enough items to fill a screen-size window. This smart zooming helps you make best use of your screen real estate after changing views, adding or removing items, rearranging icons, and so on. If you do want to zoom a window to fill the screen, press Option while clicking the zoom box.

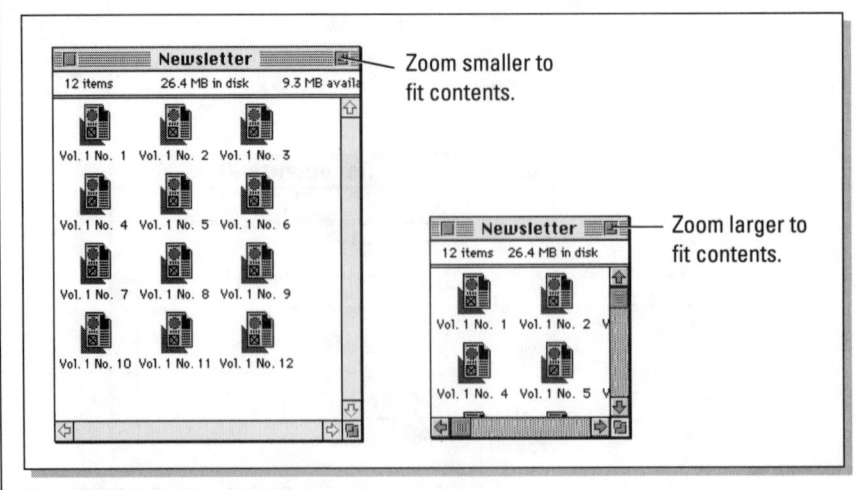

Figure 3-5: Zoom to fit.

Finding Items

An outline view helps you hunt through folders and disks for items, but Finder 7's Find command finds and fetches lost items with less effort. In its simplest form, the Find command looks through all disks whose icons are on the desktop for an item whose name contains the text you specify, as shown in Figure 3-6. It displays the first item it finds, opening the folder that contains the item to show the item in its native surroundings.

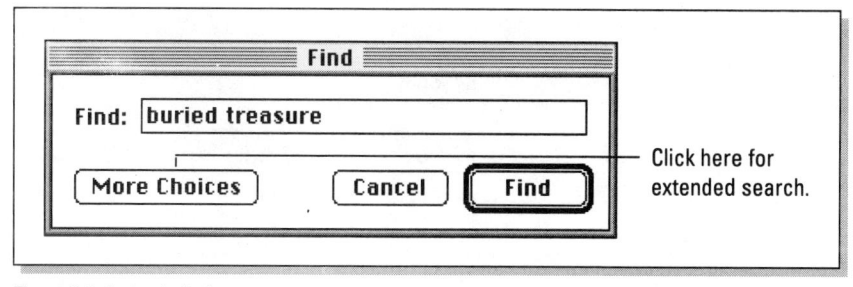

Figure 3-6: A simple find.

You can find additional matching items with the Find Again command. If the currently active window doesn't contain any more matches to the Find criteria, the Find looks in other folders and disks. If it finds another match, it closes the active window (unless it was already open) and looks for a match in another folder. If you know the active window contains several matches to the Find criteria but you know none of them is the one you want, you can skip to the next folder by closing the active window before using the Find Again command.

The Find command has an extended form as well. Clicking the More Choices button enables you to specify a wide variety of search criteria, as shown in Figure 3-7.

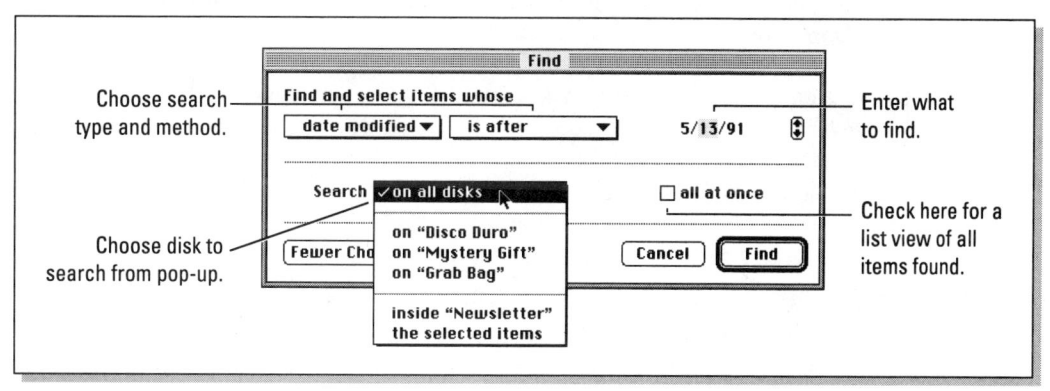

Figure 3-7: An extended find.

Table 3-1: Find criteria

Search what	Search how	Search for
name	contains/ starts with/ ends with/ is/ is not/ doesn't contain	text you enter
size	is less than/ is greater than	amount you enter
kind	contains/ doesn't contain	alias/ application/ document/ folder/ stationery/ text you enter
label	is/ is not	label you choose from pop-up menu
date created	is/ is before/ is after/ is not	date you enter
date modified	is/ is before/ is after/ is not	date you enter
version	is/ is before/ is after/ is not	text you enter
comments	contain/ do not contain	text you enter
lock	is	locked/ unlocked

You choose the type of search: by name, size, kind, label, date created, date modified, version, comments, or lock status. You also specify exactly what you want matched and how you want it matched. Table 3-1 enumerates the possible criteria combinations. For all combinations, you can restrict the search to a single disk, to the active window, or to a group of items you selected in the active window before choosing the Find command. If you do, you can also have the Finder select all the items it finds at once, in an outline view.

The Find command does not look inside the System file or suitcase files for fonts, sounds, or desk accessories. It can find those kinds of items in folders and on the desktop, though.

To return to the simple Find dialog box, click the Fewer Choices button. To end searching, click the Cancel button. The Finder remembers whether you were using the simple or the extended Find dialog box and gives you the same one the next time you use the Find command.

Opening an Enclosing Folder

When you press Command while clicking the active window's title, a menu pops up showing the path from the window through your nested folder structure to the disk that contains the active window, as shown in Figure 3-8. You can use the menu to

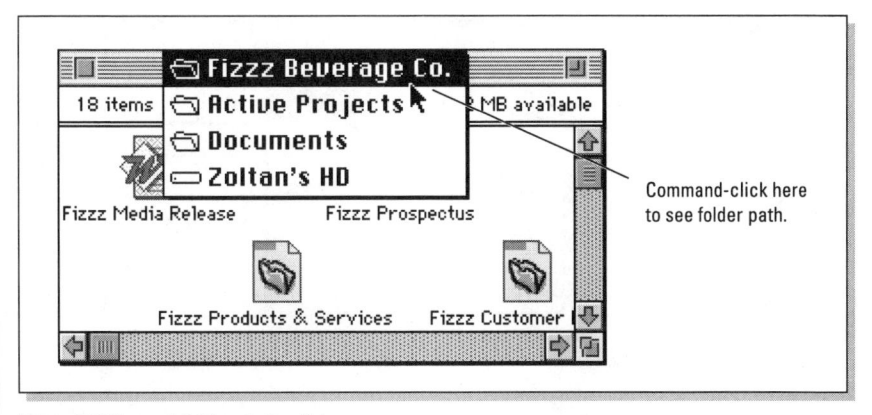

Figure 3-8: Through folders to the disk.

open the folder that contains, or encloses, the active window. The enclosing folder is sometimes called the *parent folder*. You can also use the pop-up menu to open the other folders along the path or the disk at the root of the path.

To open any folder along the path, or the disk at the end of the path, choose the container you want opened from the pop-up menu. At the same time, you can close the active window by pressing Option while choosing from the pop-up menu.

Custom Views

You can change the format and content of Finder 7's windows with the Views control panel, as shown in Figure 3-9. Control panel settings affect all Finder windows and the desktop; you can't format each window separately. After changing settings in the Views control panel, you can resize windows to fit the new format by clicking their zoom boxes.

Figure 3-9: The Views control panel.

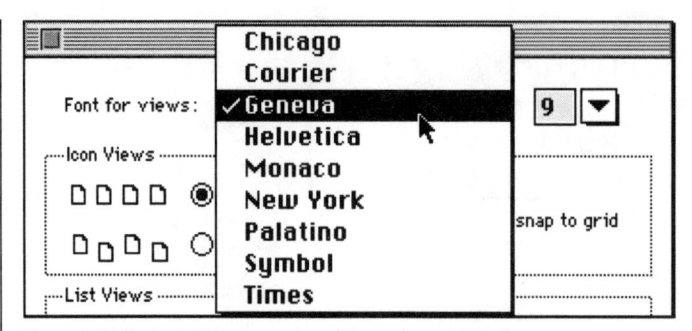

Figure 3-10: Finder text format options (Views control panel).

Setting the text font and size

Choose a text font and a text size for icon names and all the text in list views from the pop-up menus at the top of the Views control panel, as shown in Figure 3-10. If the text size you want isn't listed, you can enter any size between 6 and 36.

The Finder uses the font and size settings for icon names; the disk information header (number of items, disk space used, and disk space available); and all the text in list views. Your font and size settings affect all windows and icons.

After making the size much larger or much smaller, you may want to use the Clean Up command (Special menu) to adjust the spacing of icons on the desktop and in windows. You must clean up each window separately.

Setting icon alignment

Other settings in the Views control panel determine how the Finder aligns icons, as shown in Figure 3-11. The settings affect icons on the desktop and in all windows with icon or small icon views. You can set the type of grid the Clean Up command uses and decide whether icons automatically align with that grid when you drag them.

The Staggered Grid option makes it possible to arrange icons close together without their names overlapping. Turning on the Always Snap To Grid option makes icons you drag align to the Clean Up command's grid. You can temporarily reverse the Always Snap To Grid setting by pressing Command while dragging.

Figure 3-11: Finder icon alignment options (Views control panel).

Figure 3-12: Finder list view options (Views control panel).

Determining list view contents

To determine how much information Finder 7 shows in all windows with list views (name, size, kind, and so on), you set numerous options at the bottom of the Views control panel, as shown in Figure 3-12.

List views always include an icon and a name for every item in the window. In addition, you select which of six other columns of information to include: size, kind, label, date, version, and comments. Your selections appear as choices in the Finder's Views menu. You cannot change the order of the columns or their widths, only whether each appears or not. The version and comments columns, which you otherwise see with the Get Info command (File menu), are new in list views with Finder 7. Only the first 25 characters of an item's comments are shown in a list view.

Judicious setting of list view options keeps your list view windows as small as possible. You can make a list view window narrower by reducing the number of items checked in the Views control panel and then clicking the window's zoom box.

Finder 7, unlike older Finders, enables you to pick the size of icons it displays in all list views. Tiny-size icons are like the icons in list views of older Finders. Small-size icons are like the icons in small icon view. Standard-size icons are like desktop icons.

You can also set an option to have Finder 7 calculate and display folder sizes. Adding up the sizes of items in a large folder can take quite a while. Fortunately, Finder 7 only calculates sizes of folders you can see and it does this work in the background so you can get on with other tasks. Another list view option has Finder 7 show disk information in the header of all list view windows. The disk information includes the number of items in the window, the amount of disk space in use, and the amount of disk space available. This information is standard in icon and small icon views.

Changing List Views

You can change a window from one list view to any other available list view directly in the window, without using the Finder's View menu, as shown in Figure 3-13. Simply click the column heading that corresponds to the view you want. Finder 7

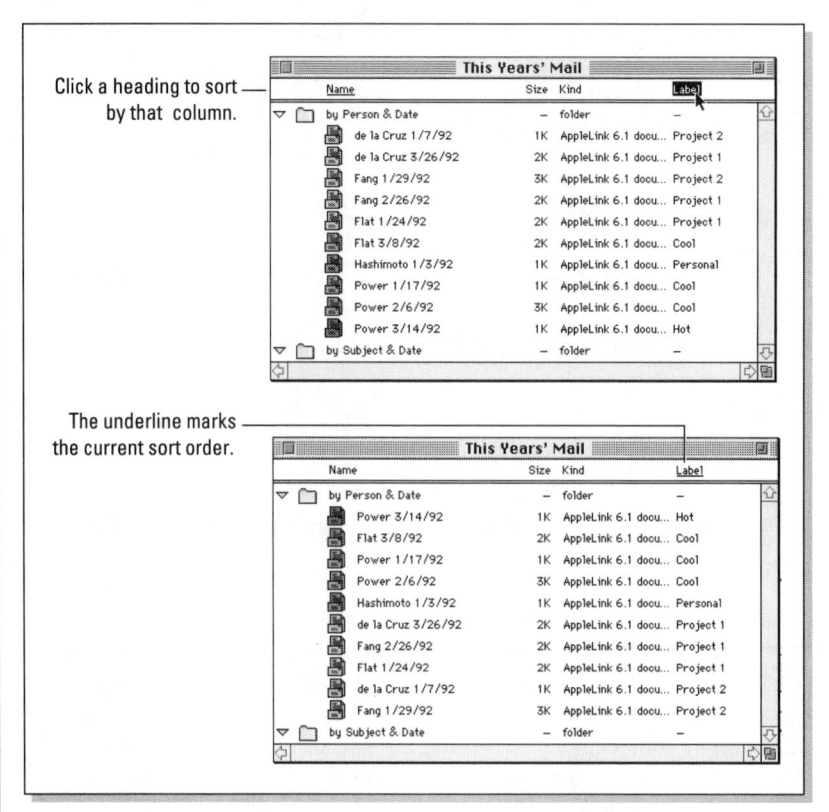

Figure 3-13: Sorting a list view.

immediately sorts all the items in the window according to the column you clicked. You can tell the current sort order by looking for the underlined column heading.

Horizontal Scrolling

All the information you have requested with the Views control panel for each item in a list view may not fit across a window even at its maximum width. If a window contains more columns out of view on the right or left, Finder 7 activates the window's horizontal scroll bar, as shown in Figure 3-14. You can use it to read all of a wide listing. Older Finders never activate the horizontal scroll bar in a list view.

Auto Scrolling

You can scroll a window in Finder 7 without using the scroll bars. Simply place the pointer in the window, press the mouse button, and drag toward the area you want to come into view, as shown in Figure 3-15. Drag the pointer up, down, left, or right past the window's active area and scrolling begins. Dragging past a window corner scrolls diagonally.

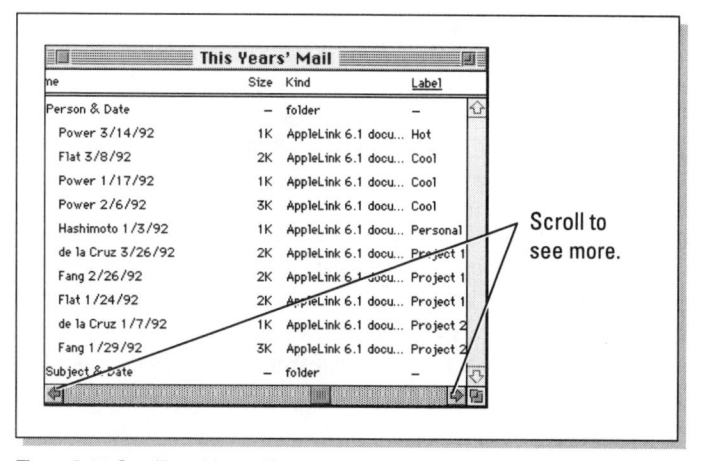

Figure 3-14: Scrolling side to side.

UNDOCUMENTED

As you drag, you can vary the scrolling speed. To scroll slowly, drag just to the window's edge (and continue pressing the mouse button). Increase scrolling speed by dragging beyond the window's edge.

You can use this scrolling technique, known as auto-scrolling, while performing the following operations:

◆ Moving an icon or group of icons to a new place in the same window (icon or small icon view)

◆ Moving an item or group of items into a folder in the same window (any view)

◆ Dragging a selection rectangle around adjacent items in the same window to select them all (any view)

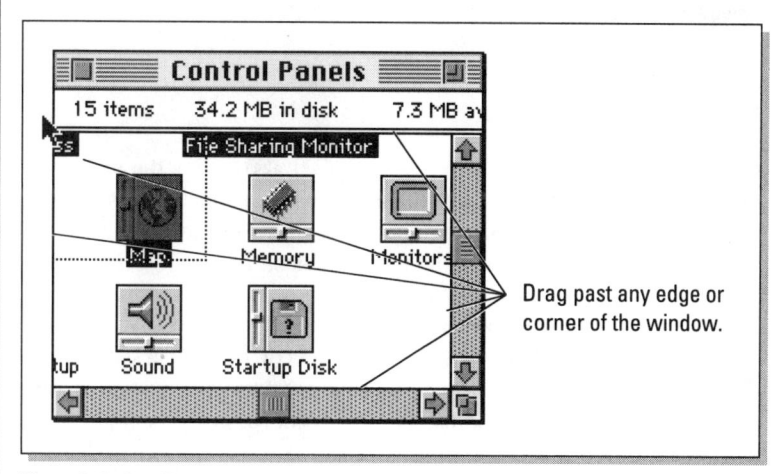

Figure 3-15: Scrolling automatically.

Selecting by Dragging

All versions of the Finder enable you to select adjacent icons by dragging a selection rectangle (which looks to some people like marching ants), across them. Finder 7 is the first to allow this type of selection in any view, not just icon and small icon views, as shown in Figure 3-16.

The selection rectangle selects every item whose icon or icon name it touches. All items must be on the desktop or in a single window. Items are highlighted one-by-one as you drag over them, not en masse when you stop dragging. As a side effect of this behavior, you must click within some text or on an icon to select an item in any list view. Older Finders select an item when you click anywhere on a line, even in blank spaces.

Figure 3-16: Selecting adjacent items.

Renaming Items

Clicking an icon selects the icon but no longer also selects the icon name for editing. On the good side, your cat can no longer rename a selected icon by walking across the keyboard. Also, you can now open an icon by double-clicking its name. On the bad side, you have to relearn how to change icon names.

To rename a disk, folder, program, document, or other item, you must explicitly select its name. You either click the name directly or you click the item's icon and then press Return or Enter. When the name is selected for editing, it has a box around it in addition to being highlighted, as shown in Figure 3-17. The box does not appear if you just click the icon.

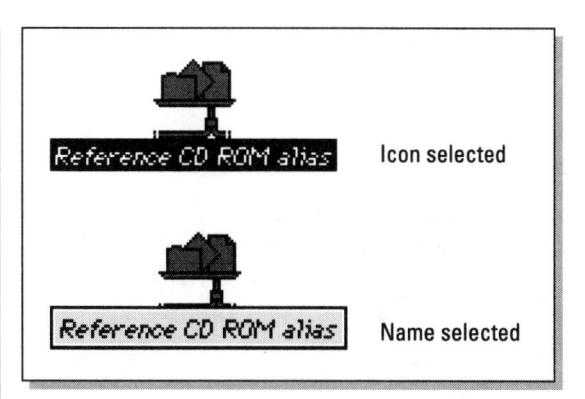

Figure 3-17: Selecting an icon name.

For an additional visual cue that you have selected a name on a color or grayscale monitor, use the Colors control panel to set the text highlight color to something other than black and white. Then you know a name highlighted in color (or gray) is ready for editing, whereas a name highlighted in black and white is not.

After selecting a name, you can replace it completely by typing a new name. If instead you want to select an insertion point, a word, or a range of text, don't click, double-click, or drag right away. Wait until a box appears around the name. The length of time you must wait depends on the duration of a double-click interval — approximately 1.9 seconds, 1.3 seconds, or 0.9 second, as set in the Mouse control panel. If you click again too soon, the Finder thinks you're double-clicking the icon and opens it. If you have trouble editing icon names without opening the item, try setting a briefer Double-Click Speed with the Mouse control panel.

You don't have to wait after clicking an icon's name if you immediately move the pointer; just twitch the mouse and the name is highlighted for editing. Another way to avoid waiting after clicking an icon's name is to move the insertion point by pressing the arrow keys. Pressing up arrow moves the insertion point to the beginning of the name, down arrow moves it to the end, left arrow moves it left, and right arrow moves it right.

While editing a name, you can use the Undo, Cut, Copy, and Paste commands in the Edit menu. You cannot undo your changes to a name after you finish editing it, only while it is still selected for editing. You can also copy the entire name of any item by selecting its icon (or its whole name) and using the Copy command (Edit menu). This capability comes in handy when you're copying a disk and want to name the copy the same as the original.

You can copy the names of multiple icons by selecting the icons and using the Copy command. If the total lengths of all selected icon names exceeds 256 characters, Finder 7 only copies the first 256 characters to the Clipboard.

The name of a locked item can't be changed. (Unlock an item with the Get Info command, or if it's a disk, by sliding its locking tab.) However, you can copy its entire name as just described.

Naming Duplicates

The Finder constructs the name of a duplicate item you create with the Duplicate command (File menu) by suffixing the name with the word *copy*. Additional copies of the same item also have a serial number suffixed, as shown in Figure 3-18.

Figure 3-18: Names of duplicate items.

If any suffixes result in a name longer than 31 characters, the Finder removes characters from the end of the original item's name. For example, duplicating an item named *5/91 Income and Expense Report* would result in an item named *5/91 Income and Expense Re copy*.

These same rules come into play when an item you drag to the Trash has the same name as another item already there. Suppose, for example, the Trash contained an item named *Untitled* and you dragged another like-named item there. The Finder would rename the item already there to *Untitled copy*. If you later added another item named *Untitled*, the Finder would change *Untitled copy* to *Untitled copy 2*, change *Untitled* to *Untitled copy*, and leave the name of the item you just added unchanged. In other words, the item most recently added has the plain name and the next most recently added has the highest number suffix.

The Finder uses similar rules to construct names of aliases. See Chapter 6.

Labeling Items

Finder 7 enables you to classify folders, programs, and documents by labeling them with a word or phrase. On monitors displaying at least 16 colors, labeling an item also colorizes it.

Using labels

To label an item, select it and choose a label from the Finder's Label menu, as shown in Figure 3-19. If the icon has an icon with natural color, the Finder blends the label color as if you covered the icon with a piece of acetate the color of the label. To label an item without colorizing it, change the label color to solid black as described in the next section.

After labeling items, you can view Finder window contents arranged by label, as shown in Figure 3-20. You can also search for items by label using the Finder's Find command, as shown in Figure 3-21. Label colors also show up in the Apple menu and in the directory dialog boxes used by many programs' Open and Save commands.

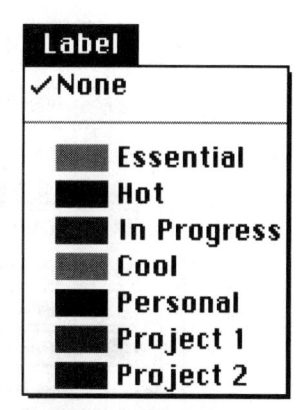

Figure 3-19: The Label menu.

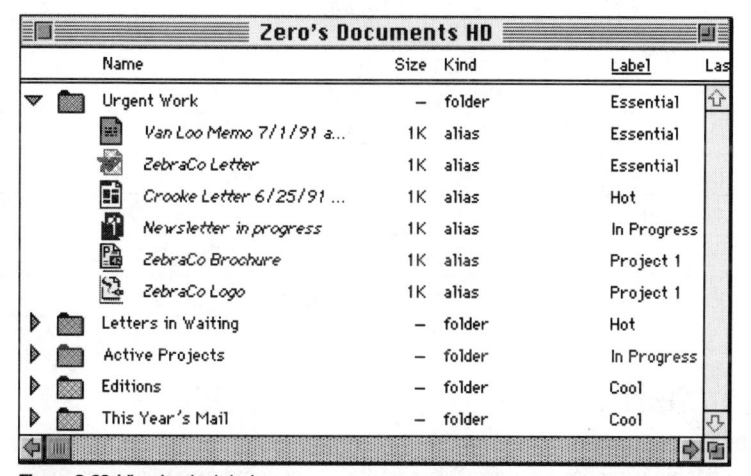

Figure 3-20: Viewing by label.

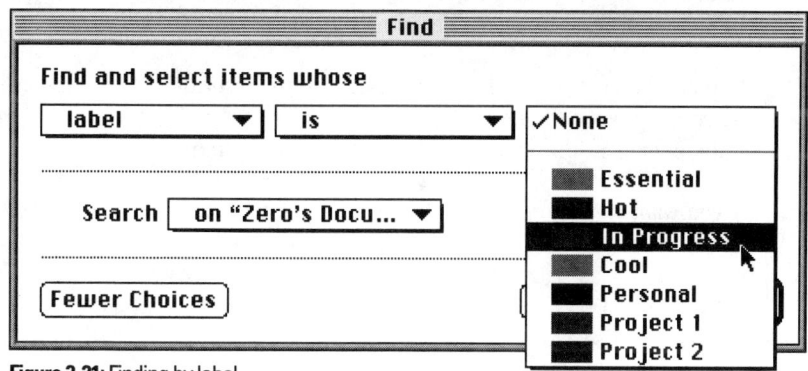

Figure 3-21: Finding by label.

Changing label names and colors

You change the standard label names and colors using the Labels control panel, as shown in Figure 3-22. If you click a label color to change it, the Finder displays a dialog box in which you specify a new color. You can click a color on the color wheel or you can enter values between 0 and 65535 either for hue, saturation, and brightness or for red, green, and blue. Table 3-2 lists the hue, saturation, and brightness values for the standard colors (in case you want to reset them after experimenting).

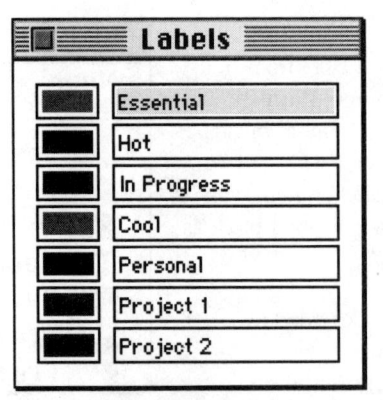

Figure 3-22: The Labels control panel.

Table 3-2:   Values for standard label colors

Label	Hue	Saturation	Brightness
Essential	4223	64884	65535
Hot	108	63573	56683
In Progress	59733	63286	62167
Cool	35756	64907	60159
Personal	43690	65535	54272
Project 1	23764	65535	25775
Project 2	5332	61619	22016

Polite Drag

When you move or copy an item by dragging it from one window to a folder in an overlapping window, Finder 7 keeps the target window in front of the source window so the destination folder is always in view, as shown in Figure 3-23. Older Finders rudely bring the source window in front of an overlapping target window as soon as you begin dragging, sometimes covering the destination folder.

In other words, Finder 7 brings a window to the front only if the pointer is in it when you release the mouse. In contrast, older Finders bring a window to the front if the pointer is in it when you press the mouse button.

If you want to drag more than one item at a time to an overlapping window, start by selecting the items in the source window. Next, activate the destination window by clicking along its right edge or its bottom edge (where its scroll bars would be if it were active). Don't click anywhere inside the destination window or in its title bar, or you will deselect the items in the source window. Finally, drag the selected items

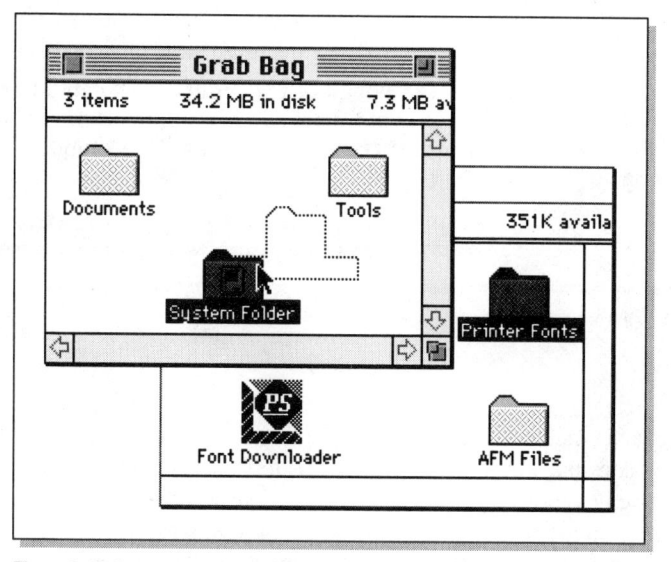

Figure 3-23: Dragging to an overlapping window.

from the now-inactive source window to the now-active destination window. You can drag the whole group of selected items by dragging any one of them, even if they aren't all visible in the inactive source window.

Desktop Database

Finder 7 handles hard disks containing hundreds or thousands of items more efficiently than older Finders. The increased efficiency comes from System 7's improved desktop database, which keeps track of the following items:

- ✦ How icons look
- ✦ What kind of file each icon refers to
- ✦ Where programs are
- ✦ Comments you have entered with the Finder's Get Info command

System 7 creates a new desktop database on every disk larger than 2MB. Each smaller disk has an old-style desktop file, because those disks can usually be ejected and inserted into other systems that are using old system software.

A desktop database (or old-style desktop file) can become corrupt, not through greed or false pride, but as a side effect of programs quitting unexpectedly or system crashes. Typical symptoms are blank icons or the Finder being unable to find the program to open a document, as shown in Figure 3-24. These symptoms also occur when the program that created a document is on an ejected disk (or you don't have the program).

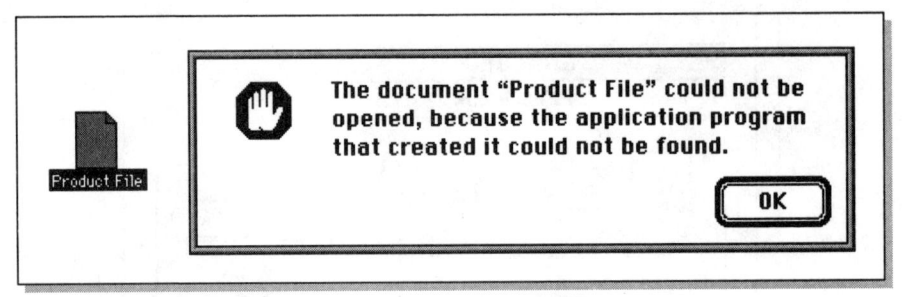

Figure 3-24: Signs of a corrupt desktop.

Restarting your Macintosh may eliminate the blank icons. If not, rebuilding the desktop usually does the trick. To rebuild the desktop, simply press Command-Option while starting up, and wait for the Finder to inquire whether you indeed wish to rebuild the desktop on the startup disk. If you have multiple hard disks, the Finder asks about rebuilding each one in turn. To rebuild the desktop on a floppy disk, press Command-Option while inserting the floppy.

Rebuilding the desktop erases all comments you have entered in Get Info windows for items on the disks involved. See Chapter 13 for a description of software you can use to retain Get Info window comments while rebuilding the desktop.

Background Work

Copying files can take a while, but Finder 7 can do the work in the background while you use another program, as shown in Figure 3-25. Background copying is especially useful during a lengthy copy, such as from or to a shared folder or disk. In addition, Finder 7's Duplicate, Empty Trash, and Find commands work in the background. Notice the dialog boxes of these commands have title bars; you can drag a title bar to move a dialog box.

After starting a copy, duplicate, empty-Trash, or find process, you can switch to another program by clicking in any of its windows or by choosing it from the Application menu or the Apple menu. You can't open a program or document by double-clicking its icon or using the Finder's Open command (File menu) while the Finder copies, duplicates, empties Trash, or finds, but you can open programs and documents listed in the Apple menu. And after switching from the Finder to another program, you can use that program's Open command to open documents. Control panels are considered part of the Finder, so you can't use them while the Finder performs one of the tasks it can do in the background.

The performance of your Macintosh suffers while the Finder works on a task in the background. The background task proceeds more slowly than it would in the foreground. The pointer jerks across the screen. The mouse button and keyboard may seem to stop working for a few seconds from time to time. If you keep typing blind (characters are not displayed on screen), the system remembers the most recent 20

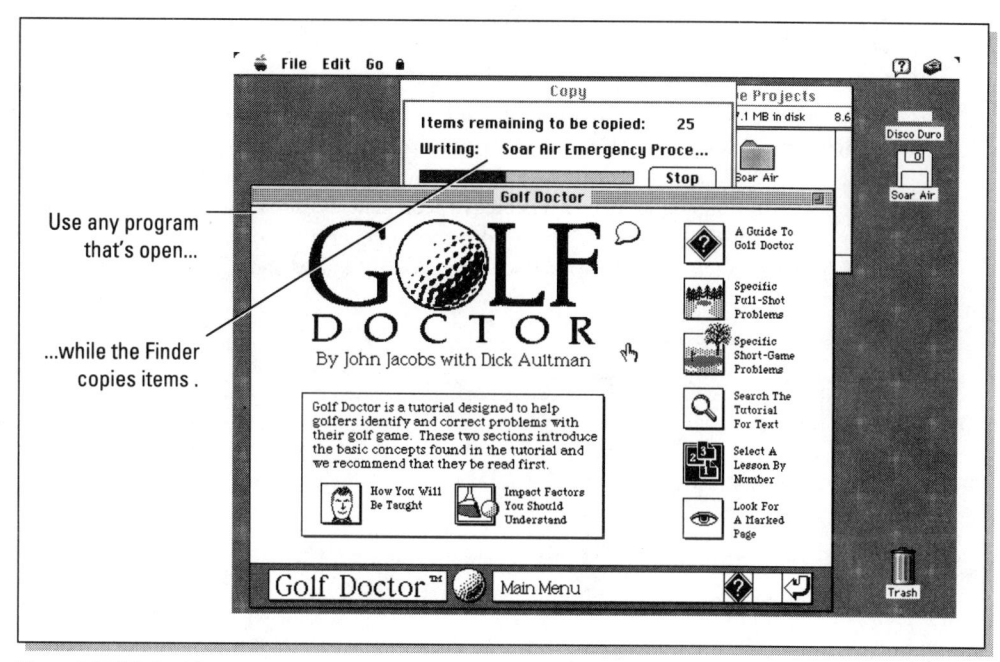

Figure 3-25: Work while you copy.

characters you type (about five seconds of typing at 40 words per minute). The system can also remember one click or double-click, or it can catch up with your dragging as long as you don't release the mouse button.

Smarter Copying

When you copy an item to a disk or folder that already contains an item by the same name, Finder 7 does more than older Finders. It asks you whether you want to replace the item at the destination and it tells you which item is newer, as shown in Figure 3-26.

Finder 7 is also smart about copying a floppy disk to a hard disk. It puts the floppy disk's contents into a new folder on the hard disk and names the folder the same as the floppy. You can even copy a floppy to a folder on a hard disk.

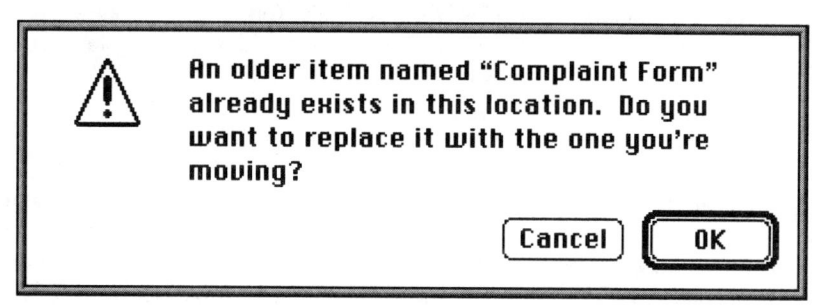

Figure 3-26: Verifying replacement.

Stationery Pads

Rather than copy a document for its format and content, you can make it a stationery pad. Opening a stationery pad with the Finder is like tearing a page from a pad of preprinted forms. You get a new document with preset format and contents.

Stationery pad documents have a distinctive icon that looks like a stack of document icons, as shown in Figure 3-27. The Finder uses a generic stationery pad icon if the program that handles that type of document doesn't know about System 7's stationery.

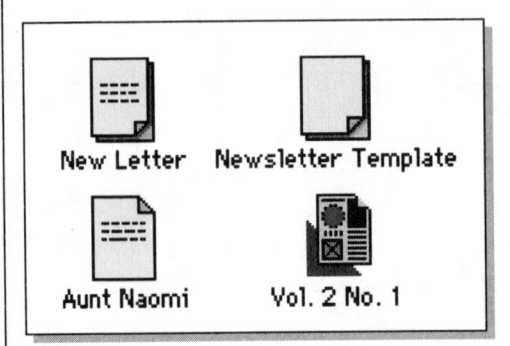

Figure 3-27: Stationery pad icons and ordinary icons.

Making stationery pads

You can make any document a stationery pad by selecting it in the Finder, choosing the Get Info command, and setting the Stationery Pad option in the Get Info window, as shown in Figure 3-28. Some programs enable you to directly save a document as a stationery pad by setting a Stationery Pad option when you save the document using the Save or Save As commands (Figure 3-29). These programs have been upgraded specifically to work with System 7's stationery pads.

Using stationery pads

Programs that know about stationery pads open an untitled document with the format and contents of the stationery pad. For programs that don't know about stationery pads, the Finder automatically creates a new document by making a copy of the stationery pad, asking you to name it, and having the program open the copy. However, opening a stationery pad from within a program that doesn't know about them (as opposed to opening from the Finder) opens the stationery pad itself, not a copy. A message warns you that you are opening a master stationery pad, as shown in Figure 3-30.

Opening a stationery document always creates a new document.

If you don't want to do this every time you open a template, don't make the template a stationery pad. Instead, make the template an ordinary document, but lock it using the Finder's Get Info command. You may want to use this method with templates for printing single envelopes and mailing labels, for example. Then you could open the locked template, type or paste the recipient's address, print, and close without saving.

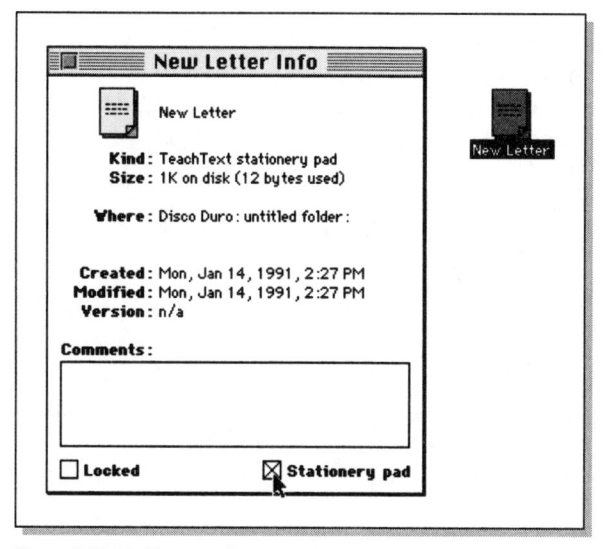

Figure 3-28: Making a stationery pad.

Figure 3-29: Saving a stationery pad.

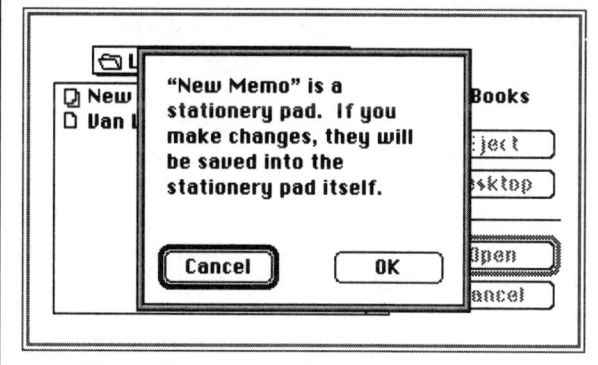

Figure 3-30: Opening stationery within a program.

Custom Icons

Would you like to see dinosaurs or hummingbirds on your desktop instead of ordinary icons? Finder 7 enables you to replace the icons of individual documents, programs, folders, and disks with your own pictures, as shown in Figure 3-31.

Figure 3-31: Icons your way.

The color, grayscale, or black-and-white picture you use for an icon can come from any one of the following sources:

- Clip-art disk
- Photo or drawing on paper converted to an electronic image with a scanner
- Video image captured with special hardware accessories
- Your own picture made with a painting or drawing program

Making a custom icon

To replace an icon with your icon, first select the picture and copy it with the Copy command (Edit menu). Then go to the Finder and find the icon you want to replace. Select the icon (click it once) and choose Get Info from the Finder's File menu. In the Get Info window, click the icon to select it and use the Paste command (Edit menu) to replace it with the picture you just copied, as shown in Figure 3-32. You can also copy an icon from a Get Info window and paste it into a different Get Info window.

For best results, your picture should measure 32 × 32 pixels (dots), or at least 64 × 64, 128 × 128, or 256 × 256. If your picture is larger than 32 × 32, the Finder reduces it proportionally to fit that amount of space when you replace an icon with it. Reducing a picture distorts it, especially if the original size is an odd or fractional multiple of the final size. If your picture is smaller than 32 × 32, the Finder centers it on a white 32 × 32 square.

Figure 3-32: Customizing an icon.

When an item with a custom icon appears in a small icon view, in the Apple Menu or in the Application menu, the Finder reduces the standard-size icon by half, as shown in Figure 3-33. If you duplicate or make an alias of an item with a custom icon, the duplicate or alias inherits the custom icon.

You cannot replace the icon of a locked item, an open document, or an open program. Nor can you replace any system software icons such as the System Folder, Finder, Control Panels Folder, and Trash. (You can replace individual control panel icons, however.)

When you paste a color picture into an item's Get Info window, you don't always get the custom icon you expect because the Finder is partly color blind. It sees light colors like yellow or orange at the picture's edge as transparent parts of the icon and omits them from the mask it makes for the custom icon. The defective mask punches an incomplete hole in the desktop for the icon to show through. For instructions on fixing a defective icon mask see "Fixing Custom Color Icons" in Chapter 13.

Figure 3-33: Custom icons in standard and small sizes.

Reverting to a standard icon

To revert to an item's standard icon, select the item, choose Get Info from the Finder's File menu, select the icon in the Get Info window, and choose Clear or Cut from the Edit menu.

Removing Disk Icons

Dragging a disk icon to the Trash does not permanently remove anything from the disk, as you might reasonably fear. Instead this process, known as unmounting a disk, removes the icon from the desktop and makes the disk's contents unavailable. If the disk is a floppy disk or other removable disk, dragging its icon to the Trash ejects the disk from the disk drive.

With Finder 7, you can also remove a disk icon by selecting the disk icon and choosing Put Away from the File menu, as shown in Figure 3-34. The Put Away command ejects floppy disks and other removable disks.

To eject a disk without removing its icon from the desktop, select the icon and choose Eject from the Special menu. The ejected disk's icon becomes gray to show it is unavailable. With older Finders, the Eject command is in the File menu and you put away a disk by pressing Option while choosing the Eject command.

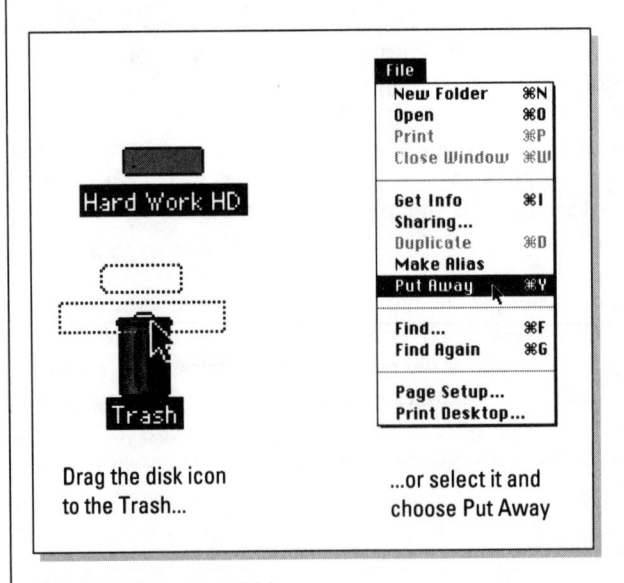

Figure 3-34: Removing a disk icon.

Trash Disposal

The Trash icon looks the same with System 7 as with older system software, but the Trash works differently. The Finder no longer automatically empties the Trash. You must remove items from the Trash explicitly by choosing Empty Trash from the Finder's Special menu. Until you do, the contents of the Trash remain there even if you open another program, shut down, or restart.

Finder 7 doesn't allow you to leave items from 400K (single-sided) disks in the Trash, however. When you drag items from a 400K disk to the Trash, a message asks whether you want to delete them immediately or cancel.

Trash warnings

When you choose the Empty Trash command, Finder 7 tells you how many items the Trash contains and how much disk space they occupy, as shown in Figure 3-35. Invisible items in the Trash also count toward the total number of items to be permanently removed. (For example, any folder that has a custom icon contains an invisible item named *Icon.*) You decide whether to discard them all or cancel.

You can disable the Trash warning by pressing Option while choosing the Empty Trash command. To more permanently muzzle the warnings, select the Trash icon, choose the Get Info command, and turn off the appropriate option, as shown in Figure 3-36.

Unlike older Finders, Finder 7 does not display a warning when you drag locked items, application programs, or system software items to the Trash. However, the Finder does not remove locked items. It advises you the Trash contains locked items, and asks whether you want to remove the other items or cancel. To get rid of locked items in the Trash, press Option while choosing the Empty Trash command.

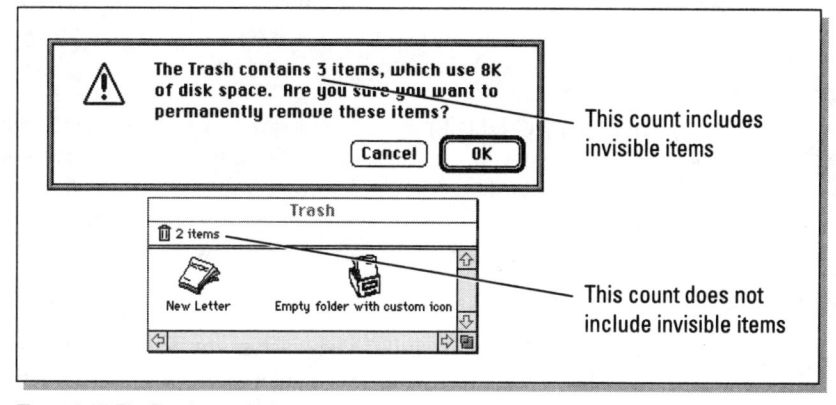

Figure 3-35: The Trash warning.

```
┌─────────────────────────────────────────┐
│ ▪ ═══════════ Trash Info ═══════════    │
│                                         │
│    🗑  Trash                             │
│                                         │
│   Where: On the desktop                 │
│                                         │
│   Contents: 2 files and 1 folder are in the Trash │
│             for a total of 8K.          │
│                                         │
│                                         │
│   Modified: Wed, Mar 27, 1991, 12:21 PM │
│                                         │
│   ☒ Warn before emptying                │
│                                         │
└─────────────────────────────────────────┘
```

Turn Trash warnings on and off here.

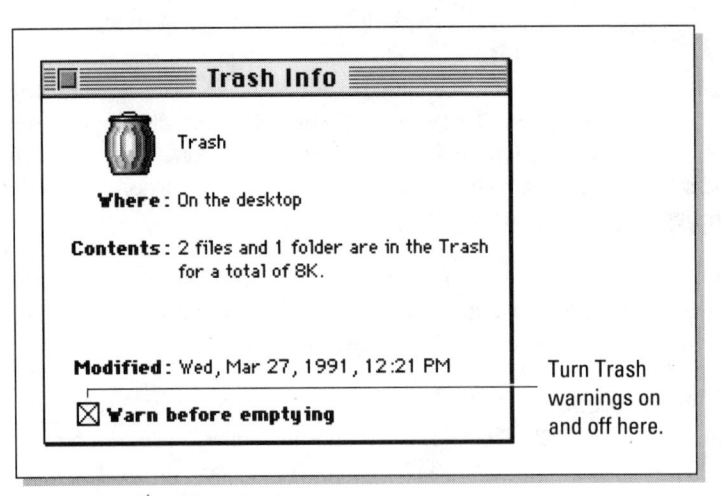

Figure 3-36: Get Info for the Trash.

Trash retrieval

To put items now in the Trash back where they came from, open the Trash, select the items, and choose Put Away from the Finder's File menu. The Finder returns each selected item to its previous folder, though not necessarily to the same place in the folder window.

Trash contents

The Trash contains all the items that have been dragged to it from all the disks whose icons are on the desktop. The Empty Trash command removes the items from all disks involved. To remove items from only one disk, first put away the icons of the disks whose trash you don't want affected (either drag the disk icons to the Trash or select the icons and choose Put Away from the File menu). The Empty Trash command doesn't affect disks whose icons are not on the desktop. Alternatively, you can open the Trash and drag the items you don't want removed to the desktop or to another folder. Then use the Empty Trash Command.

If you eject a floppy disk (and put away its icon) after dragging items from that disk to the Trash, those items disappear from the Trash but the Finder has not deleted them. They reappear in the Trash the next time you insert that disk. If you insert that floppy disk in another Mac, they appear in its Trash. They appear in a folder named Trash when you use that disk with older system software.

If you're sharing someone else's disk or folder over a network and you drag an item from the shared disk to the Trash on your desktop, the item does not go into the Trash on the Mac where the shared disk or folder resides. The item is removed from that disk or folder if you use the Empty Trash command on your Mac, however. From the opposite viewpoint, this means you do not know if someone sharing your disk or folder drags items from it to his or her Trash. (The owner of a shared disk or folder can set access privileges to keep unauthorized people from dragging items from it to their Trash.)

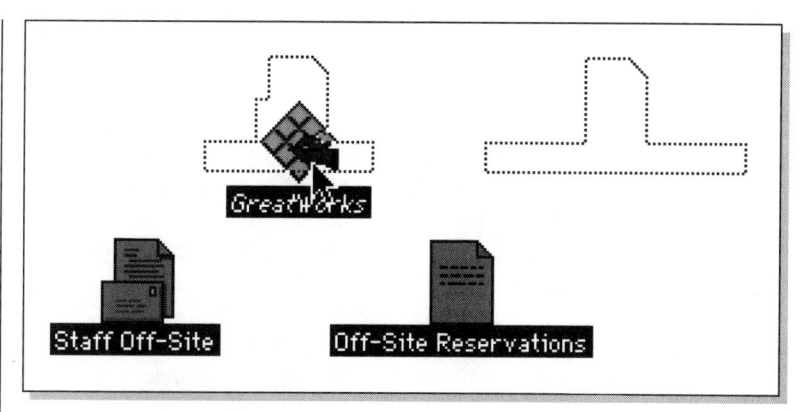

Figure 3-37: Dragging a document to open it.

> Sometimes the Trash contains a folder named *Rescued Items*. It contains formerly invisible temporary files found when you started up your Macintosh. The Rescued Items folder only appears after a system crash. You may be able to recreate your work up to the time of the system crash from the contents of the Rescued Items folder.

Drag open

You can open a document from the Finder by dragging its icon to the icon of any application program that can open it. The program need not have created the document but must be compatible with it. For example, most ReadMe documents are plain text documents that any word processor can open. Dragging a document over a compatible program without releasing the mouse button highlights the program's icon, as if you had dragged the document over a folder, as shown in Figure 3-37. Then releasing the mouse button removes the highlighting, opens the program (unless it's already open), and opens the document. If a program can't open a document you drag to it, nothing happens — no highlighting, no opening.

Cleaning Up Options

New wrinkles in Finder 7's Clean Up command help keep your icons neat and organized. As in older Finders, choosing Clean Up from the Special menu aligns the active window's icons (or the desktop icons, if no window is active) in neat rows and columns. But Finder 7 doesn't move icons into positions that make their names unreadable. If aligning an icon would make its name overlap a neighboring icon's name, the Finder moves it somewhere nearby where the names won't collide.

> As Finder 7 cleans up your icons, you can have it sort them by any of the choices in the View menu. First you choose the sort order you want from the View menu (temporarily changing the view). Then use the View menu again to choose by Icon or by

Small Icon. Finally, press Option while you choose the Clean Up command. The Finder rearranges all icons in the window, putting the one lowest in the sort order in the upper-left corner and then filling the window from left to right and top to bottom.

If you press Option while cleaning up the desktop (instead of a window), the Finder aligns all desktop icons in a standard configuration. It moves the startup disk's icon to the upper-right corner of the desktop; lines up other disk icons below it; puts the Trash in the lower-right corner; and arranges all other desktop icons in rows and columns next to the disk icons.

You can also use System 7's Clean Up command to align just the icons you have selected in a window or on the desktop. Pressing Shift changes Clean Up to Clean Up Selection.

Finder Power

The Finder has a great deal of hidden power, which you tap by pressing Command and Option at the opportune moment. In addition, much of what you can do with the mouse you can also do with the keyboard alone. Tables 3-3, 3-4, 3-5, and 3-6 list power methods and keyboard equivalents for selecting items in windows or on the desktop; opening and closing items; expanding and collapsing outlines of folders in list views; and more. For the most part, these tables do not list keyboard equivalents for menu commands because you can review them on screen by pulling down the menus.

Table 3-3:	Selecting items
Objective	*Action*
Select an item	Type the item's partial or full name
Select the next item alphabetically	Press Tab
Select the previous item alphabetically	Press Shift-Tab
Select the next item up	Press Up Arrow
Select the next item down	Press Down Arrow
Select the next item left	Press Left Arrow
Select the next item right	Press Right Arrow
Select the desktop item nearest the upper-right corner	Press Command-Shift-Up Arrow
Select multiple items	Press Shift while clicking each item or while dragging to enclose them

Table 3-4: Opening and closing

Objective	Action
Open the selected item	Press Command-O or press Command-Down Arrow
Open the selected item and close the active window	Press Command-Option-O or press Command-Option-Down Arrow
Open the folder or disk that contains the selected item	Press Command while clicking the window's title or press Command-Up Arrow
Open the folder or disk that contains the selected item and close the active window	Press Command-Option while clicking the window's title or press Command-Option-Up Arrow
Close a window while opening an item in it	Press Option while opening the item
Close all windows	Press Option while clicking the active window's close box

At Ease

In some situations the Finder offers too much power, flexibility, and access to items on the hard disk. The Finder's flexibility and power can confuse novice Macintosh users. Combine the Finder's flexibility and power with the full access it provides to the hard disk, put that in a setting where several people share the same Mac, and you have a recipe for confusion. For example, everyone has a different idea about how the Finder's desktop ought to be arranged.

Table 3-5: Manipulating outlines of folders

Objective	Action
Expand the selected folder	Press Command-Right Arrow
Expand the selected folder and its nested folders	Press Option while clicking the triangle next to the folder or press Command-Option-Right Arrow
Expand all folders in the active window	Press Command-A and then press Command-Option-Right Arrow
Collapse the selected folder	Press Command-Left Arrow
Collapse the selected folder and its nested folders	Press Option while clicking the triangle next to the folder or press Command-Option-Left Arrow
Collapse all folders in the active window	Press Command-A and then press Command-Option-Left Arrow

Table 3-6: More power methods

Objective	Action
Make the desktop active	Press Command-Shift-Up Arrow
Begin editing the selected item's name	Return or Enter
Zoom a window to fill the screen	Press Option while clicking the window's zoom box
Move a window without making it active	Press Command while dragging the inactive window
Copy an item to another folder on the same disk	Press Option while dragging the item to the folder or to the folder's open window
Copy an item to the desktop	Press Option while dragging the item to the desktop
Align (or don't align) icons to invisible grid as you move them (countermands the Views control panel's Always Snap To Grid setting)	Press Command while dragging the icons
See the path from the current window to the disk it's on	Press Command while clicking the window's title
Erase a disk	Press Command-Option-Tab as you insert the disk
Skip installing all system extensions during one startup	Hold down Shift during startup
Rebuild the desktop	Hold down Command-Option during startup or when inserting a disk
Force the active program to quit (restart your Macintosh as soon as possible afterwards)	Press Command-Option-Esc

As an alternative to the Finder's standard desktop, Apple's At Ease system extension provides a simplified view of the Macintosh environment with restricted access to programs and documents on the hard disk. At Ease is not included with System 7; it must be purchased and installed separately.

The At Ease desktop has two panels that look like tabbed file folders, as shown in Figure 3-38. One panel has buttons for programs, and the other has buttons for documents. Each panel can display 12 or more large buttons at a time, and can have multiple pages for additional buttons. The number of buttons per page depends on the screen size. You only click a button once to open the item it represents. At Ease has no Trash, so you can't throw away anything. (You have to go to the Finder to discard items.)

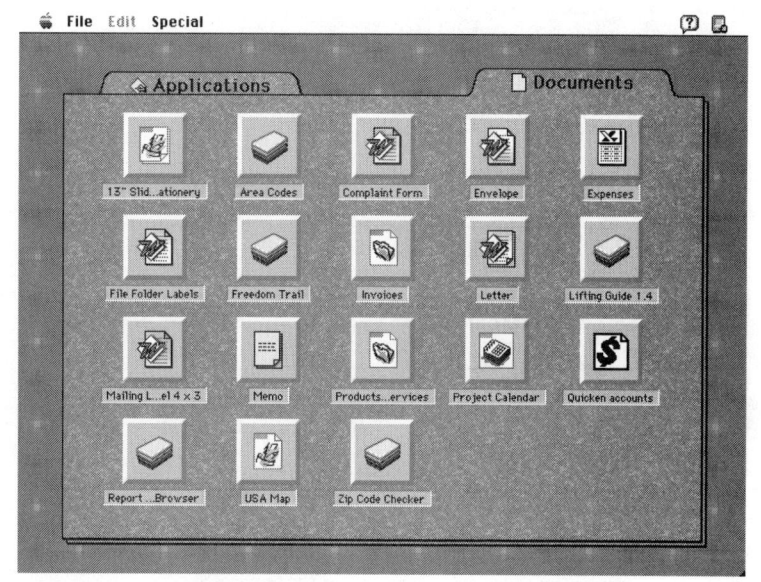

Figure 3-38: The At Ease desktop.

As usual, the Apple menu lists items from the Apple Menu Items folder (see "Apple Menu Items Folder" in Chapter 4). At Ease prevents the Control Panels folder from appearing in the Apple menu, although individual control panels may appear.

At Ease's File and Special menus are simplified versions of the Finder's menus. The File menu contains an Open Other command for opening items not displayed as At Ease buttons. Also in the File menu is a Go To Finder command, which opens the Finder. The use of both of these commands can be restricted by requiring entry of a password. A short Special menu has these commands: Eject Disk, Restart, Shut Down, and on battery-powered Macs, Sleep.

The Edit menu is dimmed in At Ease because there is nothing to edit. You can't change the name of At Ease buttons from At Ease, only from the Finder.

You set up At Ease with the At Ease Setup control panel, (see Figure 3-39), which is normally accessible only from the Finder (not from At Ease). This control panel has several buttons. Two buttons are for setting At Ease to be on and off at startup. Another button brings up a dialog box in which you add programs and documents to, or remove them from At Ease, as shown in Figure 3-40. A third button brings up a dialog box in which you can set two options to save new documents, as shown in Figure 3-41. The fourth button in the At Ease Setup control panel brings up a dialog box in which you set the password that restricts access through At Ease's Open Other and Go To Finder commands to items not displayed as At Ease buttons, as shown in Figure 3-42.

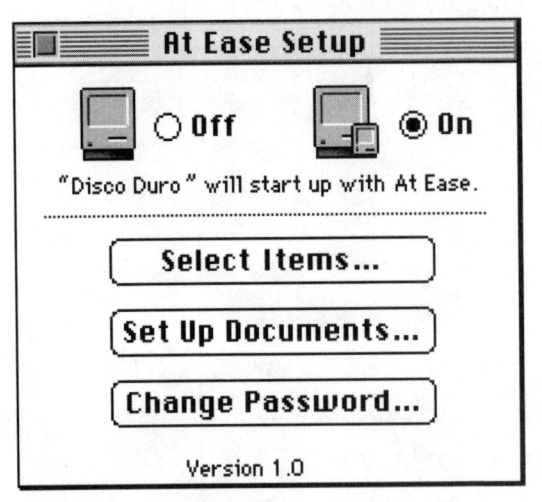

Figure 3-39: The At Ease Setup control panel.

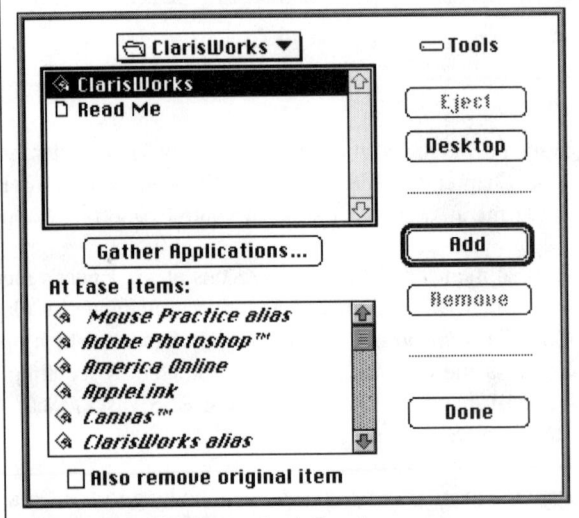

Figure 3-40: Adding or removing At Ease items.

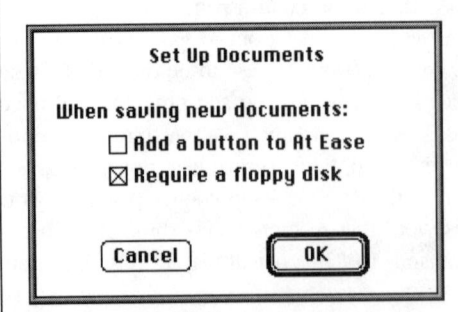

Figure 3-41: Setting At Ease options for saving new documents.

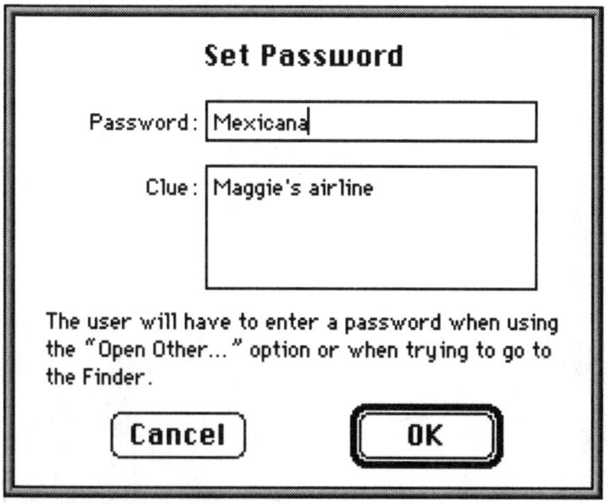

Figure 3-42: Setting the At Ease password.

All items displayed as At Ease buttons are stored as aliases in the special folder At Ease Items, which is inside the System Folder. You can rename At Ease buttons by changing the names of the corresponding aliases in the At Ease Items folder. You can add At Ease buttons by adding aliases to that folder, and remove At Ease buttons by removing aliases from that folder. For more information on making aliases, see Chapter 6.

There are two ways to switch back to At Ease from the Finder. The best method is to choose Go To At Ease from the Finder's File menu. This quits the Finder, eliminating the possibility of accidentally switching back to the Finder by clicking the desktop. You can also switch to At Ease by choosing it from the Application menu. Switching to At Ease frees about 200K for opening other programs.

Summary

- The versatile Find command locates items in your disks quickly.
- You can see, select, and reorganize items from different folders in one window using the outline folder structure in all list views.
- You can customize the format and content of Finder windows.
- Under System 7, all Finder windows are smarter about zooming, scrolling, and selecting.
- Finder 7 can copy, find, and duplicate items in the background.
- Finder 7 no longer automatically empties the Trash; you must explicitly remove items by choosing the Empty Trash command.
- Stationery pads, which are documents with preset format and contents, simplify working with document templates.
- At Ease provides a simpler alternative to the Finder's desktop, and it enables you to restrict access to specific programs and documents.
- You can classify items in a window or on the desktop using words and colors.

Part II
System 7 in Detail

Chapter 4
Organized at Last

In This Chapter

✔ Exploring the new folders inside the System Folder that make it more manageable.

✔ Working with some of the System file's contents for the first time.

✔ A look at the additional special folders outside the System Folder.

✔ Putting control panels, system extensions, fonts, sounds, keyboard layouts, or language scripts where they belong.

✔ Choosing a language and keyboard layout.

✔ Assisting the Finder in placing items in the special folders.

✔ Removing items from the System Folder.

✔ Tips on troubleshooting conflicts between system extensions.

Your Macintosh has one, my Macintosh has one, everyone's Macintosh has one. It stores the essential software that gives your Macintosh its unique appearance and behavior. It gets overcrowded and unmanageable with dozens if not hundreds of items. What is it? The System Folder!

System 7 organizes this chaos. Many of the items that formerly floated loose inside the System Folder now go in one of several new folders inside it. All the new folders have distinctive folder icons, as shown in Figure 4-1. In addition, the System file has a new look and a new openness.

Still at large in the System Folder are the Finder, the Scrapbook File, and the Clipboard. Moreover, many preferences files and other items crowd the System Folder to maintain compatibility with older application programs and desk accessories. These leftovers will gradually find their way into the Preferences folder and other special folders as the programs that use them are upgraded for System 7.

This chapter describes each new folder and the System file in separate sections. Another section describes some other special folders outside the System Folder. At the end of the chapter are four sections that explain some ways to work with the special folders and the System file.

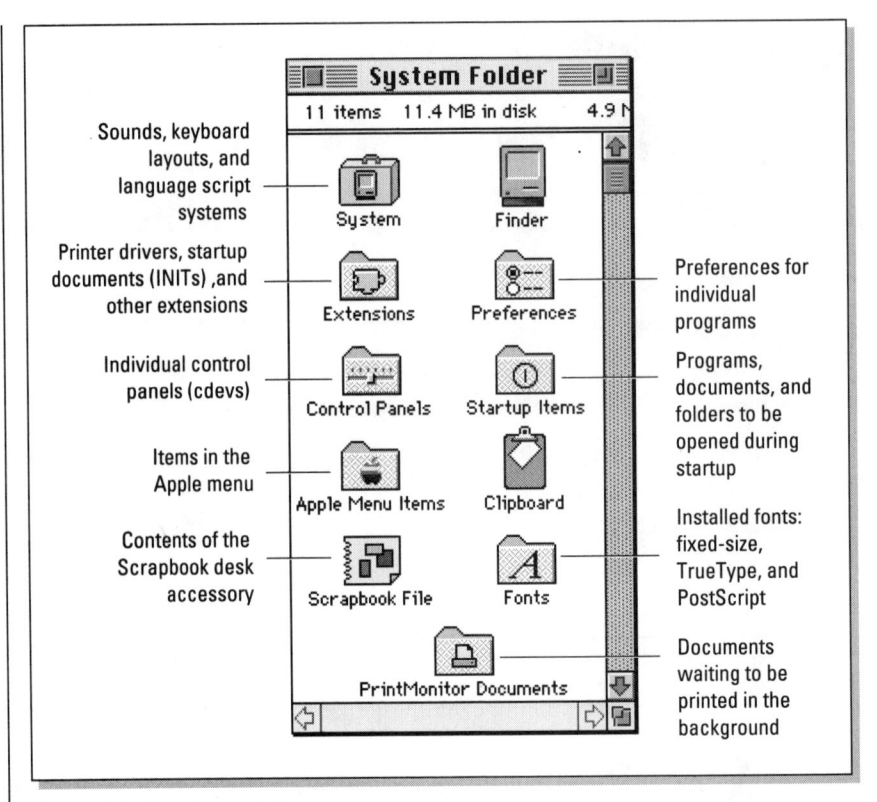

Figure 4-1: Inside a System Folder.

System File

The System file has long been terra incognita to all but the most intrepid resource-hacking Macintosh users. Although a large part of it remains an uncharted wilderness of basic system software, Finder 7 enables everyday Macintosh users to see and work with some of the System file's contents for the first time.

Seeing System file contents

You can open the System file as if it were a folder and see which alert sounds, keyboard layouts, and script systems for foreign languages it contains, as shown in Figure 4-2. Several items do not appear when you open the System file because they are permanently installed in every Macintosh that can use System 7. They include the standard beep sound (sounds different from the Simple Beep), the US keyboard layout, and the Roman script system for Western languages.

In Systems 7.0 and 7.0.1, the System file contains two types of fonts, fixed-size (also called bitmap) and TrueType (also called variable-size or outline). In older system software, the System file contains fonts and desk accessories. In System 7, desk accessories stand alone in folders or on the desktop like application programs (see "Desk Accessories" in Chapter 5).

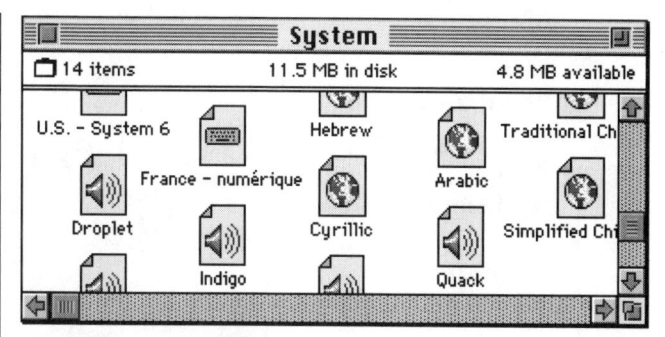

Figure 4-2: System file contents.

Working with System file contents

Not only can you see the contents of the System file, you can also drag items in and out of it as if it were a folder. Changes to sounds (and fonts in System 7.0 or 7.0.1) take effect as soon as you close the System file, but changes to other items require restarting your Macintosh first. The Finder doesn't enable you to drag items in or out of the System file if other programs are open. You must quit all open programs, make your changes to the System file contents, and then open the programs again.

Items you drag out of the System file become independent files. You can move them to any folder or the desktop and copy them to other disks. You can rename sounds but not other items in the System file. You can open a sound that's in or out of the System file, making the Macintosh play it.

Opening a sound makes the Macintosh play it.

Installing sounds in the System file makes them available as the system alert sound, which you choose with the Sound control panel. These sounds are not HyperCard sounds. The sounds used in HyperCard are a special format that don't work properly as system alert sounds.

Keyboard layouts you install appear in the Keyboard control panel. Selecting a different keyboard layout there changes how your Mac sees the arrangement of keys on your keyboard. Selecting the Español (Spanish) layout, for example, makes the semicolon key on a US keyboard produce an ñ.

Multiple languages

If your Systems file contains more than one language script system, a Keyboard menu appears between the Help menu and the Application menu near the right end of the menu bar, as shown in Figure 4-3. You choose a keyboard layout and language from it.

Systems 7.0, 7.0.1, and earlier system software works with multiple keyboard layouts and European languages that use the Roman and Cyrillic script systems. Those versions of system software have also been translated to Japanese, Chinese, Hebrew,

Figure 4-3: Keyboard menu.

Arabic, and other languages that use bidirectional, contextual, and large-alphabet script systems.

System 7.1 is the first Macintosh system software capable of handling all these multiple languages without modification. Two system extensions give System 7.1 this international capability. WorldScript I handles bidirectional and contextual scripts, and WorldScript II handles scripts with large alphabets. Each script system installed in the System file supplies fonts, keyboard layouts, rules for text sorting and word breaks, and rules for formatting dates, times, and numbers in languages that do not use the Roman script system.

Fonts Folder

Prior to System 7.1, fonts were kept in the System file and the Extensions folder, both inside the System Folder. System 7.1 simplifies font organization by keeping all fonts — TrueType, fixed-size (bitmap), and PostScript — in a special Fonts folder inside the System Folder, as shown in Figure 4-4. Installing fonts in the Fonts folder makes them available in programs that enable you to pick fonts. Some programs have you choose a font from a menu. Others have you select a font in a dialog box. Newly installed fonts may not be available in programs that are already open until you quit and reopen the programs. (For more information on fonts, see Chapter 7.)

Note that Aldus PageMaker versions 4.01 and earlier, and Adobe Type Manager (ATM) versions 2.0 and earlier can only find PostScript fonts in the System Folder. PageMaker 4.2 and ATM versions 2.0.2 and 2.0.3 also look for PostScript fonts in the Extensions folder, but not in the Fonts folder. If you use these products or if text looks bad on your PostScript printer, you should put PostScript fonts in the Extensions folder or the System Folder itself.

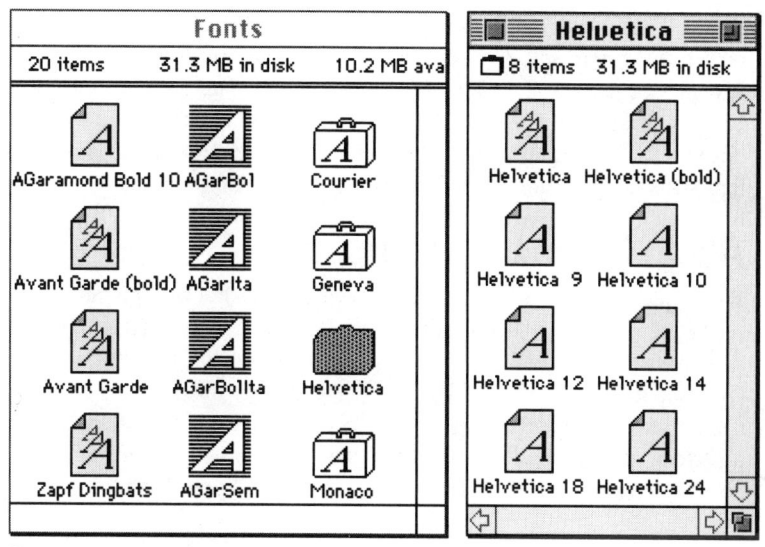

Figure 4-4: Fonts folder, font files, and font suitcase files.

Viewing font samples
All versions of System 7 enable you to open TrueType and fixed-size fonts as you would any ordinary document. Opening a font displays some sample text using that font, as shown in Figure 4-5.

Exchanging fonts with older systems
With System 7 you can also open font suitcase files and old System files. You can drag items in and out of these files. Old System files contain fonts, sounds, and desk accessories. Font suitcase files contain only fonts.

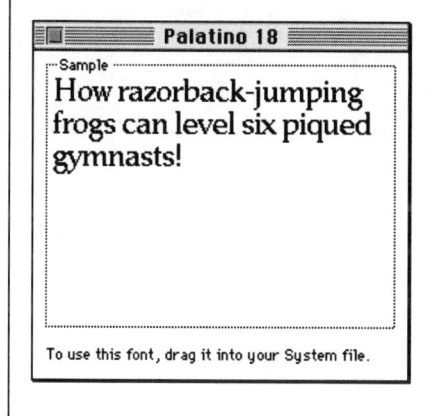

Figure 4-5: Sample text windows.

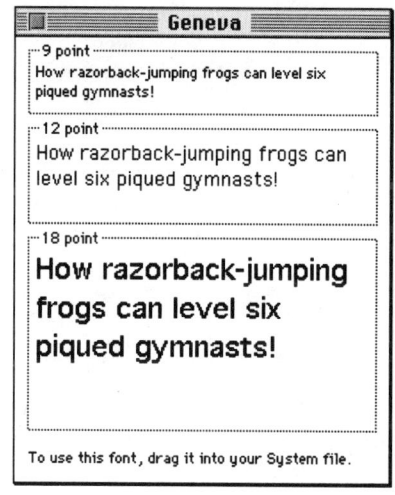

You only need font suitcases if you use the Font/DA Mover program to move fonts with older system software. You do not need the Font/DA Mover program with System 7 because System 7 enables you to manipulate fonts directly. You can create a new font suitcase file with System 7 by duplicating an existing font suitcase file, opening the duplicate, and dragging its contents to the Trash. You can also create font suitcase files using version 4.1 of the Font/DA Mover with System 7.

Apple Menu Items Folder

The Apple Menu Items folder enables you to quickly open anything you use often. All the items in the folder appear on the Apple menu (see Figure 4-6) and choosing an item from the menu has the same effect as opening (double-clicking) the corresponding item in the folder. The Apple menu plays a larger role in System 7 than in older system software because it isn't needed for opening desk accessories or for switching among open programs any more. (For more information, see "Opening Multiple Programs" in Chapter 2 and "Your Own Apple Menu" in Chapter 5.)

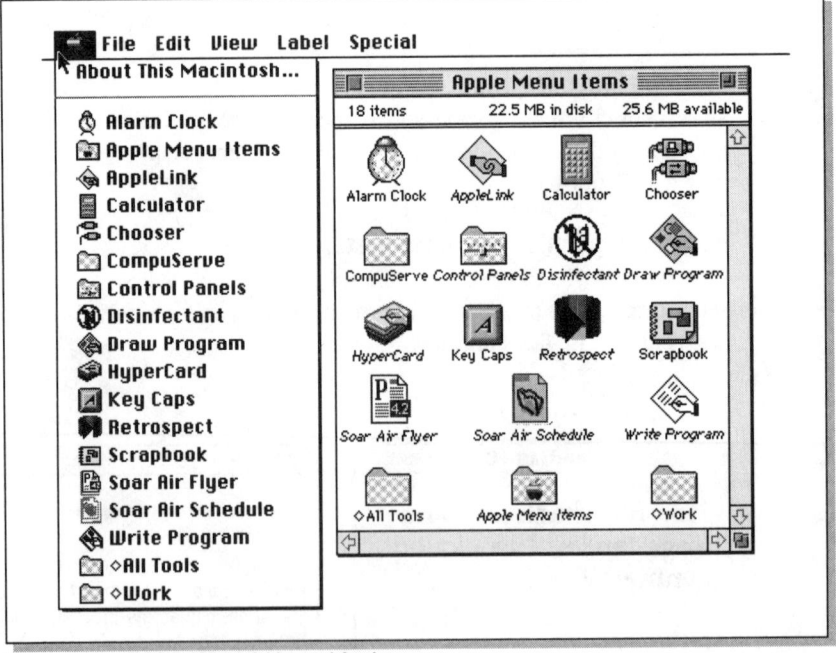

Figure 4-6: Apple Menu Items folder and Apple menu.

Startup Items Folder

Everything you put in the Startup Items folder — application programs, desk accessories, documents, control panels, sounds, and so on — gets opened when you start up your Macintosh, as shown in Figure 4-7. Items in the folder are opened in alphabetical order.

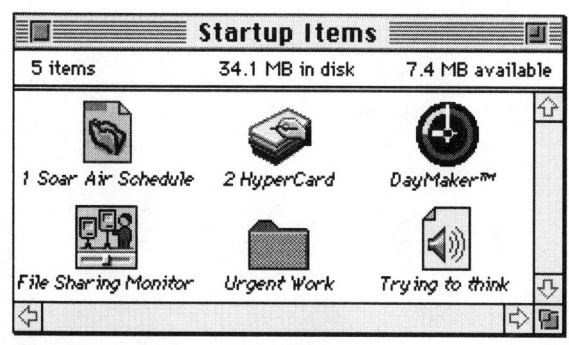

Figure 4-7: Inside a Startup Items folder.

To have an item opened for you at startup time, drag it or an alias of it to the Startup Items folder. Dragging it out of that folder removes it from the startup sequence.

If you have several programs opened during startup, you may later have to quit some of them to free up memory for opening another. Naturally you'll want to quit the programs least important to you. You'll get maximum benefit from quitting them if they were the last items opened during startup. To make that happen, rename the programs in your Startup Items folder so the most important comes first alphabetically, the next-most important comes second, and so on. You can avoid renaming original programs by putting aliases in the Startup Items folder, as described in Chapter 6.

Don't bother renaming desk accessories, control panels, folders, or the aliases of any of those items that are in the Startup Items folder, however. During startup, the Finder first opens applications alphabetically, next aliases alphabetically, then documents alphabetically, and last, desk accessories, control panels, and folders as a group alphabetically. For example, the Finder opens aliases of MacDraw Pro and QuarkXPress before it opens the Control Panels folder, the File Sharing Monitor control panel, or the Key Caps desk accessory.

Including desk accessories and folders or control panels in the Startup Items folder can disrupt the automatic startup sequence. Whenever a folder or control panel follows a desk accessory alphabetically, the Finder stops opening items and flashes its icon at the right end of the menu bar. You must switch to the Finder, for example, by choosing it from the Application menu, whereupon it opens the folders and control panels that come next alphabetically. For example, you must manually switch to the Finder after it opens the Alarming Events desk accessory before it will open the Control Panels folder.

Control Panels Folder

The items in the Control Panels folder give you control over system appearance and behavior as do the sections of the Control Panel desk accessory found with older system software. The folder contains small programs called control panels, as shown in Figure 4-8. They are also known as control panel devices, control panel sections, and cdevs. Each affects one aspect of the system. Some control panels also add functions to the basic system software during startup. (For information on using individual control panels, see "Control Panels" in Chapter 5.)

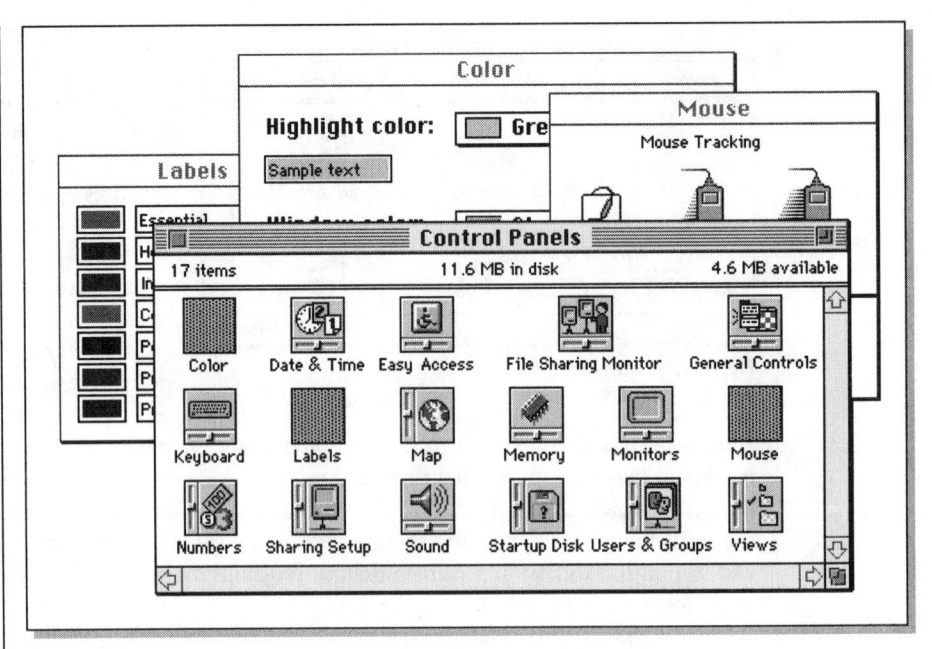

Figure 4-8: Control panels.

Extensions Folder

The items in the Extensions folder customize your Macintosh by extending the services and functions of the system software, as shown in Figure 4-9. These items, which are small software modules called system extensions, include some of the following:

- LaserWriter, StyleWriter, ImageWriter, and other Chooser extensions that enable your system to print on a specific type of printer (also called printer drivers)

- The PrintMonitor program, which enables you to continue working while documents print on a LaserWriter printer

- QuickTime, which enables you to see movies on your Mac

- AppleShare, a Chooser extension that enables you to share folders and disks from other computers connected to yours

- File Sharing Extension and Network Extension, which enable you to share your folders and disks with other people in your network

- DAL, which adds simplified database-accessing services to programs designed to use them (DAL is included with Systems 7.0 and 7.01, but not with System 7.1. Get it separately from Apple.)

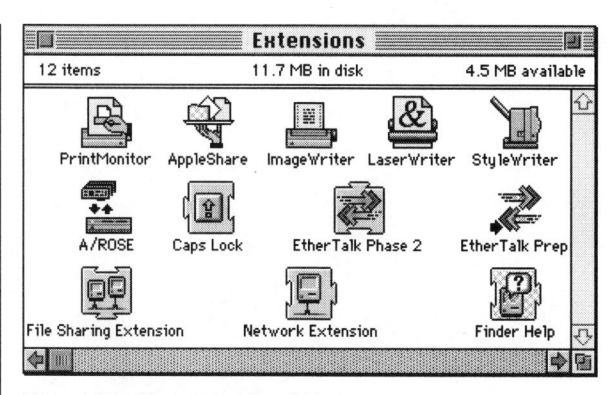

Figure 4-9: Inside an Extensions folder.

- EtherTalk and TokenTalk, which enable you to connect some Macintosh models to EtherTalk and Token-Ring networks
- Help systems like Finder Help, which provides on-screen help for the Finder
- System enablers, which override system resources during startup to make system software compatible with new Macintosh models

To use a system extension, you simply put it in the Extensions folder and restart your Macintosh. If you remove a system extension from the Extensions folder, you must again restart for the removal to take effect.

Preferences Folder

Some programs save preference settings in the Preferences folder. Most programs with commands for publishing and subscribing information also save an alias named Last Edition Used whenever they save an edition (as described in Chapter 9). Also, the system software saves the following items in the Preferences folder (see Figure 4-10):

- DAL Preferences: procedures the system software uses for connecting to relational databases
- File Sharing folder: file sharing access privileges for your disks and folders
- Finder Preferences: many of the settings you make with control panels
- Users & Groups Data File: names and privileges for registered users and groups to whom you have given access to your computer

Most of the preference files of older programs are loose in the System Folder, where they must remain until the programs are upgraded to work with System 7. If you drag a preferences file from the System Folder to the Preferences folder, the program that uses it probably won't be able to find it and will use its standard settings by default.

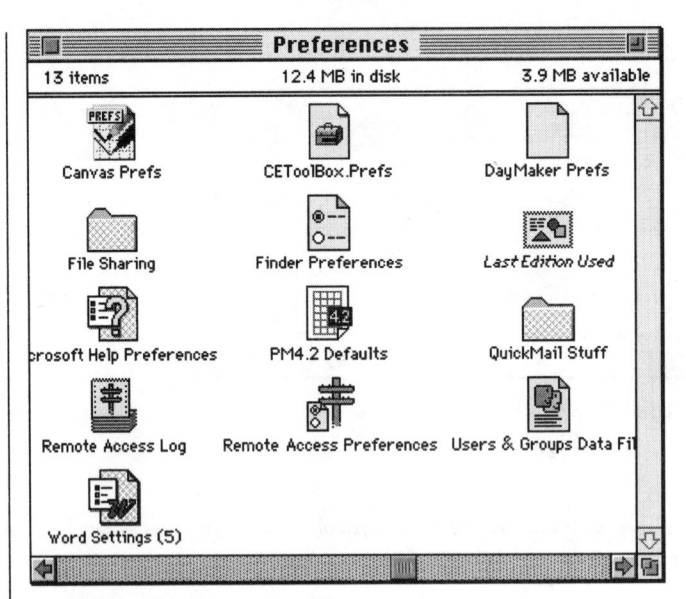

Figure 4-10: Inside a Preferences folder.

More Special Folders Outside

System 7 further organizes your disks with additional special folders outside the System Folder. The Finder creates the following special folders as needed on each disk:

✦ Temporary Items folder: Contains temporary files created by programs you are using. A program normally deletes its temporary files automatically when you quit it. This folder is invisible.

✦ Trash folder: Contains the items you have dragged from the disk to the Trash icon. Your disks' Trash folders are invisible, but you see their consolidated contents when you open the Trash icon. A visible Trash folder in a shared disk contains items from the disk that are in the owner's Trash.

✦ Network Trash folder: Contains items that people who are sharing the disk have dragged from the shared disk to their Trash icons. Inside this folder are folders named *Trash Can #2, Trash Can #3,* and so on. They contain items from your shared disk or folder that someone has dragged to the Trash — but has not yet permanently removed — on another Macintosh. These items appear in his or her Trash, not yours.

✦ Rescued Items folder: Contains items the Finder found in the Temporary Items folder when you restarted after a system crash (or after switching off the power without using the Shut Down command — tsk, tsk!). You may be able to reconstruct your work by opening them. If the Rescued Items folder exists, you can always see it by opening the Trash.

✦ Desktop Folder: Contains items located on the desktop. This folder is invisible on your disks, but the visible Desktop Folder of a shared disk is visible and contains items from the disk that are on the owner's desktop.

All these special folders become visible if you start up your Macintosh with older system software.

Adding to the System Folder

Putting control panels, system extensions, fonts, sounds, keyboard layouts, or language scripts where they belong is just as easy as putting them all in the System Folder. You simply drag the items to the System Folder icon. The Finder recognizes items that go in special folders or the System file and asks whether you want the items put into their proper places, as shown in Figure 4-11.

If you consent, the Finder puts control panels in the Control Panels folder; Chooser extensions, the PrintMonitor program, database extensions, network extensions, and system extensions in the Extensions folder; desk accessories in the Apple Menu Items folder; TrueType, fixed-size, and PostScript fonts in the Fonts folder; and sounds, keyboard layouts, and language script systems into the System file. All other items go into the System Folder itself. (In Systems 7.0 and 7.0.1, the Finder puts TrueType and fixed-size fonts into the System file and puts PostScript fonts into the Extensions folder.)

If you drag folders to the System Folder, the Finder looks inside them and puts items it recognizes in the Control Panels, Extensions, Fonts, or Apple Menu Items folders. If a folder you drag contains items the Finder doesn't recognize, the Finder leaves them in the folder and puts the folder loose in the System Folder. If an item you drag to the System Folder has the same name as an item already there, the Finder not only asks whether you want to replace the latter with the former, but tells you which is newer.

When the Finder finishes putting items into their places, it tells you how many items of each type it moved, as shown in Figure 4-12. (It counts a folder and its contents as one item no matter how numerous the contents may be.)

If you drag items to the System Folder window instead of the System Folder icon, the Finder does not put them in the inner folders for you.

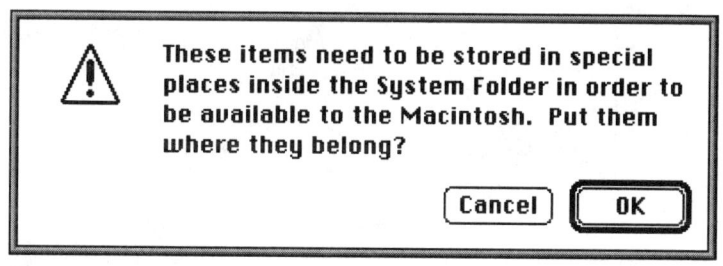

⚠ These items need to be stored in special places inside the System Folder in order to be available to the Macintosh. Put them where they belong?

[Cancel]　[OK]

Figure 4-11: Upon dragging items to the System Folder.

> 1 desk accessory was put into the Apple Menu Items folder.
> 1 control panel was put into the Control Panels folder.
> 3 extensions were put into the Extensions folder.
> 1 item was put into the System Folder.
>
> [OK]

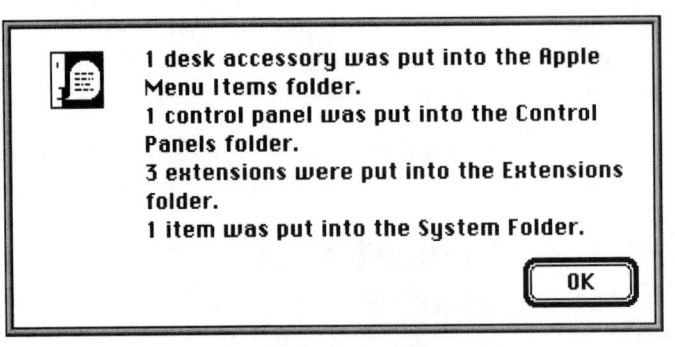

Figure 4-12: After dragging items to the System Folder.

Should you happen to discard one of the special folders, you can make a replacement using the Finder's New Folder command (File menu). After creating a new folder, change its name to be the same as the special folder you want. Wait a few seconds and you'll see its icon get the distinctive look of the special folder you're creating.

Fooling the Finder

The Finder sometimes makes mistakes when it puts items in the special folders for you. It may put some items in the correct places and incorrectly leave others in the System Folder itself. For example, it may put a control panel in the Control Panels folder but leave that control panel's auxiliary folder in the System Folder. That control panel won't work right because it expects to find its auxiliary folder in the same folder as it is in. You must open the System Folder and drag the auxiliary folder to the Control Panels folder yourself, as shown in Figure 4-13.

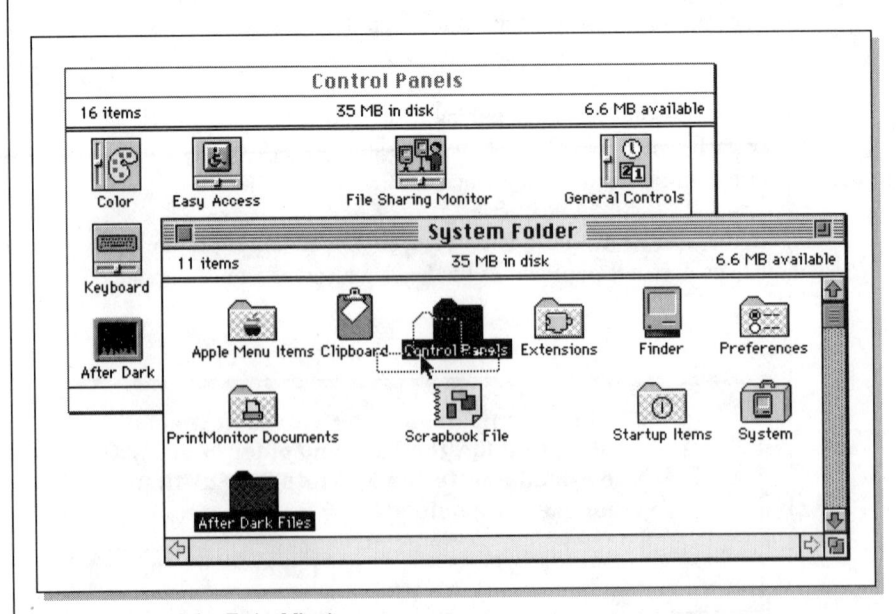

Figure 4-13: Correcting Finder Mistakes.

Additionally, the Finder never puts anything you drag to the System Folder icon into the Preferences folder or the Startup Items folder. You must open the System Folder and drag items to those folders directly.

Some items from old System Folders don't work right when they're put in the Extensions, Fonts, Control Panel, or Preferences folders. If you have trouble with an item in one of the special folders, try dragging the item from the special folder to the System Folder window.

Removing from the System Folder

Before you can remove an item from the System Folder, you must know which inner folder it is in. If you're not sure, use the Finder's Find command to locate the item (see "Finding Items" in Chapter 3). Be sure to put items you drag from the special folders onto the desktop or into an ordinary folder. Many items you drag out of special folders are still effective if you merely drag them to the System Folder window.

Troubleshooting a Conflict

If items you add to the System Folder, Extensions folder, or Control Panels folder don't work, or if your Macintosh refuses to start up, then some of the system extensions in those places may be in conflict during startup. Sometimes changing the order in which the Macintosh installs system extensions resolves the conflict.

Whereas older system software installs system extensions in strict alphabetical order, System 7 installs them in three groups. First, it goes through the Extensions folder in alphabetical order. Then, it installs the extensions that are built into items in the Control Panels folder, again alphabetically. Finally, it checks the System Folder itself and alphabetically installs system extensions it finds there. This change in the installation sequence can cause problems for older system extensions and control panels.

Some system extensions and control panels have peculiar names meant to put the items first or last in the installation sequence, as shown in Figure 4-14. Names of items meant to come first usually begin with blank spaces. Names meant to come last often begin with a tilde (~) or diamond (◊).

To have control panels whose names begin with blank spaces installed first during startup, put them in the Extensions folder. To have control panels whose names start with tildes or diamonds installed last during startup, put them in the System Folder. For convenient access to the control panels you move out of the Control Panels folder, make aliases for them and put the aliases in the Control Panels folder.

To have system extensions whose names begin with tildes and diamonds installed last during startup, drag them from the Extensions folder to the System Folder. Leave system extensions whose names begin with blank spaces in the Extensions folder so they install first during startup.

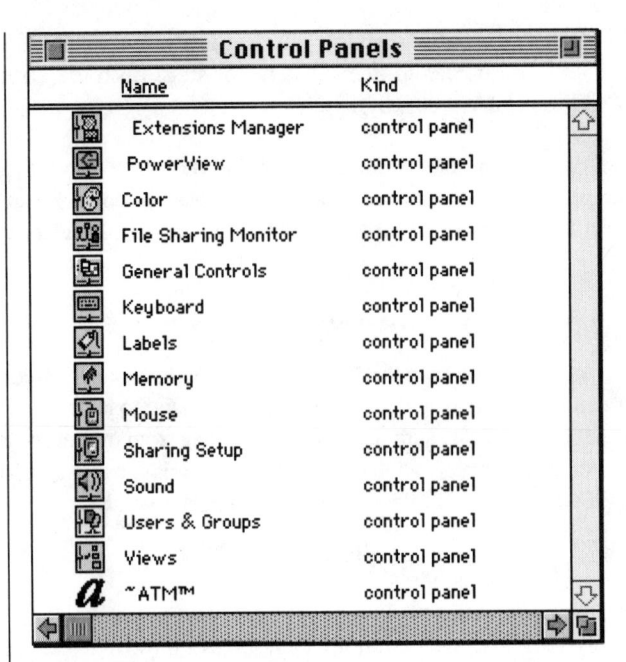

Name	Kind
Extensions Manager	control panel
PowerView	control panel
Color	control panel
File Sharing Monitor	control panel
General Controls	control panel
Keyboard	control panel
Labels	control panel
Memory	control panel
Mouse	control panel
Sharing Setup	control panel
Sound	control panel
Users & Groups	control panel
Views	control panel
~ATM™	control panel

Figure 4-14: Name prefixes affect startup sequence.

Fixing other conflicts between system extensions and control panels involves experimenting. Start by removing all the items you have added to the System Folder and its inner folders since the trouble began. Then drag half the extensions and control panels to the desktop and restart. If this solves the problem, the offending item is among the half you removed to the desktop; if not, it is among the other half. In either case, leave only half the group containing the offending item (one quarter of all extensions and control panels) on the desktop and restart. If the problem occurs, the offender is among the group you just put back; if not, it is among the group on the desktop. Continue halving the offending group until you reduce it to a single item (the troublemaker). Instead of dragging control panels and extensions to and from the desktop, you can drag them to and from a new folder you create for that purpose. Alternatively, you can use an extension manager utility such as Extension Manager to turn them on and off individually without dragging them in and out of folders (see "Extension Manager" in Chapter 13).

When you find an item that causes a conflict, try renaming it so it comes before or after other system extensions in the same folder. By experimenting with names you may find a startup sequence that works.

As a last resort, remove all system extensions and control panels to the desktop. Then put them in the System Folder (not the Extensions or Control Panels folders) one at a time, from most important to least. Restart your Macintosh each time you add another item to the System Folder. When you find an item that causes a conflict, discard it and try the next item you previously moved to the desktop. You may be able to resume using the items you discarded when they are next upgraded.

(If a conflict prevents starting up from your hard disk, start from a floppy disk with any version of system software. Make a change to the System Folder on the hard disk and try restarting from it.)

Summary

- Three folders — the Control Panels folder, the Extensions folder, and the Preferences folder — go a long way toward cleaning up the sprawling growth going on in so many System Folders. Other new folders inside the System Folder improve your access to programs, documents, and other items that can be opened.
- The Fonts folder contains all fonts — TrueType, fixed-size, and PostScript.
- The Apple Menu Items folder enables you to decide what items are listed on the Apple menu for quick opening.
- The Startup Items folder contains the things you want opened automatically at startup time.
- The Finder helps you keep the System Folder organized by putting many of the items you drag to its icon into the proper inner folders.
- In addition to the special folders found inside the System Folder are more special folders — Temporary Items, Trash, Network Trash, Rescued Items, and Desktop — created by the Finder as needed on each disk.
- To round out the redevelopment of the System Folder, System 7 unseals the System file. You now add and remove sounds, keyboard layouts, and language systems by dragging them in and out of the System file.

Part II
System 7 in Detail

Chapter 5
Tailored to Fit

In This Chapter

✔ Desk accessories move to the desktop and behave like ordinary application programs.

✔ A look at the Apple menu's expanded role: opening any program, document, folder, or other desktop icon.

✔ Individual control panels look and act like independent Finder documents.

✔ Opening more programs and bigger documents with virtual memory and 32-Bit Addressing.

✔ Managing your memory in the face of increasingly intense memory usage.

Fitting the Macintosh to your work environment just got easier. System 7 removes the special rules of older system software for installing and using desk accessories and control panels. Now you use them in a manner more consistent with ordinary programs and documents. At the same time, ordinary programs and documents acquire a trait formerly unique to desk accessories: being in the Apple menu where you can find and open them quickly.

System 7's multitasking capabilities enable you to keep multiple programs open simultaneously if your Macintosh has enough memory available. Virtual memory enables you to use hard disk space as additional memory, and 32-Bit Addressing increases the amount of memory some Macintosh models can use. To effectively use your computer's memory, you must adjust program memory size and monitor when you open and quit programs.

Related topics discussed elsewhere in this book include aliases (Chapter 6), multitasking ("Opening Multiple Programs" in Chapter 2), installing fonts ("Adding and Removing Fonts" in Chapter 7), custom views of Finder windows ("Custom Views" in Chapter 3), making and using template documents ("Stationery Pads" in Chapter 3), customizing icons ("Custom Icons" in Chapter 3), and system folder organization (Chapter 4).

Desk Accessories

Very little differentiates desk accessories and application programs in System 7. You can put both in folders, on the desktop, or in the Apple menu, as shown in Figure 5-1. Each desk accessory can have its own family of icons, consisting of small and standard sizes each in black-and-white, 16 colors, and 256 colors. However, most older desk accessories use the generic desk accessory icons, which look like generic application program icons.

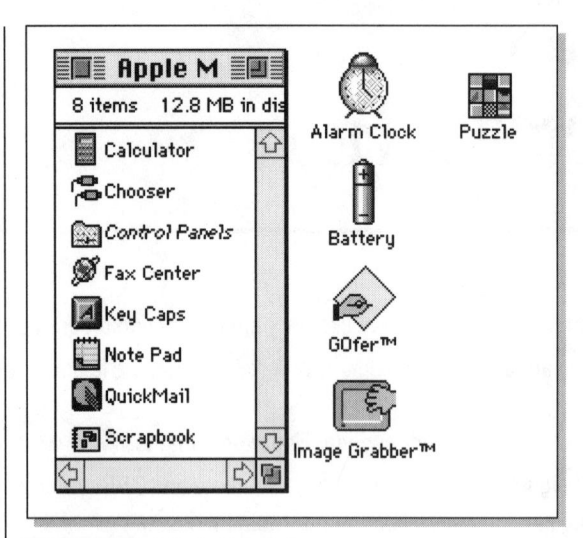

Figure 5-1: Some desk accessories.

You move and copy desk accessories by dragging their icons in the Finder. If you want to install a desk accessory in the Apple menu, you simply drag it to the System Folder icon. You do not use the Font/DA Mover utility program. For compatibility with older system software, desk accessories can exist in suitcase files, which the Font/DA Mover program creates. You can use Font/DA Mover version 4.1 (but not earlier versions) with System 7.

Opening desk accessories

System 7's full-time multitasking always enables you to open any desk accessory or application program without quitting the program you're using (available memory permitting). You open a desk accessory like an application program, by double-clicking it or by selecting it and using the Finder's Open command. Unlike an application program, however, you can't open a desk accessory by opening one of its documents. Also, desk accessories in a suitcase file can't be opened. You must first drag them out of the suitcase into a folder or onto the desktop.

Using desk accessories

System 7 puts each desk accessory you open in its own memory partition and adds its name to the Application menu. You make a single desk accessory the active program by choosing it from the Application menu or clicking its window, just like an application program. While a desk accessory is the active program, it has its own About command in the Apple menu that includes the name of the desk accessory. Older system software lumps all open desk accessories together in one partition when MultiFinder is active or includes them with the open application program when MultiFinder is inactive.

All desk accessories have a File menu with Close and Quit commands. These commands work differently in System 7 than in older system software. The Close command closes the desk accessory's active window and — in most desk accessories — it quits the active desk accessory. The Quit command quits the active desk accessory (not all open desk accessories as in older system software).

Some older desk accessories depend on being open in the same memory partition as an application program. They don't work quite right with System 7, where they must be independent. A thesaurus desk accessory, for example, may be unable to automatically look up a word you have selected. A screen capture utility may be unable to take a picture of a program's menu. You can work around these problems by pressing Option while choosing the desk accessory from the Apple menu, thereby opening the desk accessory in the active application's memory partition. This trick only works with desk accessories in the Apple menu.

System 7 comes with the same seven desk accessories as older system software: Alarm Clock, Calculator, Chooser, Key Caps, Note Pad, Puzzle, and Scrapbook. The System 7 versions of these standard desk accessories use color and gray shades on color and grayscale monitors; on black-and-white monitors they look similar to their older counterparts. These desk accessories are described in the following sections.

Alarm Clock
The Alarm Clock desk accessory shows the time of day, as shown in Figure 5-2. It can be expanded to show the date, set the time or date, or set an alarm. When the alarm goes off, you hear the system alert sound (as set in the Sound control panel) and the Alarm Clock icon flashes on top of the Apple Menu icon at the left end of the menu bar. To stop the flashing, you need only open the Alarm Clock desk accessory.

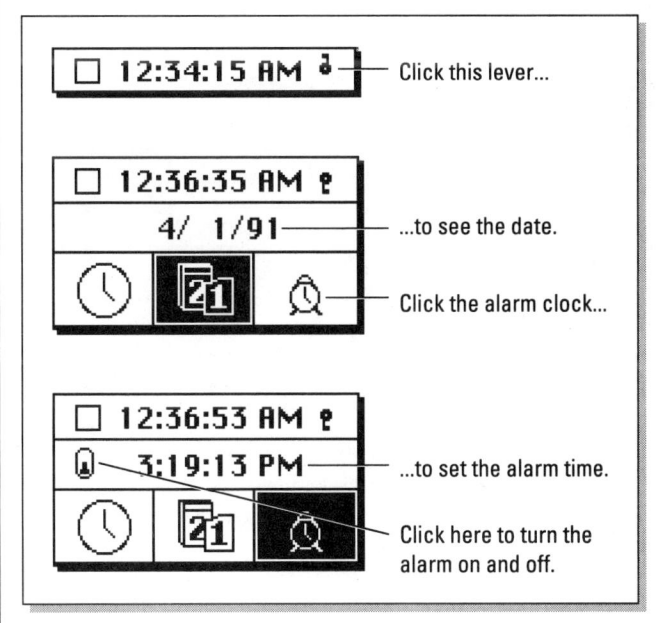

Figure 5-2: The Alarm Clock desk accessory.

Calculator

The Calculator desk accessory adds, subtracts, multiplies, and divides numbers you enter, as shown in Figure 5-3. You can type numbers and operation symbols or click the keys in the desk accessory. In addition, you can copy the text of a calculation — for example, 69.95+26.98+14.99*.0725 — and paste it into the Calculator.

Chooser

The Chooser desk accessory enables you to select a printer or other output device and make connections with other computers networked to yours, as shown in Figure 5-4. Chooser 7 is larger than older versions to make room for more devices and network zones. Also, you no longer enter the Macintosh owner's name in the Chooser, but in the Sharing Setup control panel (described in Chapter 8).

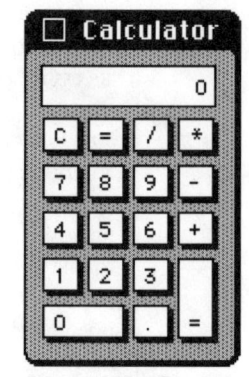

Figure 5-3: The Calculator desk accessory.

Key Caps

The Key Caps desk accessory shows all the characters you can type in any font installed in your system, as shown in Figure 5-5. You choose the font from the Key Caps menu, which appears to the right of the Edit menu when the Key Caps desk accessory is active. Key Caps changes to show the effect of pressing Shift, Option, or Control separately or in combination.

In Key Caps 7, pressing Option outlines the keys that, when pressed along with Option, don't directly produce a character, as shown in Figure 5-6. Each of those Option-key combinations, called *dead keys*, adds an accent or other diacritic to cer-

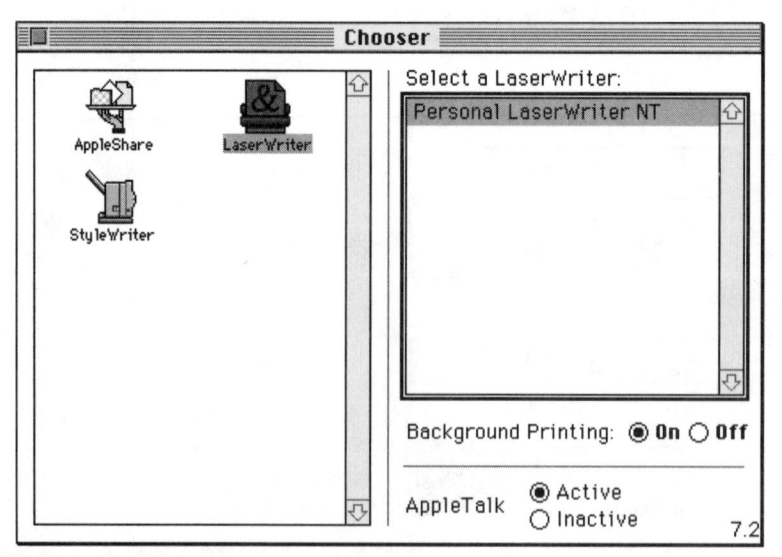

Figure 5-4: The Chooser desk accessory.

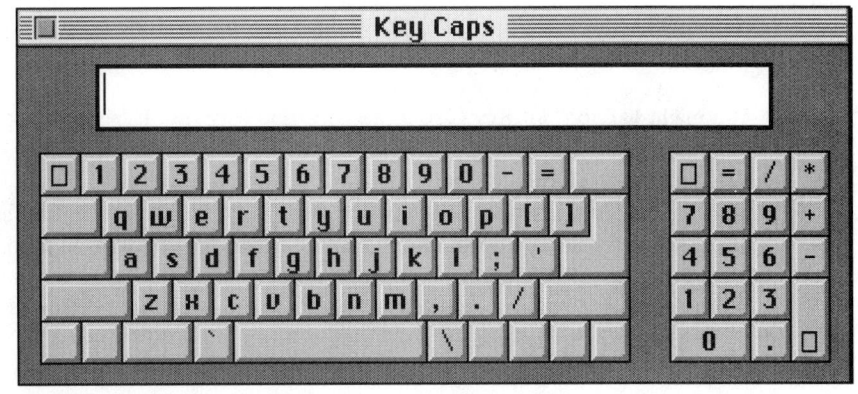

Figure 5-5: The Key Caps desk accessory.

Pressing Option outlines keys that can add a diacritic, and pressing one of them while pressing Option...

outlines the keys that can have that diacritic added.

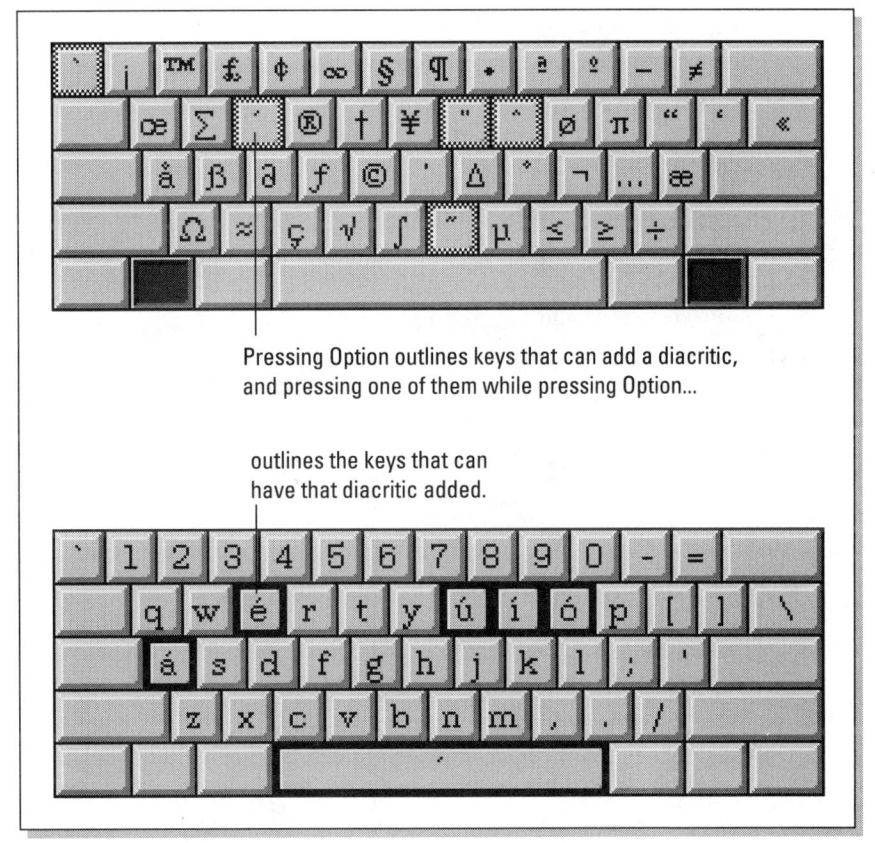

Figure 5-6: Reviewing dead keys.

tain subsequently typed keys. Pressing a dead key, for example Option-E for an accent, outlines the keys that can have that diacritic added.

You might like to print Key Caps as a handy reference, but it has no Print command. To work around this, take a picture of the screen and print that as follows: Open Key Caps, choose the font you want it to show, and press any modifier keys (Shift, Option, Control, or Command) you want in effect. Move the pointer to an empty area of the menu bar, hold down the mouse button, temporarily release the modifier keys, press Command-Shift-3, again press the modifier keys you released temporarily, and finally release the mouse button. Your gyrations should be rewarded by the sound of a camera shutter as the system snaps a picture of the screen. Open your startup disk and look for a document named Picture 1. Print this document using TeachText or any graphics program. Cut out the Key Caps window with scissors after printing or crop it out with a graphics program before printing. If you take additional snapshots, they are numbered sequentially.

Note Pad

The Note Pad desk accessory records brief messages you type or paste into it, as shown in Figure 5-7.

Puzzle

The Puzzle desk accessory is a game in which you unscramble tiles to make a picture, as shown in Figure 5-8. Push a tile in the same row or column as the vacant space toward the vacant space by clicking the tile. Also, Puzzle 7 has two games, one with numbered tiles and another with a picture of the Apple logo. Choose Clear from the Edit menu to switch between them.

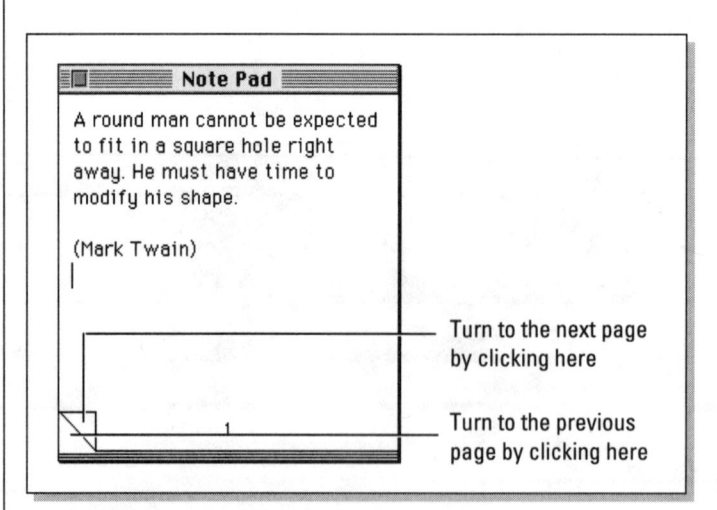

Figure 5-7: The Note Pad desk accessory.

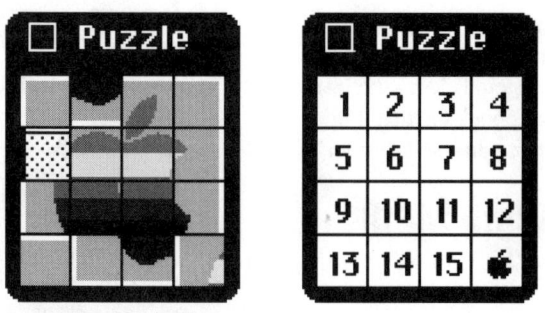

Figure 5-8: The Puzzle desk accessory.

You can replace the picture of the Apple logo. Just copy a picture in another program, switch to the Puzzle, and paste. For example, the next-to-last picture in the standard System 7 Scrapbook provides a challenging puzzle.

Scrapbook

The Scrapbook desk accessory stores and retrieves text, pictures, sounds, and other types of information that you paste into it, one item at a time, as shown in Figure 5-9. Scrapbook 7 can play sounds as well as show pictures and text.

QUICK TIPS

After extensive use, your Scrapbook may become cluttered with old clippings. If you can't bear to throw them out, make a copy of the Scrapbook File in your System Folder (use the Finder's Duplicate command) before you start weeding. Later you can use the old copy you made by dragging the current Scrapbook File out of the System Folder, dragging the old copy in, and changing its name to Scrapbook File.

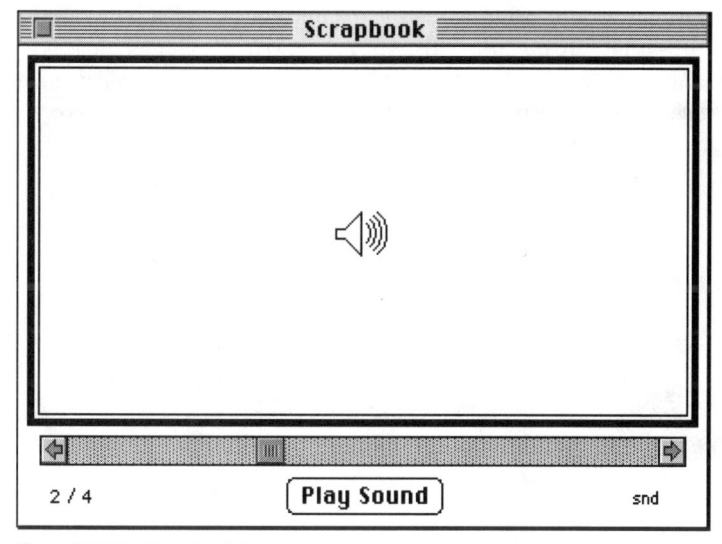

Figure 5-9: The Scrapbook desk accessory.

To get the standard System 7 Scrapbook file, you must install System 7 on a disk that has no Scrapbook file in its System Folder. The Installer does not replace a Scrapbook file that it finds in the System Folder when you install System 7.

Your Own Apple Menu

The Apple menu's role has expanded because desk accessories do not have to be in it any longer. Now the Apple menu expedites opening anything you use frequently. Anything you could double-click in the Finder you can now put in the Apple menu and open it by choosing it there. This includes documents, application programs, desk accessories, folders, control panels, and even fonts and sounds, as shown in Figure 5-10.

Adding and removing items

You put an item in the Apple menu by dragging it into the Apple Menu Items folder, which is inside the System Folder, as shown in Figure 5-11. The item becomes instantly available in the Apple menu. (No need to restart your Macintosh.)

Figure 5-10: An Apple menu.

To remove an item from the Apple menu, drag its icon or alias out of the Apple Menu Items folder onto the desktop or into another folder.

Apple menu organization

Items are always listed alphabetically in the Apple menu using plain Chicago 12-point text. Alias names are not italicized in the menu even though they are italicized in the Apple Menu Items folder. Rearranging the contents of the Apple Menu Items folder by dragging icons in its window, clicking column headings in a list view, or using the Finder's Views menu doesn't affect the Apple menu.

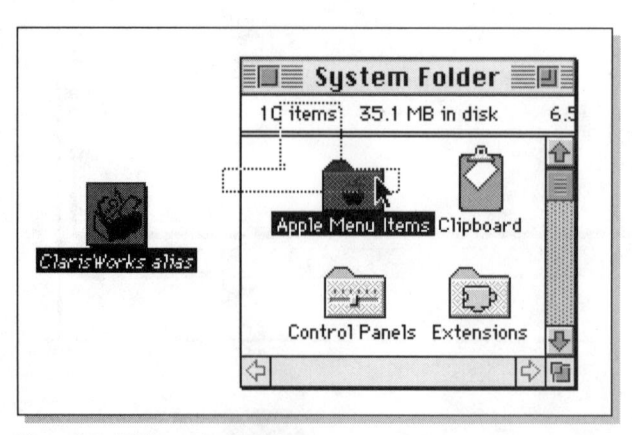

Figure 5-11: Adding to the Apple menu.

Making your own arrangements

You can make an item appear at the top of the Apple menu by prefixing its name with a blank space. Alternatively, you can prefix the name with an Apple logo or solid diamond (♦) symbol. You do that by setting the Key Caps desk accessory to the Chicago font, typing Control-T for the Apple logo or Control-S for the solid diamond, copying the symbol, and pasting it at the beginning of the item name. These special symbols look like boxes in the Apple Menu Items window because they're not part of the Geneva font, which the Finder uses for text in windows unless you specify another font with the Views control panel. They look right in the Apple menu, which uses the Chicago font.

To make items appear at the bottom of the Apple menu, prefix with a hollow diamond (◊) or a bullet (•). Type Shift-Option-V for the hollow diamond or Option-8 for the bullet.

Grouping and separating items

You can group different types of items by prefixing different numbers of blank spaces to their names — the more blank spaces, the higher on the Apple menu, as shown in Figure 5-12. For example, you might prefix three blank spaces to control panel names, two blanks to desk accessory names, one blank to application programs, and none to other items.

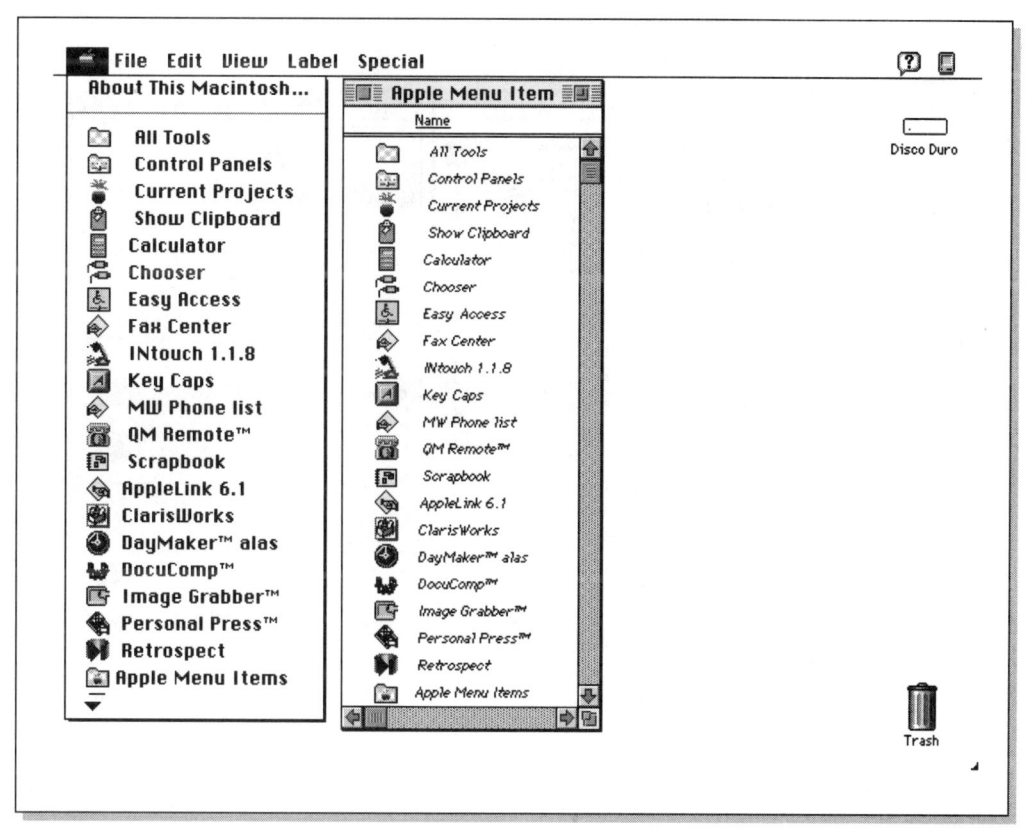

Figure 5-12: Grouping Apple menu items.

A giant list arranged by type can be hard to scan quickly. It helps to visually separate the different types of items. You can make separators by naming extra aliases with hyphens and prefixing the right number of blank spaces to the names so each one appears between two different types of items, as shown in Figure 5-13. Aliases of the Finder work well as separators because accidentally opening one results in a message saying that item can't be opened. You can also use ordinary folders instead of aliases to make separators in the Apple menu.

To further refine your Apple menu, you can hide the icons of the separators you make. First you copy some white space in any painting program (even HyperCard will do). Next you select a separator item's icon and use the Finder's Get Info command to display the item's info window. Then you select the icon in that window and paste the white space over it.

Hierarchical Apple menu

If your Apple menu has so many items that you must scroll it to see them all, consider consolidating the less-used items in a folder or two within the Apple Menu Items folder. You can make the contents of folders within the Apple Menu Items folder appear as submenus of the Apple menu (see Figure 5-14), by adding a control panel or system

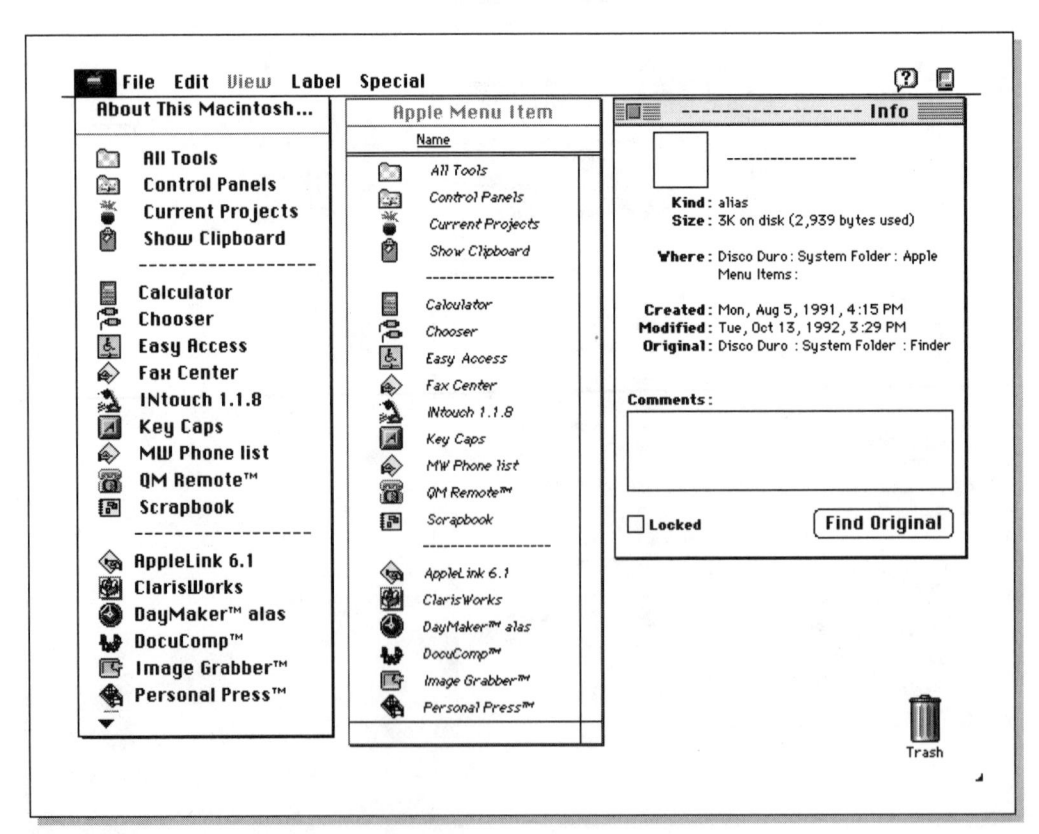

Figure 5-13: Dividing Apple menu items.

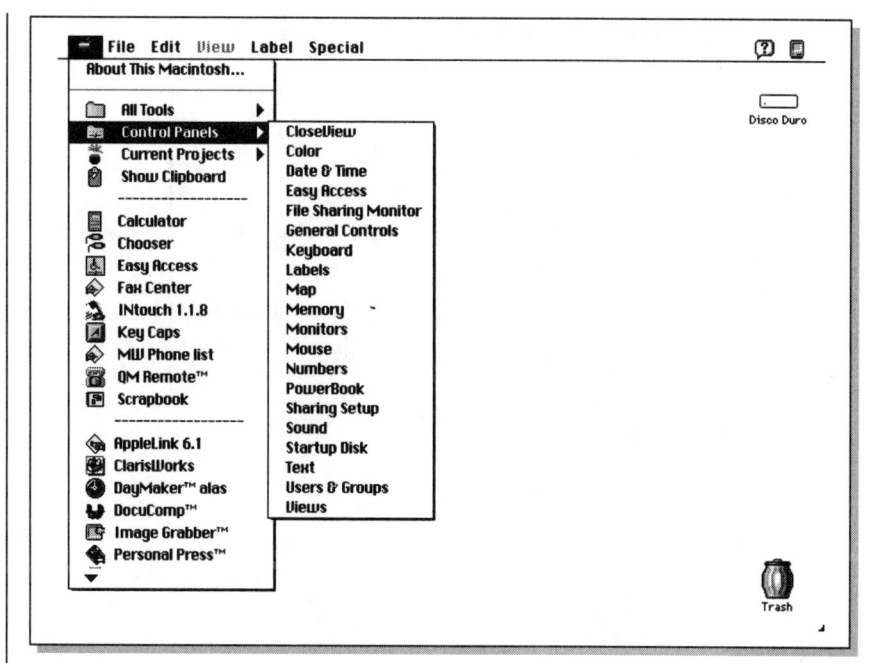

[Figure 5-14 screenshot of Apple menu with submenus showing Control Panels submenu]

Figure 5-14: Apple menu with submenus.

extension such as BeHierarchic, which is described in Chapter 13. Commercial products that add submenus to the Apple menu include HAM from Microseeds and Now Utilities 4.0 from Now Software.

Control Panels

Like desk accessories, control panels are more versatile in System 7 than in older system software. You open one or more individual control panels as you would any document, for example by double-clicking it. Each open control panel appears in its own window. Control panels now come in all sizes and shapes because they no longer have to fit in a fixed-size section of the old Control Panel desk accessory.

By convention, control panels go in the special Control Panels folder inside the System Folder. When you open the Control Panels folder, its window acts as a master control panel, as shown in Figure 5-15. You can rearrange the individual control panels in it by using the Finder's View menu or by dragging icons. So that you can open the Control Panels folder easily, it is listed in the Apple menu. (The Apple Menu Items folder contains an alias of the Control Panels icon.)

Many control panels work fine if you drag them out of the Control Panels folder. However, control panels that extend the system software during startup won't work unless they're located in the Control Panels folder, the Extensions folder, or the System Folder. The system only looks in those places during startup for system software extensions. To

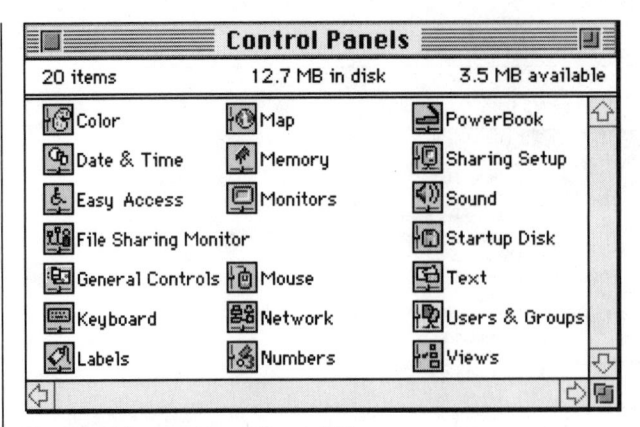

```
┌─────────────────────────────────────────────┐
│ ▤▤▤▤▤▤▤▤▤▤▤  Control Panels  ▤▤▤▤▤▤▤▤ ▣   │
├─────────────────────────────────────────────┤
│  20 items         12.7 MB in disk    3.5 MB available │
├─────────────────────────────────────────────┤
│  Color              Map              PowerBook        │
│  Date & Time        Memory           Sharing Setup    │
│  Easy Access        Monitors         Sound            │
│  File Sharing Monitor                Startup Disk     │
│  General Controls   Mouse            Text             │
│  Keyboard           Network          Users & Groups   │
│  Labels             Numbers          Views            │
└─────────────────────────────────────────────┘
```

Figure 5-15: An open Control Panels folder.

tell whether a control panel extends the system software, watch for its icon to appear at the bottom of the screen during startup. A few control panels that extend system software don't display their icons during startup (notably the standard Close View, Easy Access, and in some cases, Memory), but most do.

Control panels aren't listed in the Application menu at the right end of the menu bar along with application programs and desk accessories. They're considered part of the Finder. To use a control panel that's already open, switch to the Finder (by choosing it from the Application menu or by clicking the desktop) and find the control panel's window.

Some old control panel documents (also called *cdevs*) work properly only if you put them in the System Folder itself, not in the Control Panels folder. You should make an alias of each control panel you put in the System Folder and put the alias in the Control Panels folder so you can open that control panel from the Control Panels window (which you see upon choosing Control Panels from the Apple menu).

Standard control panels
System 7 comes with many control panels. The following seven are covered in other chapters:

- ✦ Color has settings for text highlighting color and window shading color. See "Choosing a window color" in Chapter 2.

- ✦ File Sharing Monitor lists the disks and folders you're sharing with others, identifies who is connected to your Macintosh, and enables you to disconnect them individually. See "Monitoring File Sharing Activity" in Chapter 8.

- ✦ Labels sets the names and colors (on a color or grayscale monitor) of items in the Finder's Labels menu. See "Changing label names and colors" in Chapter 3.

- ✦ Network determines which network connection to use if your Macintosh has more than one available. See "Selecting Your Network" in Chapter 8.

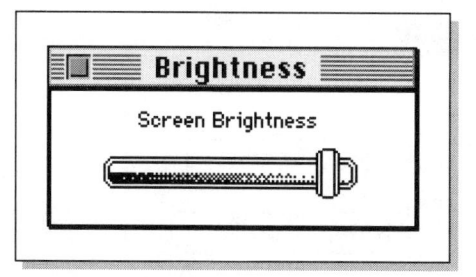

Figure 5-16: The Brightness control panel.

♦ Sharing Setup names your Macintosh and its owner on its network, sets the owner's network password, and starts or stops file sharing and program linking. See "Starting file sharing" in Chapter 8 and "Using program linking" in Chapter 11.

♦ Users & Groups identifies people and groups whom you allow specific access privileges for file sharing and program linking. See "Who Can Access Your Shared Items" in Chapter 8.

♦ Views sets format and content options for Finder windows. See "Custom Views" in Chapter 3.

The other standard control panels are described in the following sections of this chapter.

Brightness

On some Macintosh models, you adjust the brightness of your monitor by dragging the slide control in the Brightness control panel, as shown in Figure 5-16. If a message advises that you can't use the Brightness control panel when you try to open it, use the brightness knob on the monitor instead.

CloseView

You can use the CloseView control panel to magnify your screen two to 16 times and to invert the displayed colors, as shown in Figure 5-17. CloseView is not installed automatically with the rest of the control panels. You must drag it manually from the Tidbits installation disk to your Control Panels folder.

Date & Time

The Date & Time control panel, new with System 7.1, enables you to set the current date and the current time (like the General Controls control panel described below). It also enables you to set

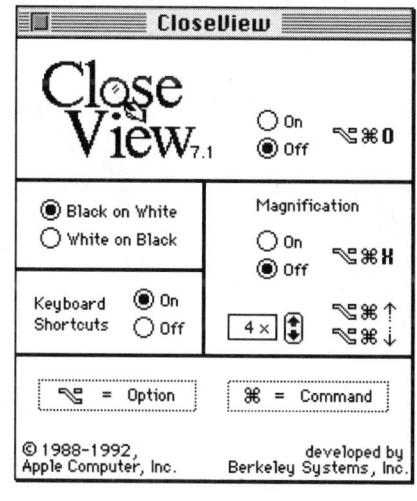

Figure 5-17: The CloseView control panel.

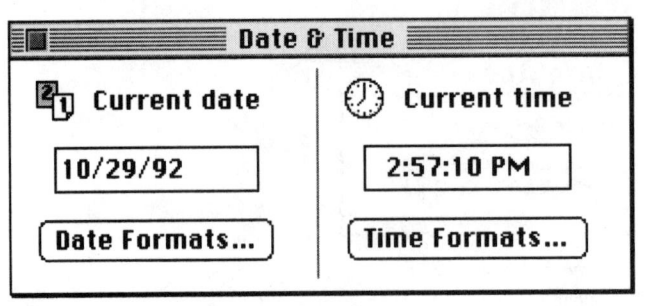

Figure 5-18: The Date & Time control panel.

how the date and time are displayed to suit your personal preference or the language you're using, as shown in Figure 5-18.

Easy Access

The Easy Access control panel sets up three alternative methods of using the keyboard and mouse (see Figure 5-19): Mouse Keys, Slow Keys, and Sticky Keys. In System 7, Easy Access whistles when you turn any of these features on or off. You can silence the whistle by turning off the audio feedback option at the top of the Easy Access control panel. To work, Easy Access must be in the Control Panels folder at startup time.

Mouse Keys enables you to click, drag, and move the pointer with the keypad instead of the mouse. You can turn on Mouse Keys by pressing Command-Shift-Clear instead of using the Easy Access control panel. You can also turn it off by pressing Clear. With Mouse Keys on, 5 on the keypad acts like a mouse button. Press once to click; press twice to double-click; or hold it down. The eight keys around 5 move the pointer left,

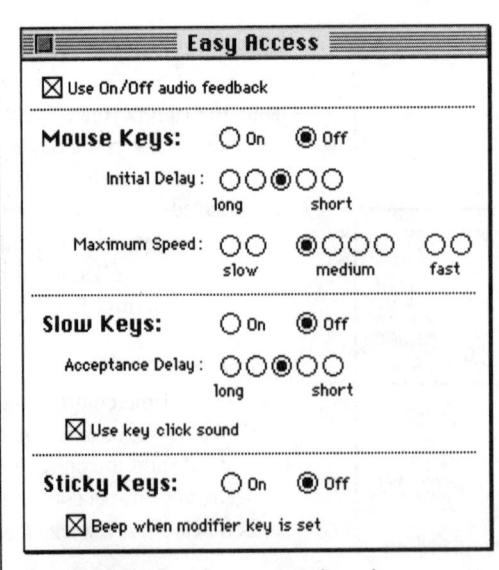

Figure 5-19: The Easy Access control panel.

right, up, down, and diagonally. Pressing 0 locks the mouse button down until you press Period on the keypad.

Slow Keys makes the Macintosh wait before it accepts a keystroke, thereby filtering out accidental keystrokes.

Sticky Keys enables you to type combination keystrokes such as Command-Shift-3 (which puts a snapshot of your screen in a picture document most graphics programs can open) one key at a time. Sticky Keys also enables you to lock down any modifier key by pressing it two times in a row. You can turn on Sticky Keys by pressing Shift five times in succession. When Sticky Keys is on, an icon at the right end of the menu bar shows its status, as shown in Figure 5-20. You can turn Sticky Keys off by pressing Shift five times again or by pressing any two modifier keys simultaneously.

General Controls
The General Controls control panel sets the desktop pattern, clock, calendar, menu flashing, and insertion point flashing, as shown in Figure 5-21. Selecting a pattern and making a custom pattern are covered in the "Desktop" section of Chapter 2.

Keyboard
The Keyboard control panel sets the key repeat rate and the delay time until key repeating begins, as shown in Figure 5-22. If your system has multiple keyboard layouts installed, you can select among them using the Keyboard control panel.

Map
The Map control panel sets the world location (latitude and longitude) and the time zone of your Macintosh, as shown in Figure 5-23. It can also compute the time difference and distance between any two places. Tiny flashing dots on the map mark known places. Click one to see its name or drag the pointer around until a name comes up. The map

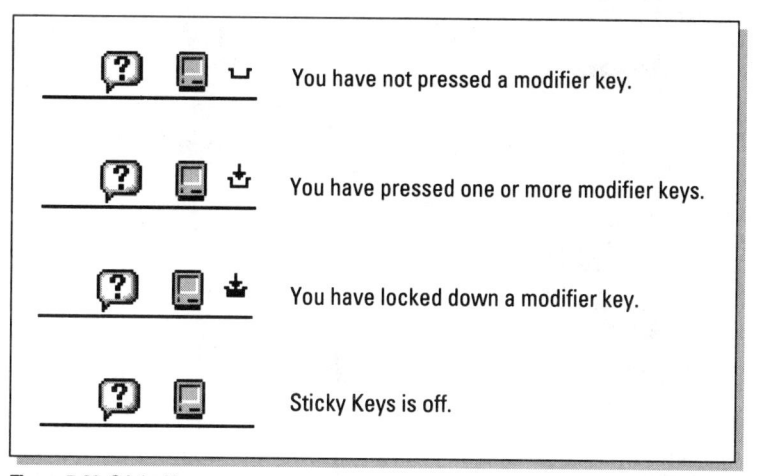

Figure 5-20: Sticky Keys status.

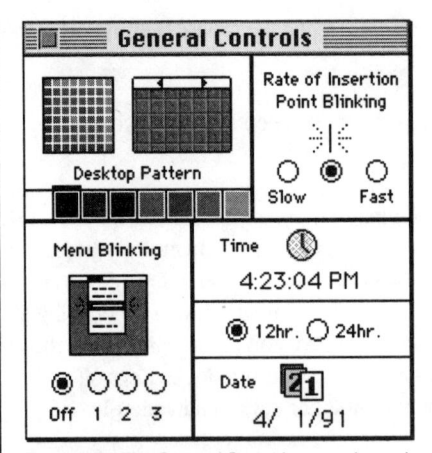

Figure 5-21: The General Controls control panel.

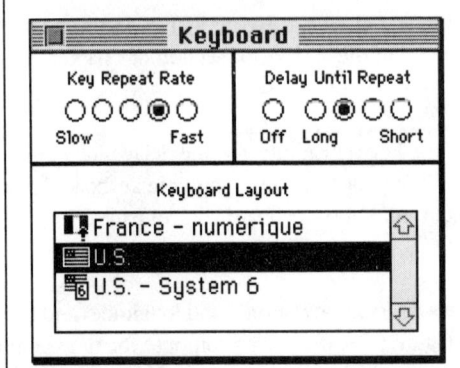

Figure 5-22: The Keyboard control panel.

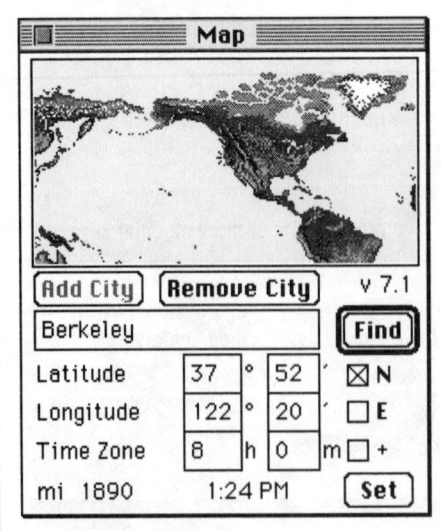

Figure 5-23: The Map control panel.

scrolls if you drag beyond its boundaries. You can also type a place name in the space provided and click the Find button or go through the list of known places alphabetically by pressing Option while clicking Find. The latitude, longitude, and time zone pertain to the most recently selected place. Map marks that location with a flashing star.

To add a new place, specify its latitude and longitude by clicking, by dragging, or by typing the coordinates in the spaces provided. Then type the place name and click the Add City button. After adding a new place, verify the estimated time zone and correct it if necessary.

Map marks the location of your Macintosh with a flashing dark cross. Set it by finding or adding the proper location and then clicking the Set button. Map automatically adjusts the time and date of your system's clock according to the difference between the old and new locations. Your Macintosh stores its location in battery-powered memory along with the time of day and other semipermanent settings.

The distance or compass direction from your Macintosh to the place marked with the flashing star appears at the bottom of the control panel along with the time at the distant place. Change from distance in miles to distance in kilometers or direction in degrees by clicking the unit of measure in the lower-left corner of the control panel. To see the time difference between that place and your Macintosh, click the words Time Differ in the control panel.

You can enlarge the map by pressing Option while opening the Map control panel. To magnify more, press Shift-Option while opening.

The Map control panel normally displays a black-and-white map of the world, but you can replace it with a color map from the standard System 7 Scrapbook. Simply scroll in the Scrapbook to the color world map, copy it, open the Map control panel, and paste. If you can't find a color map in your Scrapbook, you don't have the standard System 7 Scrapbook file. To get it, temporarily move the Scrapbook file from your System Folder to the desktop. Next copy the Scrapbook file from the Tidbits installation disk to your System Folder. Copy the color map as described above. Finally, select the Scrapbook file on the desktop, choose Put Away from the Finder's file menu, and click OK when the Finder asks if it's OK to replace the Scrapbook file in the System Folder with the one you're moving (putting away) from the desktop.

Monitors

The Monitors control panel sets the number of colors or grays of one or more monitors, as shown in Figure 5-24. Changes to these settings take place immediately.

If your Macintosh has multiple monitors, you can drag images of them around to determine their relative positions and can drag the menu bar to the monitor on which you want it to appear. Changes to monitor positions take effect when you close the Monitors control panel. You can also designate which monitor displays startup messages and icons. Press Option to reveal a tiny Macintosh icon and drag it to the monitor you want

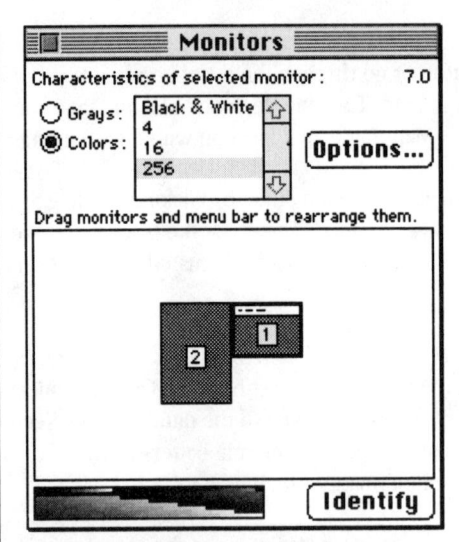

Figure 5-24: The Monitors control panel.

used during startup. Settings that affect the menu bar and startup monitor take place when you next restart your Macintosh.

On a Macintosh IIci or IIsi, you can also use the Monitors control panel to limit the number of colors or grays available with built-in video. The higher the limit, the more memory the built-in video uses. You set the limit in the Monitors Options panel, as shown in Figure 5-25. To see it, press Option while clicking the Options button in the Monitors control panel. With a 640 × 480 color monitor, 256 colors require 320K, 16 colors require 160K, four colors require 96K, and black-and-white requires 74K.

Figure 5-25: The Monitors Options panel.

Mouse

The Mouse control panel sets the mouse-to-pointer tracking speed and the double-click interval, as shown in Figure 5-26. The double-click interval also determines how long you have to wait after selecting an icon name before it is ready for editing (see "Renaming Icons" in Chapter 3).

Numbers

The Numbers control panel sets the number format — decimal separator, thousand separators, and currency symbol — for a region of the world that you choose from a pop-up menu of the languages installed in the System file, as shown in Figure 5-27. This control panel is new with System 7.1.

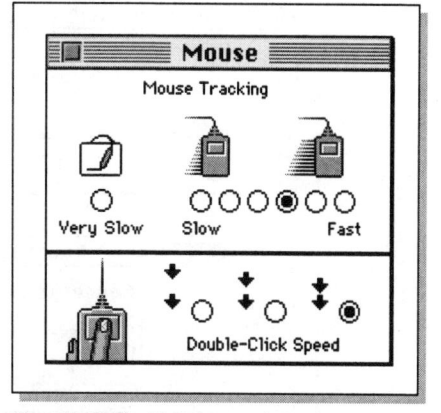

Figure 5-26: The Mouse control panel.

Portable and PowerBook

The Portable and PowerBook control panels set special features of the Macintosh Portable or PowerBook models. Portable comes with Systems 7.0 and 7.0.1, and PowerBook comes with System 7.1, as shown in Figure 5-28.

Sound

The Sound control panel sets the speaker volume and the system alert sound, as shown in Figure 5-29. It also includes controls for recording new alert sounds if your Macintosh has sound input equipment.

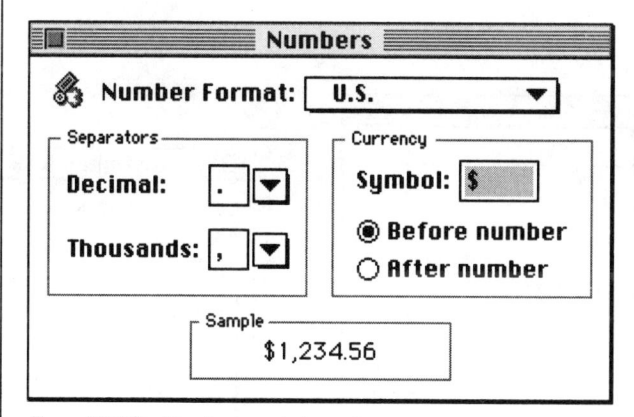

Figure 5-27: The Numbers control panel.

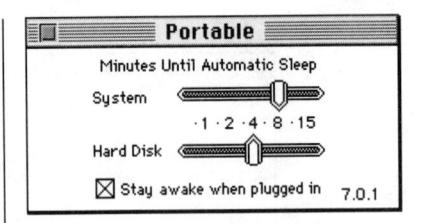

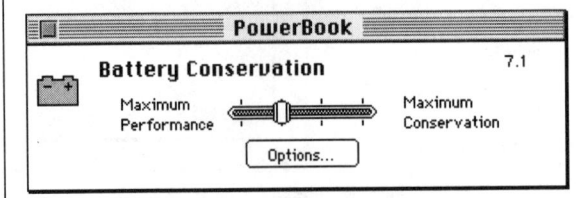

Figure 5-28: The Portable and PowerBook control panels.

Startup Disk

The Startup Disk control panel sets which hard disk your Macintosh uses the next time it starts up, as shown in Figure 5-30. This control panel doesn't work with a Macintosh Plus. It has no effect unless your Macintosh has more than one hard disk with a System Folder. And in most cases it won't enable you to choose among multiple partitions on a single hard disk.

Text

The Text control panel enables you to choose from among the installed language script systems such as Roman, Cyrillic, Arabic, Japanese, and Chinese. For the chosen script system you can also choose among the installed languages that it supports. For example, the Cyrillic language system supports Russian and several other Eastern European languages, as shown in Figure 5-31. Choosing a language affects rules for alphabetizing, capitalizing, and distinguishing words.

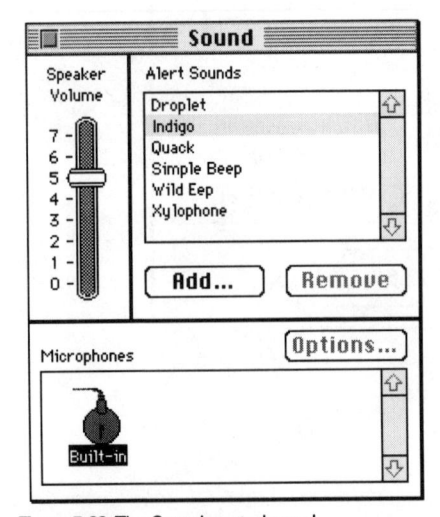

Figure 5-29: The Sound control panel.

Figure 5-30: The Startup Disk control panel.

Figure 5-31: The Text control panel.

Memory Management Tactics

The Memory control panel, new with System 7, helps you manage your computer's memory. You can ignore that control panel and the burden of memory management in general if you never open more than one program at a time and don't care about your computer's performance or effectiveness (not to mention your own). To get the most from your Macintosh, you must pay attention to how you use its memory.

Think of your computer's memory as a pie, as shown in Figure 5-32. You need to know the size of the pie, how much of the pie each open program uses, and how much is unused and available for opening additional programs. You also need to know how big a piece of the memory pie each of those additional programs would need if you opened it.

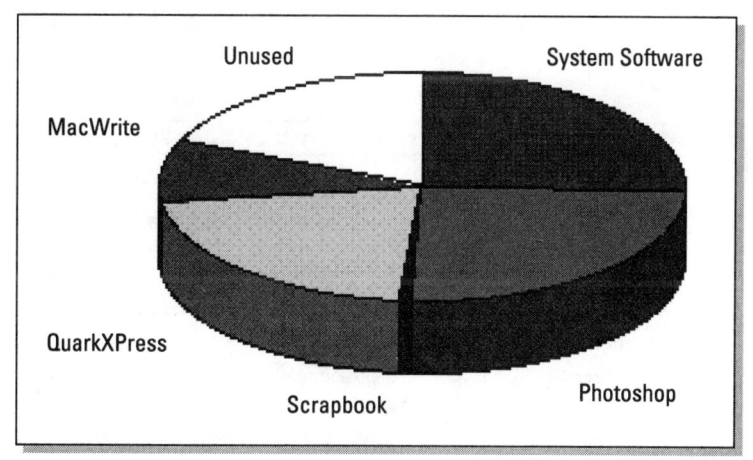

Figure 5-32: Memory pie.

Analyzing memory use

For information on the condition of your Macintosh memory pie, switch to the Finder and choose About This Macintosh from the Apple menu. The Finder displays a window that reports the total amount of memory installed in your Macintosh and the largest amount available for opening another program. It also graphs the amount allocated to and currently used by the system software and by each open program, as shown in Figure 5-33. To learn the exact amount the system software or an open program is using at the moment, turn on Balloon Help and point at the memory-use bar for the item.

If you add up the amounts of memory allocated to system software and to each open program, you may come up with a total that's less than the reported amount of total memory. Built-in video uses 40K to 340K on some Mac models and this amount is not reported by About This Macintosh. There may be an additional discrepancy of several K due to rounding errors.

System memory size

As reported by About This Macintosh, the system software (which includes the Finder) takes up a large chunk of memory. You can reduce the system software's memory size to its minimum by pressing Shift while restarting your Macintosh. Look for the message "Extensions Off" during startup. It confirms that you have suppressed loading of all items in the Extensions folder, Control Panels folder, and System Folder that would increase the system software's memory size. You have also bypassed opening items in the Startup Items folder, reduced the RAM cache to 16K, forced virtual memory off, and prevented file sharing from starting. None of these changes persist when you restart without pressing Shift. To make persistent changes you must drag items out of the special folders and change settings in the Memory and File Sharing control panels.

All items listed as system extensions in a By Kind view of the Extensions folder or System Folder (except PostScript fonts with Systems 7.0 and 7.0.1) increase the system software's memory size during startup. So do some other items, but not Chooser extensions

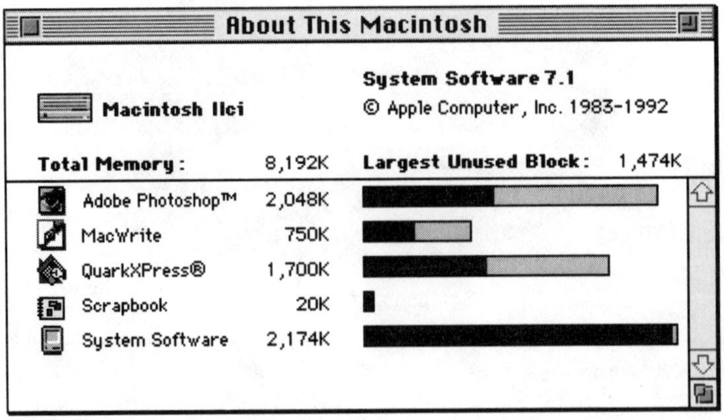

Figure 5-33: An About This Macintosh window.

for printers (LaserWriter, StyleWriter, ImageWriter, and so on), communications tools, MNPLinkTool documents, Finder Help, or the PrintMonitor application. Control panels that display an icon at the bottom of the screen during startup (or offer the option of doing so) have system extensions built in and increase the system software's memory size. Control panels that don't display startup icons generally don't increase system software's memory size, though there are exceptions such as Easy Access.

The amount of memory you recover by removing a particular item from the Extensions folder, Control Panels folder, or System Folder depends partly on what items remain, so you'll have to experiment. On a test system, for example, Adobe Type Manager 2.0.2 (ATM) added 193K, QuicKeys 2.1.1 with CE Toolbox 1.6.4 added 209K, and After Dark 2.0v added 108K. Other items had smaller memory appetites. Easy Access 7.0 added only 12K and Capture 4.0 22K, for instance. Compare your system software's memory size before and after removing an item and weigh the potential memory savings against the benefit the item provides.

For big memory savings, turn off file sharing and virtual memory if you're not using them. (The test system recouped 267K from the first and 380K from the second.) Reducing the RAM cache size reduces the system software's memory size K for K — and slows system performance.

Program memory size

When you open a program, the system software gives it a chunk of the memory pie. You can change how much an application program gets by setting its memory size in its info window (see Figure 5-34), which the Finder's Get Info command displays. You must quit an open program before changing its memory size.

The info window lists a suggested memory size, which the program's developer has recommended as the least amount needed for standard performance. The amount of memory the program gets when you open it is between two other sizes you can enter. The Finder tries to give the program the preferred memory size, but opens the program in as little as the specified minimum memory size.

Setting the preferred size higher than the suggested size may improve performance or enable you to open more documents or larger documents. Setting the preferred size below the suggested size usually has the opposite effect. For example, setting Hyper-Card's preferred size below the suggested 1,000K reduces the number of stacks you can have open simultaneously, limits your access to painting tools and scripting, and prevents opening some stacks altogether. (The preferred size is called the current size in versions of system software older than System 7.1.)

Initially, the minimum size is set to a value recommended by the program developer, and setting the minimum size lower than the recommended minimum may cause the program to crash. For example, HyperCard does not work properly if you set its minimum size below Claris's recommended minimum of 750K. (Systems 7.0 and 7.0.1 know about the recommended minimum but don't display it or enable you to change it in the Get Info window.)

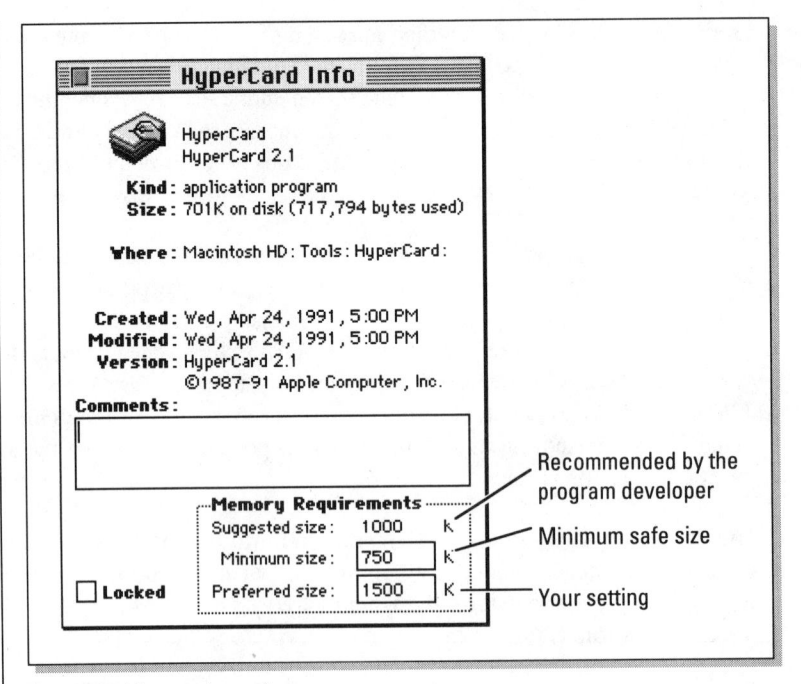

Figure 5-34: Memory size settings.

If your Macintosh has just the minimum 2MB of RAM required to use System 7, you should pare program memory sizes to the bone. For example, giving your favorite word processing program the full amount of memory available after the system software takes its chunk leaves you no room to use the Chooser to select a printer or share someone's files. (Though you can work around the file sharing limitation by making aliases of the items you most often share, as described in Chapter 8.) Also, there wouldn't be any memory left for background printing.

You can't change the memory size of a desk accessory. Each desk accessory gets 20K and it generally increases the system software memory size by a good deal more.

Memory fragmentation

As you open and quit a series of programs, the unused portion of the memory pie tends to become fragmented into multiple small chunks, as shown in Figure 5-35. You may find yourself unable to open a program because it needs a chunk of memory bigger than the biggest unused chunk (the Largest Unused Block amount in the About This Macintosh window). The total of all unused chunks may be large enough to open the program, but System 7 cannot consolidate fragmented memory nor open a program in multiple chunks of memory.

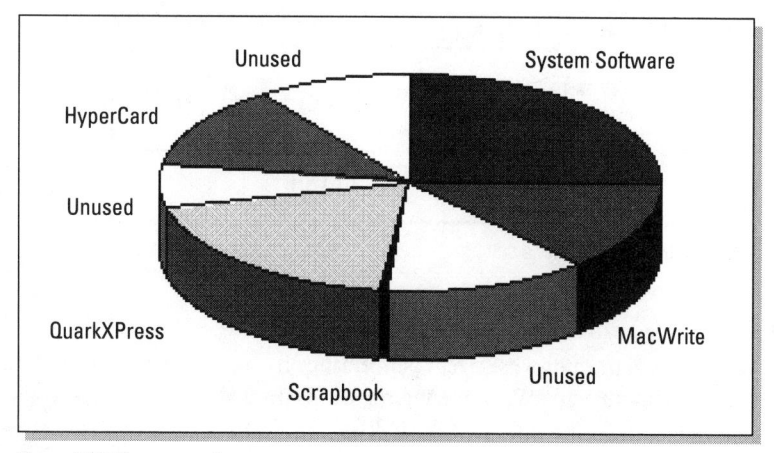

Figure 5-35: Fragmented memory.

To check for fragmentation, add up the memory sizes of all the open programs and the system software as listed in the About This Macintosh window. If you have a monitor connected to the built-in video on a Macintosh IIsi or IIci, add another 320K (or less if you have limited the number of colors to less than 256 as described in "Monitors" earlier in this chapter). If the total exceeds the Largest Unused Block amount by more than 50K or so, the unused memory is fragmented into two or more chunks.

To consolidate fragmented memory, quit all open programs and then open them again. Restarting your Macintosh also fixes fragmentation and may reduce the amount of memory used by system software as well.

You can avoid memory fragmentation by planning the order in which you open and quit programs. Open the programs you're least likely to quit first, and open the programs you're most likely to quit last. When you need more memory to open another program, quit the most recently opened program. If that doesn't free enough memory, quit the next most recently opened program, and so on. This method frees up a contiguous chunk of memory. Quitting programs helter-skelter leads to memory fragmentation.

System 7.1, and Systems 7.0 and 7.0.1 with Apple's Tune-Up installed, sometimes hasten memory fragmentation in low-memory situations. If you try to open an application that needs more memory than is available, System 7.1 (and a tuned-up 7.0 or 7.0.1) suggests quitting all programs with no open windows — or the largest open program, if all have open windows. Accepting the Finder's suggestion can fragment memory. To avoid memory fragmentation, you must quit programs in the reverse of the order in which they were opened. (For more information on the System 7 Tune-Up, see Appendix C.)

Disk Cache

The system software takes up a considerable chunk of your memory pie. A goodly portion of that goes to the Disk Cache, which improves system performance. You can use the Memory control panel to adjust the amount of memory allocated for the Disk Cache, as shown in Figure 5-36. You cannot turn off the Disk Cache as you can its equivalent in older system software, the RAM Cache control in the General section of the Control Panel.

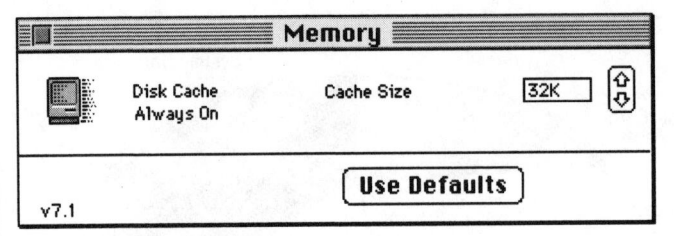

Figure 5-36: The Disk Cache setting.

The Disk Cache improves system performance by storing frequently used information from disk in memory. When the information is needed again, it can be copied quickly from memory instead of slowly from disk.

If you have a Mac IIsi and you set the number of colors or grays for its built-in video to four or more, you can improve system performance by setting the Disk Cache to 768K. Then the Disk Cache and the built-in video together use up all the memory that's soldered to the main circuit board. This forces the system software and your programs into the part of memory in the four SIMM sockets. Programs may work much slower if they are located in the soldered-on memory along with the built-in video.

The same trick works on a Mac IIci with 5MB, 9MB, or 17MB of RAM. To get the performance boost, the 256K SIMMs must be installed in the four sockets nearest the disk drive. Realizing a performance increase on a IIci with other RAM capacities isn't feasible because you would have to set the Disk Cache so high as to waste a large amount of memory.

32-Bit Addressing

Some Macintosh models can access a larger memory pie by using System 7's 32-Bit Addressing capability. To turn it on and off, you use the Memory control panel, as shown in Figure 5-37.

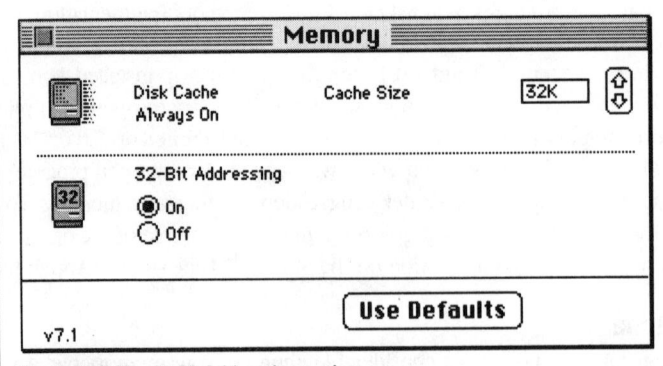

Figure 5-37: The 32-Bit Addressing setting.

With 4MB RAM SIMMs installed, for example, turning on 32-Bit Addressing enables you to use 10MB of RAM on a Mac LC, LC II, Classic II, Performa 200, or Performa 400; 17MB on a IIsi; 20MB on a Performa 600, IIvx, IIvi, or Quadra 700; 32MB on a IIci or IIfx; and 64MB on a Quadra 900 or Quadra 950. If 32-Bit Addressing is off (as it always is with older system software), you can only use 8MB of RAM regardless of the amount installed.

Your programs may not all be compatible with 32-Bit Addressing. Apple began exhorting developers to make their products "32-Bit Clean" in 1987, but not all have. For help in determining whether your programs are 32-Bit Clean, see Appendix A. If you need to use programs that are not 32-Bit Clean, you can open programs and documents in up to 14MB of RAM by installing the MAXIMA utility software from Connectix. If your Mac has more than 14MB, MAXIMA enables you to use the amount beyond 14MB as a RAM disk.

Mac Classic, SE, Plus, Portable, and PowerBook 100 models can't use 32-Bit Addressing because their 68000 central processing units can't access more than 8MB. The Power-Book 140, 145, and 170 models can use 32-Bit Addressing, but because only 8MB can be installed in those models, it is not useful.

The 68020 and 68030 central processing units in Mac SE/30, II, IIx, and IIcx models can access more than 8MB, but the ROMs (permanent read-only memory) in those models are not 32-Bit Clean. You can get around the ROM problem and use 32-Bit Addressing on a Mac SE/30, II, IIx, or IIcx by installing the MODE 32 utility software, which Apple distributes free through dealers, user groups, and on-line information services.

Virtual memory

You may be able to increase the size of your memory pie without buying and installing more RAM modules. System 7 can transparently use part of a hard disk as additional memory. This extra memory, called virtual memory, enables you to get by with less RAM. You buy only as much as you need for average use, not for peak use.

To turn virtual memory on and off, you use the Memory control panel, as shown in Figure 5-38. You also set the size of total memory and select a hard disk that has a block of available space as large as the total amount of memory you want available (RAM plus virtual memory). The hard disk space cannot be on a removable hard disk.

Virtual memory controls are only available on a Macintosh equipped with a PMMU (paged memory-management unit). The Classic II, LC II, SE/30, IIcx, IIx, IIsi, IIci, IIvx, IIvi, and IIfx models all have PMMUs, and so do all Performas, all Quadras, and all Power-Books except the 100. A Mac II can be retrofitted with a PMMU, and an LC can be upgraded with an accelerator card containing a PMMU. However, a Mac Plus, SE, Classic, or Portable with such an accelerator can't use System 7's virtual memory because the ROMs in those models are missing some information System 7 needs to implement virtual memory. To use virtual memory on those models, install Connectix's utility software Virtual.

Figure 5-38: Virtual memory settings.

With virtual memory on, the About This Macintosh window reports the total amount of memory and the amount of built-in memory (that is, RAM). It also tells you how much disk space is used for virtual memory storage and on which disk the storage file is located, as shown in Figure 5-39.

Total memory size (virtual memory plus RAM) cannot exceed 14MB unless you turn on the 32-Bit Addressing option in the Memory control panel. On Macintosh models with NuBus cards installed, that limit is 1MB lower for each installed card. Furthermore, virtual memory will be fragmented unless you install all NuBus cards consecutively starting at one end slot or the other. On a IIcx, fill slots from left to right. With 32-Bit Addressing

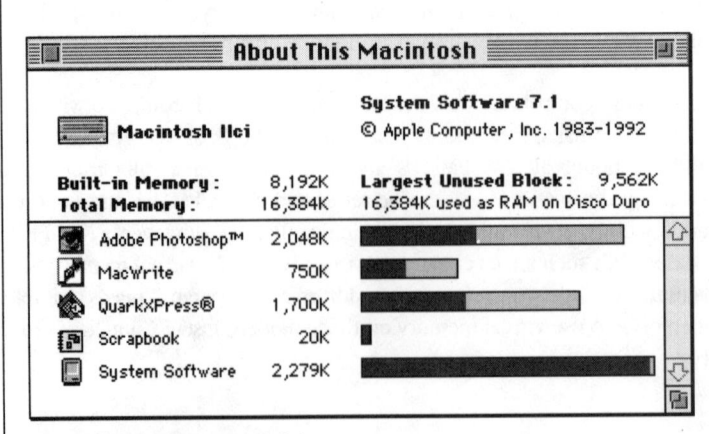

Figure 5-39: Virtual memory statistics.

on, the limit on total memory is one gigabyte (1024MB). NuBus cards are not an issue. Virtual memory works by keeping the most active program and document segments in RAM. Less-used segments of open programs and documents are kept in an invisible file named VM Storage on the hard disk. (The VM Storage file becomes visible if you start up with system software older than System 7.) When a program needs a segment not currently in physical memory, System 7 automatically swaps the least-used segment in RAM with the needed segment on disk. A swap often occurs when you switch programs, for example.

Because a hard disk is much slower than RAM, using virtual memory can degrade system performance. The performance penalty is barely noticeable if a swap happens when you switch programs. The slowdown may be severe if you use virtual memory to open a program that's bigger than the amount of RAM left after system software gets its share. The disk may thrash for several minutes as it tries to swap segments back and forth. For best results, set virtual memory no higher than double the installed RAM and use it for opening multiple small programs.

You can usually improve system performance by using the Hide Others command in the Application menu. Hidden windows don't require updating, which may require disk access when virtual memory is on.

Old Drivers Cause Trouble

Some old driver software for hard disks does not work with System 7's virtual memory or 32-Bit Addressing options turned on. Every hard disk contains driver software, which the Mac copies to its RAM while starting up, and acts as an intermediary between the system software and the hard disk. You install or update the driver software with hard disk utility software from the maker of your drive. Usually, you can do this without any loss of data. Check Appendix A for the oldest version of driver software your hard disk can use with System 7's virtual memory and 32-Bit Addressing.

Several companies sell driver software that works with a wide variety of hard disks. In tests on a Mac IIci with several different hard disks, Drive7 from Casa Blanca and Hard Disk ToolKit from FWB delivered practically identical performance. Hard Disk ToolKit has many options for tweaking the software and the hard disk that you probably wouldn't try, even after reading the manual's detailed descriptions of hard disks and SCSI. For $120 less, Drive7 has the basic features you need.

Summary

- Desk accessories work outside the Apple menu, in folders and on the desktop, and can be used like ordinary application programs.
- The Apple menu lists every item you put in the Apple Menu Items folder. Choosing an item from the Apple menu opens the item.
- The old Control Panel desk accessory gives way to individual control panels that you open like Finder documents.
- Virtual memory enables you to use disk space as memory, and 32-Bit Addressing increases the amount of memory some Macintosh models can use.
- Managing memory becomes more important as you use more of it and as you use it for keeping more programs open at the same time.

Chapter 6
Fast Access with Aliases

In This Chapter
- Learning what aliases are, how to make them, and how to use them.
- Opening any item from the desktop without moving it from its folder.
- Cutting laterally across your folder structure in directory dialog boxes.
- Adding items to the Apple menu or the Startup Items folder without moving the items from their folders.
- Organizing documents and folders according to multiple filing schemes without duplicating items.
- Opening items on floppy disks that are not inserted.
- Accessing files, folders, and disks shared from other computers on your network.
- Using a floppy disk on any Macintosh in your network to access your hard disks.

The hierarchical order of the Macintosh universe enables you to organize programs and documents into folders. Nesting folders within folders keeps related items together but can turn your disk into a labyrinth. Finder 7's Find command helps you locate items without digging through folders, but it's no substitute for well-organized disks.

Finder aliases cut through the organizational maze. Aliases act like real items when you open them or drag items to them. Think of an alias as a stand-in or an agent for a real program, document, folder, or disk. You can place these agents at your beck and call in any handy location such as the desktop or the Apple menu. When you open aliases or drag items to them, they act like the real items they represent. Aliases even look like the items they represent, except their names are italicized.

Understanding Aliases

Like the documents, programs, and other items on your disks, aliases are files. Each alias contains a pointer to the original item it represents, as shown in Figure 6-1. An alias always remembers where its original item is located, even when you move or rename the original item. The only way you can break the connection between an alias and its original item is to drag the original item to the Trash and empty the Trash.

When you open an alias, the Finder follows the pointer to the original item and actually opens the original. Dragging an item to the alias of a folder or disk has the same effect as dragging it to the original folder or disk: the Finder follows the pointer to the

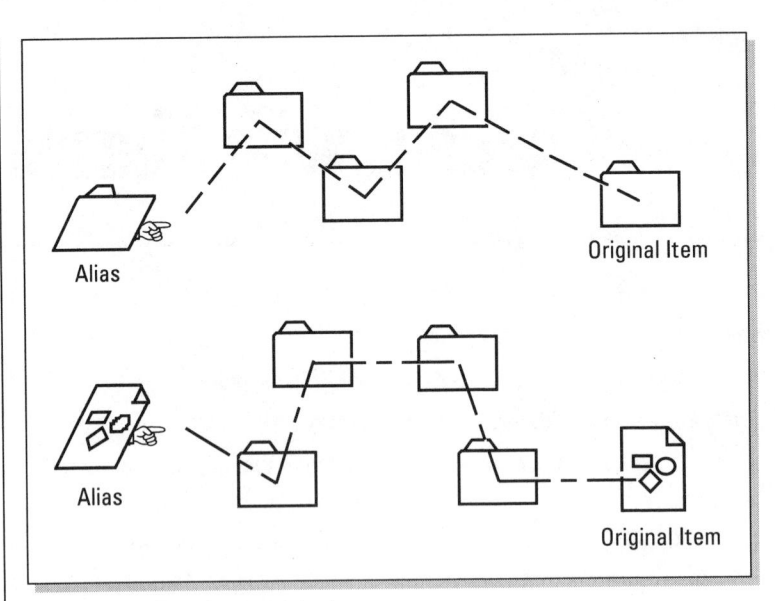

Figure 6-1: An alias points to another item.

original folder or disk and that's where it places the item you dragged. Likewise, a document you drag to an alias of a compatible program follows the pointer to the program itself, which opens the document. You can even drag an alias to an alias; the Finder follows both pointers and deals with the original items.

Aliases vary in size from 1K to 3K or more, depending on the capacity of the disk they're on. For example, an alias takes up 1K of a floppy disk, a 20MB hard disk, or a 40MB hard disk. On an 80MB hard disk, an alias takes up 2K, and aliases on CD-ROM occupy 10K each. If a hard disk is partitioned into multiple volumes (each having its own icon on the desktop), the volume capacity determines the size of aliases on it.

Old files may show up as aliases (they may have italicized names) because Finder 7 flags a file as an alias by setting a bit (a single binary digit) that older Finders reserved for a disused file-locking scheme or they contain stray data in the part of the file that Finder 7 uses to mark aliases. The Finder detects these problems and fixes them, explaining "Sorry, this item is not an alias (oops!). The problem has now been corrected. Please try again." or "The alias 'FileName' could not be opened, because this item is really not an alias (oops!). The problem has now been corrected. Please try again."

Making an Alias

You can make an alias for any item you can open from the Finder. That includes documents, application programs, desk accessories, folders, disks, control panels, and even fonts and sounds. Making an alias is a simple procedure. Select the item

Figure 6-2: Using the Make Alias command.

you want to create an alias for and choose Make Alias from the File menu. A new item appears with the same icon as the original item and an italicized name the same as the original item's name plus the suffix *alias*, as shown in Figure 6-2.

Immediately after creating an alias, its name is selected for editing. You can change the name by typing a replacement or by using other standard text-editing techniques (see "Renaming Items" in Chapter 3). To keep the name as is, click anywhere outside the name or press Return or Enter.

You can create multiple aliases for the same original item to access the original item from different locations. The number of aliases you can create is limited only by disk space.

To make aliases for several items in the same window at once, select them all and use the Make Alias command. An alias appears for every item you selected. All the new aliases are automatically selected so you can immediately drag them to another place without having to manually select them as a group.

Changing an Alias

Once you make an alias, you can manipulate it as you would any item. Move it to another folder on the same disk or to the desktop. The alias still knows where to find its original item.

Copy an alias by using the Finder's Duplicate command or by dragging the alias to another disk or to a folder on another disk. To copy an alias or other item to another folder on the same disk, press Option while dragging. All copies of the alias point to the same original item.

You rename an alias as you would any other item on the desktop or in a Finder window (see "Renaming Items" in Chapter 3). If you want an alias to have the same name as its original item, they can't be in the same folder. You must move one out.

To quickly remove the word *alias* from the end of the name, click the name once to select it for editing, pause briefly (or avoid the pause by moving the mouse slightly right after you click the alias name), double-click the last word of the name, and press Delete twice (once to delete the selected word alias and the second time to delete the space before that word). If you double-click too quickly after selecting the name, the Finder opens the item that the alias points to instead of selecting the last word of the name. Alternatively, you can select the name for editing, press the down-arrow key or right-arrow key to move the insertion point to the end of the name, and press Delete six times to erase the last word and the space preceding it. To conclude your name editing, click anywhere outside the name or press Return or Enter. If you want the Finder never to add the word alias as a suffix, you can modify the Finder as described in "Suffix for New Alias Names" in Chapter 12.

Like any item, you remove an alias by dragging it to the Trash. Remember, throwing away an alias doesn't affect the original item. You're throwing away just the alias, not the item it points to.

An alias inherits its icon from the original item. If you subsequently change the original item's icon, the alias icon is updated automatically the next time you open (but don't drag something to) the alias. Like most other icons, you can customize an alias's icon in its info window. You see the info window by using the Finder's Get Info command (see "Custom Icons" in Chapter 3). The alias's custom icon won't be affected by changes to the icon of the original item. You can also type comments about the alias and lock it in its info window.

Changing an Original Item

Aliases are truly amazing at finding items. Not only can you rename and move an alias's original item, you can replace it with another file having the same name, all without breaking the alias. You might wonder how an alias can find the original item after you rename or move the original item. If the alias can't find an item having the same name and folder location as the original, it searches for the original item's unique file ID number, which the system software internally assigns to each file. Once the alias finds the original item using this ID number, it remembers the original item's current name and folder location.

If you copy the original item referenced by an alias, the alias still points to the original item, not the copy. Sounds reasonable unless you forget the difference between copying an item and moving it. In many cases, copying and moving an item feels and

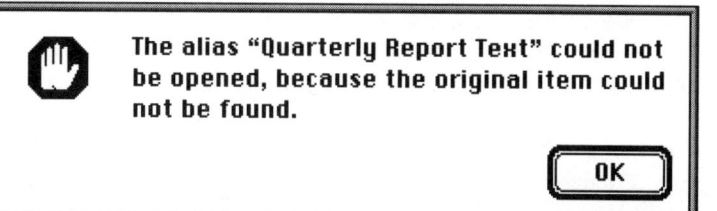

> ✋ The alias "Quarterly Report Text" could not be opened, because the original item could not be found.
>
> [OK]

Figure 6-3: After deleting an original item.

looks the same. Both copying and moving involve the same action — dragging an item to another place. If that other place is a folder in the same disk as the item you're dragging, the item is moved and the item's alias knows where to find the moved item. If the other place is a folder in another disk, the item is copied. The alias knows where the original item is, but not the copy. Deleting the original item breaks the alias's link to the item, even though a copy of the item exists on another disk. If you use an alias for which the original item has been deleted, the Finder tells you it couldn't find the original item, as shown in Figure 6-3. You can use utility software to connect an orphaned alias to its original file or to a copy of the original (see "Alias Assistance" in Chapter 13).

Finding an Original Item

You can find an alias's original item by using the Get Info command to display the alias's info window, as shown in Figure 6-4. The disk and folder path to the original item appears above the Comments box next to the heading Original. Clicking the Find Original button in the info window opens the folder that contains the original item and selects the original item.

```
≡≡≡ Fizzz Poster alias Info ≡≡≡

    📄  Fizzz Poster alias

      Kind: alias
      Size: 1K on disk (605 bytes used)

     Where: Aphrodite's Hard Disk : Icons :

   Created: Fri, Oct 30, 1992, 10:37 AM
  Modified: Fri, Oct 30, 1992, 10:37 AM
  Original: Aphrodite's Hard Disk : Documents
            : Active Projects : Fizzz Beverage
            Co. : Fizzz PR : Fizzz Poster
  Comments:
  ┌──────────────────────────────────┐
  │                                  │
  │                                  │
  └──────────────────────────────────┘

  ☐ Locked              [ Find Original ]
```

Figure 6-4: An alias's info window.

If the original item is on a disk whose icon is not on the desktop, the Finder asks you to insert that disk. If the missing disk is a removable hard disk cartridge, the Finder will be unable to find the original item unless some removable cartridge has appeared on the desktop since you started up or restarted your computer. Also, the needed removable cartridge must have the same hard disk driver software as the first cartridge mounted during or after startup.

Using Aliases

There are many useful applications for aliases. The most common is quick access to programs and documents you frequently work with. For example, you can make an alias of a spreadsheet you regularly use for updating sales figures and place the alias in a convenient location, such as the desktop. Some of the most important uses of aliases include adding items to the Apple menu or to the list of items opened at startup time, adding desktop convenience for accessing items, accessing archived information from floppy disks, streamlining access to shared items, and more. The following sections provide a collection of scenarios to leverage the power of aliases, providing express service to a wide range of items.

Aliases in the Apple menu

With System 7, the most convenient place from which to open application programs, desk accessories, control panels, documents, folders, and other items is the Apple menu. Because the Apple menu is always on the menu bar, items in the Apple menu are never more than a mouse click away. You can add any item to the Apple menu that you can open using the Finder, including aliases.

Placing an alias in the Apple menu is as easy as dragging the alias icon to the Apple Menu Items folder, which is in the System Folder. The alias and the original item it points to become instantly available without having to restart your Macintosh. Items in the Apple Menu are displayed alphabetically in plain (not italic) text. You may want to change the name of your alias to adjust its position in the Apple menu.

You can add as many aliases as you want to the Apple Menu Items folder. However, it's a good idea to keep the number within a reasonable range to prevent constant scrolling through a long menu. To remove an alias from the Apple menu, drag its icon out of the Apple Menu Items folder.

One of the most useful aliases you can add to the Apple menu is an alias of the Apple Menu Items folder. Adding this alias allows you to quickly open the Apple Menu Items folder and easily customize the Apple menu anywhere, anytime.

Universal Show Clipboard

Some application programs lack a Show Clipboard command and others that have one use a private clipboard whose contents may look different when pasted into another program. With a System 7 alias you can put a Show Clipboard command in your Apple menu for reviewing the standard Clipboard contents from any application program. First, you make an alias of the Clipboard file, which is in the System

Folder. Then, you place the alias in the Apple Menu Items folder and rename the alias Show Clipboard. Now choosing Show Clipboard from the Apple menu switches to the Finder and opens the Clipboard.

Aliases as startup items

Every time you start up (or restart) your Macintosh, Finder 7 automatically opens everything in the Startup Items folder. For example, if you regularly use a program, such as PageMaker, you may want it ready to go immediately after starting up your Macintosh. But some programs don't work correctly from the Startup Items folder. Furthermore, returning items to their previous locations when you no longer want them opened at startup time can be a drag. Moving an alias of a program, document, or other item to the Startup Items folder has the same effect as moving the original item there. To remove an alias from the startup sequence, drag the alias out of the folder.

Application programs in the Startup Items folder open in alphabetical order, so you can rename the alias of an application program to determine when it starts relative to other application programs in the folder. Aliases of other types of desk accessories, control panels, and folders open alphabetically after all application programs have opened. For more information on the Startup Items folder, see "Startup Items Folder" in Chapter 4.

Aliases on the desktop

Other than the Apple menu, the desktop is the most accessible place for opening items, and it's the most accessible place for folders to which you want to drag items. Rather than drag frequently used programs, control panels, documents, and folders themselves into the desktop, make aliases of them and put the aliases on the desktop. Putting aliases of nested items on the desktop gives you quick access to the folders without digging through folders to find them.

Putting aliases of programs on the desktop avoids problems that can occur if you move the programs themselves onto the desktop. Such programs depend on support files being in the same folder (or on the desktop) with them. For example, a word processor on the desktop may also need a dictionary file on the desktop in order to check spelling. Aliases save you the hassle of guessing which support files a program needs in order to run correctly and avoid the mess that results if you place those support files on the desktop. By creating an alias for an application, the alias accesses the original application in its folder, saving you from moving the application and supporting files to get full access to the application.

By making aliases of documents and programs you use frequently and putting the aliases on the desktop, you never have to remember where you have put the original items. Also, you can open several related items at the same time, even if the original items happen to be in different folders or on different disks, by opening aliases on the desktop.

QUICK TIPS

If the windows of open programs obscure desktop aliases, you can hide those windows by choosing Hide Others from the Application menu while the Finder is active. If Finder windows cover desktop aliases, you can close all those windows at once by pressing Option while clicking the close box of any Finder window.

If your desktop becomes too cluttered with aliases, you can put related aliases together in a folder on the desktop. For example, you can make aliases of the Trash and hard disk, put the aliases in a folder, and put the folder in your Apple menu for instant access. Leave that folder open and its window comes to the front along with the other Finder windows whenever you switch to the Finder.

If you're lucky enough to have two monitors, put a Trash alias on the desktop of the second monitor. You'll never again have to drag icons across two screens to throw them away.

Aliases in directory dialog boxes

QUICK TIPS

Aliases on the desktop appear at the desktop level in the directory dialog boxes you get when you use Open, Save, and other disk-related commands. Alias names appear in italics in directory dialog boxes, as shown in Figure 6-5, and opening an alias there opens its original item. You can also quickly go to an alias's original item in a directory dialog box by pressing Option while opening the alias (by double-clicking it, for example). In this case, System 7 opens the folder containing the original item and selects the original item.

Abridged System Folder

Aliases can help you quickly find folders inside the System Folder whose contents you need to get at, such as the Startup Items folder and the folder containing your incoming electronic mail. Make aliases for the System Folder items you access often — including an alias of the System Folder itself — and put all those aliases in a

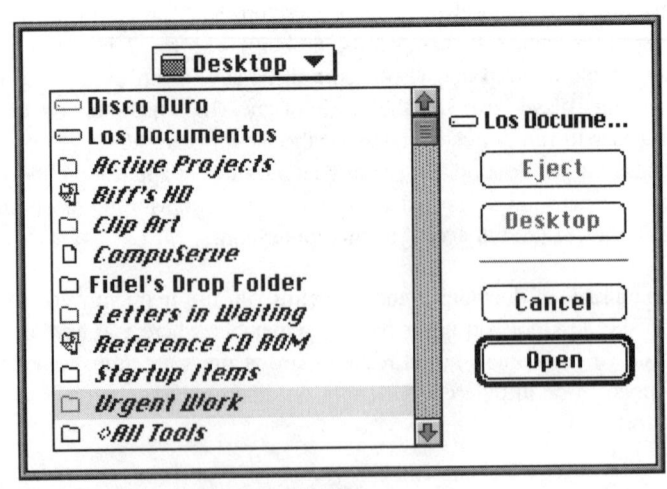

Figure 6-5: Aliases in a directory dialog box.

new folder. You can open and find an item in that new folder faster than in the System Folder. To make the new folder look like a System Folder, copy the icon from the System Folder's Get Info window and paste it into the new folder's Get Info window.

Aliases for favorite folders
Putting aliases of your favorite folders on the desktop or inside disk windows enables you to quickly open a favorite folder from a directory dialog box. Instead of working your way down through one branch of your folder structure and then working your way up another branch to the folder you want, you zip to the desktop level or the disk level and there open the alias of the folder you want. It's as if you could jump from one branch of a tree to the root level and then jump to a spot on another branch without crawling up the trunk and along the other branch.

You can quickly get to aliases of favorite folders on the desktop by clicking the Desktop button. Get to aliases at the disk window level by choosing the disk from the directory dialog's pop-up menu.

Aliases of items on floppy disks
You can use aliases to keep track of and quickly open items on floppy disks — even floppies that aren't inserted in your Macintosh. For example, suppose you're keeping track of your company's bills, and one month, March, doesn't balance. You want to close out the quarter and archive the monthly detail files to floppy disk, but you know that you may need to access the file for March later. Instead of keeping the monthly detail files on your hard disk, go ahead and copy them all to a floppy with a unique name, such as First Qtr. Select the March file on the floppy and choose Make Alias from the File menu. Copy the alias to your hard disk. When you need the March file again, open its alias on the hard disk. The system tells you the name of the disk to insert so it can open the alias's original item, as shown in Figure 6-6. If you change your mind or can't find the needed disk, click the Cancel button.

Keeping aliases on your hard disk and the original items on floppies saves valuable hard disk space because aliases almost always take up less space than the original items they represent. Just be sure you make aliases of the archived items after copying them to floppies, not before. If you make aliases of the items while they are still on the hard disk, the aliases stop working when you delete the original items from the hard disk after copying them to floppies. (Remember, aliases point to the original items, not to copies of the originals on other disks.)

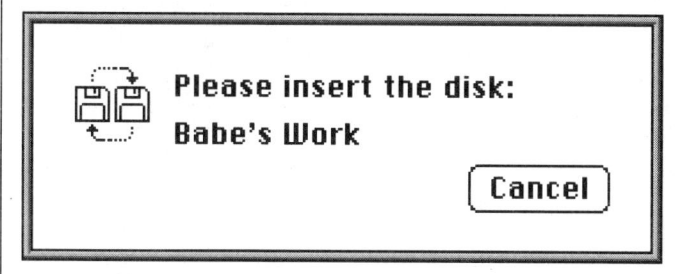

Please insert the disk:
Babe's Work

[Cancel]

Figure 6-6: Opening an item archived to a floppy disk.

Aliases and CD-ROM

Slowly wading through folders on a CD-ROM can be a royal pain (unless you can somehow see the experience as stately pomp and circumstance). Cut through the drudgery by making aliases of items inside the CD-ROM folders. Because CD-ROMs are permanently locked, you must put the aliases on your hard disk (or a floppy disk). Opening an alias makes a beeline to the original item on the CD-ROM.

Aliases of shared items

System 7's file sharing capabilities enable you to share items from someone else's Macintosh connected to the same network as yours, but getting access to shared items involves wading through a fair amount of bureaucracy in the Chooser. Aliases cut through the red tape. Here's how: You access a shared disk or folder once using the Chooser (see "Sharing Someone Else's Folders and Disks" in Chapter 8). Next, you select the shared item or any folder or file in it and choose Make Alias from the File menu. Finally, you copy the alias to your desktop or hard disk, as shown in Figure 6-7. An alias keeps track of its original item even if the original item is on another networked Macintosh.

Once you have made an alias of a shared item, you can access the shared item by opening the alias either from the Finder or from an Open command's directory dialog box. Dragging something to the alias of a shared disk or folder also automatically accesses that shared item. You still must enter a password unless you initially accessed the original item as a guest. If the shared item is not available — for example, because the Macintosh where it resides is turned off — the Finder tells you it could not find the alias on the network.

Aliases keep shared documents current

Besides providing easy access to shared items from other computers, aliases can help you make sure others who share your documents have the latest version. Suppose, for example, you create a letter template that you want the rest of your group to share. By making an alias of the template and copying it to a shared folder, other users can copy the alias to their disks and use the alias to open the original template. If you later replace the original template with a version having the same name, the aliases that people already copied will open the new version. People who share the alias always get the newest version of the original item it represents, even if the original frequently changes.

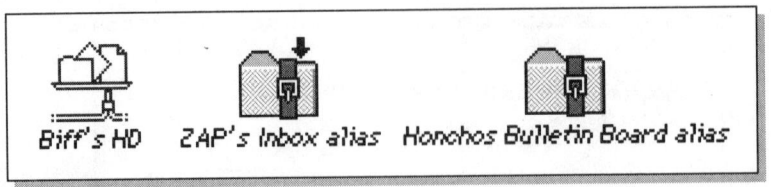

Figure 6-7: Aliases of shared items.

The only drawback to using an alias to share a template is that unless you're using a program that allows more than one person to open the same document, only one person can have access to the template document at a time. However, anyone who opens the template can quickly and easily save it with a different name and then close it to free it for someone else to open.

Your office on a disk

Aliases can give you nearly automatic access to your Macintosh's hard disks using a floppy disk in any other Macintosh on the same network. To easily access your disks from another Macintosh, open the Sharing Setup control panel (see Figure 6-8) and check the File Sharing status. If it is off, click the Start button and wait until it is on (the Start button becomes a Stop button at that time).

Next, select all your hard disk icons and choose Sharing from the File menu, opening a Sharing info window for each disk. In each window turn on the "Share this item and its contents" option and turn off the See Folders, See Files, and Make Changes options for the User/Group and Everyone categories, as shown in Figure 6-9. These settings restrict access to your disks so that only you can make changes or see files or folders. Make an alias of each hard disk and copy the aliases to a floppy disk. As long as file sharing is active on your Macintosh, you can use that floppy disk to access your hard disk from any Macintosh on your network. You simply insert the disk, open the alias for the disk you want to use, and enter your password when asked. Correctly entering your password allows you access to all applications, folders, and documents on your disk from any remote Macintosh. You don't have to bother with opening the Chooser, selecting Apple Share, selecting your computer, and typing your name as the registered user.

Figure 6-8: The Sharing Setup control panel.

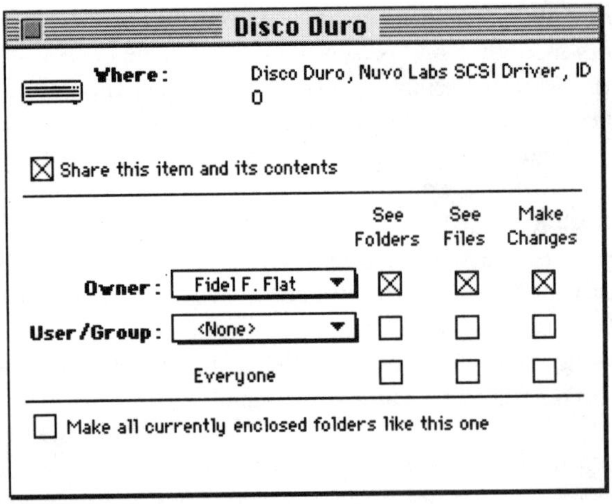

Figure 6-9: Access privileges for your office on a disk.

Summary

- Aliases look and act like the real programs, documents, folders, disks, or other items they represent. But aliases are actually small pointer files.
- Use aliases to add items to the Apple menu without moving those items from the folders they are in.
- Use aliases to increase the flexibility of the Startup Items folder.
- Use aliases to open frequently used programs, documents, folders, and control panels from the desktop while the real items remain buried in nested folders.
- Use aliases to speed access from directory dialog boxes to items buried in nested folders.
- Use aliases to speed access to archived items stored on disks that are not inserted and to items buried on CD-ROMs.
- Use aliases to streamline access to shared items from another Macintosh on your network and to keep items you share with other network users current.
- Use aliases to get nearly automatic access to your Macintosh's hard disks using a floppy disk in any other Macintosh on the same network.

Chapter 7
Smooth Text Everywhere

In This Chapter
- Comparing TrueType, fixed-size, and PostScript font technologies.
- Displaying samples of TrueType and fixed-size fonts.
- Installing and removing fonts.
- When to mix and not mix TrueType with fixed-size fonts.
- Printing with TrueType, PostScript, and fixed-size fonts.
- How TrueType fonts work.
- Samples of low-cost TrueType fonts.

Text looks great when displayed or printed with old Macintosh font technology if you stick to a half-dozen font sizes, usually 9, 10, 12, 14, 18, and 24 points. Apple's TrueType font technology, a standard part of System 7, makes odd sizes and big sizes like 11, 13, 36, 100, and 197 look just as good.

TrueType fonts work with the programs you already have. You can mix them with the fixed-size fonts and PostScript fonts you already have. They work with all Macintosh models and all types of printers, including PostScript printers.

Three Font Technologies

Your Macintosh can display and print text using three types of fonts: fixed-size, TrueType, and PostScript. Which looks best depends on the font size and the output device (display screen or type of printer).

About fixed-size fonts

Before the advent of TrueType fonts, the Macintosh system software used fixed-size fonts for displaying text on screen and for printing on many types of printers. A fixed-size font contains exact pictures of every letter, digit, and symbol for one size of a font, as shown in Figure 7-1. Fixed-size fonts are often called bitmap fonts because each picture precisely maps the dots, or bits, to be displayed or printed for one character.

Each fixed-size font looks great in one size only, so fixed-size fonts are usually installed in sets. A typical set includes 9-, 10-, 12-, 14-, 18-, and 24-point sizes. If you need text in a size for which no fixed-size font is installed, the system must scale a

Figure 7-1: Times capital A and G bitmaps in sizes 12, 14, and 18.

fixed-size font's character bitmaps up or down to the size you want. The results are lumpy, misshapen, or blocky, as shown in Figure 7-2.

About TrueType fonts

TrueType fonts don't use fixed bitmaps to define characters. Instead they use curves and straight lines to outline each character's shape. Because of this methodology, they are sometimes called outline fonts, as shown in Figure 7-3.

Figure 7-2: Fixed-size Times (9, 10, 12, 14, 18, and 24 installed).

TrueType fonts are variable-size fonts. The Macintosh system software can smoothly scale a single TrueType font's character outlines to any size, large or small, with good results, as shown in Figure 7-4.

About PostScript fonts

TrueType fonts look great in any size on screen or output on any printer, but this is nothing new. Adobe Type Manager (ATM) has done the same with PostScript fonts since 1989. Like TrueType fonts, PostScript fonts use outlines to define character shapes, and consequently they look good at any size.

Figure 7-3: Outline for TrueType Times capital G.

Although PostScript fonts were originally designed for printing on LaserWriters and other PostScript output devices, ATM smoothly scales PostScript fonts to any size for non-PostScript printers and the display screen, just like TrueType. With ATM and PostScript fonts, you don't need a set of fixed-size or TrueType fonts for the screen display.

Many longtime Macintosh users have invested thousands of dollars in PostScript fonts, and for them it makes sense to stick with PostScript and ATM. Recognizing that these people and people with PostScript printers may prefer ATM to PostScript, Apple teamed with Adobe and they now practically give away ATM in the US and Canada (ask your authorized Apple dealer or call the Apple assistance center at 800-776-2333). Apple and Adobe have agreed to put ATM technology in a future version of System 7.

Figure 7-4: TrueType Times.

If you don't already have a collection of PostScript fonts, you may prefer to go with TrueType instead. There are more PostScript fonts than TrueType, but TrueType fonts generally cost less and some are free. For example, TrueType versions of the 11 standard LaserWriter fonts come free with System 7. To make use of ATM, you must buy PostScript fonts for your System Folder; fonts built into your printer don't help. For example, Adobe sells the basic four LaserWriter fonts — Times, Helvetica, Courier, and Symbol — for $49 (with the "purchase" of ATM). The Adobe Plus Pack, which includes the other seven standard LaserWriter fonts — Avant Garde, Bookman, Helvetica Narrow, New Century Schoolbook, Palatino, Zapf Chancery, and Zapf Dingbats — costs $198. Think of TrueType not as a challenger for PostScript fonts, but as a replacement for fixed-size (bitmap) fonts.

Recognizing best font sizes

You can usually tell which font sizes will look good on screen by inspecting the Font menu of a program you're using. The program highlights the best-looking sizes with outline-style numbers. All sizes of a TrueType font are so highlighted. Only the installed sizes of fixed-size fonts are highlighted, as shown in Figure 7-5.

About font styles

Text varies by style as well as size. The Macintosh system software can display and print four basic styles — plain, bold, italic, and bold italic — and many others (as listed in your friendly Style menu). The system can derive various styles by modifying the plain style, but you get better-looking results by installing separate styled versions of fonts, as shown in Figure 7-6.

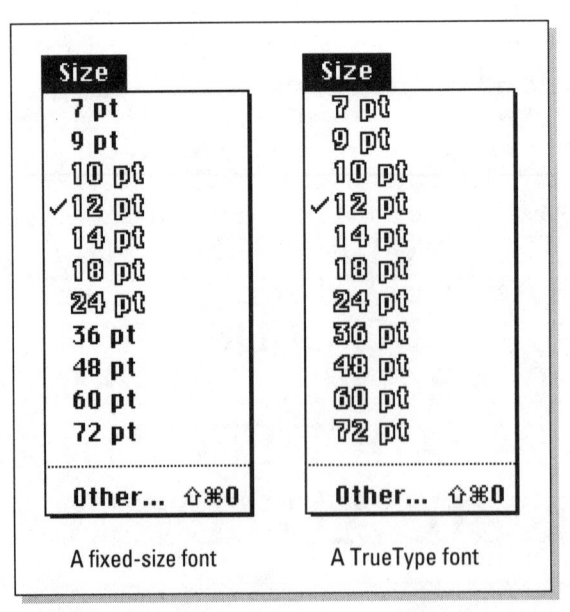

Figure 7-5: Smooth sizes are outlined.

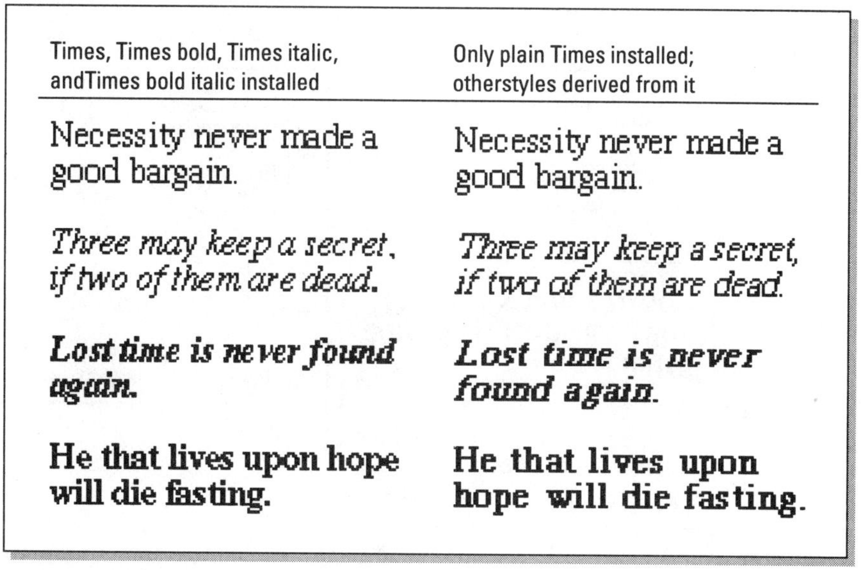

Times, Times bold, Times italic, andTimes bold italic installed	Only plain Times installed; otherstyles derived from it
Necessity never made a good bargain.	Necessity never made a good bargain.
Three may keep a secret, if two of them are dead.	*Three may keep a secret, if two of them are dead.*
Lost time is never found again.	*Lost time is never found again.*
He that lives upon hope will die fasting.	**He that lives upon hope will die fasting.**

Figure 7-6: Installed styles vs. derived styles.

Many fixed-size, TrueType, and PostScript fonts come in the four basic styles. Some PostScript font families include 20 or more styled versions. Collectively, all the styled versions together with the plain version of a font are known as a *font family*.

Seeing Font Samples

In System 7, all fonts can exist as individual items, each with its own icon, as shown in Figure 7-7. Icons of fixed-size fonts have a single capital *A* on them. Icons of TrueType fonts have three capital *A*'s, each a different size to suggest the variable sizing of the font. Icons of PostScript fonts may look like a generic laser printer or they may have custom graphics designed by the companies that make the fonts.

TrueType	Fixed-size	Adobe PostScript	Generic PostScript
Helvetica	Helvetica 12	Helve	SansSer

Figure 7-7: Font icons.

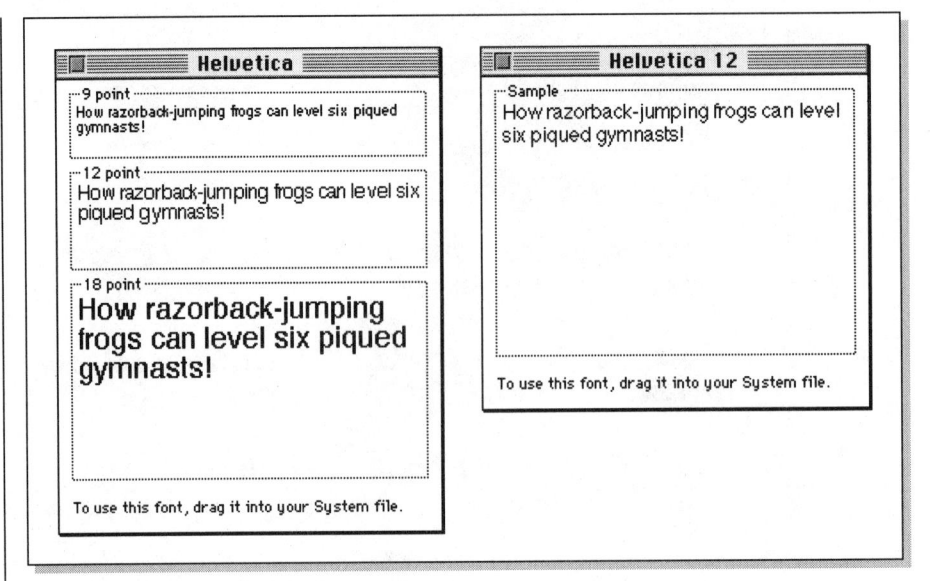

Figure 7-8: TrueType and fixed-size font samples.

You can see a sample of any TrueType or fixed-size font by opening the font from the Finder, as shown in Figure 7-8.

The fonts you're not using can be kept in any folder or on the desktop. You can also store spare TrueType and fixed-size fonts in font suitcases, which are created with the Font/DA Mover program for storing and distributing fonts in older system software. You do not need the Font/DA Mover program with System 7 because it enables you to manipulate fonts directly. You can create a new font suitcase file with System 7 by duplicating an existing font suitcase file, opening the duplicate, and dragging its contents to the Trash. You can also use version 4.1 of the Font/DA Mover with System 7 to create font suitcases.

The Fonts folder (the System file in System 7.0 or 7.0.1) is the place you install the TrueType and fixed-size fonts you want to show up in your Font menus. The PostScript fonts you want to use can go in the Fonts folder, the Extensions folder, or directly in the System Folder. With System 7.1, the Fonts folder is the preferred location for all types of fonts. With System 7.0 and 7.0.1, PostScript fonts should go into the Extensions folder. However, old software may not look in the right folders. If text prints in the wrong font on a PostScript printer or looks lumpy on screen, try putting PostScript fonts in the System Folder itself (not the Fonts folder or the Extensions folder). For example, Aldus PageMaker versions 4.01 and earlier and ATM versions 2.0 and earlier can't find PostScript fonts in the Extensions folder. ATM versions 2.0.2 and 2.0.3 look in the Extensions folder but not the Fonts folder, and PageMaker 4.2 knows about both the Extensions folder and the Fonts folder.

Adding and Removing Fonts

When you install System 7.1, Apple's Installer program puts a basic set of TrueType fonts and fixed-size fonts in the Fonts folder for you. You can add or remove both types of fonts at any time with Finder 7.1.

To add more TrueType or fixed-size fonts, you must first quit all programs that are open except the Finder. Then you drag the additional fonts to the System Folder icon, as shown in Figure 7-9. You can drag font suitcases, folders containing fonts, or loose fonts to the System Folder icon. You do not use the Font/DA Mover program as in older system software.

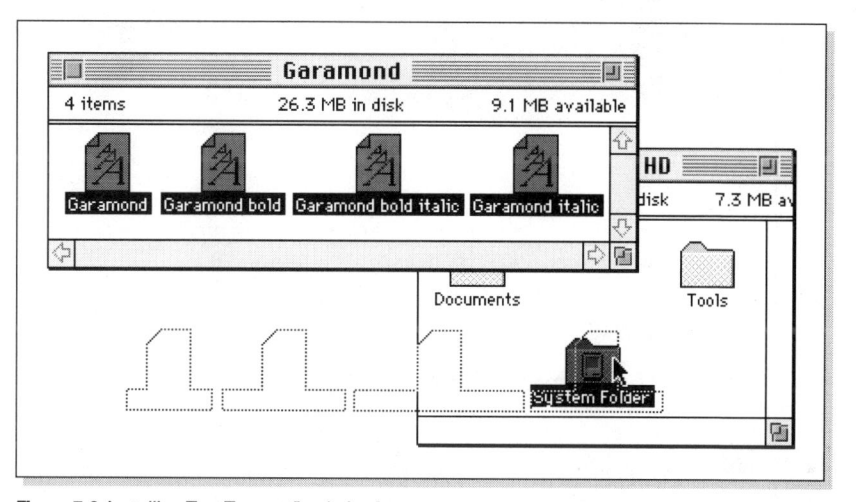

Figure 7-9: Installing TrueType or fixed-size fonts.

When you drag fonts to the System Folder icon, Finder 7.1 knows to put them in the Fonts folder where they belong, as shown in Figure 7-10. It automatically extracts fonts and font suitcases from folders that you drag to the System Folder icon. If a folder contains items other than fonts or font suitcases, Finder 7.1 puts the other items in the places where they belong (see "Adding to the System Folder" in Chapter 4). The Finder does not distribute items for you if you drag them to the System Folder window instead of the System Folder icon.

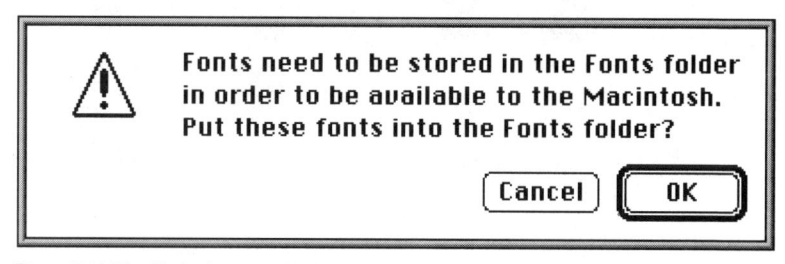

Figure 7-10: The Finder knows where fonts go.

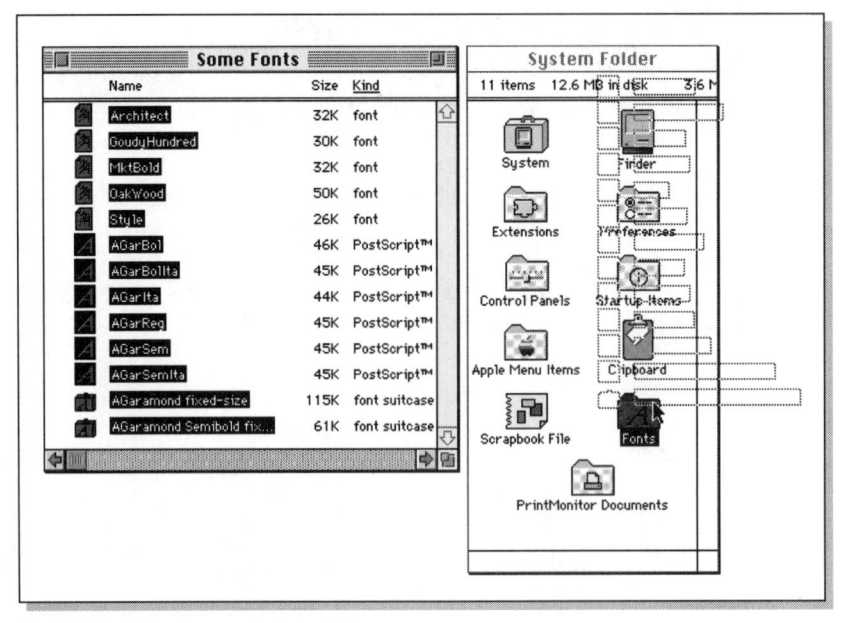

Figure 7-11: Adding fonts to the Fonts folder.

If you prefer, you can drag TrueType, PostScript, and fixed-size fonts directly to the Fonts folder icon, as shown in Figure 7-11. You can also open the Fonts folder and drag TrueType, PostScript, and fixed-size fonts to its window.

To remove fonts from your system, open the Fonts folder and drag the fonts to another folder, the desktop, or the Trash, as shown in Figure 7-12.

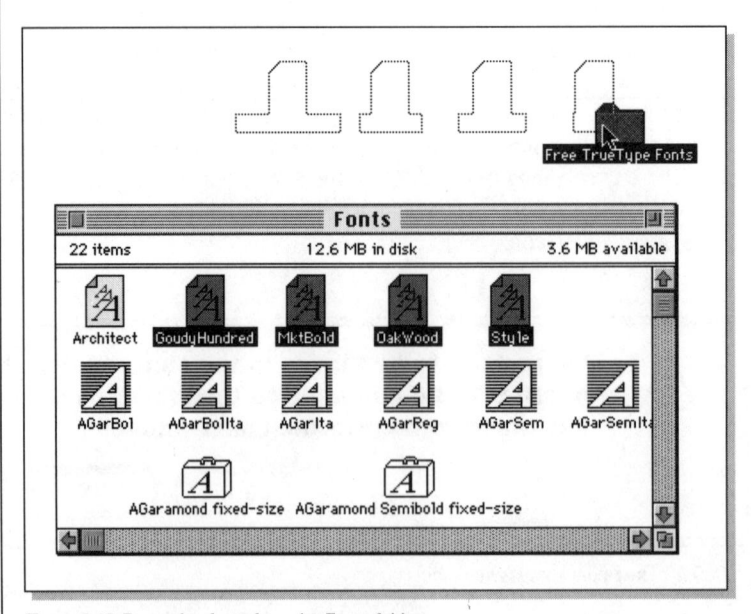

Figure 7-12: Removing fonts from the Fonts folder.

You can add or remove PostScript fonts from the Fonts folder any time, but you must quit all open programs before adding or removing TrueType or fixed-size fonts. (Inspect the Application menu to see what's open.) Changes take effect immediately, without restarting your Macintosh.

Combining Fixed-Size and TrueType Fonts

Look closely at some text in a TrueType font and the same text in an equivalent fixed-size font. You'll see differences in letter shape, width, and height that may affect text spacing, as shown in Figure 7-13. The TrueType fonts match the PostScript fonts used on printers better than fixed-size fonts. Fixed-size fonts display faster and many of them look better on screen in sizes below 18 points, however.

You can install TrueType and fixed-size versions of the same font together in the System file. For each font and size, the system software's first choice is a fixed-size font with its hand-tuned bitmaps. If the system can't find the right fixed-size font, it scales a TrueType font to the needed size. Note that when you install both fixed-size and TrueType versions of the same font, the system software always derives styled fonts from the fixed-size version, even if a styled TrueType version is installed. For

Today we are on the verge of creating new tools that will empower individuals, unlock worlds of knowledge, and forge a new community of ideas.	TrueType Times 12-point plain
Today we are on the verge of creating new tools that will empower individuals, unlock worlds of knowledge, and forge a new community of ideas.	Fixed-size Times 12-point plain
Today we are on the verge of creating new tools that will empower individuals, unlock worlds of knowledge, and forge a new community of ideas.	Fixed-size Times 12-point bold italic
Today we are on the verge of creating new tools that will empower individuals, unlock worlds of knowledge, and forge a new community of ideas.	TrueType Times 12-point bold italic

Figure 7-13: Comparison of letter shape, width, and height.

example, if you have a fixed-size 12-point Times and a TrueType Times italic installed (but no fixed-size 12-point Times italic), the system software derives a 12-point Times italic by slanting the fixed-size 12-point Times.

Individual programs can tell the system to ignore fixed-size fonts if a TrueType equivalent is available. You may be able to turn this behavior on and off in some of your programs. Check each program's preference settings for one that tells the program you prefer outline fonts. A decision to ignore fixed-size fonts in one program does not affect other programs. The general system preference for fixed-size fonts dominates in a program unless specifically overridden for that program.

Printing with TrueType

As much as TrueType fonts improve text displayed on screen, they improve printed text more. They work directly with printers that don't use PostScript. TrueType fonts also work in conjunction with PostScript fonts on printers that use them.

TrueType alone

With TrueType fonts in your System file, you're no longer limited to a few font sizes when printing on an ImageWriter or other non-PostScript output device. You can print any font size that fits on the page at the best resolution the printer can manage, as shown in Figure 7-14.

Without TrueType fonts, printers that don't use PostScript require extra-large fixed-size fonts to achieve their highest resolution. When you select Best quality for an ImageWriter II, for example, the system prints double-size fonts at a 50 percent reduction to get 144 dpi (dot per inch) resolution, twice the screen's 72 dpi. The scarcity of extra-large fixed-size fonts limits the number of font sizes you can print. Moreover, the extra-large fixed-size fonts take up 25K to 50K apiece on your startup disk. After installing System 7, you no longer need these extra-large fixed-size fonts. Remove them to free up disk space.

TrueType and fixed-size

If you have both fixed-size and TrueType fonts installed, text may not look quite the same on screen as it does on paper. Character shapes may be different. More importantly, spacing of words on the line may not match. When this happens, the system software has used a fixed-size font for display (at 72 dots per inch) and a TrueType font for printing (at a higher resolution). You can fix the problem by removing the fixed-size font from your System file. Some programs may also enable you to set an option that causes fixed-size fonts to be ignored.

TrueType and PostScript

Where System 7 displays TrueType fonts on screen, LaserWriters and other PostScript devices print PostScript fonts if the system software can find ones that match the screen fonts. The printer contains a basic set of PostScript fonts in its own permanent memory and you can put others in your System Folder. When used in conjunction with PostScript fonts, smoothly scaled TrueType fonts provide a much better match than fixed-size fonts between the screen and the printed page.

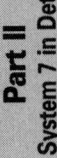

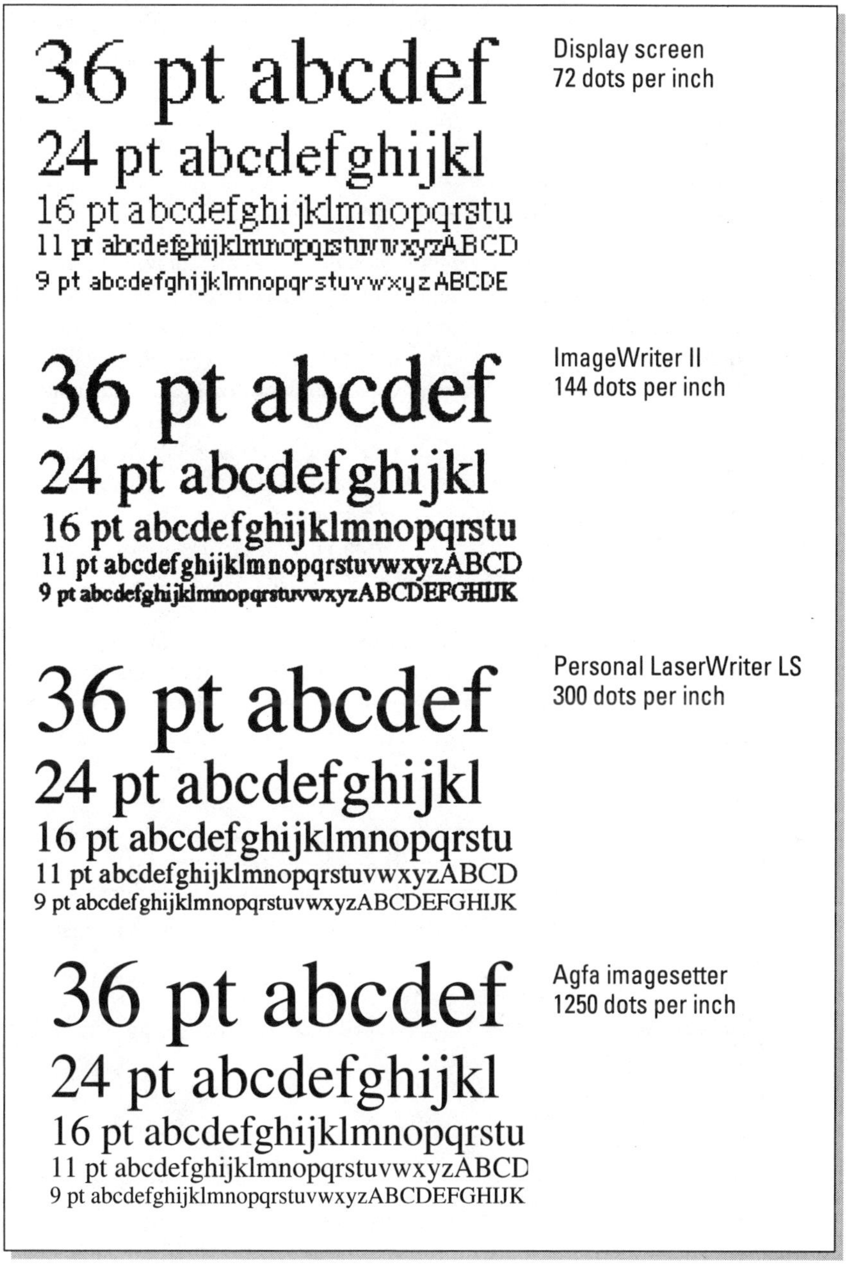

36 pt abcdef
Display screen
72 dots per inch

24 pt abcdefghijkl
16 pt abcdefghijklmnopqrstu
11 pt abcdefghijklmnopqrstuvwxyzABCD
9 pt abcdefghijklmnopqrstuvwxyzABCDE

36 pt abcdef
ImageWriter II
144 dots per inch

24 pt abcdefghijkl
16 pt abcdefghijklmnopqrstu
11 pt abcdefghijklmnopqrstuvwxyzABCD
9 pt abcdefghijklmnopqrstuvwxyzABCDEFGHIJK

36 pt abcdef
Personal LaserWriter LS
300 dots per inch

24 pt abcdefghijkl
16 pt abcdefghijklmnopqrstu
11 pt abcdefghijklmnopqrstuvwxyzABCD
9 pt abcdefghijklmnopqrstuvwxyzABCDEFGHIJK

36 pt abcdef
Agfa imagesetter
1250 dots per inch

24 pt abcdefghijkl
16 pt abcdefghijklmnopqrstu
11 pt abcdefghijklmnopqrstuvwxyzABCD
9 pt abcdefghijklmnopqrstuvwxyzABCDEFGHIJK

Figure 7-14: TrueType on various output devices.

If the system can find no PostScript equivalent for a TrueType font, it smoothly scales the TrueType font to the resolution of the printer. The PostScript printer prints the scaled TrueType font with quality equal to a PostScript font.

TrueType fonts do not signal an end to PostScript output devices for a number of reasons. For one, there are far more PostScript fonts available than TrueType fonts. In addition, PostScript can set text at any angle or along a curve or other nonlinear path. Also, PostScript offers more than outline fonts; it is a complete page description language.

Understanding TrueType Fonts

To understand why TrueType fonts look different from equivalent fixed-size fonts, you need to know how outline font technology works. Like any outline font, a TrueType font defines each character mathematically as a set of points that, when connected, outline the character's shape. The Macintosh system software can vary the font size by moving the points closer together or farther apart and drawing the character again.

After scaling the outline to the size you want, the system fills the outline with the dots that make up the text you see on screen and on paper. The dot size, which is determined by the resolution of the screen or other output device, governs how smooth the result is at a given size, as shown in Figure 7-15. Devices with more dots per inch produce smoother results, particularly at smaller point sizes.

At small sizes, however, simply scaling the font outlines results in text with unpleasant problems, such as gaps in diagonal lines or unwanted dots on the edges of curves. These imperfections happen because the outline does not precisely fit the

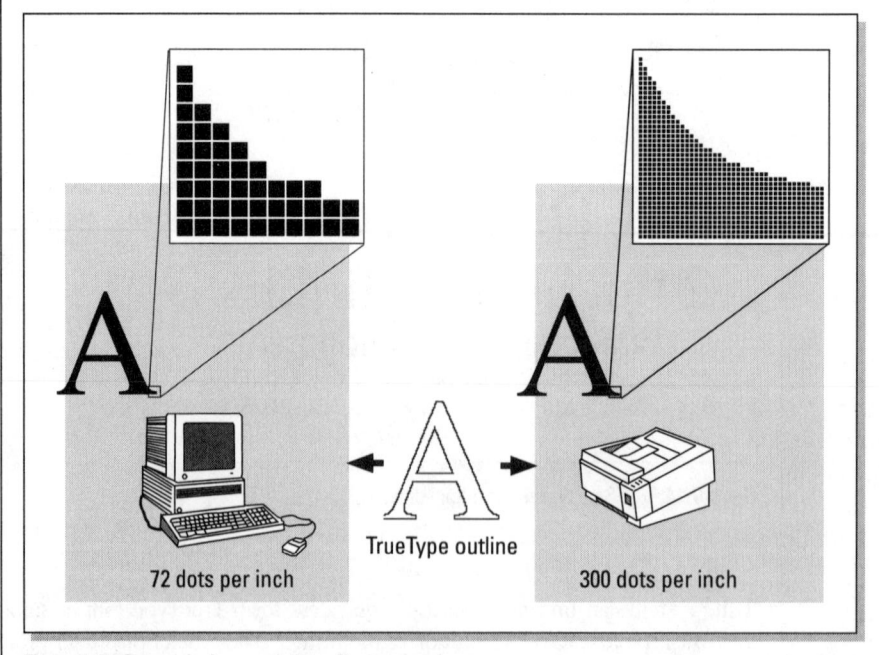

Figure 7-15: Output device resolution affects smoothness.

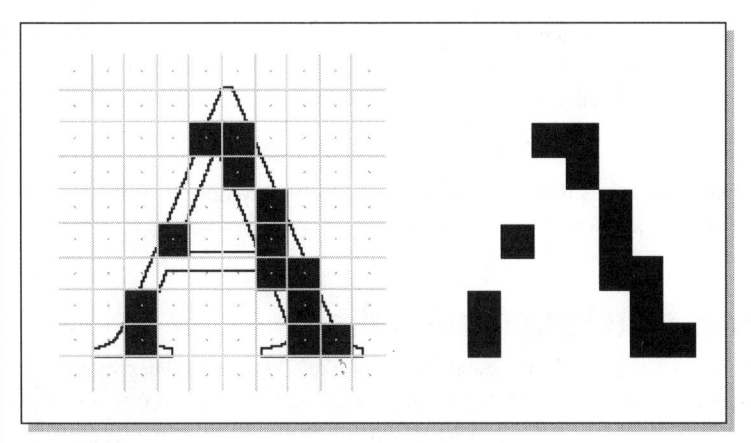

Figure 7-16: Grid fitting problems at small sizes.

grid of small point sizes, especially if the dots are relatively large as they are on the Macintosh's 72 dpi screen. On the display screen the system software must draw a typical 12-point letter in a space eight dots square. At small sizes and relatively low resolutions, deciding which dots to darken is difficult. The system reduces the True-Type outline, lays it over the grid, and darkens the dots whose center points fall inside the outline, as shown in Figure 7-16.

TrueType includes a mechanism for adjusting the outline at small sizes on low-resolution devices. The font designer provides a set of instructions, also known as hints, that tell the system how to modify character outlines so they fit the grid, as shown in Figure 7-17. This process is called grid fitting.

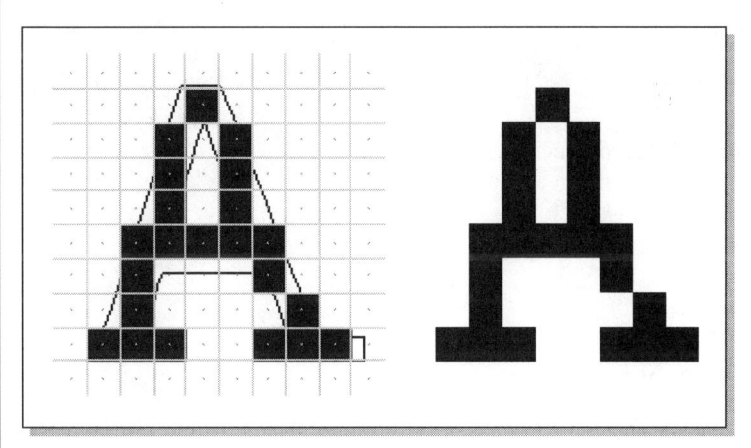

Figure 7-17: Hints modify outlines at small sizes.

High-resolution devices such as typesetters and film recorders usually don't need grid-fitting instructions. Their grid is so fine that the character outlines don't need adjusting to get filled with dots. A 300 dpi grid is four times finer than a 72 dpi grid, and a 1270 dpi grid is over 16 times finer.

Scaling and grid fitting happens so quickly you may not even notice it, especially if you have a fast Macintosh model. However, TrueType fonts are not as fast as fixed-size fonts and the lag is perceptible on screen.

TrueType Font Availability

System 7.1 comes with a standard set of TrueType fonts. They include TrueType versions of the PostScript fonts Times, Helvetica, Palatino, Courier, and Symbol; and the standard Apple fonts Chicago, Geneva, Monaco, and New York. Apple may add other TrueType fonts to System 7 over time, and may make more fonts available separately.

You can also get a variety of TrueType fonts at nominal cost from user groups and online information services. Figure 7-18 illustrates some of the available freeware and shareware fonts that are available. For more information on obtaining freeware and shareware products, see Chapter 13.

In addition, many type companies make TrueType fonts, including the following companies:

Agfa Compugraphic
200 Ballardvale Street
Wilmington, MA 01887
508-658-5600

Bitstream Inc.
215 First Street
Cambridge, MA 02142-1270
617-497-6222

Casady & Greene, Inc.
22734 Portola Dr.
Salinas, CA 93908
408-484-9228

Letraset
40 Eisenhower Drive
Paramus, NJ 07653
201-845-6100

Linotype-Hell Company
425 Oser Avenue
Hauppauge, NY 11788
516-434-2000

Monotype Typography Inc.
53 West Jackson Boulevard
Suite 504
Chicago, IL 60604
312-855-1440

Architect 18

ABCDEFGHIJKLMNOPQRSTUVWXYZab
cdefghijklmnopqrstuvwxyz123456789
0I'm tryin' to think, but nuttin' happens.

GoudyHundred 18

ABCDEFGHIJKLMNOPQRSTUVWXY
Zabcdefghijklmnopqrstuvwxyz1234567890I'
m tryin' to think, but nuttin' happens.

Market Bold 14

ABCDEFGHIJKLMNOPQRSTUVWXYZabc
defghijklmnopqrstuvwxyz1234567890I'm
tryin' to think, but nuttin' happens.

Oakwood 18

ABCDEFGHIJKLMNOPQRSTUVWXYZabcd
efghijklmnopqrstuvwxyz1234567890I'm
tryin' to think, but nuttin' happens.

Style 16

ABCDEFGHIJKLMNOPQRSTUVWXYZab
cdefghijklmnopqrstuvwxyz1234567890I'm
tryin' to think, but nuttin' happens.

Figure 7-18: Some freeware and shareware TrueType fonts.

Summary

- Fixed-size fonts look best at their installed sizes; TrueType fonts look good at any size on any screen or printer; and PostScript fonts look good at any size on any PostScript printer.
- With Adobe Type Manager (ATM) software installed, PostScript fonts look good at any size on screen or output on any printer (not just PostScript printers).
- You can see samples of fixed-size and TrueType fonts by opening them in the Finder.
- You add and remove fonts by dragging icons in the Finder.
- Fixed-size fonts look better on the display screen than many TrueType fonts at sizes below 18 points, but TrueType fonts look better when printed. You can mix both types in the same system.
- The system chooses the fixed-size version of a font over the TrueType version when both are present.
- Where System 7 displays TrueType or fixed-size fonts on screen, PostScript printers substitute PostScript fonts if the system software can find ones that match the screen fonts.

Chapter 8
File Sharing for the Rest of Us

In This Chapter

✔ A description of networks and network services, including file sharing.

✔ Building a network, identifying yourself on it, and making your Macintosh available to others on the same network.

✔ Accessing a network over standard telephone lines.

✔ Designating which folders and disks you want to share, with guidelines for optimizing sharing and preventing potential problems.

✔ Who can access your shared items: all about the owner, guests, and registered users.

✔ Granting privileges that determine who can see and change your files and folders, with instructions for making a private in-box folder and a bulletin-board folder.

✔ Seeing which folders and disks you are sharing and who is connected to your computer.

✔ Sharing folders and disks from someone else's Macintosh.

Similar to a library, file sharing enbales you to share files, folders, and disks with people whose computers are connected to yours in a network. You can share items from your Macintosh with others, they can share their items with you, and they can share their items with each other. In effect, these network users become librarians of their shared information, controlling who has access to shared items and determining what a user can do to files. Your network may consist of two computers in the same room, several computers located near each other, or a number of computers scattered throughout a building. Your computer can even join the network from a distance by telephone. This chapter explains how to use System 7's new file sharing capabilities to manage the flow of shared information across a network of any complexity.

System 7's Distributed File Sharing

System 7's built-in networking capabilities make sharing items across a network surprisingly easy. Previously, to create a network to share items, you needed to purchase additional networking software, such as AppleShare or Tops. With System 7 and LocalTalk or LocalTalk-compatible connectors, you can easily create a ready-to-use network for sharing files, folders, and disks. File sharing is one type of network service; networks can also provide printing services, modem and fax modem services, and more.

File sharing can be implemented in either a distributed or centralized fashion. In a distributed file sharing network, each Macintosh user makes files, folders, and disks available to other people using the network. While you are sharing your files you are free to use your Macintosh for normal tasks. In contrast, a centralized file sharing network enables everyone to share items from a computer dedicated to provide file sharing services, referred to as a *dedicated file server*. Usually, the Macintosh acting as a dedicated file server needs more than minimal processing capabilities, such as a Macintosh LC, LC II, Classic II, or SE/30 with a large hard disk, to handle network demands.

System 7's file sharing capabilities are designed for distributed file sharing among up to ten users at once. (More than ten can be connected to the network, but only ten can share files at the same time.) You can also use System 7's file sharing capabilities on a Macintosh dedicated to sharing files, making it a dedicated file server. Many people can access a shared folder or disk at the same time, but only one person can use a shared file at a time unless the application program involved is a network version, which enables multiple users to work with the same program or document. For best performance, multiuser application programs and their documents are usually kept on a dedicated file server.

AppleShare 3.0 dedicated file server

A network with more than ten people actively sharing files needs a dedicated file server like Apple's AppleShare Server 3.0 software. It extends network file sharing and background printing services beyond System 7's standard capabilities. Installing AppleShare Server 3.0 software turns any Macintosh into an efficient centralized file server capable of sharing the files and folders on its hard disk (or disks) among 120 users of Macintosh, Apple II, and MS-DOS computers on an AppleTalk network.

Centralized disk storage reduces the amount of local disk storage required by each networked computer, while providing a way for people who work together to share information. People can store files on the server's disks where other people can open or copy them. Many people can access the server's disks and folders simultaneously, and new files become instantly available to everyone. Unlike the file sharing provided by System 7, no one uses the server's Macintosh to do personal work because it is dedicated to providing network services. Conversely, your Macintosh is never burdened when someone else on the network accesses one of your shared items on the AppleShare server's disk.

A centralized file server is set up and maintained by a trained person called a network administrator. The AppleShare Server 3.0 software includes organizational, administrative, and security features to manage file access on the network. The network administrator does not control access to folders and files on the server's disks; that is the responsibility of each person putting items there.

AppleShare's file sharing capabilities are compatible with System 7's. You use the same methods (described in this chapter) to share your files with others, to control access to them, and to access files others have made available to you.

Connecting Your Network

You establish a LocalTalk network by simply plugging Apple's LocalTalk connectors into the printer ports of two or more Macintosh computers and connecting them with LocalTalk wiring. For a less expensive network that actually performs better, you can also use Farallon's PhoneNet connectors and ordinary telephone cables. Either way you have a basic LocalTalk network.

System 7 includes optional software for connecting your Macintosh to two other types of networks: EtherTalk and TokenTalk. These are sophisticated networking options that provide more powerful networking capabilities than LocalTalk, but require more expensive wiring and extra-cost internal or external adapters. You install EtherTalk or TokenTalk software using the same Installer program that installs System 7.

Your Macintosh can connect to an AppleTalk network through another Macintosh over standard telephone lines. Both computers need compatible modems and copies of Apple's AppleTalk Remote Access software. Once connected, you can use System 7's file sharing to access shared files on the computers connected to the network, and you can access other network services as well. AppleTalk Remote Access can call into any type of AppleTalk network — LocalTalk, PhoneNet, EtherTalk, or TokenTalk.

You set up AppleTalk Remote Access with the Remote Access control panel, as shown in Figure 8-1, specifying the type of modem you have and the port it's connected to. To connect, you have your copy of AppleTalk Remote Access call AppleTalk Remote Access on the computer whose network you want to access, as shown in Figure 8-2. Data travels over the phone lines as sounds, and the modems convert between the sounds and the computer's digital data. You can't let anyone on the network access your shared files, but you can access files (using the methods described in this chapter) that people on the network have made available for sharing exactly as if you were connected locally to the network.

Figure 8-1: The Remote Access Setup control panel.

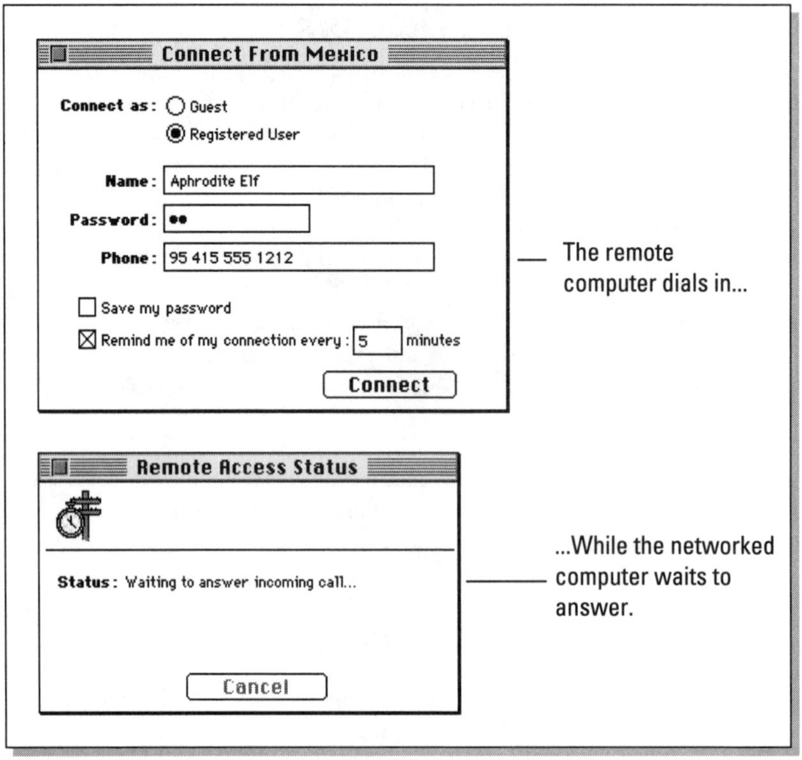

Figure 8-2: Connecting to a distant network with AppleTalk Remote Access.

Selecting Your Network

If your Macintosh has an EtherTalk or TokenTalk network connection, you switch between LocalTalk and the other network or networks using the Network control panel. If your Macintosh is using AppleTalk Remote Access to connect to a remote network, you can use the Network control panel to disconnect from your local network (if any). You would do this if you were unable to access a device on the remote network because it was being masked by a device on your local network, or if you had no local network and needed to use your Printer port for a nonnetworked printer such as a StyleWriter. You don't usually find the Network control panel in your Control Panels folder unless your Macintosh is directly connected to a network other than LocalTalk (such as EtherTalk) or you use AppleTalk Remote Access.

The Network control panel displays the network option icons, as shown in Figure 8-3. To select a network, click its icon. A message warns that you'll lose any network services you're using with your current network connection, because you can only maintain a connection to one network at a time. When you switch to a different network, you'll no longer be able to access any file servers, printers, or other network services on the original network.

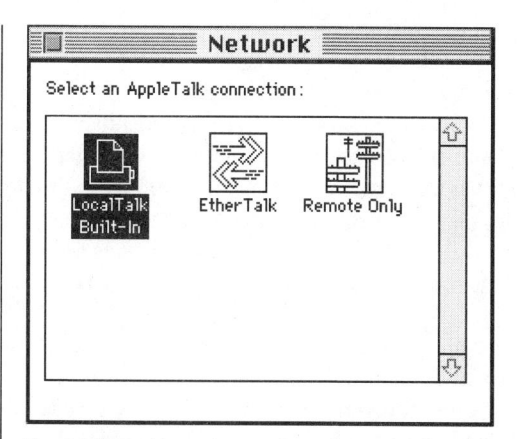

Figure 8-3: The Network control panel.

Turning AppleTalk on and off

As soon as you connect to a network and turn on your Macintosh, AppleTalk is automatically turned on for you. AppleTalk is the built-in software that allows your Macintosh to communicate with a network. In some cases, you may need to turn AppleTalk off, meaning you want to disconnect your Macintosh from the network. To turn AppleTalk off, use the Chooser desk accessory, as shown in Figure 8-4. Click the Inactive button to turn AppleTalk off. If you attempt to turn off AppleTalk when you're currently connected to a network service, such as file sharing, you get a message warning you these services will be disconnected. In this case, click the Cancel button, close the Chooser, and then close any shared items. Remember, if you turn off AppleTalk, it remains turned off until you turn it on again by clicking on the Active button in the Chooser.

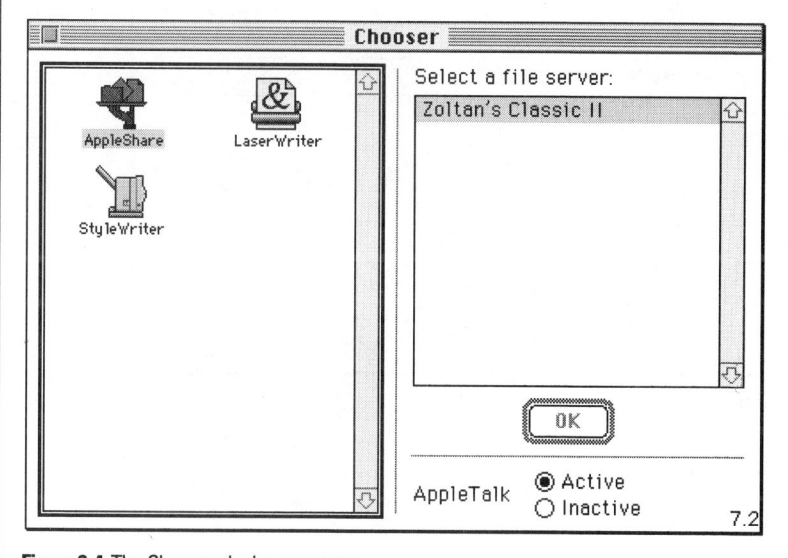

Figure 8-4: The Chooser desk accessory.

Identifying Your Macintosh

Before you can begin sharing files, you must identify your Macintosh to the network using the Sharing Setup control panel, as shown in Figure 8-5. Identifying your Macintosh involves entering the name of its owner, a password to prevent other users from connecting to your Macintosh as its owner, and a name for your Macintosh. Identifying the owner of your Macintosh plays an important role in determining who has access to your shared items. When people on the network want to share items from your Macintosh, they first select your Macintosh by name from a list in their Chooser.

The Owner Password can be up to eight characters in length. A password is case sensitive, meaning if you create a password that includes uppercase and lowercase letters, it must be reentered using the same uppercase and lowercase letters to gain access. Select a password that is easy to remember but difficult for others to guess. For better security, mix letters with numbers; try replacing the letters *I* and *O* with the numbers 1 and 0. You must know the Owner Password to access your Macintosh from another Macintosh on the network. After entering your password, the Sharing Setup control panel displays bullets in place of the actual password to prevent others from seeing the password.

In the Macintosh Name text box, give your Macintosh a name that others will easily recognize when they see it in their Choosers. If a name already appears in the Macintosh Name text box, you can use that name or type a new one. You can change any of these settings at a later time by returning to the Sharing Setup control panel.

Figure 8-5: The Sharing Setup control panel.

Starting File Sharing

You also use the Sharing Setup control panel to start up, or activate, file sharing. This enables the network users to access your computer and its shared items. To start file sharing, click the Start button in the File Sharing section of the Sharing Setup control panel. The Start button's label changes to Cancel, and the status message next to the button describes what is happening while file sharing is starting up. When the status line says, "File sharing is now on" and the button's label changes to Stop, your Macintosh is ready to share files. You can close the Sharing Setup control panel any time after clicking the Start button, but you won't know precisely when file sharing is enabled if you do.

If you shut down or restart your Macintosh while file sharing is on, System 7 automatically starts up file sharing when the Macintosh is next started up. In other words, file sharing stays on until you explicitly stop it.

You can stop file sharing so other users on the network cannot access your computer. Stopping file sharing does not unshare items you've already designated as shared (as described in the next section), but instead denies other users on the network all access to any of your shared items until you turn on file sharing again. To stop file sharing, click the Stop button in the Sharing Setup control panel. The system asks you to enter the number of minutes' warning to be given to anyone sharing items from your Macintosh. Allow enough time for people sharing items from your Macintosh to be able to close any shared items. Every Macintosh sharing items from your Macintosh sees a message indicating that access to your computer is going to be disconnected at the end of the time you specified, as shown in Figure 8-6. The same message goes out when you shut down or restart your Macintosh with file sharing on. Caution: People sharing your items receive no notification of impending shutdown if you shut down or restart your Macintosh with the At Ease Special menu (instead of the Finder).

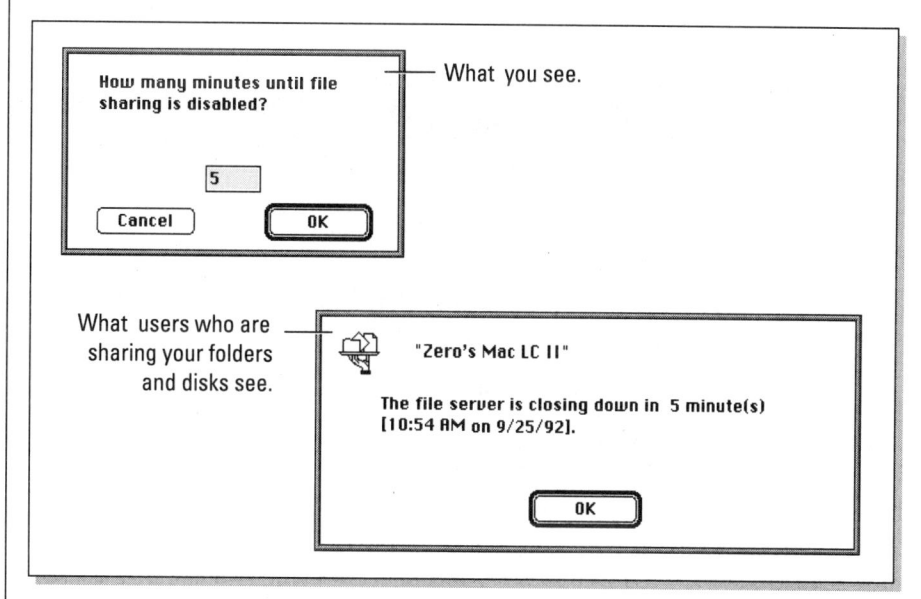

Figure 8-6: When you stop file sharing.

If you're planning to share a CD-ROM or removable hard disk, you must insert the disk before starting up file sharing with the Sharing Setup control panel. You can only share disks whose icons are on your desktop when you start up file sharing. Conversely, be sure to eject a CD-ROM or removable hard disk that you do not want to share before starting file sharing. You cannot eject a CD-ROM or removable hard disk that was mounted when sharing started; you have to turn off sharing before ejecting.

Sharing Your Folders and Hard Disks

After identifying your Macintosh and activating file sharing, you designate the folders and hard disks you want to share. You can share up to ten folders and hard disks (including CD-ROMs and removable hard disks) at one time. To share just one file, you must drag it into a folder and share the folder.

When you share a folder or hard disk, every item it contains is shared, including enclosed folders. You can't share a document by itself (outside a folder) or an item located on a floppy disk. Once you share a folder or hard disk, you can drag unshared items into the shared folder or hard disk to share them.

To make a folder or hard disk available for sharing, select the item and then choose Sharing from the File menu to see the Sharing info window, in which you specify access privileges, as shown in Figure 8-7. Turn on the "Share this item and its contents" option. The remaining options in the Sharing info window establish which users can access the shared item and what privileges they have, as explained in "Controlling Access to Shared Items" later in this chapter. The initial settings for a shared item enable anyone on the network to access it and make any changes he or she wants. When you close the Sharing info window, the system asks if you want to save the changes to the access privileges that you've just made. If you click the Save button, the item is shared and available to everyone on the network. All items contained within the selected folder or hard disk are also available.

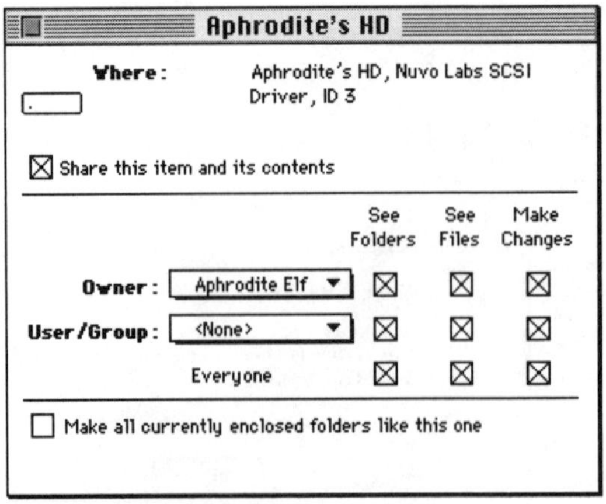

Figure 8-7: The Sharing info window.

Settings you make in an item's Sharing info window persist until you use the Sharing command again to change them. Shutting down or restarting your Macintosh does not affect Sharing info window settings, nor does stopping file sharing with the Sharing Setup control panel.

The icon of a shared folder on your Macintosh appears with network cables and a tabbed folder, indicating its shared status. When people on your network are connected to a shared folder, the folder icon displays faces in the center to indicate that it's in use, as shown in Figure 8-8. Note that shared hard disk icons, unlike folders, don't change. You can use the Views control panel to set icon size so you'll see the network folder icons. You can move a shared folder anywhere on your Macintosh, except a floppy disk.

You can't rename a shared folder or disk. Neither can you drag it to the Trash. Also, you can't eject and put away a removable hard disk or CD ROM that you are sharing. To do any of these things, you must first stop sharing with the Sharing Setup control panel or unshare the item.

You unshare any folder or disk with the Sharing command. In the item's Sharing info window, turn off the "Share this item and its contents" option and close the Sharing info window.

UNDOCUMENTED

If another user throws away a shared item from your Macintosh, a folder appears on your Macintosh with the label *Network Trash Folder*. As long as the user doesn't empty the Trash, the items thrown away appear inside the Network Trash Folder in folders labeled *Trash Can #1, Trash Can #2,* and so on, one for each Macintosh with something of yours in its Trash. To restore an item someone else has trashed, simply drag it out of the *Trash Can #* folder and rename it. You can set access privileges to prevent others from trashing your shared items, as described in "Controlling Access to Shared Items" later in this chapter.

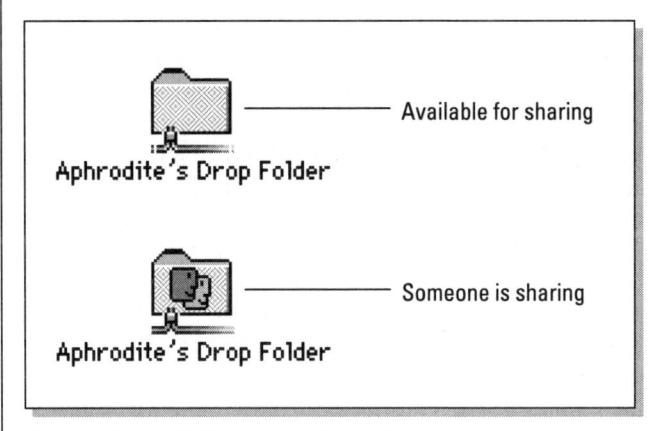

Figure 8-8: Shared folders on your Macintosh.

Guidelines for sharing folders and disks

There are several things you can do to optimize file sharing and prevent potential problems. The following are some guidelines and tips for sharing folders and disks:

+ **Share from the highest level of your disk and folder structure.** For example, a disk can't be shared if it contains an already-shared folder (no matter how deeply nested in the unshared disk). If you attempt to share a disk or folder that contains an already-shared folder, you get a message telling you the disk or folder cannot be shared because there is a shared folder inside it. To work around this situation, use the File Sharing monitor to identify the shared items (as explained in "Monitoring File Sharing Activity" later in this chapter), unshare it, and then share the enclosing disk or folder.

+ **Share as few folders as possible.** The more shared folders being accessed, the greater the memory demands on your Macintosh. Sharing too many folders can slow your system to a crawl.

+ **Check with any applicable licensing agreements before sharing folders containing programs, artwork, or sounds.** Often, licensing agreements or copyright laws restrict use of these items to a single computer.

+ **Set up a dedicated Macintosh to act as a centralized file server for the shared information.** This is often the most efficient way to share numerous files or share folders simultaneously with several users.

Who Can Access Your Shared Items

When you initially share a folder or disk with Systems 7.0 and 7.0.1, it's made available to every user on the network. Every network user can access the shared items on your Macintosh as a guest without any restrictions. This arrangement may be fine if you know and trust absolutely everyone who might use another network Macintosh to access your shared items. Otherwise, you should take steps to restrict access. System 7.1 is more secure than 7.0 and 7.0.1 because it does not permit guest access by default.

The Users & Groups control panel enables you to specify which users can access the shared folders and disks on your Macintosh, as shown in Figure 8-9. When you first open the Users & Groups control panel, there are two user icons already created. The one with the dark border is for your Macintosh's owner and the other is for guests (that is, anyone on your network). You create additional icons for registered users to whom you want to grant greater access privileges than guests have. Registered users must enter their names and any passwords you've assigned them before they can access your Macintosh to share information.

Once you create your set of registered users, you can use the Sharing command to specify the kind of access each user has to an individual shared item. You can also create groups of registered users and assign a group special access privileges to any item (again with the Sharing command). As many as 100 registered users and groups can be created in the Users & Groups control panel; however, you shouldn't name more than 50 for optimal performance.

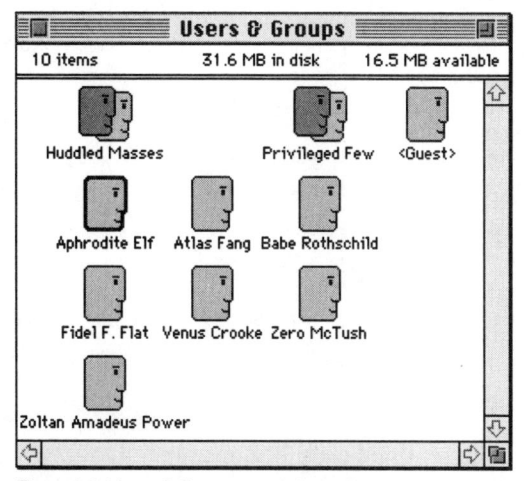

Figure 8-9: Users & Groups control panel.

The Owner

The Owner icon in bold outline in the Users & Groups control panel represents the owner of your Macintosh as a registered user. It's created automatically when you identify your Macintosh using the Sharing Setup control panel. The name of the Owner icon comes from the name in the Sharing Setup control panel's Owner Name text box. You have special access rights when you connect to your Macintosh as its owner from any other Macintosh on the network. Opening the Owner icon displays the owner privileges window, as shown in Figure 8-10. Turning on the "Allow user to connect" option gives you access to your Macintosh from another Macintosh connected to the network. Turn-

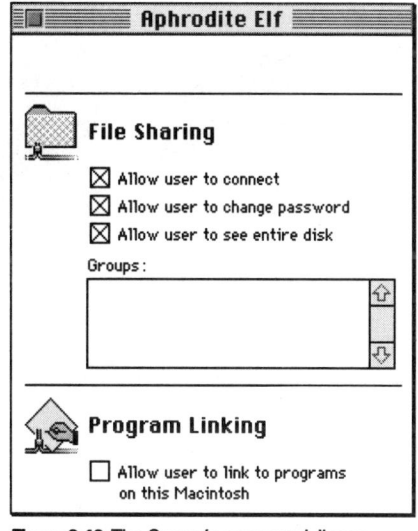

Figure 8-10: The Owner's access privileges.

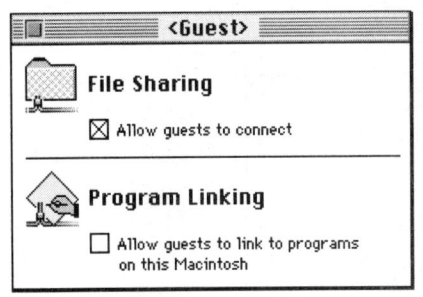

Figure 8-11: A Guest's access privileges.

ing on the "Allow user to change password" option enables changing your password remotely. The option "Allow user to see entire disk" enables you to see and use any items on any hard disk attached to your Macintosh. This setting gives you access to all shared or unshared disks and folders on your Macintosh (while connected to it from another Macintosh), whether or not you're named the owner of a shared folder and regardless of the privileges assigned to them.

Guests

The Guest icon in the Users & Groups window enables anyone connected to the network to access your shared information; however, you can restrict Guest access to your Macintosh. Generally, it's a good idea to prevent unwelcome users from accessing your Macintosh by restricting Guest access and granting specific access privileges to registered users. To restrict access privileges for individual shared items, see "Controlling Access to Shared Items" in this chapter. To disable all Guest access, open the Guest icon in the Users & Groups control panel to display the Guest privileges window (see Figure 8-11), and turn off the "Allow guests to connect" option in it. Now only registered users are allowed to share items on your Macintosh.

Figure 8-12: A new registered user.

Registered users

Establishing registered users helps secure your shared items from unauthorized access. To identify a registered user, first open the Users & Groups control panel. Next choose New User from the File menu to create a New User icon in the Users & Groups control panel, as shown in Figure 8-12. The New User command is only available when the Users & Groups control panel is opened.

Replace the name New User with the name of the user you want by typing the user's name while the icon name is selected. Registered user names are not case sensitive, so it doesn't matter how you mix uppercase and lowercase letters. You can save the user's time when connecting to your Macintosh if you use the Owner Name from his or her Sharing Setup control panel. Contact the user to get the right name. If you use a different name than the Owner Name, you need to notify the user of the name you enter here, since the user must type the exact name to be able to connect to your Macintosh. The user is now registered on your Macintosh and you can grant him or her special access

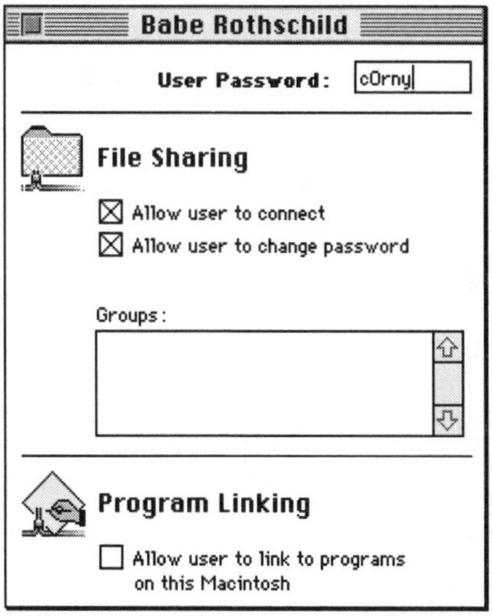

Figure 8-13: A registered user's access privileges.

privileges to specific shared items on your Macintosh. For information on setting access privileges of your shared items, see "Controlling Access to Shared Items" in this chapter.

You can add another level of security by assigning a registered user a password that he or she needs to type to access your shared items. You assign a password by opening the user's icon to see the registered-user privileges window, as shown in Figure 8-13. Enter a password up to eight characters long. Keep in mind that the user must type the password exactly as you type it here, including uppercase and lowercase letters.

Two additional settings in the registered-user privileges window enable you to specify the user's general access privileges. Turning on the "Allow user to connect" option permits the user to access your Macintosh. If you want to let this user change the password you assign, turn on the "Allow user to change password" option. When you're done setting the registered user's access privileges, close the registered-user privileges window to make them take effect.

You can modify a registered user's access privileges or remove the user from your set of registered users at any time. To remove a registered user, drag its icon from the Users & Groups control panel to the Trash.

AppleTalk Remote Access privileges

If you have installed the AppleTalk Remote Access software, the various user privileges windows include additional settings, as shown in Figure 8-14. You can allow or deny remote access to the owner, to guests, and to each registered user individually. For the owner and for each registered guest you can specify a call-back phone number. When AppleTalk Remote Access gets a call from a user who has a call-back number, the pro-

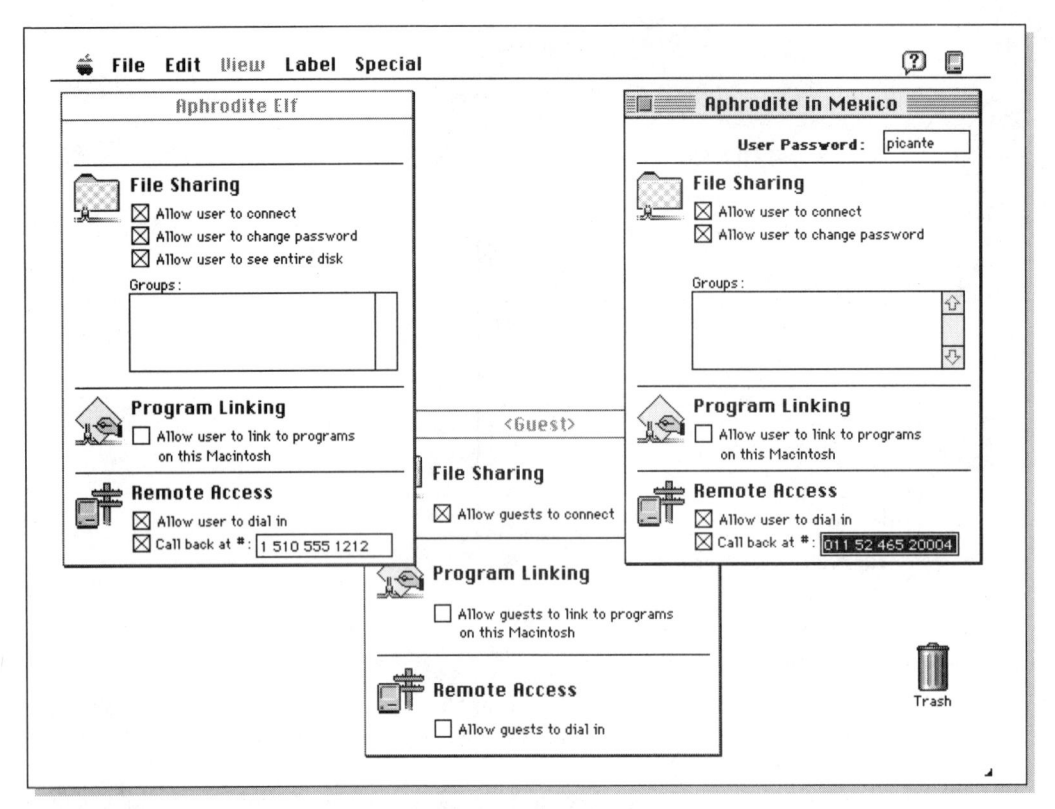

Figure 8-14: Remote access privileges for owner, guests, and registered users.

gram hangs up and calls the user back at the specified number. This safeguards against an unauthorized person gaining access to your computer by learning a registered user's password and trying to call from an unauthorized location. With a call-back number specified you have to pay the cost of the phone call for the connection, but you know the person accessing your computer has the correct password and is calling from the user's computer.

Groups of users

Office or work environments usually consist of groups of people, such as departments or project teams, who need to share common items. System 7's file sharing enables you to specify special access privileges for groups as well as individual users. Groups are simply collections of individual registered users, and you can grant specific access privileges for a shared item to a group instead of a single user. See "Controlling Access to Shared Items" in this chapter for information on setting access privileges of your shared items.

Figure 8-15: A new group.

To establish a group of users, open the Users & Groups control panel and choose New Group from the File menu. A new icon named New Group appears in the Users & Groups control panel, as shown in Figure 8-15. Notice the group icon is different from the single-user icon.

Replace the name New Group with your own group name by typing while the icon name is selected.

To add registered users to a group, drag their icons to the group icon. The system displays a message indicating the user or users are being added to the group. The registered-user icons are copied into the group icon. You can also drag the group icon to a user icon to add the user to the group. To speed up the process of adding users to groups, Shift-click to select all the registered users at once and then drag them to the group icon. You don't need to include the owner icon in groups.

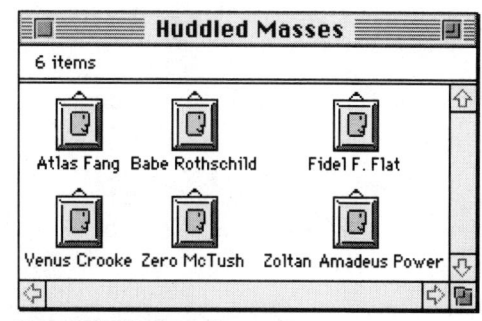

Figure 8-16: Members of a group.

To see the members of the group, open the group icon. The group window shows a member icon for every user in the group, as shown in Figure 8-16. If you want to see or change information for a registered user, you can open either the user icon or the member icon. You cannot create a new registered user from within the group window however.

To see all the groups that an individual user belongs to, open the registered or member user icon. In both cases, the user's access privileges window displays a list of groups the registered user belongs to, as shown in Figure 8-17.

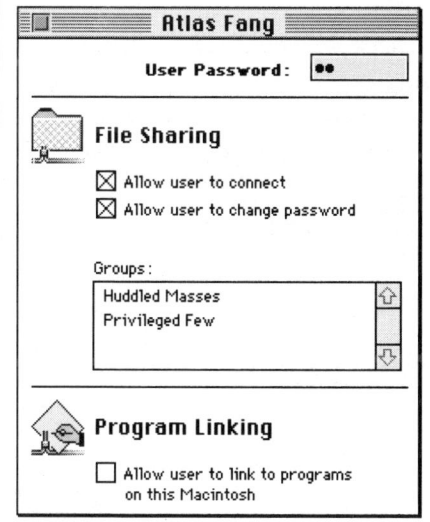

Figure 8-17: The groups a registered user belongs to.

Controlling Access to Shared Items

Anyone can use and make changes to a shared folder or disk and its contents when you first share the folder or disk. System 7 provides access privilege settings with which you control who can see and change your shared files, folders, and disks. You specify access privileges for three categories of users: the owner, one user or group, and everyone. For example, you might want to ensure that a user or group of users can access templates on your Macintosh but not be allowed to modify them. Access privileges also enable you to selectively share confidential documents, such as an employee's review.

You set the access privileges of a folder or disk in its Sharing info window, which appears when you select the folder or disk and choose the Sharing command from the File menu, as shown in Figure 8-18. You can't set a file's access privileges directly. Instead, you put the file in a shared folder and set the folder's access privileges.

Setting access privileges

There are three types of access privileges you can grant to each user category in the Sharing info window. Table 8-1 describes each of these access privilege settings.

Additional settings in the Sharing info window enable access privilege uniformity and more security for shared items. Turning on the "Make all currently enclosed folders like this one" option for a shared disk or folder assigns its privileges to folders you have recently moved into it and to folders in it that previously had different privilege settings. This option makes the privileges of all enclosed folders the same as the enclosing folder. When you're sharing a disk or folder for the first time, you don't need to turn on this option because the shared item's contents, as well as any new folders you later create in it, are automatically set to the same privileges as the shared item.

To prevent anyone on the network, including yourself, from moving, deleting, or renaming a shared folder, turn on the "Can't be moved, renamed, or deleted" option. This option is always in force for shared disks so it is not listed for them. You can set different privileges for a folder inside a shared folder or disk by turning off the "Same as enclosing folder" option in the enclosed folder's Sharing info window, as shown in Figure 8-19.

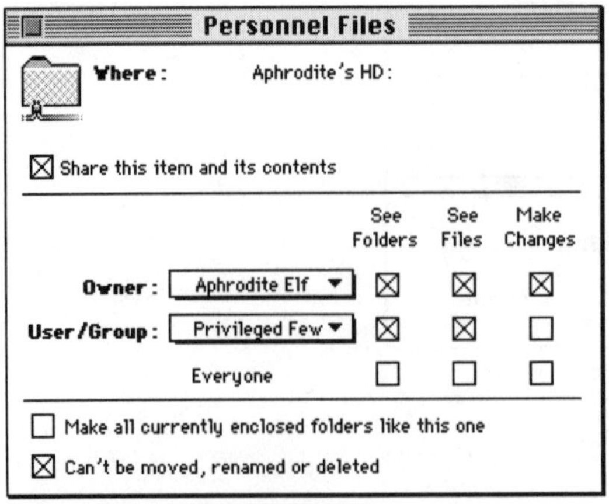

Figure 8-18: A Sharing info window.

Table 8-1:	Disk and folder access privilege settings
Privilege	*Purpose*
See Folders	Shows or hides folders enclosed in a shared folder or disk. Users who don't have this privilege can't see the folders enclosed in the shared folder or disk.
See Files	Shows or hides files enclosed in a shared folder or disk. Users who don't have this privilege can't see files enclosed in the shared folder or disk.
Make Changes	Allows designated users to make changes to the shared item, including duplicating, deleting, and saving.

Specifying who has access privileges

The Sharing info window displays three categories of users to whom you can grant or deny access privileges. The Owner category is the person or group that created the shared folder (not necessarily your Macintosh's owner). The User/Group category refers to one registered user or one group of users. The Everyone category refers to anyone who connects to your Macintosh as a guest. The three categories of users appear dimmed if the "Share this item and its contents" option is off or, for enclosed folders, if the "Same as enclosing folder" option is on.

Ownership of a folder or disk gives you the right to modify its access privileges. You can transfer ownership of a folder or disk to a registered user, to a group, or to any user on the network. To change ownership of a folder or disk located on your Macintosh, use the Owner pop-up menu in the Sharing info window. The Owner pop-up menu lists the registered users and groups to whom you can transfer the ownership of the folder, as shown in Figure 8-20. You can also change ownership of a folder or disk you own on someone else's Macintosh. In this case there is no Owner pop-up menu so you must type the new owner's name.

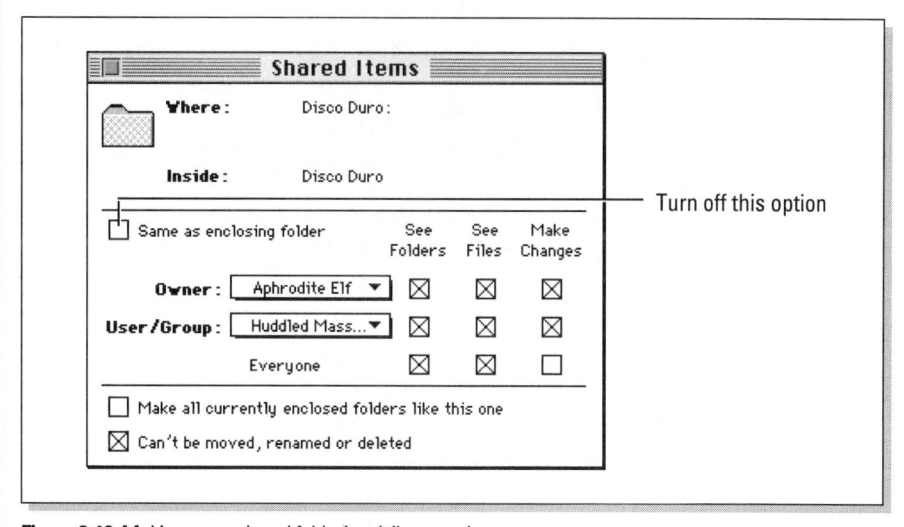

Figure 8-19: Making an enclosed folder's privileges unique.

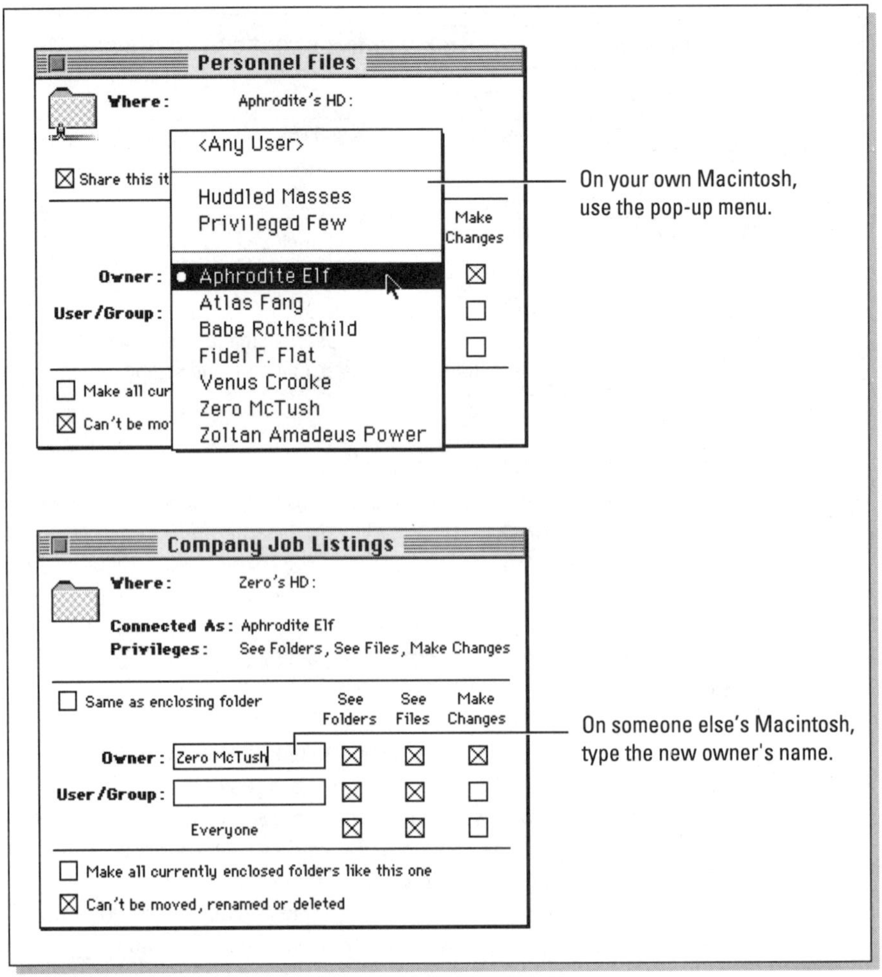

```
┌─────────────────────────────────────────────────┐
│  ▣════════ Personnel Files ══════════▣          │
│  ┌──┐  Where:      Aphrodite's HD:              │
│  │📁│                                            │
│  └──┘      <Any User>                           │
│  ☒ Share this it                                │
│            Huddled Masses          Make         │
│            Privileged Few         Changes       │
│                                                 │
│  Owner:  ● Aphrodite Elf           ☒            │
│            Atlas Fang                           │
│  User/Group:                       ☐            │
│            Babe Rothschild         ☐            │
│            Fidel F. Flat                        │
│  ☐ Make all cur                                 │
│            Venus Crooke                         │
│  ☒ Can't be mo                                  │
│            Zero McTush                          │
│            Zoltan Amadeus Power                 │
└─────────────────────────────────────────────────┘
```

— On your own Macintosh, use the pop-up menu.

```
┌─────────────────────────────────────────────────┐
│  ▣════════ Company Job Listings ══════════▣     │
│  ┌──┐  Where:       Zero's HD:                  │
│  │📁│                                            │
│  └──┘  Connected As: Aphrodite Elf              │
│        Privileges:   See Folders, See Files, Make Changes │
│                                                 │
│                             See   See    Make   │
│  ☐ Same as enclosing folder Folders Files Changes │
│                                                 │
│  Owner:  [Zero McTush]      ☒     ☒      ☒      │
│  User/Group:  [        ]    ☒     ☒      ☐      │
│              Everyone       ☒     ☒      ☐      │
│                                                 │
│  ☐ Make all currently enclosed folders like this one │
│  ☒ Can't be moved, renamed or deleted           │
└─────────────────────────────────────────────────┘
```

— On someone else's Macintosh, type the new owner's name.

Figure 8-20: Changing an item's owner.

Keep in mind that once you transfer ownership of a folder or disk, the new owner can restrict your access to that item and its contents — but only when you try to access the folder from another Mac on your network. Giving away ownership of a folder or disk on your Macintosh doesn't take away your ability to open, use, or modify it from your own Mac. In effect, an item can have dual ownership, giving two users ownership privileges. If you make another user the owner of an item on your Macintosh, both you and that other user have ownership privileges. Of course, you can reclaim sole ownership at any time by making yourself the owner in the item's Sharing info window.

You choose the registered user or a group to which you want to grant specific access privileges by choosing from the User/Group pop-up menu. It lists all the registered users and groups in your Users & Groups control panel, as shown in Figure 8-21. You can also change the User/Group setting for an item you own on another computer (or on your computer when you're accessing it from another computer on the network). In this

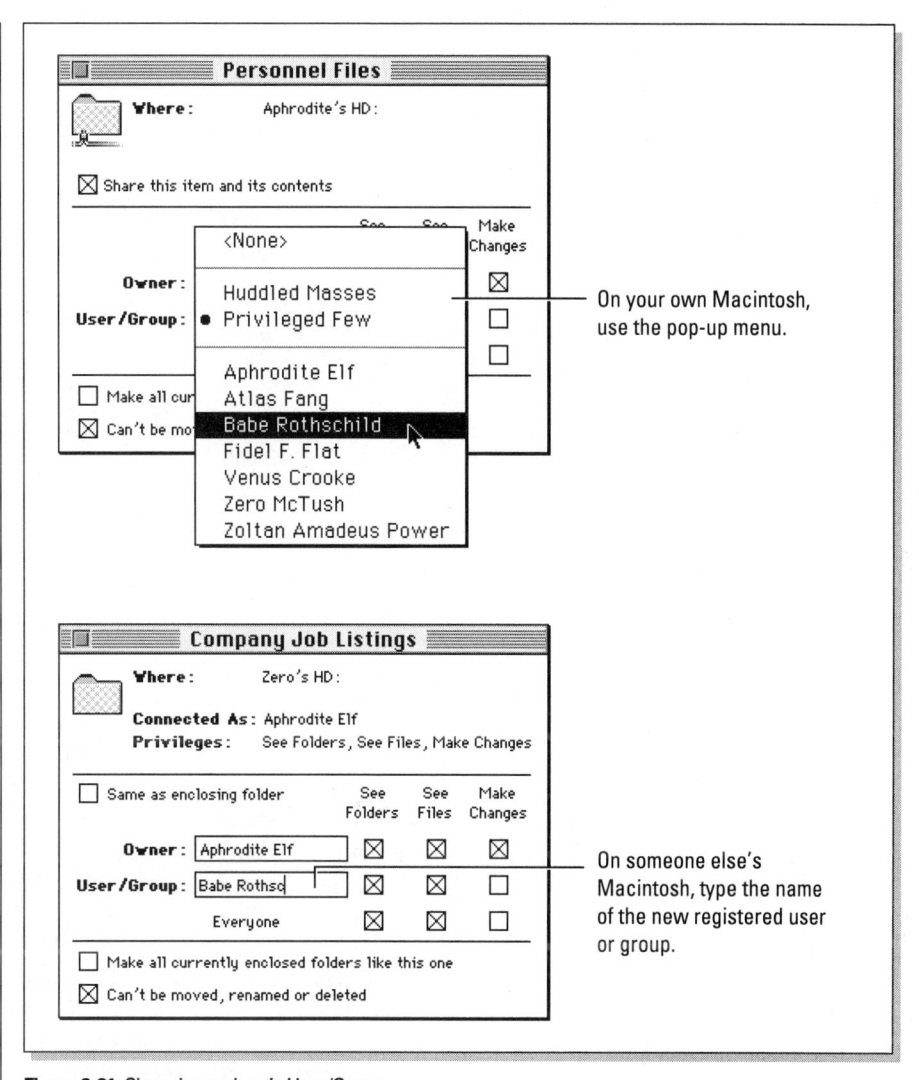

Figure 8-21: Changing an item's User/Group.

case, you must type the name of the registered user or group because the pop-up menu does not appear.

It's important to remember to set Everyone's access privileges less than or the same as the designated user or group, because the Mac does not grant registered users or the owner less privileges than guests. Furthermore, you want to set the User/Group privileges lower than the Owner privileges. For example, granting broad access privileges to the User/Group category is useless if you don't also restrict access privileges of the Everyone category. Just remember, rank hath its privileges.

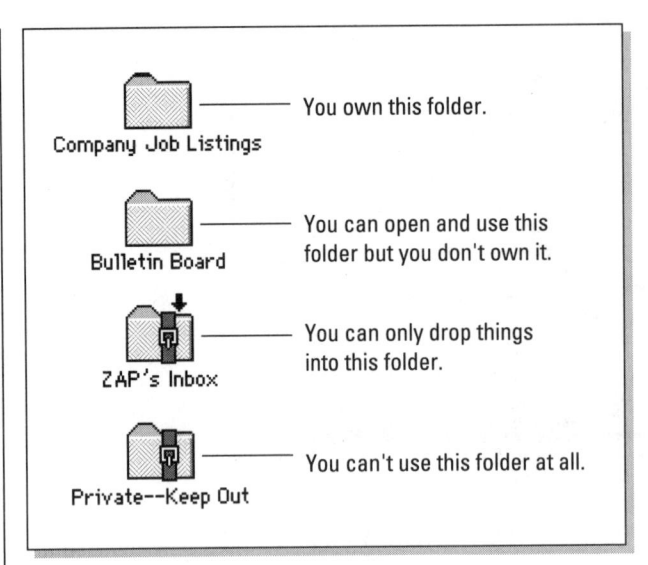

Figure 8-22: The four shared-folder icons.

Icon indicators for access privileges

People who share your folders can easily see the privileges you have assigned to a folder by looking at its icon, as shown in Figure 8-22. A folder icon with a belt around it indicates that the user doesn't have access privileges. A belt-strapped folder icon with an accompanying down arrow acts like a mailbox; the user can drop items in the folder but cannot open it or use anything inside it. A tabbed folder icon tells the user he or she is the folder's owner. A plain folder icon means the user can open and use the folder.

When you open a folder that belongs to someone else, look for one to three icons under the window's close box. The icons indicate any privileges the folder's owner has denied you. A pencil with a line through it means you can't make changes to items in the window. A document with a line through it means you can't see files in the window. A folder with a line through it means you can't see folders in the window.

Access Privilege Scenarios

Controlling who can do what with files in shared areas opens up new possibilities for working in groups. Using access privilege settings, you can keep folders private between two users or make them accessible to everyone on the network and lots of combinations between these extremes. The following sections explain setting access privileges for five interesting file sharing scenarios.

Universal access

Allowing everyone on the network access to a shared item and its contents is easy. Just grant the See Files, See Folders, and Make Changes privileges to the Everyone category, and it doesn't matter how you set the User/Group and Owner categories, as shown in Figure 8-23.

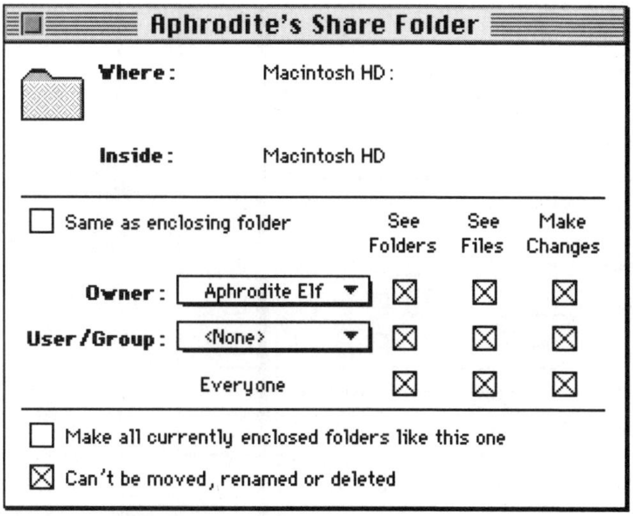

Figure 8-23: Access privileges for universal access.

Restricted access

If you want to allow one registered user or one group access to a shared item, but deny access to guests, turn on all privileges in the User/Group category and turn off all privileges in the Everyone category, as shown in Figure 8-24.

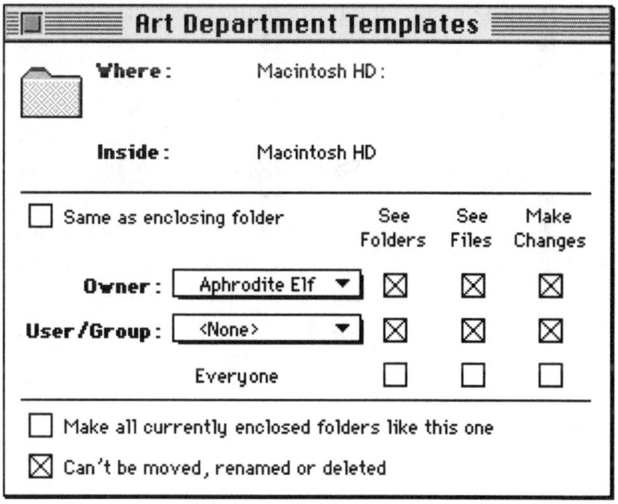

Figure 8-24: Access privileges for restricted access.

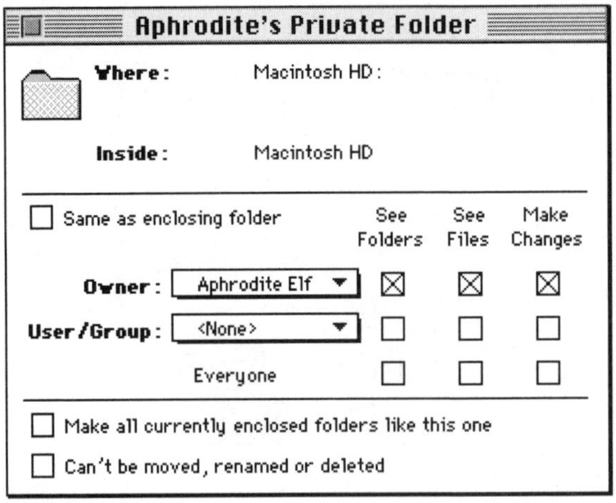

[Screenshot of "Aphrodite's Private Folder" Get Info window showing access privileges, with Owner: Aphrodite Elf having See Folders, See Files, and Make Changes checked; User/Group: <None> with no boxes checked; Everyone with no boxes checked.]

Figure 8-25: Access privileges for private access.

Private access

If you own a folder on someone else's computer, you can keep it private by turning off all privileges in the User/Group and Everyone categories, as shown in Figure 8-25. Only you and the user of that Macintosh can access your folder. Anyone connecting to that Macintosh sees a strapped folder without a down arrow, indicating he or she can't use the folder at all.

To keep a folder or disk on your own computer private, make sure its "Share this item and its contents" option is off; use the Finder's Sharing command to check.

A private in-box folder

Setting up a folder to act as an in-box, or in-basket, enables other network users to deposit documents, folders, and other items into it. This in-box is sometimes referred to as a drop folder, meaning other users can drop in items, but only you can take them out.

You prevent all other people from seeing, removing, or changing your folder's contents by denying the User/Group and Everyone access privileges to see folders and files, as shown in Figure 8-26. Anyone connecting to your Macintosh sees a strapped folder accompanied by a down arrow, indicating that they can only add folders and documents to the folder.

A user or group bulletin board

Another useful configuration of access privileges is to set up a folder to act as a bulletin board, enabling other users to open and read documents, but preventing them from adding or changing documents. To establish a bulletin board folder, create and name an empty folder. Select the folder and choose Sharing from the File menu. If you don't want

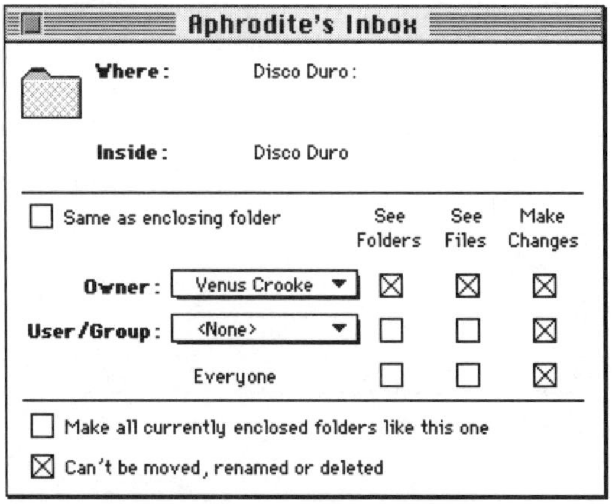

Figure 8-26: Access privileges for an in-box folder.

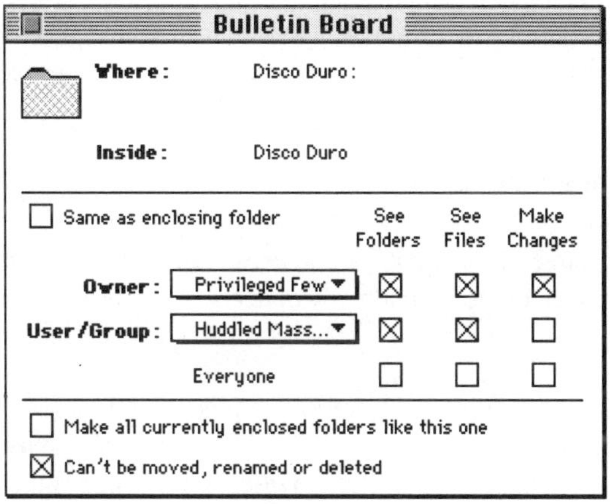

Figure 8-27: Access privileges for a bulletin board folder.

to share your bulletin board folder with everyone, select the user or group you want to have access to the bulletin board folder and set their access privileges to see folders and files. Deny privileges to make changes for the User/Group and Everyone categories, as shown in Figure 8-27. If you only want a user or group to access your bulletin board folder, deny all privileges to the Everyone category.

Monitoring File Sharing Activity

When file sharing is on, you can view who is connected to your Macintosh and list which of your folders and disks you are sharing. To monitor file sharing activity, open the File Sharing Monitor control panel, as shown in Figure 8-28. A list of your shared folders and disks appears on the left side of the File Sharing Monitor control panel. Only

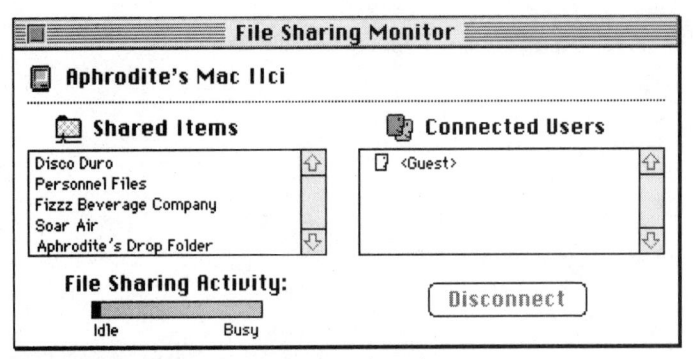

Figure 8-28: The File Sharing Monitor control panel.

the folders and disks you're sharing using the Sharing command are displayed; all the files and folders contained in them are also accessible although they aren't explicitly listed. A list of network computer users currently connected to your Macintosh appears on the right side of the control panel window. The File Sharing Activity indicator shows you how much of your Macintosh's total processing time is now being spent handling file sharing.

Temporarily disconnecting users

The File Sharing Monitor control panel also enables you to disconnect a user currently connected to your Macintosh. This disconnection doesn't turn off file sharing, like the Sharing Setup control panel, but temporarily disconnects all, or selected users, from sharing items on your Macintosh.

To disconnect a user, select the user you want to disconnect from the list of connected users in the File Sharing Monitor control panel. To select more than one user, press Shift while clicking the names of the users you want to disconnect. When you click the Disconnect button, the system asks you to specify the number of minutes you want to elapse before the disconnection occurs. It's good networking etiquette to give people enough time to save any changes they have made to the files before disconnecting them. To disconnect a user immediately, specify 0 minutes. Remember, this only temporarily disconnects the user; he or she can still connect again and access your shared folders.

Sharing Someone Else's Folders and Disks

Until now, you've created and set access privileges for items you're sharing with other network users. Other users on the network who are sharing their items have performed similar tasks to make folders or disks available to you and other users. Before you can access another user's shared items as a guest, you need to know the name of the Macintosh you want to access. To access the shared items as a registered user, you must also know your registered name and password on the other computer. If your network has zones, you also need to find out the name of the zone the other Macintosh is in.

Connecting as a registered user or guest

To make a connection to another Macintosh, open the Chooser. Make sure that Apple-Talk is active in order to connect to another Macintosh on the network, and click the AppleShare icon. If your network contains zones, click the zone in which the other Macintosh you want to connect to resides. The Chooser then displays a list of computers whose folders and disks you can share. From the list, select the name of a Macintosh to which you want to connect and click the OK button. A dialog box appears in which you identify yourself as a registered user or guest, as shown in Figure 8-29.

To connect as a registered user, click the Registered User button and enter your registered name and password in the spaces provided. This name and password must have been previously assigned by the owner of the Macintosh you want to access. Type your password exactly as assigned, including uppercase and lowercase letters, and then click the OK button. If you're not a registered user and the Guest option isn't dimmed, you can access the other Macintosh as a guest. If the Guest option is dimmed, guests are not permitted access to the selected Macintosh. If you're accessing your own Macintosh from another Macintosh, you enter your password (the owner password in the Sharing Setup control panel on your Macintosh). You can connect to another Macintosh on the network automatically by using aliases (see Chapter 6).

You change your password by clicking the Set Password button. A dimmed Set Password button indicates the owner of the Macintosh which you want to connect to does not allow you to change your password.

Selecting shared disks and folders

After connecting as a registered user or guest, the Chooser displays a list of the items you can share, as shown in Figure 8-30. A dimmed name indicates either that you're already sharing that folder or disk, or that its user hasn't granted you access privileges to see it.

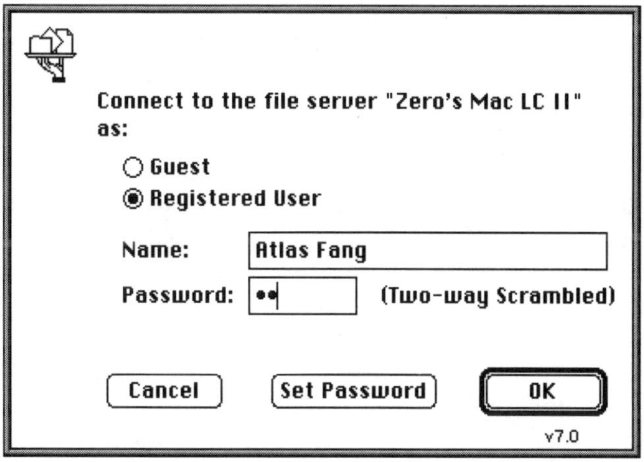

Figure 8-29: Identifying yourself to another computer.

Figure 8-30: The Chooser's list of shareable items.

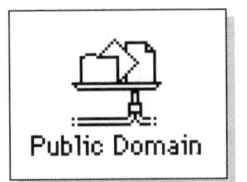

Figure 8-31: The icon of a shared disk or folder.

Select the name of the shared folders and disks you want to use. To select more than one, press Shift while clicking the names of the shared folders or disks you want. You can scroll through the list or type the first few letters of a shared item's name to find it. When you click OK to close the dialog box, a shared volume icon appears on your desktop, as shown in Figure 8-31. Your Macintosh treats a shared volume like a disk, no matter whether it's a folder or a disk on the owner's Macintosh. Table 8-2 shows the access privileges you need to perform common tasks with a shared item.

Automatically sharing items from another Macintosh

You also use the Chooser's list of shareable items to designate which of them you want System 7 to open automatically at startup time. This feature is a real timesaver if you frequently use certain shared folders or disks. Designate the items you want automatically opened by marking the check box next to each one.

If you mark a check box and are a registered user, two options appear in the dialog box below the list. Select the "Save My Name Only" option if you want the system to ask for your password before opening the shared folder or disk during startup. Use this option to prevent unauthorized people from accessing the shared folder or disk from your Macintosh. If you select the "Save My Name and Password" option, your Macintosh automatically supplies your password when it opens the marked items.

Working with items shared from another Macintosh

You use the items shared from another Macintosh in the same manner you use items on your own Macintosh. Of course, what you can do with a shared item depends on the access privileges its owner has granted you. To see your access privileges, select the shared item and choose Sharing from the File menu. For an item shared from another Macintosh, the Sharing info window tells where the item is, the name by which you're connected, and your access privileges for that item.

Table 8-2:	Access privileges for common tasks		
To do this with a shared folder or disk:	See Folders	See Files	Make Changes
Open a file from		✔	
Save changes to a file in		✔	✔
Drag something to			✔
Copy a file from		✔	
Copy a folder from	✔		
Discard a file from		✔	✔
Discard a folder from	✔		✔
Create a new folder in	✔		✔

UNDOCUMENTED

When you open a shared document, the Finder searches your local disks for the program needed to open the document. If the program isn't found, the Finder tries to find it on the Macintosh you're sharing the file from and open it across the network. Running programs over a network is considerably slower than running a program on your Macintosh. Whenever you send or receive information across the network using System 7's file sharing, a double-arrow icon flashes in the upper-left corner of the menu bar.

If you access your own Macintosh remotely (or another Macintosh as its owner), you can see and use everything on that Macintosh. In other words, you have full access privileges to all items, whether they have been designated for sharing (using the Sharing command) or not. This is handy, for example, if you've forgotten an important file or if you need to refer to some information that you have on your Macintosh but you're no longer in your office. By connecting to your computer over the network, you can copy those files to the Macintosh you're working at and read, change, or print them. It's possible to deny the owner the ability to see unshared items, or to prevent the owner (yourself) from connecting at all, by turning off the "Allow user to see entire disk" setting or the "Allow user to connect" setting in the owner's access privilege window, as shown in Figure 8-10.

Transferring items between computers

The most common use of sharing folders and disks is to transfer items from one Macintosh to another. For the most part, you transfer items between computers just as you would copy files to a floppy disk. If you try to move a folder or file to the desktop, a message asks whether you want to copy the item to your startup disk. If you click OK, the item appears on your desktop.

Disconnecting from another Macintosh

There are three ways you can disconnect from another Macintosh. You can select the icons of all items you're sharing from it and choose Put Away from the File menu. You can also drag those file server icons to the Trash. If you're done working on your Macintosh, choose the Shut Down command from the Finder's Special menu.

Network Insecurity

Hackers invade your network? System 7's file sharing capability puts your hard disks at risk if your Mac is connected to a network. The risk of invasion exists even if you normally have file sharing turned off. Someone with 40 seconds at your keyboard can open your Sharing Setup control panel, change your owner password (without knowing your current password), start file sharing, close the control panel, and leave no sign. Then at his or her leisure from another Mac on the network, this hacker can connect to your Mac as its owner and snoop through everything on your hard disks without leaving any electronic footprints. Of course you would eventually notice if someone changed your files, or you would see that your password had been changed if you tried to connect to your Macintosh from another computer. But a less easily detectable invasion involves altering access privileges with the Users & Groups control panel and the Finder's Sharing command and takes only five to ten minutes.

Apple could make your system more secure by adding password access to the Sharing Setup and the Users & Groups control panels. In the meantime, you can install and use At Ease to prevent unauthorized access to your Control Panels folder, thereby preventing access to the Sharing Setup and Users & Groups control panels inside it (see "At Ease" in Chapter 3). On another level, you can password-protect your disks or folders using a software available from several companies, such as Folder Bolt from Kent-Marsh. Otherwise you must either remove the File Sharing extension from your Extensions folder or trust everyone with access to a Mac on your network.

Summary

- System 7's built-in file sharing makes connecting Macintosh computers and sharing files, folders, and disks easier than ever before.
- Using LocalTalk or PhoneNet connectors to connect two or more Macintosh computers, anyone can create a ready-to-use AppleTalk network to share and transfer files.
- After installing AppleTalk Remote Access, your Macintosh can connect to an AppleTalk network through another Macintosh over standard telephone lines.
- You use the Sharing Setup control panel to start and stop file sharing from your Macintosh.
- With the Users & Groups control panel, you create registered users and groups of users, and assign general access privileges to each.
- You use the Finder's Sharing command to designate which of your disks and folders you want to share with others and what each item's access privileges are for three categories of users: the owner, one registered user or group, and everyone on the network.
- The File Sharing Monitor control panel tells you which items you are sharing with others and who is presently connected to your Macintosh.
- You get access to other computers and the folders and disks on them using the Chooser desk accessory. Once you have access to a shared item, your Macintosh treats it like a disk.

Chapter 9
Creating Living Documents

In This Chapter

- Creating publishers: saving live copies of material from your documents as edition files.
- Subscribing to editions: including live copies of material in your document from other documents.
- What happens when you change a publisher (or a subscriber).
- How to have publishers and subscribers updated automatically or manually.

The United States Constitution is often referred to as a "living document" because it has the ability to change with the times. Application programs supporting System 7's new publish and subscribe capabilities enable you to create your own living documents. The Create Publisher and Subscribe To commands enable you to dynamically share information between documents. Think of the Create Publisher and Subscribe To commands as live Copy and Paste commands. For example, you can copy a group of cells or a chart from a spreadsheet and paste it into a word processing report document. Any time the selected information in the spreadsheet is changed, the report is automatically updated. In this chapter, you'll learn how to breathe life into your documents using the Create Publisher, Subscribe To, and other related commands.

About Publishers, Editions, and Subscribers

System 7 borrows concepts and terminology from the publishing industry for its publish and subscribe technology. A selected area of a document becomes a *publisher* when you make a live copy of it available to other documents. The publisher can include any information you can select within a document. Publishing material from a document creates a live copy of the material in a separate file, which is called an *edition*, as shown in Figure 9-1. You include a copy of an edition in another document by subscribing to the edition. The area of the document that contains a copy of an edition is called a *subscriber*. A document can contain any number and combination of publishers and subscribers.

Saving a document after changing a publisher in it can automatically update the publisher's edition (or you can update the edition manually). When an edition is updated, System 7 notifies all subscribers to that edition that a new edition is available. The subscriber can automatically reflect the latest information from the edition

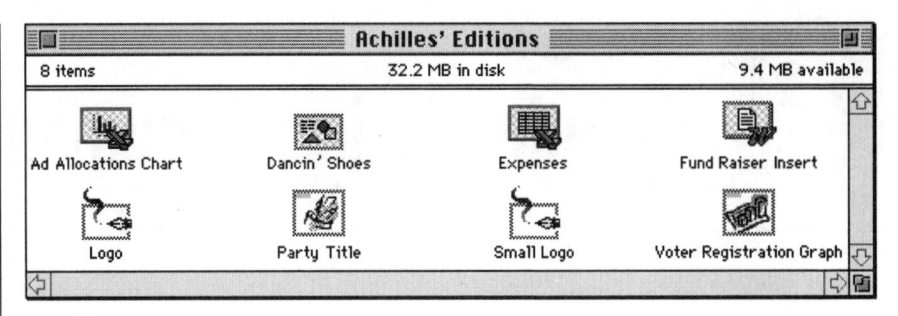

Figure 9-1: Some edition files.

or you can update it manually. Documents containing subscribers do not have to be open for the subscribers to receive edition updates. System 7 stores notices of edition updates destined to closed subscribers and forwards each stored notice when you open the document that contains the subscriber. Information always flows from the publisher to an edition and then to the edition's subscribers, as shown in Figure 9-2.

Publishing and subscribing work across a network just as well as they work locally on your Macintosh. You can subscribe and get updates to editions that are on any disk or folder you are sharing from someone else. Likewise, other people can subscribe and get updates to editions on disks or folders those people are sharing from you. If you are not sharing a disk or folder when an edition on it is updated, System 7 stores the update notice and forwards it to the subscribers on your local disks the next time you share the disk or folder. (For more information on file sharing, see Chapter 8.)

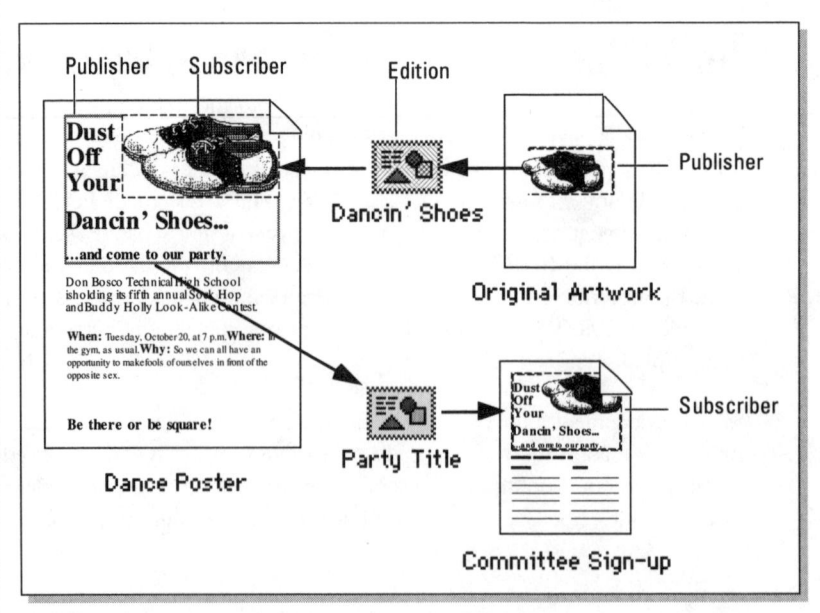

Figure 9-2: The relationship between publisher, edition, and subscriber.

Publishing and subscribing only works in programs that have been updated to offer it. You can't use System 7's publish and subscribe technology with a program that doesn't contain publishing commands in its Edit menu or in a submenu of its Edit menu. If you have a program that lacks those commands, check with the program's developer to see if an upgraded version is available.

Creating a Publisher

You create a publisher by selecting the information that you want to share and choosing Create Publisher from the Edit menu of your program, as shown in Figure 9-3. Many programs put the Create Publisher command in a Publishing submenu of the Edit menu. In most programs you need to select text or graphics in your document in order to create a publisher. If you haven't selected anything, the Create Publisher command appears dimmed. In a few programs, such as Adobe Photoshop, you can publish an entire document by choosing Create Publisher without having selected anything.

After choosing the Create Publisher command, the Publisher dialog box appears, as shown in Figure 9-4. A thumbnail view of the material you selected appears in the Preview area of the dialog box. Usually the folder in which you saved the last edition is already open. System 7 knows which folder to open because it keeps an alias of

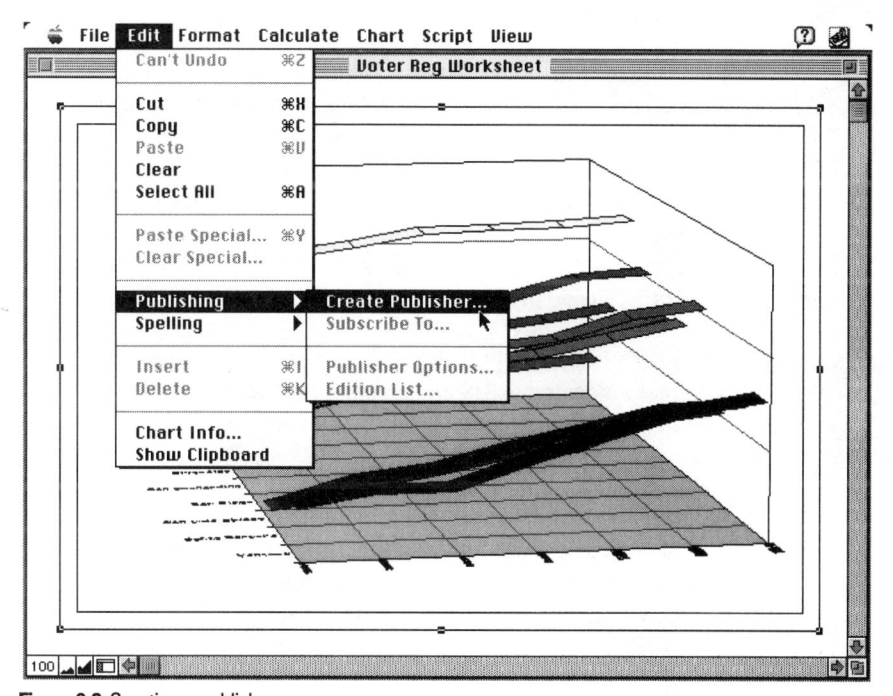

Figure 9-3: Creating a publisher.

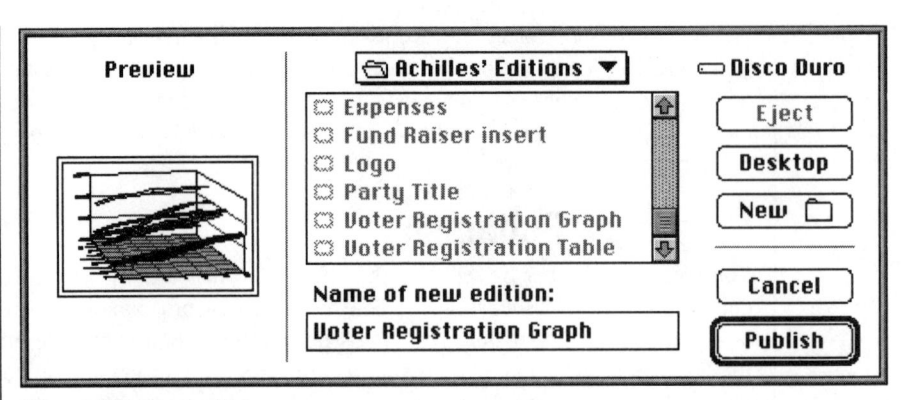

Figure 9-4: Saving an edition.

the most recently saved edition in the Preferences folder inside the System Folder. You can go to a different folder by using the same methods you would use with the Save As command. If you want to make the edition available to other users on your network, be sure to save the edition to a folder or disk you allow them to share.

To keep a new publisher you must save the document that contains it. If you close the document without saving, the program asks whether you want to save changes. You lose the publisher if you decline to save.

You can create as many independent publishers in a document as you want. Some programs permit publishers to overlap partially or completely — one publisher can include all or part of the information contained in another publisher. Apple's guidelines suggest word processing programs permit nested publishers but not overlapping publishers. Spreadsheet programs and graphics programs should permit both nesting and overlapping publishers. A program that does not allow overlapped or nested publishers dims the Create Publisher command when you select any part of a document that is already part of an existing publisher.

A publisher's format — plain text, styled text, paint-type picture, object-type graphic, and so on — is determined by the program that created the document containing the publisher. Some programs save information in several formats in an edition file. When you subscribe to a multiformat edition, the program that created the subscribing document uses the most appropriate format. Microsoft Excel, for example, saves spreadsheet cells as a picture, as a text table, and as a range of formatted Excel cells. A graphics document subscribing to an Excel edition uses the picture format; a word processor probably uses the text table (though Microsoft Word uses the formatted cells to create a formatted Word table); and another Excel worksheet uses the formatted cells.

Subscribing to an Edition

You subscribe to an edition to incorporate live information from another document into the document you're currently working on. To subscribe to an edition, select a place in your document for the edition, and choose Subscribe To from the Edit menu, as shown in Figure 9-5. Some programs put the Subscribe To command in a Publishing submenu of the Edit menu. The place you select for the edition depends on the type of document that's subscribing to it. In a word processing document, you click an insertion point. In a spreadsheet document, you select a cell or range of cells. You do not have to select a place in most graphics documents, because you can move the subscriber after it's placed in the document.

Choosing Subscribe To from the Edit menu displays the Subscribe To dialog box, as shown in Figure 9-6. The dialog box displays the highlighted name of the last edition you published or subscribed to, and you can select a different edition as if you were using an Open command. When you select an edition, a thumbnail view of its contents appears in the Preview area of the dialog box. Clicking the Subscribe button places a copy of the selected edition into your document.

A document can subscribe to any number of editions. The editions can be on a disk directly connected to your Macintosh or on a disk or folder you're sharing from another Macintosh on the same network.

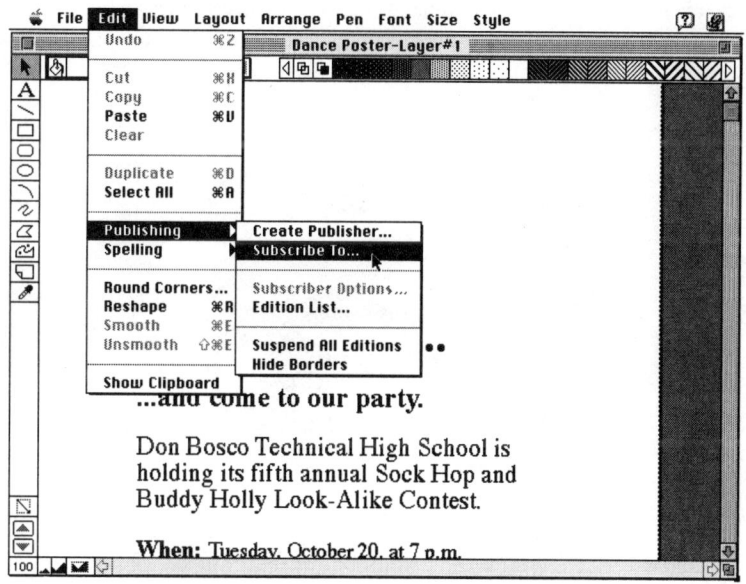

Figure 9-5: Subscribing to an edition.

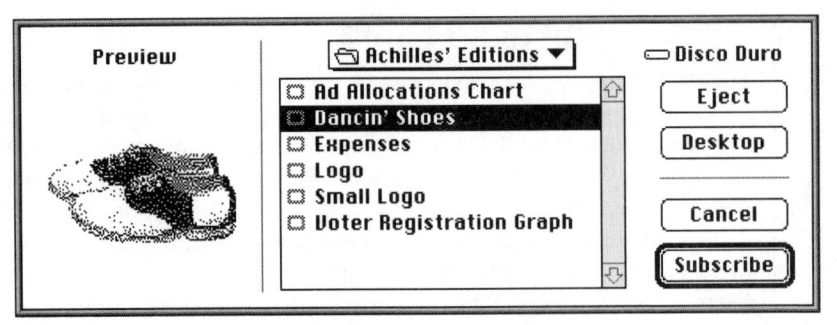

Figure 9-6: Selecting an edition to subscribe to.

Publisher and Subscriber Borders

Most programs display a gray border around a publisher or subscriber when you click or select something inside the publisher or subscriber. The border also appears if you select part of a document that contains a publisher or subscriber, as shown in Figure 9-7. The standard border lines are three pixels thick, and are medium gray (50 percent gray) for publishers and dark gray (75 percent gray) for subscribers. Clicking outside the publisher or subscriber makes the border disappear.

An optional Edit menu command, Show Borders, displays borders around all publishers and subscribers in the active document. After choosing the Show Borders command, it becomes the Hide borders command, which (surprise!) hides all borders except the one for the subscriber or publisher you have clicked. Some programs have different methods

Figure 9-7: Borders around publishers and subscribers.

of showing and hiding all borders. In Claris Resolve, for example, you choose Show from the View menu and turn the Edition Borders option on or off.

Some programs, including Microsoft Excel 4.0, don't show publisher or subscriber borders. Excel's Links command can select a publisher's range of cells (but not a chart or other type of publisher nor a subscriber). You select the publisher you want by name from a list of publishers in the document and click a Select button. Then Excel selects the range of cells and scrolls the document window so you can see it.

Publisher and Subscriber Options

System 7 provides you with several options for working with publishers and subscribers. You can adorn a subscriber (change its formatting), locate and open a subscriber's publisher, control edition updates, and cancel or suspend a publisher or subscriber.

Application programs use different methods to make publisher and subscriber options available. Some programs put a Publisher Options command in the Edit menu when a publisher is selected in the active window, or a Subscriber Options command when a subscriber is selected. Choosing one of those commands brings up a dialog box in which you set the publisher or subscriber options, as shown in Figures 9-8 and 9-9. Other programs put the Publisher Options and Subscriber Options commands in a Publishing submenu of the Edit menu. As a shortcut, many programs bring up the appropriate options dialog box when you double-click a publisher or subscriber while pressing Option. Microsoft Excel has its own eccentric methods. In Excel, you choose the Links command from the File menu to see the Links dialog box. In it you choose Publisher or Subscriber from the Link Type pop-up menu to see a list of the publishers or subscribers that are in the document. Then you select the one whose options you want to see and click an Options button. As a shortcut, you can double-click any part of a publisher or subscriber on a worksheet. (The double-click trick doesn't work for chart publishers.)

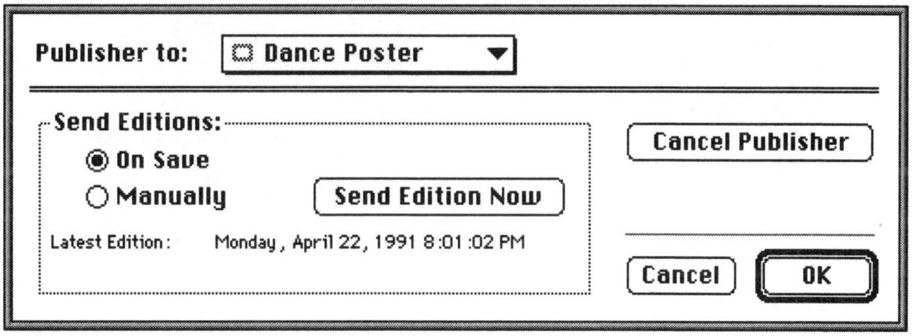

Figure 9-8: A Publisher Options dialog box.

Figure 9-9: A Subscriber Options dialog box.

Adorning a subscriber

Most programs do not permit you to change the contents of a subscriber directly, because your changes would disappear the next time the subscriber was updated. However, many programs do permit adorning a subscriber in ways that the program can reapply to a new edition. For example, you may be able to resize or crop an entire subscriber as you would resize or crop a graphic in a word processing document. You may be able to change all the text in a subscriber to a different font, style, or size. Programs that allow adornment generally have an option in the Subscriber Options dialog box that you can set to maintain adornments or not, as shown in Figure 9-10. With this option on, the program reapplies changes you have made to the subscriber the next time it is updated.

In programs that do permit modifying a subscriber, you should suspend or cancel automatic edition updating before you begin editing a subscriber, as explained later in "Updating Editions." This preserves your changes until you update the subscriber manually by clicking the Get Edition Now button in the Subscriber Options dialog box. If you don't turn off automatic updating for a subscriber, the program may warn you and do it for you, but not all programs do.

Figure 9-10: The Maintain Adornment option.

Opening a subscriber's publisher

Generally you make changes to a subscriber by opening its publisher and changing the publisher. To help you open a publisher, the Subscriber Options dialog box includes an Open Publisher button. Clicking it opens the document that contains the subscriber's publisher (and the program that created the publisher's document, if it's not already open), scrolls the publisher into view, and selects the publisher. Some programs also open a publisher when you press Option while double-clicking a subscriber.

Sometimes you can open a publisher by opening its edition icon in the Finder. When you do, an edition window appears, as shown in Figure 9-11. The window contains a miniature view of the publisher and an Open Publisher button. Clicking it is supposed to open the publisher's original document, just like the Open Publisher button in the Subscriber Options dialog box. In practice, this Open Publisher button doesn't always work.

You can always see the last edition you used by opening the Preferences folder in the System Folder. Opening the alias named Last Edition Used gets you the edition window of the last edition that was saved.

Making changes to a publisher

You can modify a publisher within a document just like any other part of a document. You can add material to a publisher or delete material from it, making the publisher get larger or smaller. You can cut an entire publisher and paste it at a different place in the document. However, it's not a good idea to copy and paste or otherwise duplicate a publisher. If you do, all duplicates of the publisher share one edition, making the contents of subscribers to that edition seem unpredictable. (The edition reflects the contents of the most recently updated duplicate publisher.)

Each time you save a document containing a revised publisher, the application program automatically updates the publisher's edition. You can turn off automatic updating and only update manually, as described in the next section.

Figure 9-11: An edition window.

Updating Editions

The Subscriber and Publisher Options dialog boxes enable you to control whether edition updates are sent or received automatically or manually. Various programs label these dialog box options differently. You can set update options individually for each publisher and subscriber. For example, you may want one subscriber in a document, such as a logo, to be updated on request and another subscriber, such as daily sales figures, updated automatically.

A publisher's Publisher Options dialog box (see Figure 9-8), controls when new editions of the publisher are sent. With the standard setting, On Save, the program automatically sends a new edition the next time you save the document (if you have modified the publisher). Setting the Manually option suspends sending new editions of the publisher until you click the Send Edition Now button in the Publishers Options dialog box.

The subscriber can receive new editions automatically or manually. If the Automatically option is set in the subscriber's Subscriber Options dialog box (see Figure 9-9), the subscriber gets updated as soon as the program receives a new edition. You can suspend automatic subscriber updating by setting the Manually option in the subscriber's Subscriber Options dialog box. To get a manual update, you click the Get Edition Now button in the Subscriber Options dialog box.

You can cancel a publisher or subscriber by clicking the Cancel Subscriber or Cancel Publisher button in its Publisher Options or Subscriber Options dialog box. Canceling a publisher or subscriber permanently breaks the link between the publisher and the subscriber.

Some programs enable you to temporarily suspend all updating activity by providing a Suspend All Editions command (or its equivalent) in the Edit menu. When this command is on, a check mark appears next to it in the menu and the program blocks all publishers from sending new editions and all subscribers from receiving new editions. Turning off the command removes the check mark from the menu and updates with any new editions all subscribers that are set to receive new editions automatically. The Stop All Editions command only affects publishers and subscribers in documents created by the program in which you use the command.

Summary

- The Create Publisher command saves a live copy of material you have selected to an edition file, and the Subscribe To command puts a copy of an edition into the document you're currently working on.
- You can publish editions to your shared folders and disks and subscribe to editions from folders and disks you're sharing from other computers on your network.
- In most programs, you can recognize publishers and subscribers by their gray borders.
- Although you can't usually change a subscriber directly, you can usually adorn it. To change the content of a subscriber, you open its publisher by clicking the Open Publisher button in the Subscriber Options dialog box or the Edition window.
- The Publisher Options and Subscriber Options dialog boxes control whether an individual publisher or subscriber is updated automatically or manually.
- Publishing and subscribing methods differ somewhat from one program to the next.

Part II
System 7 in Detail

Chapter 10
QuickTime

In This Chapter
- The tricks QuickTime uses to play back movies on a Macintosh.
- How QuickTime extends the system software.
- What's in a QuickTime movie.
- Comparing the standard compression methods.
- How you control movie playback.
- Finding and filming movie content.
- Coming to grips with data in motion.

With System 7.1 you get Apple's digital video technology, QuickTime. It's a 440K system extension that gives your Mac the capability of playing movies, animation, sound, and other time-related data. Don't throw away your TV set yet, because today's QuickTime movies are small and jerky. What's more, you need a color-capable Mac with several megabytes of hard disk space to watch a few short movies, and you may need a CD ROM drive just to get the movies. If you want to make movies, not just watch other people's work, be prepared to pay $500 to $8,000 to set up a movie-making studio on your Mac.

Why would anyone want to give up a lot of disk space to watch inferior movies? For one thing, they're fun. Besides the entertainment value, people are already applying QuickTime to training, entertainment, communications, presentations, and more. QuickTime pioneers know that its limitations, burdens, and costs will decrease over time as its technology improves and storage costs inexorably come down. Case in point: With the delivery of QuickTime version 1.5 in October 1992, less than a year after delivery of version 1.0, Apple improved picture quality fourfold and improved playback rates of movies stored on CD ROM, movies stored on network file servers, and all movies played on black-and-white Macs.

QuickTime 1.5 also works with Kodak's Photo CD technology, which enables you to have your photographs digitized onto a CD ROM. With a CD ROM drive and Quick-Time 1.5, you can easily view thumbnail miniatures of your digitized photos, see a slide show of the photo images, and paste the images as standard Mac PICT graphics in almost all applications.

The Magic Behind QuickTime

A Mac shouldn't be able to play movies any more than a bumblebee should be able to fly. A single full-screen color picture on the Mac takes a megabyte of disk space. To get 30 pictures per second, which is what you see on TV, the Mac would have to store, retrieve, and display 30MB per second. Dream on.

QuickTime pulls every trick in the book to play movies. For one, it doesn't display a full-screen picture. QuickTime 1.0 works best at 1/16 the size of a standard color screen — 160 × 120 pixels (not quite 2.25 × 1.75 inches); QuickTime 1.5, which became available in October 1992 and is the version that comes with System 7.1, ups the standard movie size by four — 320 × 240 pixels, which is about ¼ the size of a standard color screen. Moreover, QuickTime plays fewer frames per second than TV or movies. Whereas TV shows 30 fps (frames per second) in the US and other countries that use the NTSC standard (25 in Europe and other places that use the PAL or SECAM standards), QuickTime movies generally play at 15 fps. Showing smaller pictures reduces the amount of data to store, retrieve, and display, but not nearly enough. So QuickTime compresses movies, throwing out the redundant parts.

Despite compression and the small movie size, playing movies requires lots of processing power. Your Mac needs at least a 68020 central processor and 5MB of RAM. For making your own movies, plan on 8MB of RAM and a digitizer, which converts movies from a camcorder or VCR (something else you'll need) to digital data.

QuickTime Technology

QuickTime extends the standard Macintosh system software so you can incorporate time-based data, such as video and animation, into documents you create with mainstream application programs. After installing QuickTime, you can copy and paste movies as easily as you have always copied and pasted individual graphic images. You can also use QuickTime to compress individual graphics, and when you open a compressed graphic, QuickTime automatically decompresses it.

Installing QuickTime puts two new pieces of system software into your System Folder. The QuickTime extension goes into System 7's special Extensions folder. A new version of the Scrapbook desk accessory, which can play QuickTime movies, goes into System 7's Apple Menu Items folder. If the Apple Menu Items folder contains an old desk accessory named Scrapbook, the new Scrapbook desk accessory replaces it.

There is more to QuickTime than software, as shown in Figure 10-1. Video, sound, animation, and other time-related data, which Apple collectively calls QuickTime movies, are a new type of data. To represent this data in the computer's memory and on disk, QuickTime establishes a standard format called MooV. Time-based data tends to be very bulky, so QuickTime provides a mechanism for compressing and automatically decompressing it. QuickTime also extends the standard PICT graphics format to include individual compressed images. Furthermore, QuickTime establishes standard methods for you to recognize movies and control movie playback.

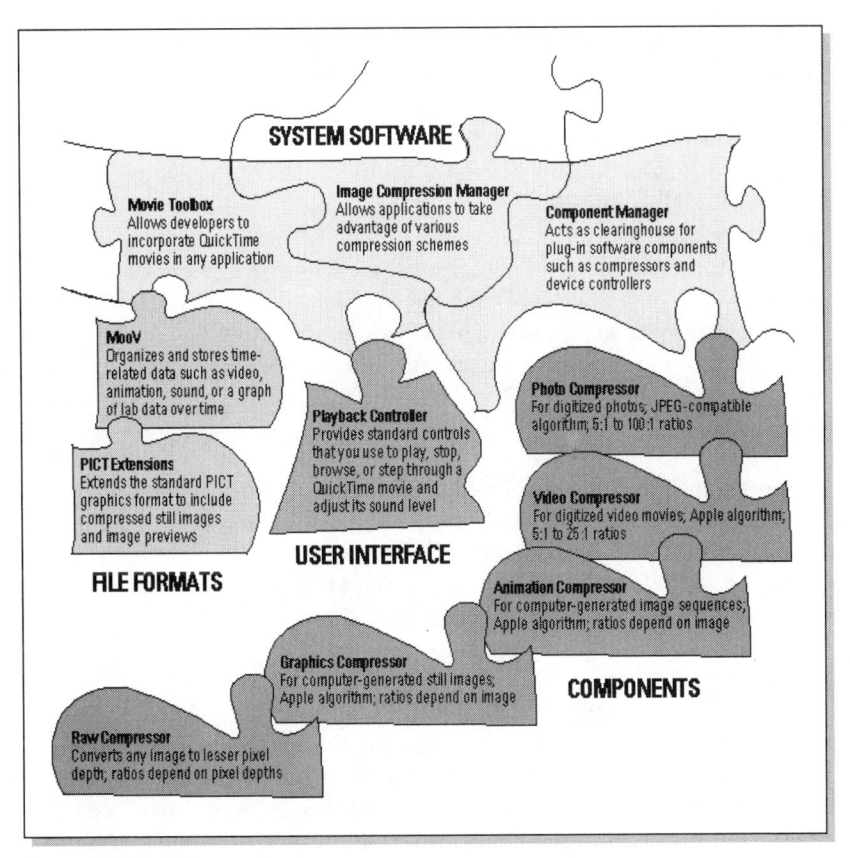

Figure 10-1: QuickTime at a glance.

System Software

The QuickTime extension provides three major pieces of new system software: the Movie Toolbox, the Image Compression Manager, and the Component Manager. Application programs take advantage of these software modules to play back or record QuickTime movies.

Movie Toolbox

The Movie Toolbox includes software tools with which application developers can easily add the capability of copying, pasting, and playing back movies to old and new programs. You can then use the Cut, Copy, and Paste commands with a QuickTime movie as if it were an ordinary graphic, and the application program has the Movie Toolbox do the work.

When you play a movie, the Movie Toolbox takes care of synchronizing audio, video, animation, and other time-related data regardless of system speed. An application doesn't have to do anything to make a QuickTime movie run at the same speed on a stripped Mac LC as on a loaded Quadra 950.

Image Compression Manager

The Image Compression Manager provides software tools for image compression and decompression. Application developers incorporate these tools in applications so you can compress movies when you record them and graphic images when you save them. You choose a compression method from a pop-up menu, which lists the compression methods available on your system that are relevant to the type of image or movie you are compressing, as shown in Figure 10-2. The Image Compression Manager controls the compression.

When you open a compressed graphic image or play back a QuickTime movie, the Image Compression Manager automatically applies the correct compressor to decompress the image or the movie. You can add or remove compressors by dragging icons in or out of the System Folder; the Image Compression Manager automatically revises the pop-up menu for the application program.

Component Manager

The Component Manager handles modular software tools called *components*. These components are to Macintosh systems what stereo components are to music systems. Some people want the simplicity of a preconfigured stereo system and others prefer to mix and match pre-amps, amps, equalizers, tuners, CD players, tape drives, and speakers. The Component Manager brings similar flexibility to application programs.

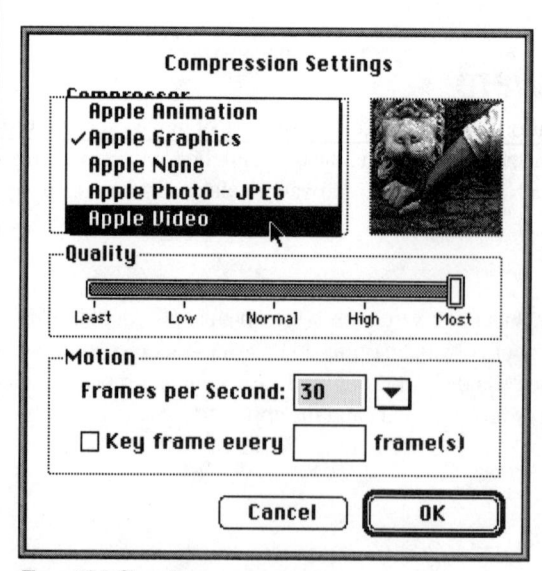

Figure 10-2: Choosing a compressor.

The QuickTime extension has the following several types of components built in:

- Clock components provide timing signals.
- Compressor components compress and decompress video, animation, and individual graphics.
- Movie controller components provide a standard interface for playing back QuickTime movies.
- Sequence grabber components enable applications to save video and sound as QuickTime movies.
- Digitizer components enable applications to control VCRs, camcorders, and other video source equipment.

You can add more components by dragging icons to the System Folder. For example, some add-on components compress and decompress graphics faster than QuickTime's built-in graphics compressor. There are even components that are entirely unrelated to QuickTime.

What's in a MooV

Although Apple's QuickTime file format is dubbed MooV, it encompasses more than just visual data. In fact, it is designed to organize, store, and exchange any time-related data. Also, Apple is publishing the specifications for the format so developers can incorporate QuickTime movies in non-Mac environments.

Each QuickTime movie contains one or more tracks; a simple movie might consist of one video track and one sound track. A more complex movie might have several video tracks, several audio tracks, and closed-caption tracks for text subtitles. Each video track could be designed specially for playback with a certain number of available colors (black and white, 256 grays, 256 colors, thousands of colors, or millions of colors). Each audio track could provide dialog in a different language (English, Spanish, Japanese, and so on). Each closed-caption track could provide subtitles in a different language.

Each track specifies one type of data, but it doesn't actually contain any data. Instead, the track identifies where the data segments are stored, the order in which the data segments are played, a playback speed, spatial properties such as image size, and a loudness level, as shown in Figure 10-3. The data might be stored in a disk file containing digitized video, digitized audio, an animation sequence, or a graphic image (PICT). The data might also be on a videodisc or on an audio CD.

The movie, its tracks, and the actual data may all have different time scales. QuickTime correlates the different time scales and synchronizes the tracks.

The MooV format also specifies a poster, which is a single image that represents the movie, and a preview, which is a brief excerpt of the movie like the trailers you see in a theater.

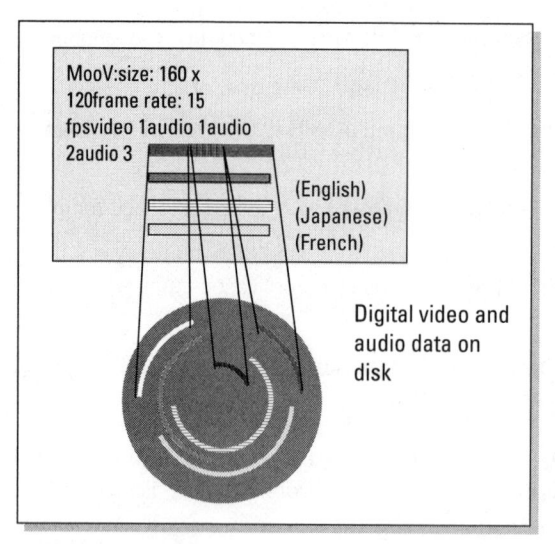

MooV:size: 160 x 120
frame rate: 15 fps
video 1 audio 1 audio 2 audio 3

(English)
(Japanese)
(French)

Digital video and audio data on disk

Figure 10-3: Storing MooV data.

Storing data segments in separate modules rather than with the movie description keeps the MooV small. The data required to play a QuickTime movie can easily occupy several megabytes, whereas the complete MooV specification only takes up a few kilobytes. This makes it practical to copy and paste or publish and subscribe QuickTime movies between documents. The modular approach also makes it easy and efficient to use one data segment several times in a single movie or in several different movies. Additionally, modularity makes it easy to use data from different sources, such as disk files, videodisc, and videotape.

On the down side, having a MooV file doesn't mean you can play the QuickTime movie it specifies. For example, you might copy a MooV file to a floppy disk on your Mac at work, take the floppy home, and open the movie on another Mac there. You wouldn't be able to play the QuickTime movie at home because its data would be at work. Even at work, some data segments may be in files on an unavailable file server on your office's network. You can throw away data files used by a movie without any word of warning or caution from the system. Eventually, the Finder and the file system will probably get smart about such linked files, but in the meantime expect to see alerts from the system when it can't find a movie file you forgot to copy or accidentally deleted.

PICT Extensions

Not only does QuickTime define the new MooV format, it also extends the standard graphics format, PICT, to handle compressed still images and image previews. An application that knows about these extensions can compress a graphic image with any software or hardware compressor available on your computer. Any application that can now open a PICT format image needs no changes to be capable of opening a compressed PICT; QuickTime automatically decompresses a compressed PICT image without requiring changes to the application program.

Updated application programs can save a small (4K to 5K) thumbnail version of a PICT image along with the image itself. You can use thumbnails to browse through image collections with a standard Open command in any program that can open PICT format images, as described in the next section.

User Interface

With QuickTime, Apple is addressing not only the issue of how application programs include movies and compressed PICTs, but how people use them. Applications may use two methods for controlling movie playback. They may display a standard VCR-like controller just below the movie, as shown in Figure 10-4. You use this playbar to play, stop, browse, or step through the movie and adjust its sound level. Some applications have variants of the standard controller and may put the controller in a palette that floats above the document window.

Applications may also display movies without controllers. In this case, a badge in the lower-left corner of the movie distinguishes it from a still graphic, as shown in Figure 10-5. To play a movie that has a badge and no controller, you double-click the movie. Clicking a playing movie stops it.

QuickTime also extends the directory dialog box you get with the Open command and similar disk-related commands to show what a movie or PICT contains before you open it, as shown in Figure 10-6.

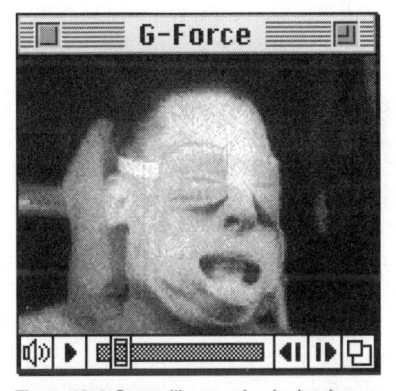

Figure 10-4: Controlling movie playback.

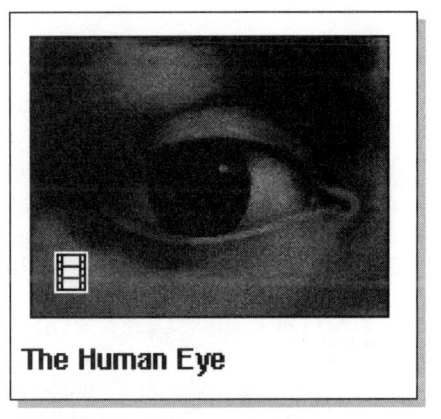

Figure 10-5: Identifying a movie without a controller.

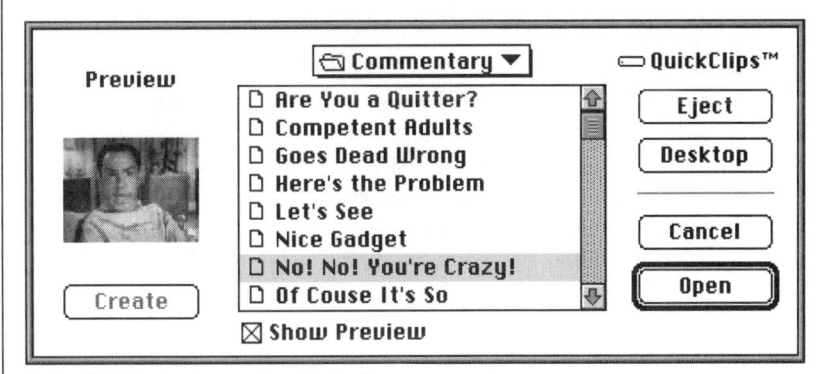

Figure 10-6: Previewing movies with the Open command.

Image Compression

It's possible, if not practical, to digitize video on the Mac without QuickTime. The problem is that digitized video involves so much data that it overwhelms disk-drive capacity and may even exceed the data-transfer rates of the fastest Mac. The solution is universal image compression, together with smaller frame sizes and slower frame rates.

QuickTime includes five standard image compressors, one for video, one for animation, one for graphics, one for photos, and one for raw compression of any image. Each compressor applies a particular method, called a *compression algorithm*, that's especially suited to one type of image. Three characteristics of a compression algorithm determine how effectively it compresses: compression ratio, image fidelity and speed.

Compression ratio

The compression ratio measures how much the algorithm reduces the size of an image. A compression ratio of 2:1 means an average image compresses to half its original size; at 20:1 the compressed image is ¹⁄₂₀ its original size. No algorithm compresses every image by exactly the same amount, because image content affects the compression ratio. For example, many compression algorithms can't compress a patterned area as much as a solid block of color. All compression algorithms remove data from an image by analyzing the data within the image, a technique called *spatial compression*. Algorithms for compressing sequences of images may also use temporal compression, also called *frame differencing*, to remove part of a frame that's unchanged from the previous frame.

Compression fidelity

The compression ratio directly affects the fidelity of the decompressed image. *Lossless compressors,* which decompress images identical to their originals, have compression ratios between 2:1 and 4:1. *Lossy compressors,* which lose some image fidelity during compression, generally achieve satisfactory results at compression ratios between 20:1 and 30:1. Lossy image compression relies on your mind's tendency to blend adjacent tiny bits of color into one color. For example, you tend to see a pattern of black and white dots on your screen as a medium gray.

Compression speed

A complex compression algorithm that tries to achieve the utmost image fidelity and greatest compression ratio will be slower than a simple algorithm. Efficient software (or hardware) that implements the algorithm and a fast computer will accelerate any compression algorithm. Decompression speed is especially important in video and animation because it affects the frame rate, frame size, and color depth. Faster decompression means you can increase one or more of those factors.

Compressors

The five software compressors that Apple supplies with QuickTime are meant for pixel-map (pixmap) images created by scanners, digitizers, painting programs, or animation programs. None of these compressors can reduce the size of object-oriented graphics created by CAD, drawing, or 3-D-modeling programs, nor of EPS (Encapsulated PostScript) graphics.

The Apple Photo compressor uses the international standard JPEG (Joint Photographic Experts Group) algorithm. It is best suited to compressing digitized photographs and other natural images, which vary smoothly and have few edges or other sharp details. The JPEG algorithm spatially compresses an image by removing data that is redundant or imperceptible to the human eye. Compression ratios range from 5:1 to 100:1, depending on image content and size.

The Apple Video compressor uses a compression algorithm developed by Apple specifically for fast decompression of digitized video movies. It spatially compresses each image in the movie and can also perform frame differencing. You can adjust the degree of frame differencing to get different levels of image quality. Color depth can be 8-, 16-, or 24-bit (256, thousands, or millions). With QuickTime 1.0, the video compressor achieves compression ratios from 5:1 to 25:1 (5:1 to 8:1 without frame differencing); you can expect to store 10 to 20 seconds of compressed video per megabyte. With QuickTime 1.5, the video compressor achieves higher compression ratios. Decompression rates permit playing back small frames (160 × 120 pixels, or 1/16 of a 13-inch monitor with QuickTime 1.0, and 320 × 240 pixels, or 1/4 of a 13-inch monitor with QuickTime 1.5) at 10 frames per second on a Macintosh LC. Smaller frame sizes play back proportionally faster. Faster Macintosh models can play back at higher frame rates, larger frame sizes, or both. Compressing a movie (while recording it) takes about five times longer than playing it back.

The Apple Animation compressor uses a compression algorithm developed by Apple for animation and other computer-generated images, such as sequences of screen images recorded by Farallon's ScreenRecorder, at any color depth (2, 4, 16, 256, thousands, or millions of colors). The compressor uses a lossless run-length encoding (RLE) technique to spatially compress each image in an animation sequence. The animation compressor can also perform lossy frame differencing to achieve full-size, real-time playback (640 × 480 at up to 30 frames per second). Actual performance and compression ratios depend greatly on the content of images in the animation sequence. The animation compressor works best with synthetically created images. Natural images, such as those captured from videotape, generally have too little edge definition and too much visual noise, making it difficult for the animation compressor to achieve a good compression ratio.

The Apple Graphics compressor uses an algorithm developed by Apple especially for 8-bit (256 color) still images where compression ratio matters more than compression speed. Generally, the graphics compressor reduces an image to half the size of the animation compressor, but takes twice as long doing it. The slow speed of the graphics compressor is less noticeable when decompressing images stored on relatively slow devices such as CD-ROM.

The Apple Raw compressor reduces image size by converting the image to a lesser pixel depth (number of available colors). For example, converting from 24-bit (actually 32-bit) to 16-bit compresses by 2:1. Some of the other Apple compressors implicitly use the raw compressor. The photo compressor, for example, only works directly with 24-bit images, so it uses the raw compressor when it needs to work with an image at a different pixel depth. Reducing the pixel depth loses image fidelity. Converting to a higher pixel depth usually does not affect image fidelity, but sometimes converting from 8-bit to 16-bit can lose information.

Content, Content, Content

Having the option to play QuickTime movies is great, but if you want to record them, where will your video content come from, and how will you get the rights to use it? Apple's QuickTime Startup Kit contains quite a bit of video on CD ROM, and other publishers are also publishing clip video on CD ROM.

You can record your own QuickTime movies directly onto your hard drive. You'll need a video capture card such as E-Machines' QuickView Studio version 2, Radius' 24stv, RasterOps' ColorBoard 364, or SuperMac's VideoSpigot. In addition, you'll need a video source: a VCR, camcorder, videodisc player, or professional video playback equipment.

You can also create QuickTime movies entirely on the computer. The Movie Converter program that comes with the QuickTime Starter Kit enables you to create QuickTime movies from PICT graphics files, PICT images in the Scrapbook, PICS animation files, or AIFF sound files. (PICT, PICS, and AIFF are standard types of Macintosh files.) Also, MacroMedia Director 3.1 can save its animations as QuickTime movies.

Unless you film your own video with a camcorder or your own animation with animation software, you must also wrestle with copyright issues. Video, being a form of expression, has international copyright protection unless it has been placed in the public domain. Legally, you must get permission from the copyright holder before you record any copyrighted video as a QuickTime movie.

Once you have QuickTime movies on disk, you can slice, dice, chop, mix, combine, and bake them with video editing and composing programs such as Adobe Premier and Diva's VideoShop.

Movie Makers

Before QuickTime even came out, several intrepid pioneers around the world began incorporating QuickTime movies into their work. In Switzerland, multimedia designers Thierry Amsallem and Fulvio Massini created an information kiosk where journalists attending the annual Montreaux Jazz Festival could get background information on performers. For each artist, the kiosk presented biographical text, photographs, and a one-minute excerpt of a prior-year's performance. The designers used HyperCard, MacroMedia Director, and QuickTime movies to create the program for the kiosk. They recorded the movies on an 8MB Mac IIfx with a fast 1.2-gigabyte hard drive and a RasterOps ColorBoard 364 for digitizing the video from an 8mm source. They had hoped the movies would play at 16 frames per second, but their 175 × 130 frames (slightly oversized for QuickTime 1.0) slowed the frame rate to around 9. With QuickTime, they were able to include sound and video without having to go through a video studio.

Holland's Veronica Broadcasting has 12,000 video clips on analog videotape and someday hopes to put QuickTime movie versions of them on AppleShare file servers. Then its news directors can use one of the company's 240 Macs to browse through the archive and quickly find just the right shot. They expect to need 25 gigabytes of hard drive storage — too costly right now. But their tests show the project is feasible. They are able to play back their undersized 120 × 110 frames at 25 frames per second from a fast hard drive, and that's using QuickTime 1.0, which is slower than version 1.5. Frame rates are slower across their EtherTalk network, but still acceptable, and two Macs can play the same video clip on a file server at the same time. To expedite browsing, they plan to imbed keywords on one extra track and time codes of the source video on another extra track in each QuickTime movie. These extra tracks will allow them to link related shots. For example, while watching a video clip filmed in San Francisco, you might see a cable car and want to see another shot of a cable car. You'll click the video to stop it and click another button to go to the related shot.

At Northwest Airlines, QuickTime movies may help flight schedulers watch worldwide weather changes so they can make the best flight plans. Without QuickTime, schedulers can only see one weather image at a time and have to remember the last image to figure out which way the wind is moving. With QuickTime, the airline's Operations Analysis and Automation team can combine the images in a QuickTime movie and store it on a network file server. Schedulers watching the time-lapse animation on their Macs can make flight plans that save fuel, reduce wear and tear on aircraft, and give passengers a smoother ride.

You won't have to work as hard as the QuickTime pioneers to make use of movies. Apple wants you to be able to copy, paste, resize, move, and play movies in any document where you can now put PICT graphics. QuickTime's Movie Toolbox makes it easy for developers to add those capabilities to their applications. By comparison, it's harder to figure out what to do with movies in a program like a word processor, which seems to exist for creating static printed documents.

WordPerfect 2.1 was one of the first ordinary applications to include QuickTime movie capabilities. It's not immediately obvious how you might use movies in a word processing document, but Don Sorensen, who works on special projects for Macintosh development at WordPerfect Corporation, has demonstrated several ideas. He created an interactive newspaper whose static illustrations of movie reviews become

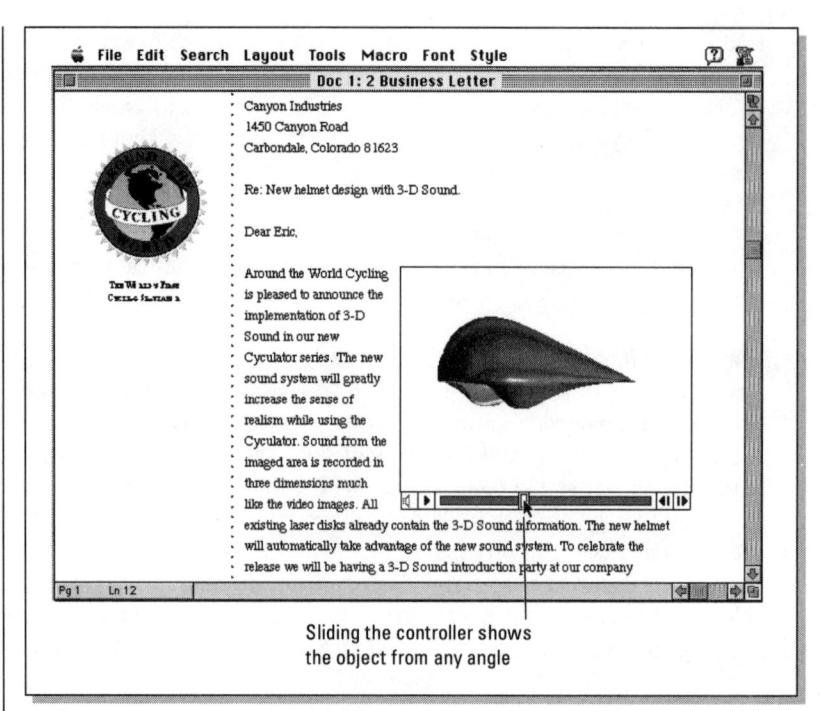

Figure 10-7: An interactive business letter using QuickTime.

movie trailers when you double-click them. Imagine seeing an interactive newspaper in a kiosk at the front of a movie theater complex.

In another example, a business letter describes a new helmet design and includes an animated 360-degree view of the helmet, as shown in Figure 10-7. You can use the movie controller to look at the helmet from any angle. The letter and the animation fit on a 50-cent floppy disk, and can be read by anyone with a QuickTime-equipped Macintosh. Larger documents, such as a student's report about travel to the moon illustrated with movies of NASA space missions, could be delivered by network.

Storing movies uses lots of disk space, but some documents are short-lived. For example, A TV news director could review several clips pasted into a memo, and make comments on them in the same document, as shown in Figure 10-8. The alternative is to hand the director a bunch of videotapes and scrawled notes. This document would probably only exist (and occupy disk space) for a day.

QuickTime in Your Life

QuickTime makes including video, sound, and animation in your documents as easy as including graphics. However, movies are a new type of data on the computer and don't lend themselves to traditional, paper-oriented ways of thinking about computer documents. Suddenly you have a dynamic new way to communicate. You have to change how you think about using your computer. It's not just for preparing messages but for delivering the messages as well.

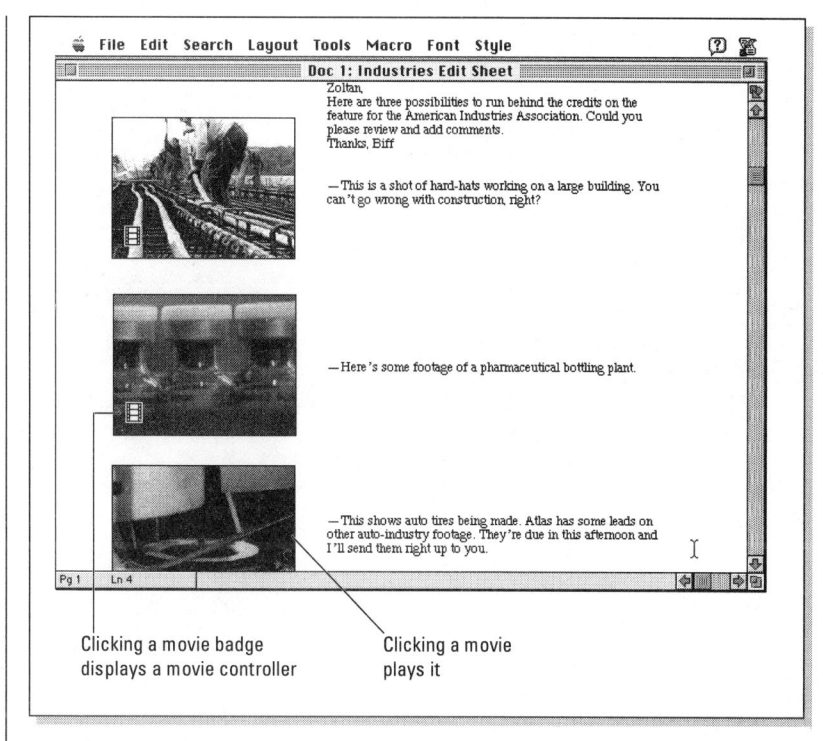

Figure 10-8: A document containing the temporary storage of QuickTime movie clips and accompanying commentary.

Summary

- QuickTime uses several tricks to enable playback of movies on a Macintosh — reduced picture size, slower playback speed, and image compression.
- The QuickTime extension provides three major pieces of new system software: the Movie Toolbox, the Image Compression Manager, and the Component Manager. Application programs take advantage of these software modules to play back or record QuickTime movies.
- To represent video, sound, animation, and other time-related data in the computer's memory and on disk, QuickTime establishes a standard format called MooV.
- Time-based data tends to be very bulky, so QuickTime provides a mechanism for compressing and automatically decompressing it. QuickTime comes with five standard compressors: video, animation, graphics, photo, and raw (none).
- QuickTime extends the standard PICT graphics format to include individual compressed images.
- QuickTime establishes standard methods for you to recognize movies and control movie playback — the movie controller and the movie badge.
- You can film your own movies and convert them to QuickTime movies with a digitizer card, or you can use existing footage (be sure to get permission from the copyright holder).

Part II
System 7 in Detail

Chapter 11
Advanced Capabilities

In This Chapter

- What program linking means to you: compound documents, mix 'n' match program modules, and system-wide user scripting.
- A look at real-world program linking using Claris's MacProject II and Resolve.
- Accessing database management systems using one menu command in some programs.
- Using query documents to access data from a database management system.

You upgrade to System 7 not only for the new capabilities it gives your Macintosh immediately, but also for its possibilities. Three of System 7's most advanced capabilities — program linking, system-wide user scripting, and data access — pave the way for future improvements in Macintosh programs.

Program Linking

People have worked together for thousands of years but personal computer programs are just beginning to. Why? People have been talking (or otherwise communicating) but programs have not — at least not aside from the limited communications that the Copy and Paste commands provide. The technology behind programs working together, which Apple calls inter-application communication (IAC), was not implemented system-wide before System 7. The publish and subscribe capabilities described in Chapter 9 together with the Copy and Paste commands are one part of IAC. The other part of IAC enables programs to link with other programs and share services.

Unlike publish and subscribe, in which you actively participate, program linking happens automatically behind the scenes when programs send and receive messages called *Apple events.* Apple events have a basic set of four messages, which Table 11-1 defines. Finder 7 uses these basic Apple events messages to open programs, open documents, print documents, and quit programs. When you double-click a program icon, the Finder sends the program an Open Application message. When you double-click a document, the Finder sends the program that created the document an Open Application message and an Open Documents message with the name of the document you double-clicked. When you select one or more documents and choose Print from the Finder's menu, the Finder sends the application an Open Application message, a Print Documents message with the names of the documents you selected, and a Quit Application message. When you choose the Shut Down or Restart commands, the Finder sends a Quit Application message to each open program. For programs that don't understand the basic Apple events, the Finder uses its traditional means of opening, printing, and quitting.

Beyond the four basic Apple events messages, Apple recommends that application programs understand another two dozen messages. They encompass actions and objects almost all programs have in common, such as close, save, undo, redo, cut, copy, and paste. Programs with related capabilities recognize additional sets of Apple events messages. For example, word processors understand messages about text manipulation, and drawing programs understand messages about graphics manipulation. Program developers can also define personal messages that only their own programs know.

System 7 provides the means of communicating Apple events messages between programs. The programs can be on the same computer or on different computers connected to the same network. A program doesn't have to be open or even accessible to receive its messages. System 7 stores messages and forwards them when the program becomes available. Only application programs can send and receive Apple events; desk accessories cannot. A desk accessory can work around this limitation by sending and receiving through a small surrogate application program that is always open in the background. This background application does not have to appear in the Application menu, and the Macintosh user does not have to know it is open.

To understand how program linking works, think of it as a telephone system. System 7 software furnishes a telephone and answering machine for each program and the wires between them. For messages sent across a network, System 7 uses the built-in AppleTalk networking software and LocalTalk or other networking connectors and cables (as described in the first two sections of Chapter 8). Application programs talk on the telephones and leave each other Apple events messages. Desk accessories aren't capable of talking on the phone, but some of them have agents who forward incoming and outgoing messages.

Table 11-1:	Basic Apple events messages
Message	*Meaning*
Open Application	Open the selected program
Open Documents	Open the selected documents
Print Documents	Print the selected documents without displaying them
Quit Application	Same as when you choose Quit from the program's File menu

Using program linking

Program linking works automatically on your own Macintosh when you use programs that understand Apple events messages. The methods for linking with a program on someone else's Macintosh vary from one program to the next. You'll have to consult your program manual for detailed information. In FileMaker Pro 2.0, for example, you define a script to send Apple events, specifying the target application program as part of a Send Apple Event step in the script, as shown in Figure 11-1. You select the target application in a dialog box as if you were opening it with the Finder's Open command. You can select any program on one of your disks or on a disk you're sharing with System 7's file sharing (see "Sharing Someone Else's Folders and Disks" in Chapter 8). If you have previously created an alias to a shared disk, you can start sharing that disk from the Open dialog box (see "Aliases of Shared Items" in Chapter 6).

Before others on your network can link to your programs, you must start, or activate, program linking on your Macintosh. Do that by clicking the Start button in the Program Linking section of the Sharing Setup control panel, as shown in Figure 11-2.

Soon after you click the Start button it changes to a Stop button. Pressing the Stop button prevents all other computers on your network from linking to your programs.

After starting program linking on your Macintosh, you must designate which application programs you want to share. To allow others to link to one of your programs, select the program and choose Sharing from the Finder's File menu. The Finder displays a program linking info window, as shown in Figure 11-3. Turn on the "Allow remote program linking" option and close the window. Turning off that option prevents others from linking to the program. If the option is dim, the program is open; you must quit a program before changing its program linking option.

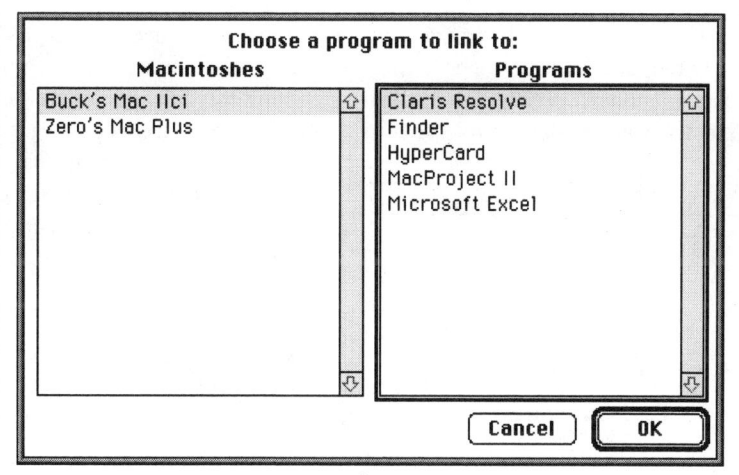

Figure 11-1: Program linking with a Claris Resolve script.

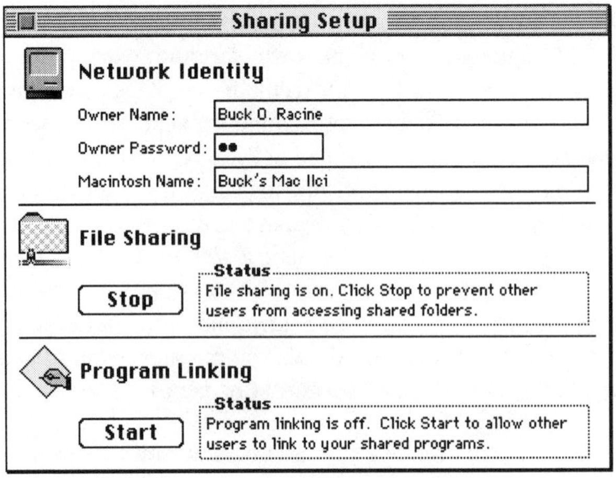

Figure 11-2: Allowing others to link to your shared programs.

Figure 11-3: A program linking info window.

You also control who on your network can share your programs. You do this with the Users & Groups control panel.

To allow everyone on your network access to your programs, open the Guest icon in the Users & Groups control panel to display the Guest privileges window (see Figure 11-4), and turn on the "Allow guests to link to programs on this Macintosh" option. Turning off that option prevents unauthorized users from sharing your programs.

If you don't allow guests program linking privileges, you need to designate which registered users in your Users & Groups control panel can share your programs. To allow a registered user to link his or her programs to yours, open that user's icon in your Users & Groups control panel to display the user's access privileges window, as shown in Figure 11-5. In that window, turn on the "Allow user to link to programs on this Macintosh" option. (For information on registering users, see "Registered Users" in Chapter 8.)

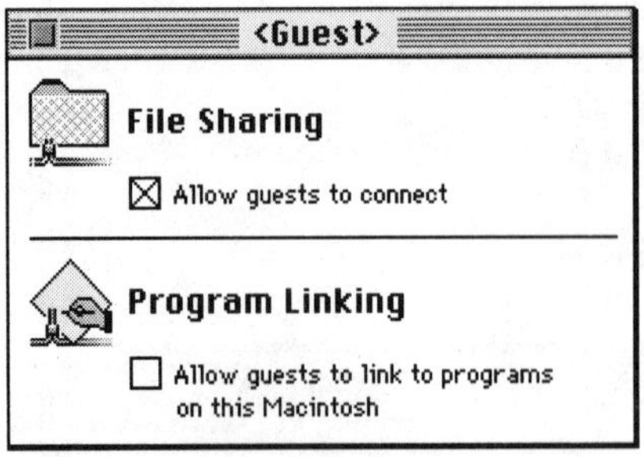

You can block any registered user from linking to your programs by turning off that user's "Allow user to link to programs on this Macintosh" option.

Figure 11-4: A Guest's access privileges.

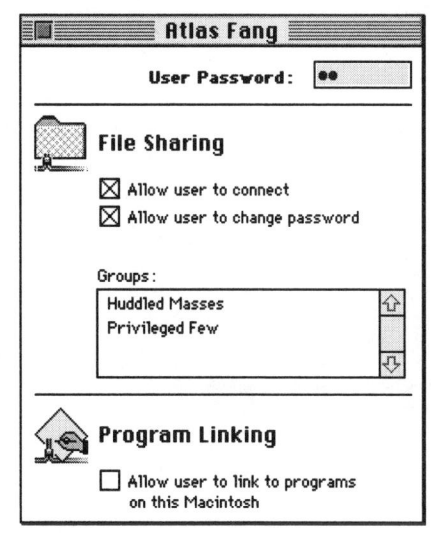

Figure 11-5: A registered user's access privileges.

Program linking example

Before System 7, program linking on the Macintosh was pure speculation. When System 7 first became available, a few Macintosh programs took advantage of program linking, and as time goes by, more and more programs know how to work together. Two of the first programs to use System 7's program linking capabilities were Claris's MacProject II v2.5 and Resolve. MacProject II keeps lots of tables of project-related information but can't graph the tabular information. Resolve can graph tabular information and can be controlled by scripts. Claris decided to write Resolve scripts that prepare graphs and summary tables in response to Apple events messages from MacProject II. Here's how it works:

1. Using MacProject II, you build a project schedule in the usual manner, as shown in Figure 11-6. As the project proceeds, you update it with actual start dates, completion dates, and costs.

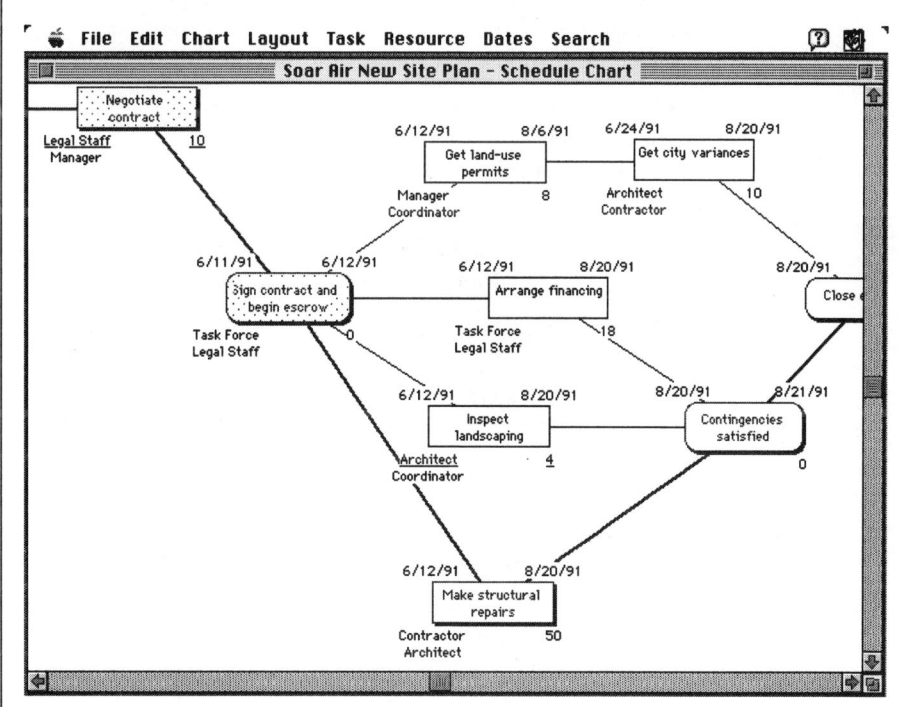

Figure 11-6: A MacProject II project schedule.

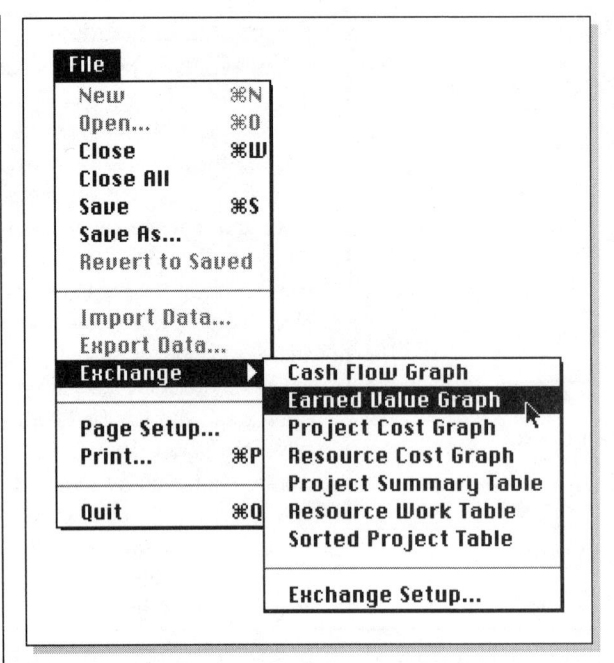

```
File
New          ⌘N
Open...       ⌘O
Close        ⌘W
Close All
Save         ⌘S
Save As...
Revert to Saved

Import Data...
Export Data...
Exchange    ▶  Cash Flow Graph
               Earned Value Graph
Page Setup...  Project Cost Graph
Print...    ⌘P Resource Cost Graph
               Project Summary Table
Quit        ⌘Q Resource Work Table
               Sorted Project Table

               Exchange Setup...
```

Figure 11-7: Choosing a MacProject II graph or summary table.

2. Whenever you want a graph or summary table based on the current status of your project, you choose the type of graph or summary you want from the Exchange submenu of MacProject II's File menu, as shown in Figure 11-7.

3. MacProject II automatically exports its Cash Flow Table, Project Table, Task Cost Entry Table, Dependency Table, and Resource Table as needed for the item you chose. That is, it saves them on disk in a plain-text format that Resolve can understand.

4. MacProject II sends an Apple events message to open Resolve if it's not already open. You see Resolve open on your Macintosh, as shown in Figure 11-8.

5. MacProject II sends Resolve a message to open the document containing the script that creates the graph or summary table you requested. Resolve recognizes that the document contains a script and runs the script. You see Resolve constructing the spreadsheet on which the graph is based and then creating a graph, as shown in Figure 11-9.

6. The Resolve script asks whether you want to copy the graph to the Clipboard and then close the graph window without saving it. You can answer no if you want to change the graph's appearance. For example, you might want to change a resource allocation bar chart to a pie chart. (You would then use Resolve's Copy command to put a copy of the revised graph on the Clipboard.)

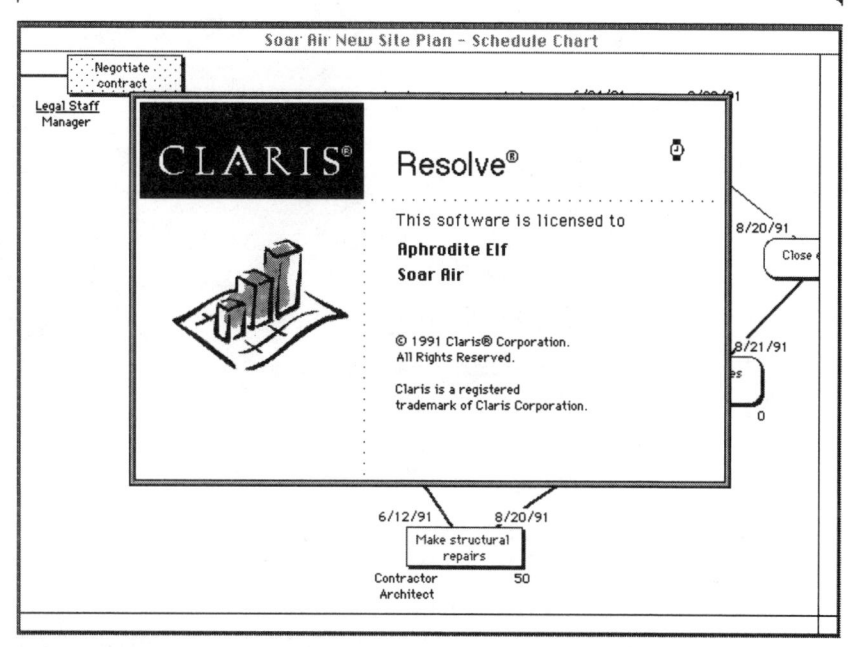

Figure 11-8: MacProject II opens Resolve.

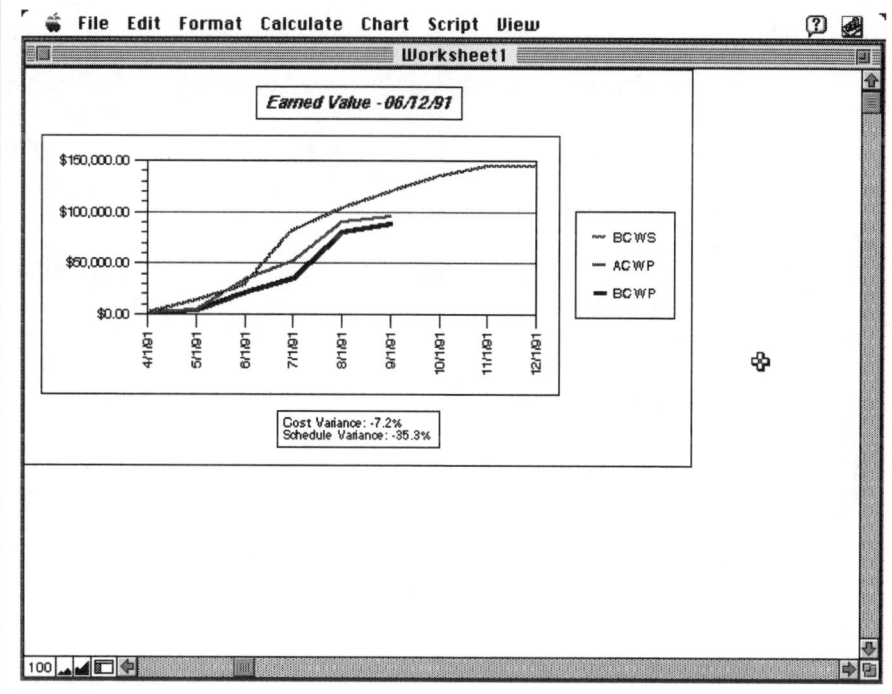

Figure 11-9: A Resolve script constructs a graph.

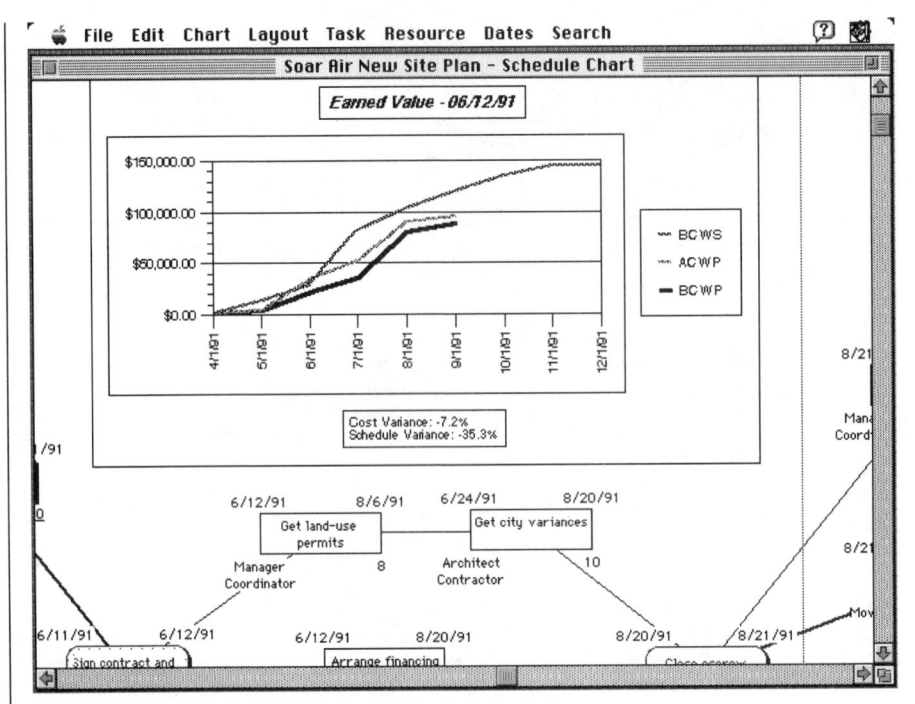

Figure 11-10: A Resolve graph in MacProject II's schedule window.

7. You make MacProject II the active program by clicking one of its windows or by choosing it from the Application menu. Then you open the MacProject II window where you want to put the Resolve graph and choose Paste from the Edit menu, placing a copy of the graph as a graphic in that window, as shown in Figure 11-10. You can drag the pasted graph to a new place in the MacProject II window and you can resize the graph by dragging any of its handles.

You can add more items to MacProject II's Exchange menu by specifying the names and folder locations of additional Resolve scripts and for each script you add, specifying which MacProject II tables you want exported.

The promise of program linking

MacProject II's use of Resolve's graphing capabilities is just a beginning. When MacProject gets publish and subscribe capabilities, it will be able to have Resolve not only create graphs but keep them up-to-date as you make changes to a project in MacProject. The result is called a compound document. The MacProject document contains a type of information that it can't directly manipulate (a graph), but the foreign information is linked to its natural environment (Resolve).

System-Wide Scripting

Resolve and many other programs can be controlled by scripts you write. Program linking makes scripting like this possible system-wide. HyperCard, for example, can use the scripting language in HyperCard version 2.1 (distributed with System 7) to send Apple events messages to savvy programs such as Resolve. Imagine being able to write a script that causes your Macintosh to do with one mouse click (or at preset times) a routine procedure that otherwise involves much tedious manual work with many programs. A script can be your agent, knowing how to complete a task and report back to you when it finishes.

UserLand's Frontier is a true scripting language — functionally like HyperCard's HyperTalk or an Excel macro but system-wide — and Apple expects to deliver its AppleScript system-wide scripting language in 1993. Simple Software has a point-and-click scripting system called Control Tower, and CE Software's QuicKeys 2.5 can send Apple events as part of a QuicKeys macro.

With a system-level script you can automate a process involving several application programs or several networked computers. For example, a network administrator's Frontier script can clean up every Macintosh in a school computer lab after students have finished for the day. The script replaces essential files accidentally deleted by students, removes extraneous files, and makes a complete report of its actions.

Useful scripting requires more than a scripting language and scripting tools; the programs you use need to respond to the scripts as well. With System 7, this means recognizing Apple events.

Data Access

Program linking and file sharing give you access to Macintosh programs and to documents that your programs can open on other computers in your local network. Like many people, you may also need access to data kept in an external database management system (DBMS), whose files your programs can't open. Typically, the DBMS is a corporate database on a large computer that is not part of your local network. System 7's data access management capabilities enable you to access an external database with one simple menu command. The same command can also provide simplified access to a database on your own Macintosh or on another computer on your local network. Macintosh program developers can easily add that command to their software products.

Systems 7.0 and 7.0.1 come with the data accessing capabilities described in the remainder of this chapter, but System 7.1 does not. With System 7.1, you must obtain the DAL system extension from Apple, which enables data access separately.

Using data access

You get data from a database management system by choosing a menu command, as shown in Figure 11-11. Apple suggests the data access command be named Open Query and be located in the File menu, but not all programs follow this suggestion. In Microsoft Excel, for example, you open the Data Access Macro, which adds four new commands to the Data menu and one to the Options menu. Then you choose Query Assistant from the Data menu and click the Open button. You'll have to consult your program manual to see if and how the program offers data access.

The Open Query command (or its equivalent) displays a directory dialog box in which you open a document that specifies what data you want from the database management system, as shown in Figure 11-12. The document contains a predefined sequence of commands, called a *query*, in a language the database management system understands. But you don't type the commands or even see them.

When you open a query document, you see a dialog box that describes the data you'll get if you click the button that starts the query, as shown in Figure 11-13. The dialog box may also contain buttons, check boxes, and text entry boxes that you use to narrow the scope of the query. If you opened a query document to get voter registration data, for example, you might have to specify the political parties and counties for which you wanted data.

After you click the button that starts the query, System 7 sends the query to the database management system and periodically checks for a response. When the database management system supplies the requested data, System 7 puts it into a table. Each column of the table can be a different type of data, such as true/false, integer number, decimal number, date, time, money value, or general text. The program in which you opened the query document can take the table as is or can have System 7

Figure 11-11: Choosing the data access command.

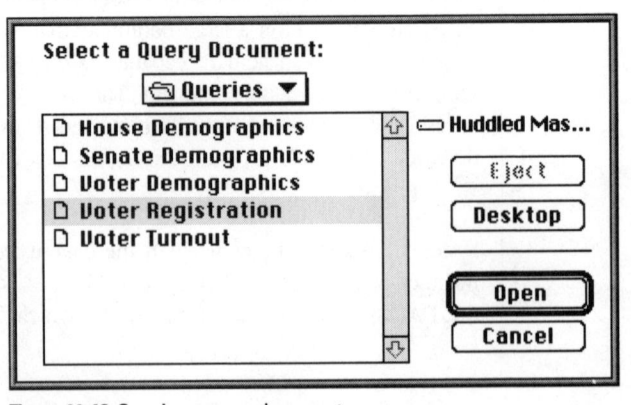

Figure 11-12: Opening a query document.

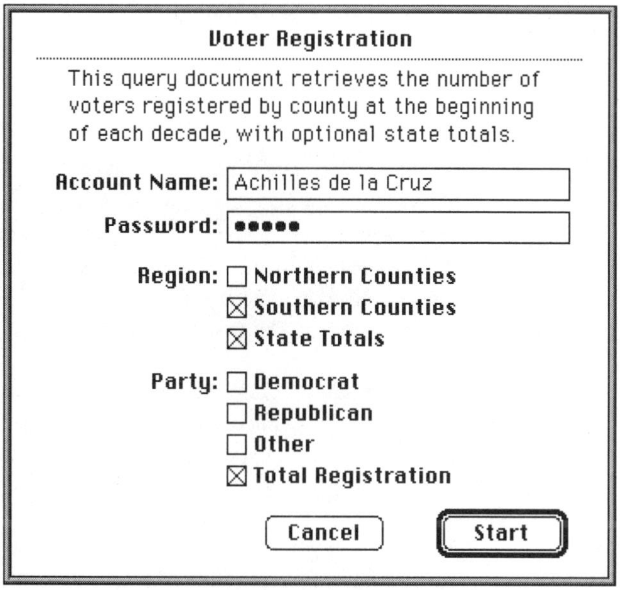

Figure 11-13: Specifying query document options.

convert it to plain text. Then the program either displays the table for you or puts it on the Clipboard so you can paste it into your document, as shown in Figure 11-14.

About query documents

Query documents work with the most popular database management systems, host computers, and networks. These include the Informix, Ingres, Rdb, Oracle, and Sybase database management systems on DEC VAX/VMS computers connected to your Macintosh via an Async or ADSP (AppleTalk Data Stream Protocol) network.

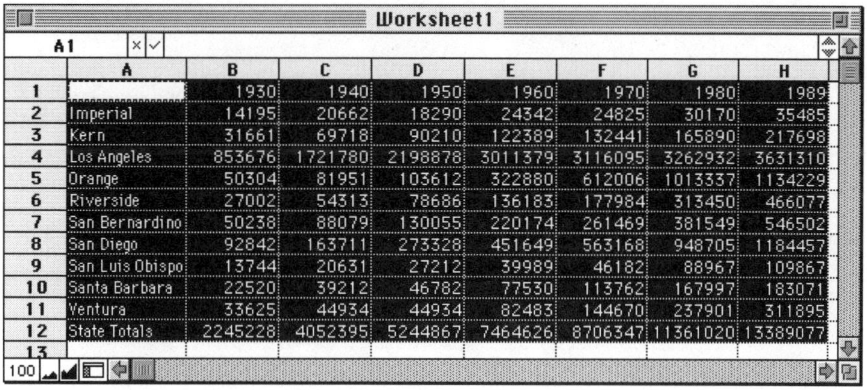

	A	B	C	D	E	F	G	H
1		1930	1940	1950	1960	1970	1980	1989
2	Imperial	14195	20662	18290	24342	24825	30170	35485
3	Kern	31661	69718	90210	122389	132441	165890	217698
4	Los Angeles	853676	1721780	2198878	3011379	3116095	3262932	3631310
5	Orange	50304	81951	103612	322880	612006	1013337	1134229
6	Riverside	27002	54313	78686	136183	177984	313450	466077
7	San Bernardino	50238	88079	130055	220174	261469	381549	546502
8	San Diego	92842	163711	273328	451649	563168	948705	1184457
9	San Luis Obispo	13744	20631	27212	39989	46182	88967	109867
10	Santa Barbara	22520	39212	46782	77530	113762	167997	183071
11	Ventura	33625	44934	44934	82483	144670	237901	311895
12	State Totals	2245228	4052395	5244867	7464626	8706347	11361020	13389077
13								

Figure 11-14: Retrieved data pasted into a spreadsheet.

Query documents also work with a DB2 database on an IBM MVS/TSO mainframe computer and a SQL/DS database on an IBM VM/CMS mainframe computer. Connecting your Macintosh to an IBM mainframe computer requires an internal network adapter card or an external network adapter.

Query documents send queries in one command language, called Data Access Language (DAL), regardless of the type of host computer, brand of database management system, or type of network. A DAL server program must be installed on the host computer to translate DAL commands to the language the particular database management system understands. Your Macintosh must have the DAL system extension in its Extensions folder, which is inside the System Folder.

A single query document works with any program that has an Open Query command (or equivalent). Most people use predefined query documents and do not create their own. The person who creates a query document must know the database structure and usually needs a special program and an understanding of the database access language.

All these installation and setup details sound complicated, but they're usually handled by a system administrator or MIS support person in your company. To get data, you just choose a menu command, select a query document, fill in its dialog box, wait, and paste.

Summary

- Programs link with each other and share services by sending and receiving Apple events messages. Some programs understand only the four basic Apple events messages but other programs understand two dozen or more.

- You control whether programs from other computers on your network can link to your programs using the Sharing Setup control panel, the Users & Groups control panel, and the Finder's Sharing command.

- Apple events also provides the foundation for system-wide user scripting. A script can perform with one mouse click a routine procedure that otherwise involves much tedious manual work with many programs.

- Some programs enable you to access data from a database management system by opening a query document and selecting a few options in its dialog box. The query document contains a hidden sequence of database-access commands, which someone familiar with the database management system has prepared in advance.

Part III:
Customizing System 7

Chapter 12 .... **257**
Tips and Secrets

Chapter 13 .... **289**
Utilities and Enhancements

Chapter 12
Tips and Secrets

In This Chapter
- Finder tips: icons, aliases, windows, folders, and the Trash.
- Directory dialog box, Apple menu, and Application menu shortcuts.
- Desk accessory, control panel, and file sharing tips.
- Memory use, performance, and troubleshooting tips.
- Printing, desktop, typing symbols, and startup time tips.

Scattered throughout the first eleven chapters of this book are scores of tips and secret methods for getting more out of System 7. For your convenience, this chapter contains a digest of the most useful six dozen. For some of these tips you need a copy of ResEdit, Apple's resource editor. You can get it from APDA (Apple Programmers and Developers Association) on-line information services, or Macintosh User Groups.

Icons

In this section, you'll find ideas for saving time and effort while editing icon names, making and using aliases on the desktop, getting icons to look the way you want, and manipulating font icons.

Spotting a name selected for editing

For a visual cue that you have selected the name of an icon on a color or grayscale monitor, use the Colors control panel to set the text highlight color to something other than black and white. Then you know a name highlighted in color (or gray) is ready for editing, whereas a name highlighted in black-and-white is not, as shown in Figure 12-1.

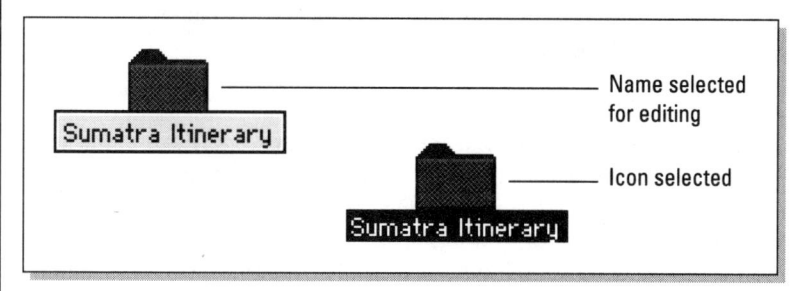

Figure 12-1: Ready for editing, or not.

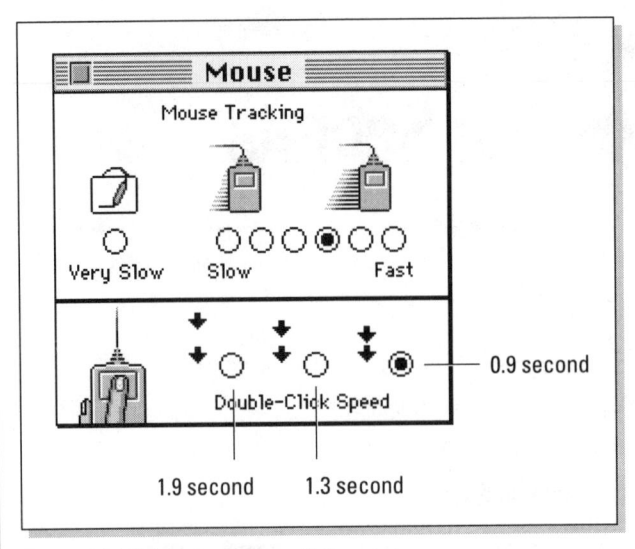

Figure 12-2: Wait this long before clicking again.

Edit, don't open
If you have trouble editing icon names without opening the item, try setting a briefer Double-Click Speed with the Mouse control panel, as shown in Figure 12-2. You must wait the duration of a double-click interval — about 1.9 second, 1.3 second, or 0.9 second, as set in the Mouse control panel — after selecting an icon name before selecting an insertion point, a word, or a range of text. If you click again too soon, the Finder thinks you're double-clicking the icon and opens it.

You don't have to wait if you move the pointer slightly right after clicking the icon name. Click the name, twitch the mouse, and the name is ready for editing. Another way to beat the wait is to click the name and then move the insertion point by pressing the arrow keys. Pressing up arrow moves the insertion point to the beginning of the name, down arrow moves it to the end, left arrow moves it left, and right arrow moves it right.

Undoing accidental name change
If you rename an icon by mistake, choose Undo from the Edit menu or press Command-Z to restore the original name. Another way to restore the icon's original name is to press Backspace or Delete until the name is empty, and then press Return or click outside the icon.

Copy/Paste icon names
While editing a name, you can use the Undo, Cut, Copy, Paste, and Select All commands in the Edit menu. You cannot undo your changes to a name after you finish editing it, only while it is still selected for editing. You can also copy the entire name of any item by selecting its icon (or its whole name) and using the Copy command (Paste menu). This capability comes in handy when you're copying a disk and want to name the copy the same as the original.

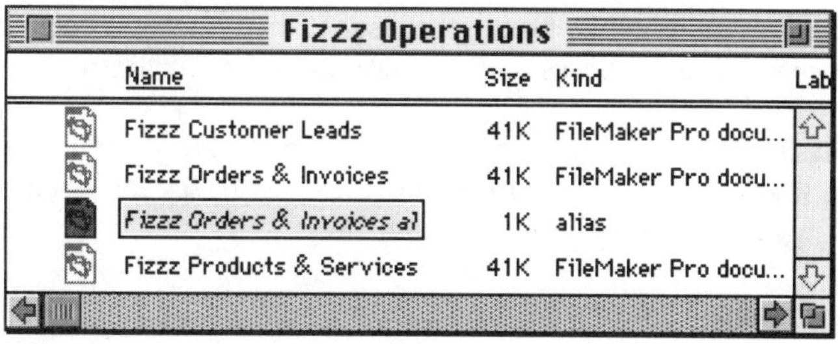

Figure 12-3: A long alias name.

You can copy the name of a locked item — select the item and use the Copy command — but you can't change the name of a locked item. (Unlock an item with the Get Info command, or if it's a disk, by sliding its locking tab.)

Finder 7 doesn't limit you to copying one icon name at a time. If you select several items and then use the Copy command, all their names are put on the Clipboard (up to 256 characters in all), one name per line.

Removing "alias"

The name the Finder constructs for an alias can be so long you can't see it all in a list view, as shown in Figure 12-3. If you want to remove the word *alias* from the end, select the icon name for editing, press the right-arrow or down-arrow key to move the insertion point to the end of the name, and press Delete six times, or five times if you want to leave a blank space at the end of the alias name to distinguish it from the original name.

You can also drag the alias to the desktop or switch the view to by Icon or by Small Icon and edit the name in icon view. In icon view you can click the name once to select it for editing, move the mouse slightly (or pause briefly), double-click the last word of the name, and press Delete twice (once if you want to retain a blank space at the end of the alias name). If you double-click too quickly after selecting the name, the Finder opens the alias instead of selecting the last word of the name.

Permanently removing "alias"

If you always remove the word *alias* from the end of new alias names, you may prefer never to have the word appended to the file name at all. You can make a change with ResEdit so the Finder never appends the word alias to the names of new aliases. Follow these steps:

1. Open ResEdit and use its Open command to open a copy of the Finder. You see a window full of icons, each representing a different type of resource in the Finder.

2. Double-click the STR# resource type, opening a window that lists all the Finder's string lists resources by number.

3. Locate STR# resource number 20500, and double-click it to open it. This is the text the Finder appends to the original file name to make up the alias name.

4. Change the string to one blank space, rather than making it completely empty, so the names of original files and their aliases will be different.

5. To finish, close all the ResEdit windows or simply quit ResEdit. Answer yes when it asks whether you want to save changes. To see the results of your work, you must restart your Macintosh.

Desktop aliases

Rather than drag frequently used programs, control panels, documents, and folders themselves into the desktop, make aliases of them and put the aliases on the desktop. You get quick access to the original items through their desktop aliases. Also, you can open several related items at the same time by opening aliases on the desktop, even if the original items happen to be in different folders or on different disks. If your desktop becomes too cluttered with aliases, you can put related aliases together in a desktop folder.

Trash everywhere

Are your Trash and hard disk icons inevitably covered by windows of other open programs? What a mess! Make aliases of the Trash and hard disk, put the aliases in a folder, and put the folder in your Apple menu for instant access. Leaving that folder open makes its window come to the front along with the other Finder windows whenever you switch to the Finder. If you're lucky enough to have two monitors, put a Trash alias on the second monitor. Beats dragging icons across two screens to throw them away.

Express access to CD-ROM

Cut through the drudgery of wading through folders on a CD-ROM by making aliases of items inside the CD-ROM folders. Because CD-ROMs are permanently locked, you must put the aliases on your hard disk (or a floppy disk). Opening an alias makes a beeline to the original item on the CD-ROM.

Cataloging items on floppy disks

You can use aliases to keep track of and quickly open items on floppy disks — even floppies that aren't inserted in your Macintosh. Make aliases of the items on a floppy disk and copy the aliases to your startup disk. (You can then delete the aliases from the floppy disk.) When you need the item again, the Finder tells you the name of the disk to insert so it can open the alias's original item, as shown in Figure 12-4. If you change your mind or can't find the needed disk, click the Cancel button.

Making many aliases

To make aliases for several items in the same window at once, select them all and use the Make Alias command. An alias appears for every item you selected. All the new aliases are automatically selected so you can immediately drag them to another place without having to manually select them as a group. If you accidentally deselect them, you can easily group them together for reselecting by changing the window's view to by Kind or by Date.

Figure 12-4: After opening an alias of an item on a floppy disk.

Duplicating fonts

Because you can't rename individual fixed-size or TrueType fonts with the Finder, you can't duplicate them in the same folder. (You can rename or duplicate font suitcases and PostScript fonts.) To duplicate a fixed-size or TrueType font, press Option and drag it to another folder or to the desktop. (Dragging to another disk automatically makes a copy of the font on the target disk.)

Making a font suitcase

You can create a new, empty font suitcase file with System 7 by duplicating an existing font suitcase file, opening the duplicate, and dragging its contents to the Trash, as shown in Figure 12-5.

Stationery workaround

You can work around the Finder asking you to name and save a new document every time you open a particular stationery pad. Instead, make an ordinary document and lock it using the Finder's Get Info command. You may want to use this method with templates for printing single envelopes and mailing labels, for example. Then you could open the locked template, type or paste the recipient's address, print, and close without saving. This method does not work with WriteNow 3.0 or other programs that do not permit making changes to locked documents.

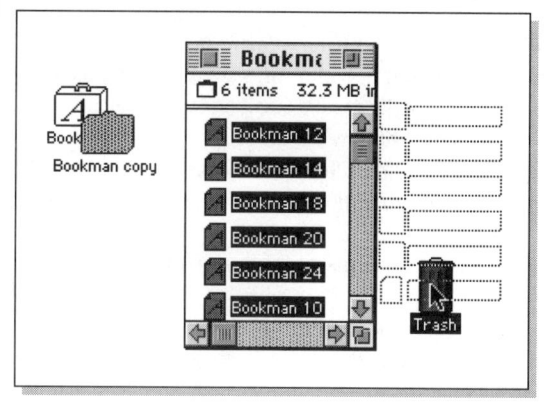

Figure 12-5: A new font suitcase.

> ⚠ Are you sure you want to rebuild the desktop file on the disk "Macintosh HD"? Comments in info windows will be lost.
>
> [Cancel] [OK]

Figure 12-6: Ready to rebuild the desktop.

Icon updating

When you install an updated program that includes redesigned icons on your disk, you may not see the new icon until you rebuild the disk's desktop. To rebuild the desktop of any disk whose icon normally appears on the desktop after startup, press Command-Option while starting your Macintosh. For each disk in turn, the Finder asks whether you want the disk's desktop rebuilt, as shown in Figure 12-6. To rebuild the desktop of a floppy disk or other removable disk whose icon is not on the desktop, press Command-Option while inserting the disk.

WARNING: Rebuilding the desktop destroys all comments in Get Info windows. You can get software that preserves the comments through rebuilding, and other software that resets the icon of any program you designate (see "Disk and File Utilities" in Chapter 13).

If you have too many boring, look-alike folders cluttering your desktop and you use System 7, you can liven them up by superimposing a relevant application icon, as shown in Figure 12-7. First copy a folder icon from its info window, which you view with the Finder's Get Info command, and paste it into a color paint program. Then open the folder that contains the application whose icon you want to use, view the folder window by Small Icon, and take a screen snapshot (press Command-Shift-3). Next open the screen snapshot file (named *Picture 1* on your startup disk) with the color paint program or with TeachText, copy the small application icon from the snapshot, and paste it over the pasted folder icon. Finally copy the composite icon from the paint program, paste it into the folder's info window, and close the info window.

Fixing blank icons

Sometimes a file you copy onto your disk ends up with a generic (blank) icon. You don't really want to rebuild your desktop just to fix one icon (especially if you have a large drive). Instead, open the Get Info window for the icon. Click the icon in the info window and a box appears around it, indicating you have selected the icon. Now copy, paste, and cut the icon — in that order. If you are lucky, the correct icon shows its face.

Here's how it works: Copying the icon makes it possible to paste; pasting the icon causes the system to internally mark the file as one that has a custom icon; and cutting the icon causes the system to unmark the file and restore its standard icon. You can't do the cutting step unless you have done the pasting step, and you can't do the pasting step unless you have done the copying step.

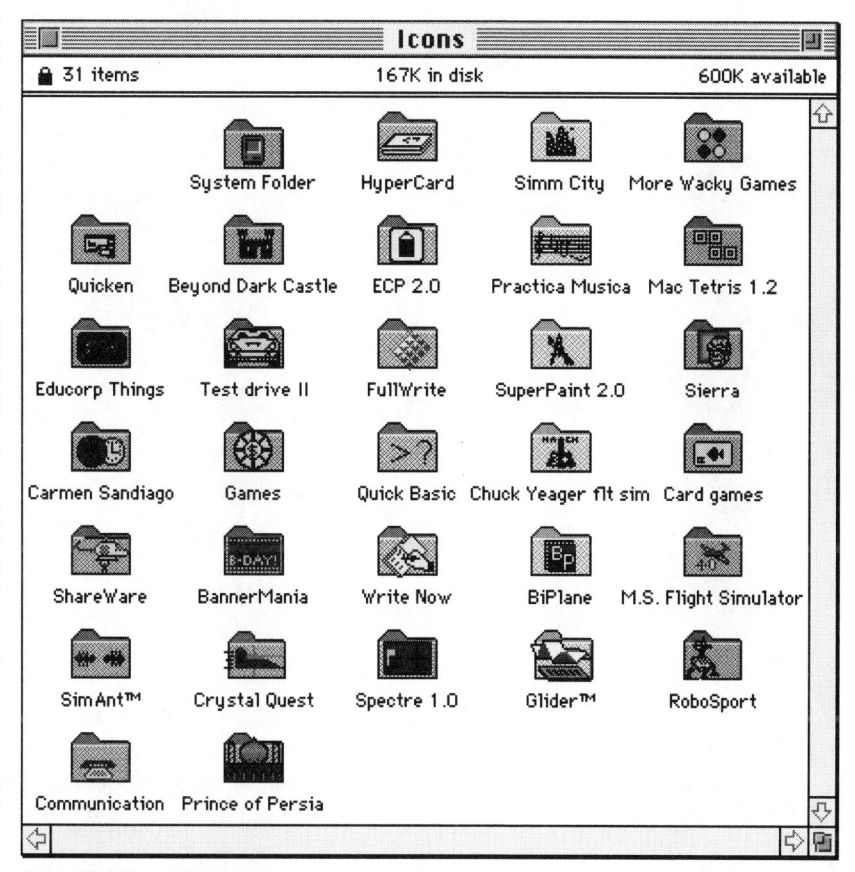

Figure 12-7: Composite folder icons.

Problems with custom color icons

When you paste a color picture into an item's Get Info window, you don't always get the custom icon you expect, because the Finder is partly color blind. It sees light colors like yellow or orange at the picture's edge as transparent parts of the icon and omits them from the mask it makes for the custom icon. The defective mask punches an incomplete hole in the desktop for the icon to show through, as shown in Figure 12-8. You can fix a defective icon mask with ResEdit version 2.1 or later (see the beginning of this chapter for more details). Use the following steps:

1. Open ResEdit and use its Open command to open the item whose custom icon you want to fix. To get at the custom icon of a folder or disk, open the file named *Icon* inside the folder or disk (this file is invisible in the Finder). You can't fix the custom icon of an alias directly because you can't open the alias itself. Instead, make a new folder, paste the custom icon into that folder's info window, fix the folder's icon as described here, and copy the fixed icon to the alias's info window.

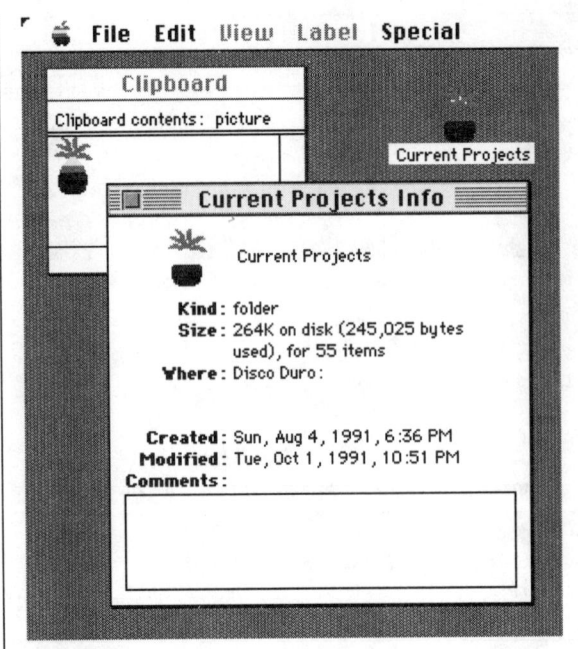

Figure 12-8: A color icon with an incomplete mask.

2. After opening the item whose icon you want to fix, double-click the icl4 resource type. A window opens containing the icon you need to fix and maybe some other icons.

3. Double-click the icon in that window to open an icon-editing window, as shown in Figure 12-9. This window contains a set of icon-editing tools and a panel in which you can edit the icon dot by dot. In addition, the window shows the icon mask and the six variations of the icon (large and small sizes in black-and-white, 16-color, and 256-color). The icon-editing window also shows what the icon looks like on the desktop in several states (not selected, selected, not open, open, and off-line).

4. To fix the large icon, drag the icl4 icon or the icl8 icon over the large mask, as shown in Figure 12-10. This creates a better mask based on the color icon. You may need to fine-tune the mask so its black dots exactly correspond to the colored dots in the icl4 icon. To edit the mask, click with the pencil tool or use other tools. To check the correspondence of dots, alternately click the icl4 icon and the large mask.

5. Repeat step 4 using the ics4 icon to make a new small mask. You may want to touch up the ics4 and ics8 icons before making the small mask.

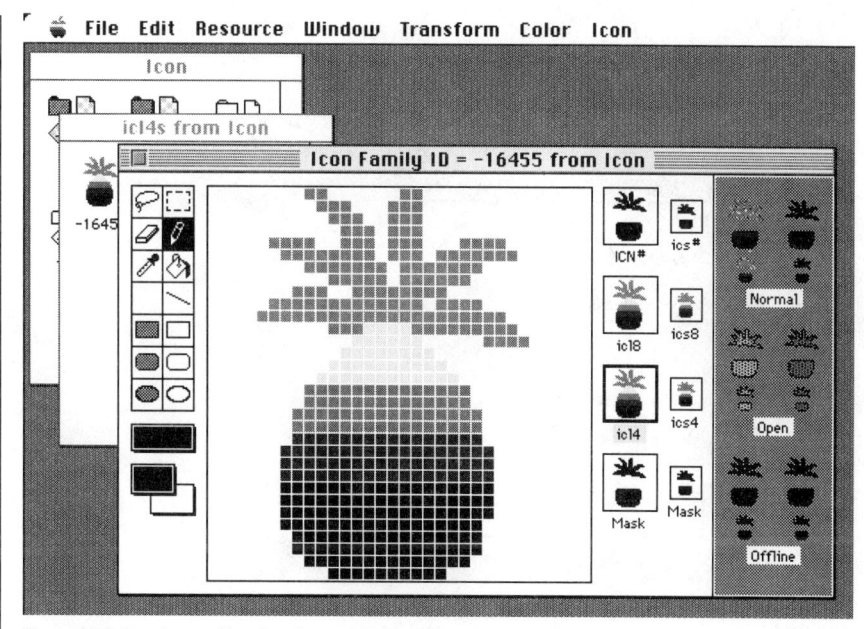

Figure 12-9: Ready to edit an icon's mask in ResEdit.

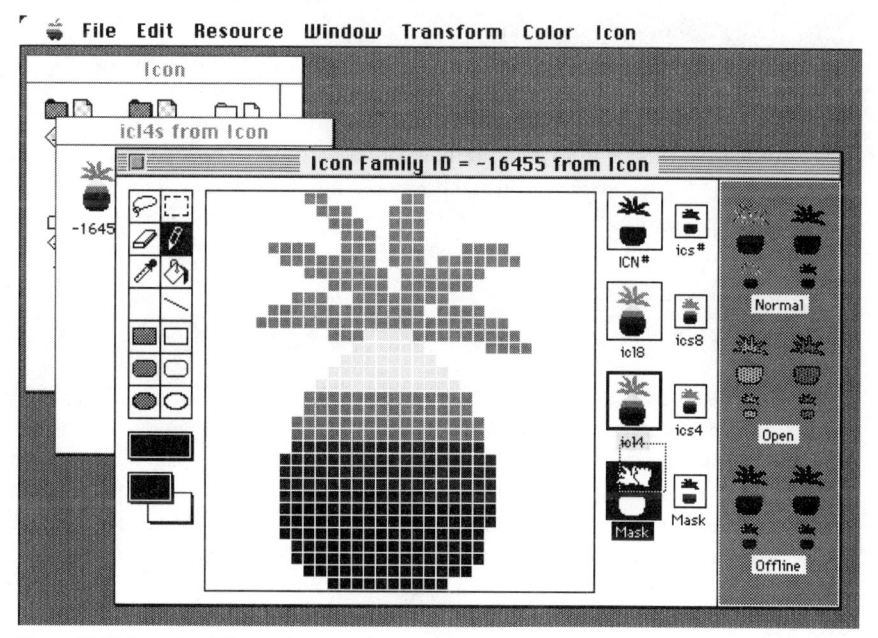

Figure 12-10: Dragging icl4 to make a new large mask.

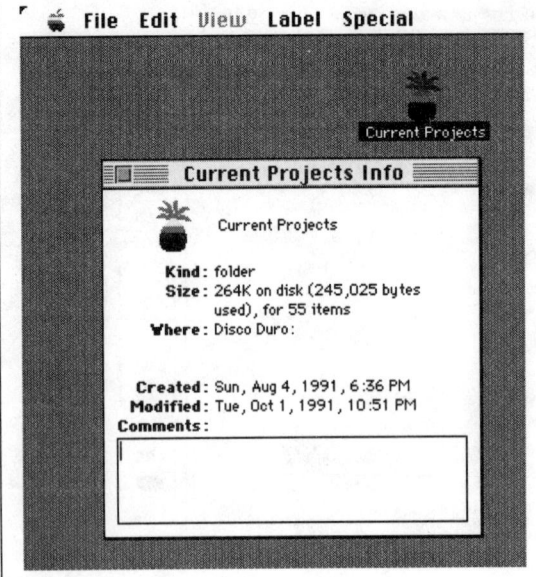

Figure 12-11: A color icon with a complete mask.

6. To finish, close all the ResEdit windows or simply quit ResEdit. Answer yes when it asks whether you want to save changes. To see the results of your work, as shown in Figure 12-11, you must restart your Macintosh.

Revert to standard icon

You can revert to an item's standard icon after having replaced the icon with custom graphics. Just select the item, choose Get Info from the Finder's File menu, select the icon in the Get Info window, and choose Clear or Cut from the Edit menu.

Folders and Windows

The tips in this section involve Finder windows and folders.

Finder power

The Finder has a great deal of hidden power, which you tap by pressing Command-Option at the opportune moment. In addition, much of what you can do with the mouse you can also do with the keyboard alone. Tables 3-3, 3-4, 3-5, and 3-6 list power methods and keyboard equivalents for selecting items in windows or on the desktop; opening and closing items; expanding and collapsing outlines of folders in list views; and more. For the most part, these tables do not list keyboard equivalents for menu commands because you can review them on-screen by pulling down the menus.

Special folder replacement

Should you happen to discard one of the special folders inside the System Folder, you can make a replacement using the Finder's New Folder command (File menu). After creating a new folder, change its name to that of the special folder you want: Apple

Menu Items, Control Panels, Extensions, Fonts, Preferences, or Startup Items. Wait a few seconds and you'll see its icon get the distinctive look of the special folder you're creating.

Special folder mistakes
The Finder sometimes makes mistakes when it puts items in the System Folder's special folders for you. It may put some items in the correct places and incorrectly leave others in the System Folder itself. For example, it may put a control panel in the Control Panels folder but leave that control panel's auxiliary folder in the System Folder. That control panel won't work right because it expects to find its auxiliary folder in the same folder as it is in. You must open the System Folder and drag the auxiliary folder to the Control Panels folder yourself.

Abridged System Folder
Does finding the Apple Menu Items folder, Startup Items folder, or some other item in your System Folder take too long? Make aliases for the System Folder items you access often — including an alias of the System Folder itself — and consolidate the aliases in a new folder. You can open and find an item in that folder faster than in the System Folder. To make the new folder look like a System Folder, copy the icon from the System Folder's info window and paste it into the new folder's info window.

Removing from the System Folder
Before you can remove an item from the System Folder, you must know which inner folder it is in. If you're not sure, use the Finder's Find command to locate the item (see "Fast File Finding" in Chapter 3). Be sure to put items you drag from the special folders within the System Folder onto the desktop or into an ordinary folder. Many items you drag out of special folders are still effective if you merely drag them to the System Folder window.

Easy startup items
If you want an item opened at startup time, put an alias of it in the Startup Items folder. Don't put original items there, because returning them to their original locations when you no longer want them opened at startup time can be a drag. When you're done with an alias, you can just drag it to the Trash. Aliases in the Startup Items folder are opened alphabetically after any applications and before any documents that are also in that folder.

Seeing desktop items
If the windows of open programs obscure desktop icons, you can hide those windows by choosing Hide Others from the Application menu while the Finder is active. If Finder windows cover desktop icons, you can close all those windows at once by pressing Option while clicking the close box of any Finder window.

Narrow Finder windows
You can reduce the width of Finder windows to show just the item names in list views without laboriously dragging the size boxes of each window. Use the Views control panel to temporarily set all List View options off. Then shrink each window

to fit the new format by clicking its zoom box. After shrinking all windows, you can turn on List View options in the Views control panel. You can scroll the contents of a narrow window horizontally to see columns that are out of view.

Viewing by size

Items in Finder windows viewed by size may be out of order right after you turn on the Calculate Folder Sizes option in the Views control panel. The Finder takes a while to calculate the sizes, and in the meantime it has already displayed the window contents. You can force the Finder to re-sort a window's contents according to size by clicking another column heading (such as Name) and then clicking the Size column heading again.

Folder size slowdown

The Calculate Folder Sizes option in the Views control panel can slow down your Mac when you're sharing someone else's files or accessing a file server. If you notice the network activity indicator flashing in the left corner of the menu bar and you're not actively using a shared item, the Finder may be getting folder sizes from another Mac. (The Finder even does that in the background while you work with another program.) To end the slowdown, either close the shared item's windows or turn off the Calculate Folder Sizes option.

Find in next window

Sometimes the Finder's Find Next command gets you bogged down in a window that contains many matches to what you specified in the Find command, but you know the window doesn't contain the item you want. To cancel searching in the active window and skip to the next folder that contains a match, close the window by clicking the close box or pressing Command-W.

Drag to scroll

You can scroll a window in Finder 7 without using the scroll bars. Simply place the pointer in the window, press the mouse button, and drag toward the area you want to come into view. Drag the pointer up, down, left, or right past the window's active area and scrolling begins. Dragging past a window corner scrolls diagonally. To scroll slowly, drag just to the window's edge (and continue pressing the mouse button). Increase scrolling speed by dragging beyond the window's edge.

Trash

This section has tips on throwing stuff away and retrieving it from the Trash afterwards.

Skip the Trash warning

To skip the standard Trash warning the next time you empty the Trash, press Option while choosing the Empty Trash command. You can also reverse the Trash Warning setting by selecting the Trash, choosing Get Info and reversing the setting of the "Skip Trash Warnings" option.

Discarding locked items
When you use the Empty Trash command, the Finder normally won't discard locked items that you have dragged to the Trash. Instead of unlocking each locked item with the Finder's Get Info command, you can simply press Option while choosing Empty Trash from the Special menu.

Trash retrieval
To put items currently in the Trash back where they came from, open the Trash, select the items, and choose Put Away from the Finder's File menu. The Finder returns each selected item to its previous folder, though not necessarily to the same place in the folder window.

Discarding items from one disk
To remove items from only one disk, try putting away the icons of the disks whose trashed items you want to retain. To put away a disk icon, either select it and choose Put Away (or press Command-Y) from the Finder's File menu, or drag the disk icon to the Trash. Alternatively you can open the Trash and drag the items you want to save onto the desktop or to another folder. Then use the Empty Trash command.

Rescued items
Sometimes the Trash contains a folder named *Rescued Items*. It usually contains formerly invisible temporary files found when you started up your Macintosh. The Rescued Items folder may appear after a system crash and you may be able to recreate your work up to the time of the system crash from the contents of the Rescued Items folder.

Directory Dialog Boxes
You can save time and effort in the directory dialog boxes you get with the Open, Save As, and other disk-related commands by using the tips in this section.

Directory dialog keystrokes
The System 7 directory dialog boxes recognize more keyboard equivalents than older versions. Table 2-1 has the details.

Find an alias's original item
You can quickly go to an alias's original item in a directory dialog box by pressing Option while opening the alias (by double-clicking it, for example). Alias names appear in italics in directory dialog boxes, just as they do in Finder windows.

Folder switching
If you find yourself frequently going back and forth between two folders, just put an alias of each folder in the other. Whichever folder you are in, you can go to the other in one step by opening its alias.

Aliases for favorite folders

Putting aliases of your favorite folders on the desktop or inside disk windows enables you to quickly open a favorite folder from a directory dialog box. Instead of working your way down through one branch of your folder structure and then working your way up another branch to the folder you want, you zip to the desktop level or the disk level and there open the alias of the folder you want. It's as if you could jump from one branch of a tree to the root level and then jump to a spot on another branch without crawling up the trunk and along the other branch.

You can quickly get to aliases of favorite folders on the desktop by clicking the Desktop button. Get to aliases at the disk window level by choosing the disk from the directory dialog's pop-up menu.

Copy and Paste

You can copy-and-paste a document's name from the document to a Save or Save As dialog box (or vice versa). If the Cut, Copy, and Paste commands are not available from the Edit menu, you can use their keyboard equivalents, Command-X, Command-C, and Command-V. When pasting, only the first 31 characters are used; any additional characters are omitted.

Double-click sidestep

As usual you can open an item in the directory window by double-clicking it. If you double-click the wrong item and realize it before you release the mouse button, continue pressing and drag the pointer to the item you want to open. When you release the mouse button, the currently selected item opens.

Double-click cancel

To cancel a double-click in a System 7 directory dialog box, hold down the mouse button on the second click and drag the pointer outside the dialog box before releasing the mouse button.

Desk Accessories

You'll find ideas for getting more from the standard desk accessories that come with System 7 in this section.

Puzzle pictures

Puzzle 7.0 has two games, one with numbered tiles and another with a picture of the Apple logo. Choose Clear from the Edit menu to switch between them. You can replace the picture of the Apple logo. Just copy a picture in another program, switch to the Puzzle, and paste. For example, the next-to-last item in the standard System 7 Scrapbook, a picture of linked rings, makes a challenging puzzle.

Scripted calculator

You can copy the text of a calculation — for example, 69.95+26.98+14.99*.0725 — and paste it into the standard Calculator desk accessory. Be sure to use the asterisk (*) symbol for multiplication and the slash (/) symbol for division.

Printed key caps

You might like to print the Key Caps desk accessory as a handy reference, but it has no Print command. To work around this, take a picture of the screen and print that as follows. Open Key Caps, choose the font you want it to show, and press any modifier keys (Shift, Option, Control, or Command) you want in effect. Move the pointer to an empty area of the menu bar, hold down the mouse button, temporarily release the modifier keys, press Command-Shift-3, again press the modifier keys you released temporarily, and finally release the mouse button. Your gyrations should be rewarded by the sound of a camera shutter as the system snaps a picture of the screen. Open your startup disk and look for a document named *Picture 1*. Print this document using TeachText or any graphics program. Cut out the Key Caps window with scissors after printing or crop it out with a graphics program before printing. If you take additional snapshots, they are numbered sequentially.

Alternate scrapbooks

After extensive use, your Scrapbook may become cluttered with old clippings. If you can't bear to throw them out forever, make a copy of the Scrapbook File in your System Folder (use the Finder's Duplicate command) before you start weeding. Later you can use the old copy you made by dragging the current Scrapbook File out of the System Folder, dragging the old copy in, and changing its name to *Scrapbook File*.

Control Panels

This section has tips on using the standard control panels that come with System 7.

Revert to standard gray desktop

After changing the standard gray desktop pattern as described in Chapter 2, you can easily revert to the standard gray colors. Simply open the General Controls control panel and scroll through the available desktop patterns until you see the standard gray pattern. Clicking that pattern in the control panel makes it take over the desktop.

Caution: Your custom pattern is not saved anywhere.

Revert to standard labels

If you want to reset the Labels control panel to factory standard colors and names, use the settings in Table 3-2.

Easy Access shortcuts

Instead of using the Easy Access control panel to turn Mouse Keys or Sticky Keys on and off, you can use the keyboard. To turn on Mouse Keys, press Command-Shift-Clear. To turn it off press Clear. (Mouse Keys requires a numeric keypad, so you can't use it from a PowerBook.) To turn on Sticky Keys, press Shift five times in succession. Turn it off by pressing Shift five times again or by pressing any two modifier keys simultaneously.

Big map

You can enlarge the world map in the Map control panel by pressing Option while opening the control panel. To magnify more, press Shift-Option while opening.

Color map

If your Map control panel displays a black-and-white world map on your color or grayscale monitor, you can colorize the map. First look through your Scrapbook for a color version of the world map used in the Map control panel. If you find one, copy it, open the Map control panel, and paste.

If you can't find a color version of the world map, you don't have the standard System 7 Scrapbook file. To get it, temporarily move the Scrapbook file from your System Folder to the desktop. Next copy the Scrapbook file from the Tidbits installation disk to your System Folder. Copy the color map as described above. Finally, select the Scrapbook file on the desktop, choose Put Away from the Finder's file menu, and click OK when the Finder asks if it's OK to replace the Scrapbook file in the System Folder with the one you're moving (putting away) from the desktop.

Hidden free beep

The System 7 Scrapbook includes an extra system alert sound that you can paste into the Sound control panel. If your Scrapbook doesn't contain the sound, you don't have the standard System 7 Scrapbook file. This usually means your System Folder had a Scrapbook file when the disk was upgraded to System 7. For instructions on getting the standard Scrapbook file, see the previous tip.

Apple and Application Menus

Use the tips in this section to get more from the Apple menu and the Application menu.

Hiding windows while switching

To hide the active program's windows as you switch to a particular program, press Option while choosing the other program from the Application menu. Or press Option while clicking another program's window. You hide windows and switch to the Finder by pressing Option while clicking the desktop or a Finder icon.

Hide windows to boost performance

With several programs open, you can spend lots of your time waiting while inactive programs redraw portions of their windows as dialog boxes come and go. This delay is particularly protracted when using virtual memory, because the window redrawing may require disk access. Eliminate all the delay by choosing Hide Others from the Application menu. Hidden windows don't require updating.

Apple menu organization

Once you add more than a few items to the Apple menu it becomes a mess. You can group different types of items by prefixing different numbers of blank spaces to their names — the more blank spaces, the higher on the Apple menu. For example, you might prefix three blank spaces to control panel names, two blanks to desk accessory names, one blank to application programs, and none to other items.

Apple menu separators

A long Apple menu, even one organized by type of item as described in the previous tip, can be hard to scan quickly. It helps to visually separate the different types of items. You can make separators by naming extra aliases with hyphens and prefixing the right number of blank spaces to the names so each one appears between two different types of items. Aliases of the Finder work well as separators because accidentally opening one results in a message saying that item can't be opened. You can also use ordinary folders instead of aliases to make separators in the Apple menu.

To further refine your Apple menu, you can hide the icons of the separators you make. First you copy some white space in any painting program. Next you select a separator item's icon and use the Finder's Get Info command to display the item's info window. Then you select the icon in that window and paste the white space over it.

Fast Apple menu changes

To quickly add or remove items to the Apple menu, list the Apple Menu Items folder on the Apple menu. How? Make an alias of the Apple Menu Items folder and put that alias in that folder.

Too-full Apple menu

If your Apple menu has so many items that you must scroll it to see them all, consider consolidating the less-used items in a folder or two within the Apple Menu Items folder. You can make the contents of folders within the Apple Menu Items folder appear as submenus of the Apple menu by adding a control panel or system extension such as BeHierarchic or MenuChoice (both described in "Menus, Folders, and Icons" in Chapter 13). Commercial products that add submenus to the Apple menu include HAM from Microseeds and Now Utilities 4.0 from Now Software.

Universal Show Clipboard

Some application programs lack a Show Clipboard command and others that have one use a private clipboard whose contents may look different when pasted into another program. With System 7 installed you can put a Show Clipboard command in your Apple menu for reviewing the standard Clipboard contents from any application program. First you make an alias of the Clipboard file, which is in the System Folder. Then you place the alias in the Apple Menu Items folder and rename the alias Show Clipboard. Now choosing Show Clipboard from the Apple menu switches to the Finder and opens the Clipboard.

File Sharing

Get more out of System 7's file sharing by using the tips in this section.

Reducing network cabling costs

For a less expensive network, use Farallon's PhoneNet connectors (or equivalent) and ordinary telephone cables instead of Apple's LocalTalk connectors and cables. Not only does PhoneNet cost less, it also works with greater cable lengths than LocalTalk.

Picking a secure password
Pick a password that is easy to remember but difficult for others to guess. For better security mix letters with numbers; try replacing the letters *I* and *O* with the numbers 1 and 0.

Allow saving, not trashing
You can allow others to save changes to a file you're sharing but prevent them from throwing the file away. Simply share an alias to the file and put the original item in a folder to which only you have privileges for making changes. If someone discards the alias, the original item isn't affected.

Share disks or outer folders
Once you share a folder, System 7 won't let you share the folder or disk that contains it, as shown in Figure 12-12. You have to drag the shared folder to another place or unshare it before you can share the outer folder or disk. To avoid this situation, share from the highest level of your disk and folder structure.

Improving file sharing performance
For best performance of your Macintosh, share as few of your folders as possible. The more items others access on your Macintosh, the greater the demands on your Macintosh's performance. Sharing too many folders can slow your system to a crawl. In situations where you need to share numerous files or share folders simultaneously with several users, consider setting up a dedicated Macintosh to act as a centralized file server for the shared information.

Cutting file sharing red tape
Getting access to shared items involves wading through a fair amount of bureaucracy. Aliases cut through the red tape. Here's how: You access a shared disk or folder once using the Chooser desk accessory, as described in Chapter 8. Next you select the

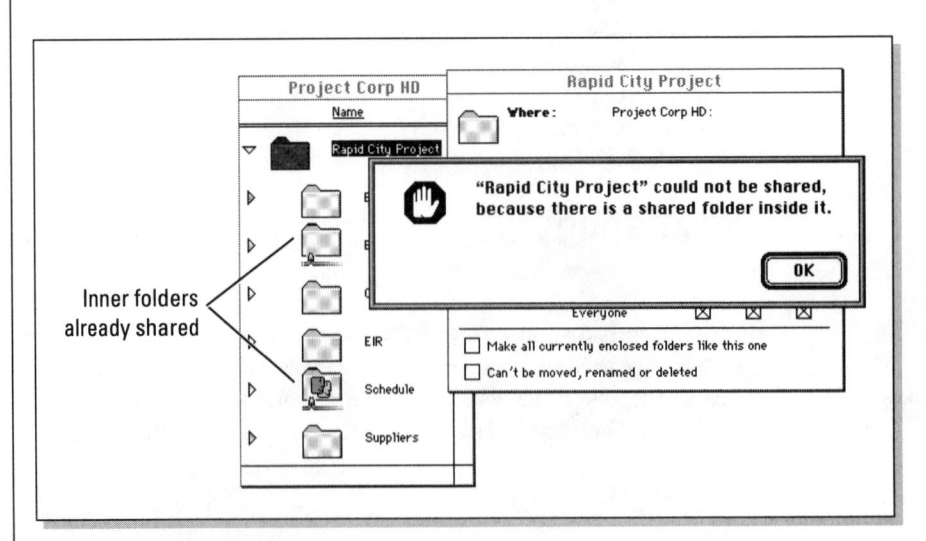

Figure 12-12: Can't share outer folder.

shared item or any folder or file in it and choose Make Alias from the File menu. Finally, you copy the alias to your desktop or hard disk. An alias keeps track of its original item even if the original item is on another networked Macintosh.

Once you make an alias of a shared item, you can access the shared item by opening the alias either from the Finder or from an Open command's directory dialog box. Dragging something to the alias of a shared disk or folder also automatically accesses that shared item. You still must enter a password unless you initially accessed the original item as a guest. If the shared item is not available — for example, because the Macintosh where it resides is turned off — a message tells you that.

Office on a disk
Aliases can give you nearly automatic access to your Macintosh's hard disks using a floppy disk in any other Macintosh on the same network. To easily access your disks from another Macintosh, open the Sharing Setup control panel and check the File Sharing status. If it is off, click the start button and wait until it is on (the Start button becomes a Stop button).

Next select all your hard disk icons and choose Sharing from the File menu to open a Sharing info window for each disk. In each window turn on the "Share this item and its contents" option and turn off the See Folders, See Files, and Make Changes options for the User/Group and Everyone categories. These settings restrict access to your disks so that only you can make changes or see files or folders. Make an alias of each disk and copy the aliases to a floppy disk.

As long as file sharing is active on your Macintosh, you use that floppy disk to access your hard disk from any Macintosh on your network. You simply insert the disk, open the alias for the disk you want to use, and enter your password when asked. Correctly entering your password allows you access to all applications, folders, and documents on your disk from any remote Macintosh. You don't have to bother with opening the Chooser, selecting AppleShare, selecting your computer, and typing your name as the registered user.

The latest shared document
To make sure others who share your documents have the latest version, share an alias of the original and keep the original in an inaccessible folder. Other users can copy the alias to their disks and use the alias to open the original document. If you later replace the original document with a version having the same name, the aliases people already copied will open the new version. People who share the alias always get the newest version of the original item it represents, even if the original frequently changes.

What people have trashed
Items from your shared disk or folder that someone has dragged to the Trash — but has not yet permanently removed — on another Macintosh don't appear in your Trash. System 7 puts those items in folders whose names begin *Trash Can #*. You can use the Finder's Find command to search for those names. To see which disk the items come from, select the Trash Can # icon and use the Finder's Get Info command.

Memory and Performance

The tips in this section help you make the most of your computer's memory and increase its performance.

Disk Cache performance boost

If you have a Macintosh IIsi and you set the number of colors or grays for its built-in video to 4 or more, you can improve system performance by setting the Disk Cache to 768K in the Memory control panel. Then the Disk Cache and the built-in video together use up all the memory that's soldered to the main circuit board. This forces the system software and your programs into the part of memory in the four SIMM sockets. Programs may work much slower if they are located in the soldered-on memory along with the built-in video.

The same trick works in a Macintosh IIci with 5MB, 9MB, or 17MB of RAM. To get the performance boost, the 256K SIMMs must be installed in the four sockets nearest the disk drive. Realizing a performance increase on a IIci with other RAM capacities isn't feasible because you would have to set the Disk Cache so high as to waste a large amount of memory.

Finder out of memory

Finder 7 is supposed to manage its memory size automatically (by borrowing from the system area of memory as the need arises). If you get a message that there wasn't enough memory to use a control panel or open a window right now, try quitting an application program or desk accessory. If quitting programs doesn't help, you must restart your Macintosh.

If you get out-of-memory messages often, you may want to try increasing the Finder's memory size. However, Finder 7 gives you no way to set its memory size. You can work around this situation by restarting your Macintosh using a version of system software older than 7.0. Then open the System Folder on your System 7 startup hard disk, select the Finder, and choose Get Info from the File menu, as shown in Figure 12-13. In the info window that appears, set the Application Memory Size to 550K or so.

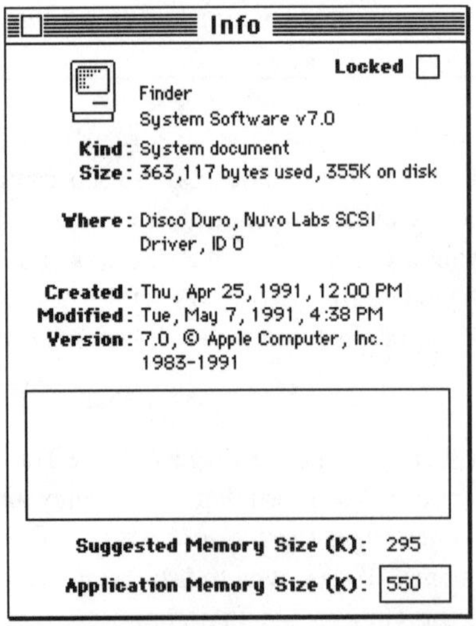

Figure 12-13: Using Finder 6 to change Finder 7's memory size.

Quitting startup programs

If you have several programs opened during startup, you may later have to quit some of them to free up memory for opening another. Naturally you'll want to quit the programs least important to you. You'll get maximum benefit from quitting them if they were the last items opened during startup. To make that happen, rename the items in your Startup Items folder so the most important comes first alphabetically, the next-most important comes second, and so on. You can avoid renaming original items by putting aliases in the Startup Items folder.

Paring memory to the bone
If your Macintosh has just the minimum 2MB of RAM required to use System 7, you should pare program memory sizes to the bone. For example, giving your favorite word processing program the full amount of memory available after the system software takes its chunk leaves you no room to use the Chooser to select a printer or share someone's files. (Though you can work around the file sharing limitation by making aliases of the items you most often share, as described in Chapter 8.) Also, there wouldn't be any memory left for background printing.

Reducing system memory size
You can reduce the system software's memory size (as reported by the About This Macintosh command) to its minimum by pressing Shift while restarting your Macintosh. Look for the message "Extensions Off" during startup. It confirms that you have suppressed loading of all items in the Extensions folder, Control Panels folder, and System Folder that would increase the system software's memory size. You have also bypassed opening items in the Startup Items folder, reduced the RAM cache to 16K, forced virtual memory off, and prevented file sharing from starting. None of these changes persist when you restart without pressing Shift. To make persistent changes, you must drag items out of the special folders and change settings in the Memory and File Sharing control panels.

For big memory savings, turn off file sharing and virtual memory if you're not using them. (I recoup 267K from the first and 380K from the second.) Reducing the RAM cache size reduces the system software's memory size K for K — and slows system performance.

Fragmented memory
To check for fragmented memory, add up the memory sizes of all the open programs and the system software as listed in the About This Macintosh window. If you have a monitor connected to the built-in video on a Macintosh IIsi or IIci, add another 320K (or less if you have limited the number of colors to less than 256 as described in "Monitor" in Chapter 5). If the total exceeds the Largest Unused Block amount by more than 50K or so, the unused memory is fragmented into two or more chunks.

To consolidate fragmented memory, quit all open programs and then open them again. Restarting your Macintosh also fixes fragmentation and may reduce the amount of memory used by system software as well.

You can avoid memory fragmentation by planning the order in which you open and quit programs. First open the programs you're least likely to quit first, and last open the programs you're most likely to quit last. When you need more memory to open another program, quit the most recently opened program. If that doesn't free enough memory, quit the next most recently opened program, and so on. This method frees up a contiguous chunk of memory. Quitting programs helter-skelter leads to memory fragmentation.

Troubleshooting

If you're having trouble with System 7, check out the tips in this section.

Printed font doesn't match display

If you have both fixed-size and TrueType fonts installed, text may not look quite the same on-screen as it does on paper. Character shapes may be different. More importantly, spacing of words on the line may not match. When this happens, the system software has used a fixed-size font for display (at 72 dots per inch) and a TrueType font for printing (at a higher resolution). You can fix the problem by removing the fixed-size font from your System file. Some programs may also provide an option that causes fixed-size fonts to be ignored.

Can't put away hard disk icon

The Finder doesn't allow removing a hard disk icon from the desktop while file sharing is turned on. If you drag the disk icon to the Trash or use the Put Away command, you get a message about items being in use, as shown in Figure 12-14. You'll have to stop file sharing using the Sharing Setup control panel, put away the disk, and then start file sharing again.

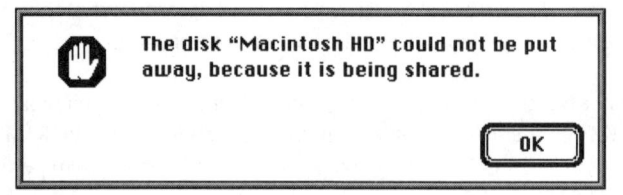

Figure 12-14: Can't put away with file sharing on.

Can't switch cartridges

If you have file sharing turned on in the Sharing Setup control panel, the Finder may not allow switching cartridges in a removable hard disk drive, CD-ROM drive, or other removable-media storage device. You must stop file sharing, put away the disk icon, and then start sharing again. Now you'll be able to switch cartridges at will, but you won't be able to share them with others (see the next tip).

Can't share a disk

To use the Finder's Sharing command with a disk or any folder in the disk, the disk must be mounted (its icon must be on the desktop) when you start file sharing using the Sharing Setup control panel, a shown in Figure 12-15. Also, the disk capacity must be at least 2MB to be shareable. If you start file sharing with no cartridge inserted in a removable hard disk drive or CD-ROM drive, for example, you won't be able to share a cartridge you insert later until you stop file sharing and then start it again while the disk icon is on the desktop.

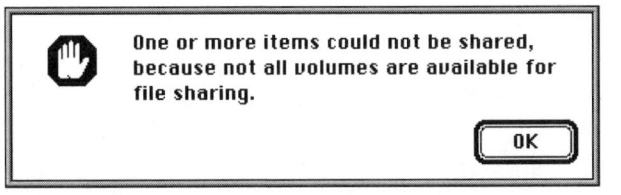

> ⚠ One or more items could not be shared, because not all volumes are available for file sharing.
>
> [OK]

Figure 12-15: Disk was unmounted when file sharing started.

Blank icons

Blank icons are a sign of a corrupt desktop database. Restarting your Macintosh may eliminate the blank icons. If not, rebuilding the desktop usually does the trick. To rebuild the desktop, simply press Command-Option while starting up, and wait for the Finder to inquire whether you indeed wish to rebuild the desktop on your hard disk. If you have multiple hard disks, the Finder asks about rebuilding each one in turn. To rebuild the desktop on a floppy disk, press Command-Option while inserting the floppy.

WARNING: Rebuilding the desktop erases all comments you have entered in Get Info windows for items on the disks involved. See Chapter 13 for a description of software you can use to retain Get Info window comments while rebuilding the desktop.

If the Finder advises it can't open a document you have double-clicked but it used to be able to do so, the desktop database may be corrupt. Try the fixes described in the previous tip. If they don't work, the program that created the document you're trying to open may be missing. Use the Finder's Find command to search for it.

Program unexpectedly quits

When a program you're using suddenly vanishes from the screen and an alert box advises that the program has quit unexpectedly, you'll never really know why the program crashed. Maybe the program suddenly ran out of memory, or you found a bug (error) in the program that the developer didn't encounter during testing. (No software is perfectly bug-free, and no testing program, no matter how rigorous, can uncover every bug.) The program crash could also be caused by another program that's open at the time, because System 7's multitasking doesn't isolate each open program in memory. A program operating in the background could have a bug that clobbers the program you're using. Chances are the error will not recur if you open the program that crashed and resume working. If the same program crashes repeatedly (especially if it does so in a predicable manner), contact the program's publisher and see if there's a bug-fix update available.

Bomb message causes

Apple hasn't yet managed to eliminate system errors and their dread bomb alert boxes. Table 2-2 lists the error messages that can appear in a system error alert box and their likely causes.

Emergency quit

Sometimes you can recover from a system error — or the related problem of a hung or frozen system — without restarting your Macintosh. Pressing Command-Option-Esc may bring up a dialog box asking whether you want to force the Finder (or some other program) to quit, as shown in Figure 12-16. If so, click the Force Quit button and cross your fingers. If you get to the Finder, immediately save all open documents and restart the computer.

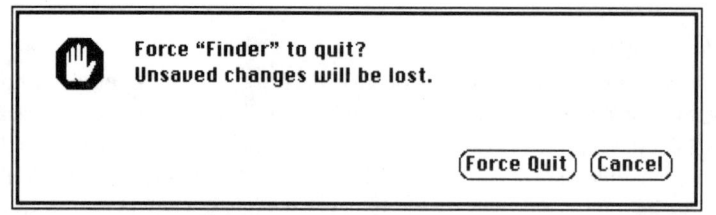

> Force "Finder" to quit?
> Unsaved changes will be lost.
>
> (Force Quit) (Cancel)

Figure 12-16: Forcing a program to quit.

Bomb recovery

If that trick doesn't work and the plastic programmer's switch is installed on your Macintosh, try pressing the Interrupt part of the switch (not the Restart part). On most Macintosh models, the Interrupt part is labeled with a tiny circle and the Restart part is labeled with a tiny arrow. Some Macs, such as the LC, LC II, and IIsi, have no programmer's switch; try pressing the Command and Power-On keys. With luck, you'll see a dialog box containing a greater-than symbol in its upper-left corner, as shown in Figure 12-17. Type G FINDER and press Return. If you get to the Finder, immediately save all open documents and restart the computer.

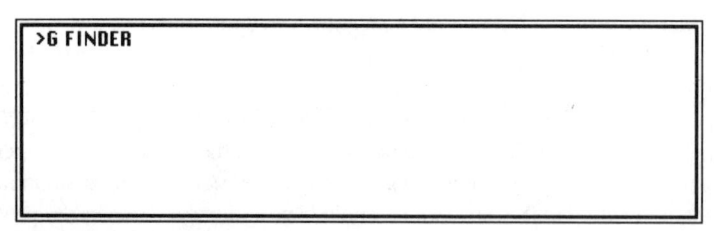

```
>G FINDER
```

Figure 12-17: Secret passage to the Finder.

System extension conflicts

If items you add to the System Folder, Extensions folder, or Control Panels folder don't work, or if your Macintosh refuses to start up, some of the system extensions in those places may be in conflict during startup. Sometimes changing the order in which the Macintosh installs system extensions resolves the conflict.

To have control panels whose names begin with blank spaces installed first during startup, put them in the Extensions folder. To have control panels whose names start with tildes or diamonds installed last during startup, put them in the System Folder. For convenient access to the control panels you move out of the Control Panels folder, make aliases of them and put the aliases in the Control Panels folder.

To have system extensions whose names begin with tildes and diamonds installed last during startup, drag them from the Extensions folder to the System Folder. Leave system extensions whose names begin with blank spaces in the Extensions folder so they will be installed first during startup.

Fixing other conflicts between system extensions and control panels involves experimenting. Start by removing all the items you have added to the System Folder and its inner folders since the trouble began. Then drag half the extensions and control panels to the desktop and restart. If this solves the problem, the offending item is among the half you removed to the desktop; if not, it is among the other half. In either case, leave only half the group containing the offending item (one quarter of all extensions and control panels) on the desktop and restart. If the problem occurs, the offender is among the group you just put back; if not, it is among the group on the desktop. Continue halving the offending group until you reduce it to a single item (the troublemaker). Instead of dragging control panels and extensions to and from the desktop, you can drag them to and from a new folder you create for that purpose. Alternatively, you can use an extension manager utility such as Extension Manager to turn them on and off individually without dragging them in and out of folders (see "Extension Manager" in Chapter 13).

As a last resort, remove all system extensions and control panels to the desktop. Then put them in the System Folder (not the Extensions or Control Panels folder) one at a time, from most important to least. Restart your Macintosh each time you add another item to the System Folder. When you find an item that causes a conflict, discard it and try the next item you previously moved to the desktop. You may be able to resume using the items you discarded when they are next upgraded.

(If a conflict prevents starting up from your hard disk, start from a floppy disk with any version of system software. Make a change to the System Folder on the hard disk and try restarting from it.)

Other

This section contains tips about the desktop, printing, typing symbols, startup time, and more.

Desktop by Name

If your desktop gets so cluttered that you can hardly find the icon for an inserted floppy disk, you may wish you could use the View menu to arrange items on the desktop by name, as you can with icons in windows. You can get this effect with System 7's custom icon capabilities. First you open a paint program, select some blank white space, and copy it. Then you use the Finder's Get Info command on each desktop item you want to view by name, and you paste the white space over the icon in each item's info window. Pasting the white space leaves only the item names visible, and six items without icons fit in the space previously occupied by two items with icons, as shown in Figure 12-18.

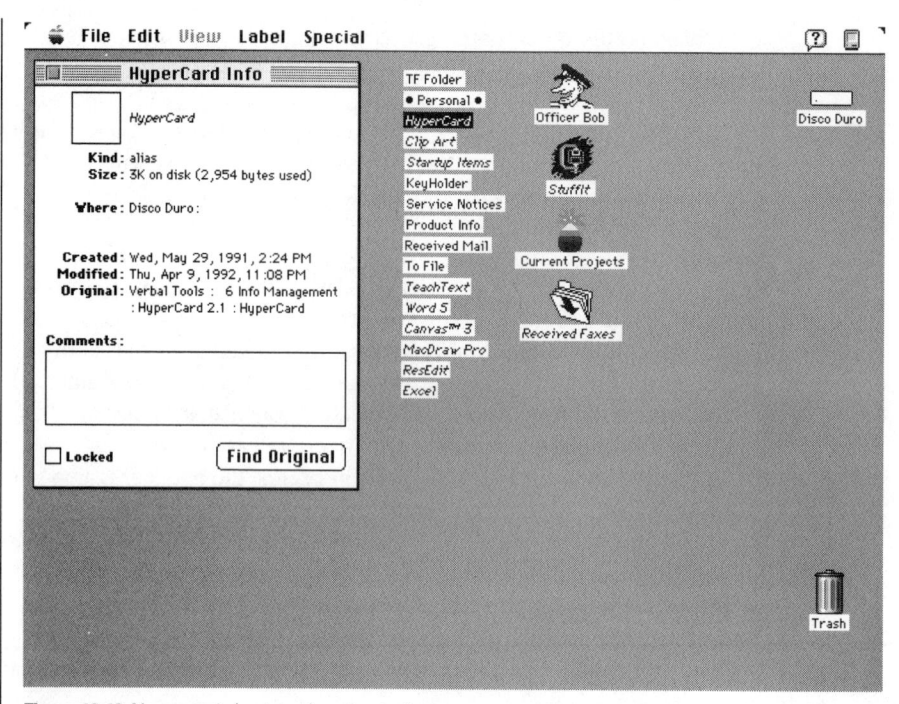

Figure 12-18: Names only (no icons) on the desktop.

LaserWriter test page

The LaserWriter Font Utility program on the Tidbits disk of the System 7 installation set (the More Tidbits disk if you have 800K disks) can turn a LaserWriter's test page on and off. The Installer does not automatically put this utility program on your hard disk when you install System 7.

Easter egg hunt

Apple's system software engineers, true to their kind, have left a few Easter eggs in their work. In the Color control panel, for example, click the sample text a few times to see authorship credits. On a Mac whose Memory control panel has a virtual memory section, try turning on virtual memory and pressing Option while clicking the Hard Disk pop-up menu. Instead of a list of disks, you see the names of virtual memory's creators.

If your Mac can use the Monitors control panel, click the version number in its upper-right corner to see a smiley face and the authors' names. Repeatedly press Option to mix up the first names and randomly replace them with the words *Blue Meanies*. (Blue Meanies are software engineers who work on system software as a whole, not solely on one aspect of it.)

In the Finder, pressing Option changes the first command in the Apple menu to About the Finder. Choose it, and instead of the usual memory usage chart, you see the mountain range picture that adorned Finder version 1.1 in 1984. Wait about 10 seconds and credits start scrolling from right to left across the bottom of the screen. Hold down

Command-Option while choosing About the Finder and the pointer becomes a wacky smiley face. You may not see the smiley face if you originally installed System 7 before its release date of May 13, 1991. If the Desktop Folder on the startup disk was created before that date, the smiley face does not appear. The Desktop Folder is normally invisible in System 7 but is visible if you restart with a System 6 floppy disk or if you access your startup hard disk from another Mac using file sharing.

More Chicago symbols

In addition to the four special symbols that have always been part of the Chicago font (⌘, ✓, ◆,), the TrueType version of Chicago shipping with System 7 has many new special symbols. They include ⌥ and ⇧ which Apple uses to represent the Option and Shift keys. You type them by pressing Control-A and Control-D. You can type other symbols by pressing Control with one of the letter keys, as shown in Figure 12-19.

However, you probably won't see any of the new special symbols if you set the font size to 12 points or any other size for which a fixed-size (bitmap) Chicago font is installed in your System file. (Chicago 12 is in the ROM of all Mac models except those older than a Plus.) Fixed-size versions of Chicago don't include the new symbols and most programs use fixed-size fonts wherever possible.

If you have trouble typing the special symbols in a particular program, try typing them in the Key Caps desk accessory. Because Key Caps always displays 12-point text, you'll see a box instead of the special symbol. Copy it anyway, paste it where you want the special symbol, and change its font there to 13-point Chicago.

One other symbol, ⌫, can't be typed in Key Caps or in most applications but can be generated by typing the following command in HyperCard's message box and pressing Return: `put numToChar(8)`. HyperCard replaces the command with a box; copy it, paste it where you want the ⌫, and change its font there to Chicago 13.

Desktop pattern

With ResEdit 2.1 or later you can modify System 7 to decorate your desktop with a custom pattern of up to 64 × 64 pixels. (The standard desktop patterns you select with the General control panel are 8 × 8.) Unfortunately, designing 64 × 64-pixel patterns can be quite tedious. The Terraform module of Berkeley Systems' More After Dark (which requires After Dark 2.0) can create striking patterns that repeat perfectly on the desktop, as shown in Figure 12-20. To create these patterns, do the following:

Figure 12-19: TrueType Chicago symbols.

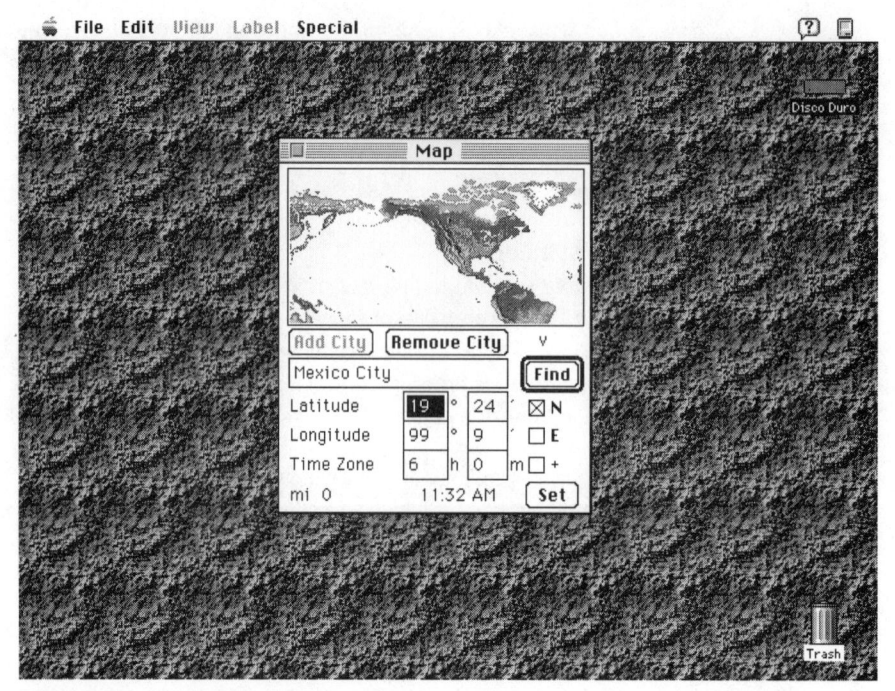

Figure 12-20: A desktop made of big pattern tiles.

1. In After Dark, select the Terraform module and set the Repeat Size option to 64. Activate After Dark by moving the pointer to the sleep corner or by clicking the Demo button. Wait until you see a pattern you like and then press Command-Shift-3 to have System 7 capture the screen in a PICT file (at the root level of your startup disk). You can experiment with colors and textures by clicking the Terraform module's Terrain button and trying different settings in the dialog box that appears.

2. Open the screen capture, named *Picture 1*, with a program that enables you to select a 64 × 64-pixel piece of it. TeachText, which comes with System 7, will do, but drawing programs such as Canvas 3.01, PixelPaint Pro, Studio/8 1.0, and SuperPaint 3.0 are more convenient because they show the size of the selection as you use the marquee tool (selection rectangle). Select the 64 × 64 area that you want to become your desktop pattern, and copy it to the Clipboard (with the Edit menu's Copy command).

3. Copy the System file with the Finder — for example, press Option while dragging it from the System Folder to the startup disk icon — and then open the copy with ResEdit 2.1 or later. In ResEdit, scroll until you see the icon for the resource named ppat (pixel pattern) and double-click it to open it. There should be one resource numbered 16; open it by double-clicking. A pattern-editing window appears along with three new menus — Transform, Color, and ppat. Choose Pattern Size from the ppat menu and set the pattern size to 64 ×

64, making the pattern-editing window larger. Paste the pattern from the Clipboard to replace the standard gray pattern. Quit ResEdit, answering yes when it asks whether you want to save changes to the System file.

4. Drag the unedited System file out of the System Folder, drag the edited System file into that folder, and restart. When the Finder's menu bar appears, you should be rewarded with a very pleasing desktop pattern.

To take desktop patterns the next step — multiple patterns in sizes up to 128×128 — you can get the Wallpaper control panel from Thought I Could. It works with System 6 (6.0.5 and later) as well as System 7 on any color-capable Mac (including an SE/30 or Classic II) and includes pattern editing tools.

With System 7, you can put a sound file in the Startup Items folder (inside the System Folder) and it will be played when you start up your Mac. If your Mac has a microphone, you can use the Sound control panel to record a message for the next person who uses the Mac or just for fun.

Cancel startup items

You can probably imagine times when hearing Darth Vader say, "What is thy bidding, Master?" while your Mac starts up would not be politically correct. You can suppress playing of sounds and opening of all other items in System 7's Startup Items folder by pressing Shift when the Finder's menu bar appears. After the opening of startup items has begun you can cancel it by pressing Command-period. The Mac immediately stops any sound it was playing and skips all startup items it has not already opened.

If you press Command-period while the Mac is opening an application, document, or desk accessory from the Startup Items folder, the Mac finishes opening that item and ignores all other startup items. Pressing Command-period also stops any sound you started playing by opening its icon in the Finder.

Keyboard changes

In System 7 Apple changed the mapping of U.S. keyboards largely to make the Caps Lock key more consistent with the Shift key. All versions of system software ignore the Shift key if you simultaneously press the Command key, and System 7 likewise ignores the Caps Lock key when you simultaneously press the Command key. System 7, unlike earlier system software versions, also ignores the Caps Lock key for Option-key combinations that produce the eight symbols © (Option-G), ° (Option-K), ® (Option-R), † (Option-T), √ (Option-V), Σ (Option-W), ≈ (Option-X), and Ω (Option-Z).

With System 7 you can directly type the accent produced by one of the dead-key combinations — ` (Option-`), ´ (Option-E), ˆ (Option-I), ˜ (Option-N), or ¨ (Option-U) — by pressing the dead-key combination with Shift or with Caps Lock. Pressing Option-Shift-I produces a true circumflex (ˆ) in System 7 instead of the caret (^) of earlier system software, and pressing Option-Shift-N produces a true tilde (˜) instead of an equivalence sign (~). As always, pressing a dead-key combination without Shift or Caps Lock applies the accent to the next character you type.

If you press a dead-key combination and then type a letter that doesn't take the accent, System 7 always produces the accent followed by the letter you typed. In contrast, System 6 substitutes a caret (^) for a circumflex (ˆ), an equivalence symbol (~) for a tilde (˜), and produces the other accents correctly. The System 7 keyboard mapping enables you to directly type four additional accents — ″, ˘, ¸, and ˌ — but you can't apply them to other characters as you can the four dead-key accents. Table 12-1 shows the characters affected by the new keyboard map and the key combinations that produce them in System 7 and in System 6.

Table 12-1: System 7 keyboard changes

	System 6 key combination	System 7 key combination
Â	Option-Shift-R Option-Caps Lock-R	Option-Shift-M Option-Caps Lock-M Option-I, then Shift-A
È	Option-Shift-I Option-Caps Lock-I	Option-`, then Shift-E
Ê	Option-Shift-T Option-Caps Lock-T	Option-I, then Shift-E
Ë	Option-Shift-U Option-Caps Lock-U	Option-U, then Shift-E
Ì	Option-Shift-G Option-Caps Lock-G	Option-`, then Shift-I
Ù	Option-Shift-X Option-Caps Lock-X	Option-`, then Shift-U
Û	Option-Shift-Z Option-Caps Lock-Z	Option-I, then Shift-U
Ÿ	Option-Shift-' Option-Caps Lock-'	Option-U, then Shift-Y
©	Option-G	Option-G Option-Caps Lock-G
°	Option-K	Option-K Option-Caps Lock-K
®	Option-R	Option-R Option-Caps Lock-R
†	Option-T	Option-T Option-Caps Lock-T
√	Option-V	Option-V Option–Caps Lock–V

continued

Table 12-1: **System 7 keyboard changes** *(continued)*

	System 6 key combination	*System 7 key combination*
Σ	Option-W	Option-W Option-Caps Lock-W
≈	Option-X	Option-X Option-Caps Lock-X
Ω	Option-Z Option-Caps Lock-Z	Option-Z
‰	Option-Shift-E Option-Caps Lock-E	Option-Shift-R
	Option-Shift-K Option-Caps Lock-K	Option-Shift-K
◊	Option-Shift-V Option-Caps Lock-V	Option-Shift-V
„	Option-Shift-W Option-Caps Lock-W	Option-Shift-W
'	Option-Caps Lock-' Caps Lock-' ' alone	Option-Shift-' Option-Caps Lock-' Caps Lock-' ' alone
´	Option-E, then Space	Option-Shift-E Option-Caps Lock-E Option-E, then Space
ˆ	Option-Shift-N Option-Caps Lock-N	Option-Shift-I Option-Caps Lock-I Option-I, then Space
^	Option-I, then Space Shift-6	Shift-6
~	Option-Shift-M Option-Caps Lock-M	Option-Shift-N Option-Caps Lock-N Option-N, then Space
~	Option-N, then Space Shift-'	Shift-'
¨	Option-U, then Space	Option-Shift-U Option-Caps Lock-U Option-U, then Space
‚	None	Option-Shift-Z
„	None	Option-Shift-G

Summary

- You can avoid opening an item when editing an icon's name by setting a briefer Double-Click Speed with the Mouse control panel.
- You can quickly access programs, control panels, documents, and folders themselves by making aliases of them and putting the aliases on the desktop.
- You can use aliases to keep track of and quickly open items on floppy disks that aren't inserted in your Macintosh.
- You can open an item at startup time by putting an alias of it in the Startup Items folder. Don't put original items there, because returning them to their original locations when you no longer want them opened at startup time can be a drag.
- You can hide windows of open programs that obscure desktop items by choosing Hide Others from the Application menu while the Finder is active.
- Sometimes the Trash contains a folder named Rescued Items that contains formerly invisible temporary files found when the Mac is started up. It only appears after a system crash, possibly allowing a user to re-create completed work up to the time of the crash.
- You can avoid going back and forth between two folders by putting an alias of each folder in the other.
- You can avoid memory fragmentation by planning the order in which programs are opened and quit. Open programs you're least likely to quit first, and then open programs you're most likely to quit last.

Chapter 13
Utilities and Enhancements

In This Chapter

- Understanding shareware and freeware.
- Alias assistance shareware and freeware.
- Disk and file utility shareware and freeware.
- Finder helper shareware and freeware.
- System management shareware and freeware.
- Window and dialog box shareware and freeware.
- Font and sound shareware and freeware.
- Menu, folder, and icon shareware and freeware.
- Networking enhancement shareware and freeware.
- PowerBook enhancement shareware and freeware.
- Summary tables telling where to find this software.

What Is Shareware or Freeware?

Although System 7 offers extensive ways to make your Macintosh computing flexible and easy, even this advanced system software can use some assistance. Many programmers have developed small adjunct applications, control panels, and system extensions that enhance the performance of the Finder and other system software. Macintosh users are an idiosyncratic lot, meaning that they want their computers to make their work easy as well as provide personalized services. These shareware and freeware utilities personalize the activities of the Finder and System so that the Macintosh does exactly what you need it to do when you need it to. With these programs, you can open specific files directly without having to know where they are located, throw away files while using an application without going to the Finder, create aliases in new ways, and make your Mac more fun.

All of the software described in this chapter is publicly distributed through user groups or electronic bulletin boards. This doesn't mean it is in the public domain; most authors of publicly distributed software retain the copyrights to their works. Publicly distributed software falls into two categories: shareware and freeware. The authors of shareware ask you to send them modest fees if you decide to use the software, whereas the authors of freeware ask for no payment. You can get both

> **Supporting shareware authors**
>
> As stated earlier, much of the software described in this chapter is shareware. Shareware authors require that you make a small payment if you decide to use their programs. Details, including the author's name and address, and the amount of the shareware payment, are typically included in each program's ReadMe file or in the About... or Help dialog boxes.
>
> Please support shareware authors by sending your payment, so you can get more great programs in the future! Some programs are freeware, meaning that the author does not require a payment.
>
> Please read the documentation that comes with the programs. If there is no ReadMe file or other documentation with the program, instructions are usually incorporated into the program itself; check the "About" selection in the Apple menu when you run the program.

types of software from Macintosh user groups or on-line information services, such as CompuServe, GEnie, or America Online. Most of the software listed below is available from the Berkeley Macintosh User's Group (BMUG), 510-849-9114, or from the Boston Computer Society Macintosh User Group (BCS•Mac), 617-864-1700. You'll find a coupon in the back of this book to order a set of disks that contains all of the software described here and much more.

This chapter is divided into subject headings defining the different types of software available. Each type of software is summarized in a table providing information on the software's type (for example, control panel, system extension, or application), size, cost, and at least one source. The items may be available from sources not listed in the table, because the software collections of user groups and on-line information services are constantly changing.

Using Shareware and Freeware

Shareware and freeware programs are typically written by interested users who do not have the economic power to support these programs in the same manner that commercial programs are technically supported. Thus, you use these programs at your own risk. In addition, although the software listed below has been tested for bugs with System 7.1 on a Macintosh IIsi with a math coprocessor, this does not mean that they are as stable as commercial programs, again for economic reasons. Be sure to follow the instructions and discussions provided by the authors in their ReadMe or Help files before using any of these programs.

There are hundreds of shareware and freeware programs available over the myriad networks accessible by your Macintosh. The software listed below has been culled from the pack based upon its use of the Macintosh interface, how complete it is, and how bug-free it is. This list is not meant to be exclusive, but rather is meant only to be an example of the types of software available to enhance the performance of your Macintosh with System 7.

Alias assistance

Software listed under this heading provide enhancements to System 7's alias generation capability. You can use this software to generate aliases on-the-fly using drag-and-drop icons, as well as to manage your aliases more efficiently.

AKA
Create aliases in the Finder by pressing Control while dragging an item to another folder, disk, or the desktop.

Alias Assassin
Finds orphaned aliases and deletes them or reunites them with their original files or folders.

Alias Director
Written to make creating and deleting aliases as easy as using them. The program operates either automatically or interactively to create aliases of your applications and to place them where you want them located, such as in the Apple menu or any folder on your desktop. Figure 13-1 displays the dialog box used in Alias Director to create an alias and save it to the Apple Menu.

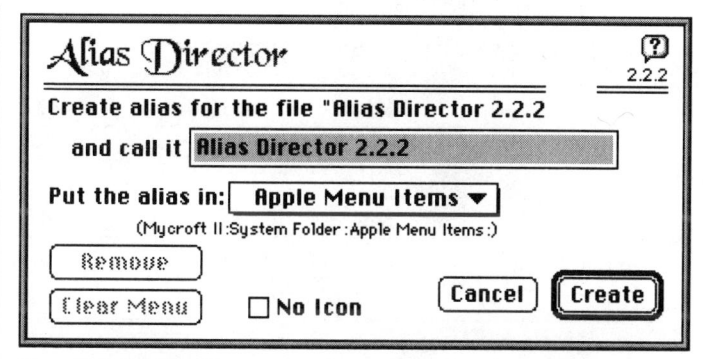

Figure 13-1: Use Alias Director to easily create and place aliases anywhere on your system.

AliasBOSS
Creates, validates, moves, and deletes alias files. You drag any icon of a file into the program's drop box to create an alias; or, by pressing Shift while dropping a volume or disk icon you can scan for files of your selected file type. You can also scan a volume for aliases by pressing and holding Option while dragging.

AliasZoo
Identifies aliases and their originating files using hierarchical menus. The program also can re-attach the alias to its rightful owner, a new owner, or delete it from the disk if you decide it is obsolete.

Easy Alias
Makes it easy to create an alias with the same name as the original file and save it in the location where it is needed.

Power Alias
Groups your application aliases for easier access. The software opens up to five applications. You can also use the program to specify which word processor should be used to open generic text files.

ZMakeAlias
Places a bullet on the Save As dialog box enabling you to create an alias within an application rather than using the Make Alias command in the Finder.

Summary of alias assistance software
Table 13-1 summarizes the pertinent data about alias assistance software. (Note that CP is a control panel, EXT is a system extension, and APP is an application program.)

Table 13-1: Alias assistance software

Software	Type	Size	Cost	Source	Author
AKA	EXT	8K	Free	BMUG/BCS•Mac	Fred Monroe
Alias Assassin	EXT	12K	$5	BMUG	
Alias Director 2.2.2	APP	38K	$5	BCS•Mac	Laurence Harris
AliasBOSS 1.0	APP	98K	$15	BMUG/AOL	Scott Johnson
AliasZoo 1.4 Information Control	APP	110K	$20	BMUG/ BCS•Mac	Optimize
Easy Alias	APP	5K	Free	BMUG	Alan Simon
PowerAlias 1.0	APP	25K	$5	BMUG	Andrew Anker
ZMakeAlias	EXT			BCS•Mac	

Disk and file utilities
These shareware and freeware programs assist you in managing your files and desktop to customize your Macintosh for the way you want to work. The software includes some items for hackers (advanced users or programmers) to edit file types and creator information, applications to maintain your Desktop file, and other useful housekeeping programs.

AppDisk
Creates a RAM disk to use extra RAM memory as if it were a really fast hard disk. The disk appears on your desktop just like any other disk, and you can copy files to it just like a normal disk. The difference between this program and most other RAM disks is that the AppDisk gets the memory for its disk from its application memory. Most RAM disks take memory away from your total system memory when you start up, so you can't get that memory back without restarting. To get the memory back with AppDisk, all you have to do is quit the AppDisk program or remove the RAM disk from your desktop by dragging it to the Trash.

BunchTyper
Changes the type or creator information of a file or group of files. The program provides detailed information on types and creators of Macintosh files, including extensive help balloons, to avoid costly mistakes.

CommentKeeper
Makes your Mac retain the comments that you have entered into Get Info windows when you rebuild your desktop database (by pressing Command-Option while restarting).

Discolour
Enables the Finder to display beautiful full-color floppy disk icons in place of the black-and-white icons when your monitor is set for 16 colors or greater.

Locksmith
Locks or unlocks files, folders, and disks quickly and easily without using the Finder's Get Info windows. You drop files or folders into the program's drop box to unlock or lock, as needed.

Put Away
A drag-and-drop utility that puts files in folders based on file types and creators, much like the System 7 Finder puts System-specific files in special folder locations. You can configure the program to recognize unlimited types, creators, and folder locations. The application moves or copies files to the destination folders as specified by using Option.

Save-A-BNDL
Gets the Finder to recognize changes in a file's icon, which is linked to the file through the file's BNDL resource. You use this program after upgrading an application to update its icon without rebuilding the desktop database or restarting your Macintosh. After Save-A-BNDL updates a BNDL resource, it interactively restarts the Finder to update the desktop database without interfering with any other currently open applications.

Scale
Counts the number of files and folders you have selected (including files and folders within folders), and calculates the total logical and physical size of that group. The software enables you to determine the size of a selected group of files and folders without using the Get Info command on each and breaking out the calculator. This application is useful when you are moving files around as a quality control check to ensure that you moved everything you wanted to, but no more.

SparedDisk
Spots floppy disks that contain bad sectors which the system spared (internally marked as unusable) when the floppy disk was formatted. Such floppy disks appear on the desktop as a disk with a band-aid.

Stationer

Creates stationery files without your having to use the Get Info command.

Summary of disk and file software

Table 13-2 summarizes the pertinent data about disk and file utility shareware. (Note that CP is a control panel, EXT is a system extension, and APP is an application program.)

Table 13-2: Disk and file utility software

Software	Type	Size	Cost	Source	Author
AppDisk 1.5	APP	39K	$15	BMUG	Mark Adams
BunchTyper 1.01	APP	97K	$10	BMUG	Kwang Lee
Comment Keeper 1.0	EXT	10K	Free	BMUG/BCS•Mac	Maurice Volaski
Discolour 1.01	EXT	11K	Free	BMUG	Andrew Welch
Locksmith 1.0	APP	20K	$2	BMUG	Robert Gibson
Put Away 1.0	APP	27K	Free	BMUG	Pete Johnson
Save-A-BNDL 1.3	APP	12K	Free	BMUG/BCS•Mac	Michael Engber
Scale 1.0	APP	19K	$2	BMUG	Robert Gibson
SparedDisk 1.0b1	EXT	2K	Free	BMUG/BCS•Mac	Martin Gannholm
Stationer 1.0	APP	21K	$2	BMUG	Robert Gibson

Finder helpers

These shareware and freeware packages assist the Finder in performing finding, opening, saving, printing, changing, copying, or moving operations.

Applicon

Provides an efficient way to access your frequently used applications. Applicon displays a *tile* (a small square window) for each application you have open. Each tile shows the icon and name of the application the tile represents. If you click a tile, the corresponding application becomes active. Option-clicking hides the currently active application as the new application becomes active. If Applicon's tiles are all hidden behind other windows, moving the mouse to a *hot spot* in a corner of the main screen will bring them forward.

AppSizer

Enables you to change your application's memory size (the suggested memory size in the Get Info window) as you open it, rather than having to use the Get Info command before opening.

Before Dark

Installs desktop patterns up to 128 × 128 pixels (the standard desktop pattern is 8 × 8). The program includes several patterns and shows you how to build your own using commercial painting programs. Figure 13-2 displays the dialog box used in Before Dark to import, apply, and install colored desktop background patterns.

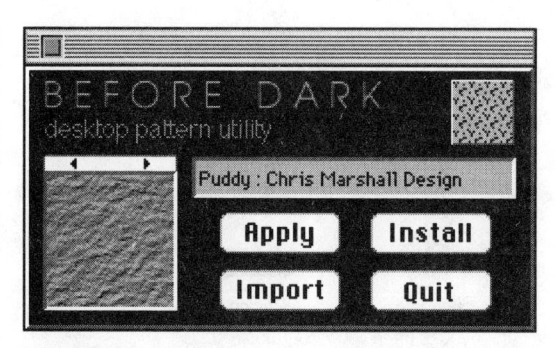

Figure 13-2: Choose among several artistic computer graphic patterns to decorate your desktop with Before Dark.

Blindfold
Hides or shows icons in the Finder as you require. The program can add security to your desktop by hiding private folders or applications, and also provides the capability of restoring these personal folders and applications to view when required.

Carpetbag
Opens all of the fonts, desk accessories, sounds, and FKeys you designate without having to previously install them into the System Folder.

DTPrinter
Enables you to drop files you want to print onto an icon that represents a particular printer, fax modem, or other output device. You can make a separate icon for every printer you use. The program replaces using the Chooser with dragging an icon on your desktop.

Find Pro II
Searches for multiple files all at once. In addition, the program opens files and connects aliases with their originating files. The author claims that the program is 10 to 20 times faster than the Finder's Find file command, because it searches for multiple files at the same time.

Finder 7 Menus!
Enables you to change the Command-key shortcuts in the Finder's menus.

Finder Palette
Creates a series of 3-D tiles representing your most frequently used programs, enabling you to open these applications by clicking their tiles. You can create palettes of tiles, each associated with a type of work you do, and save each palette. Figure 13-3 displays the tiles created using Finder Palette's menu-based commands.

Figure 13-3: Finder Palette creates full-color application tiles on your desktop to make it easier for you to open your programs.

Folder Icon Maker

Customizes the look of your folders by copying application icons without having to use the Get Info command. The program acts like a drop box, copying the icon that you drop into it onto a new folder.

It's Your Default!

Changes the default application font. You can set it for the current session (until you restart), or save the changes across restarts in Parameter RAM. Figure 13-4 displays the control panel of It's Your Default! that enables you to set the default font of your selected application.

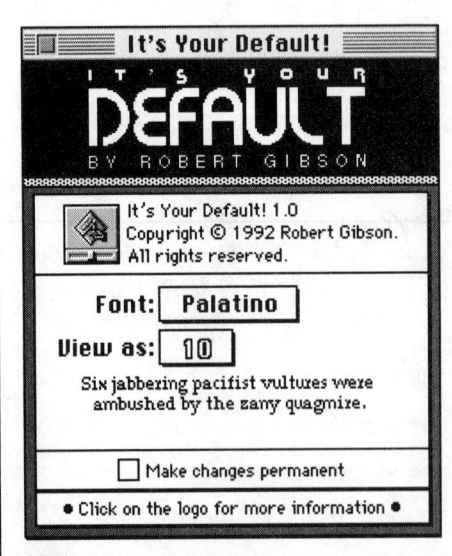

Figure 13-4: It's Your Default! provides an efficient method for changing the default font of your application.

Obliterate
Automatically deletes all files and folders dragged to its icon. The software also offers an optional shredding facility to make files totally unrecoverable. All folders dragged into this drop box are scanned, so you can throw in sets of files, folders, or even disks, or any combination of the three for permanent or semi-permanent erasing.

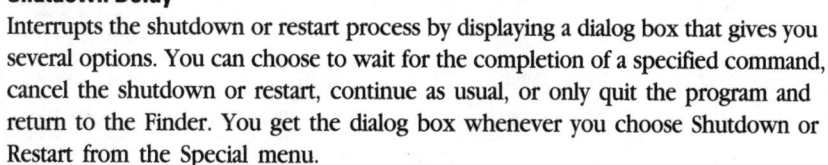

Shutdown Delay
Interrupts the shutdown or restart process by displaying a dialog box that gives you several options. You can choose to wait for the completion of a specified command, cancel the shutdown or restart, continue as usual, or only quit the program and return to the Finder. You get the dialog box whenever you choose Shutdown or Restart from the Special menu.

Suitcaser
Creates suitcases for fonts, desk accessories, FKeys, or sounds so that they can be used with System 6.

TattleTale
Presents information about your computer and its system-related software. Data provided includes: the name and number of your Macintosh, volumes and drives, monitors, NuBus cards, SCSI devices, ADB devices, serial ports, general system attributes, startup environment, System file contents, desk accessories, fonts, printer drivers, currently open files, currently active programs, available applications, and traps. In addition, it can mount volumes and close files.

Trash Chute
Automatically empties your Trash without displaying the cautionary dialog box associated with the Empty Trash command.

Trash Selector
Replaces the Empty Trash command with a Trash Selector command. This command displays a dialog box that enables you to selectively delete files that you have placed in the Trash.

TrashMan
Provides a timed deletion of items you have thrown into your Trash. It can age items in your Trash, making the action of emptying the Trash occur automatically at times you specify in the control panel.

Summary of Finder helper software
Table 13-3 summarizes the pertinent data about Finder helper software. (Note that CP is a control panel, EXT is a system extension, APP is an application program, and DA is a desk accessory.)

Table 13-3: Finder helper software

Software	Type	Size	Cost	Source	Author
Applicon 2.2	APP	84K	Free	BMUG/BCS•Mac	Rick Holzgraf
AppSizer 2.1	CP	63K	$19.95	BMUG/BCS•Mac	Peirce Software
Before Dark 1.01	APP	159K	$10	BMUG	Craig Marciniak
Blindfold	APP	20K	$2	BMUG	Robert Gibson
Carpetbag 1.02	CP	45K	$5	BMUG	James Walker
DTPrinter 1.1	APP	24K	Free	BMUG/BCS•Mac	Leonard Rosenthol
Find Pro II 1.2.1	APP	91K	Free	BCS•Mac	Ziffnet Mac
Finder 7 Menus!	APP	12K	$10	BMUG	Adam Stein
Finder Palette 1.0	APP	169K	$20	BCS•Mac	Anchor Beech Software
Folder Icon Maker 1.1	APP	20K	Free	BCS•Mac	Gregory Robbins
It's Your Default!	CP	18K	Free	BMUG	Robert Gibson
Obliterate	APP	24K	$2	BMUG	Robert Gibson
Shutdown Delay 1.27	CP	16K	$5	BMUG	Alessandro Montalcini
Suitcaser	APP	20K	Free	BMUG/BCS•Mac	Troy Gaul
TattleTale 1.5	DA	234K	Free	MAUG	John Mancino
Trash Chute 2.0	APP	6K	Free	BMUG	Milissa Rogers
Trash Selector™ 1.1	CP	38K	Free	BCS•Mac	HCS Software
Trashman 4.01	CP	193K	$10	BMUG/BCS•Mac	Dan Walkowski

System Management

These shareware and freeware programs assist you in your transition from System 6 to System 7 by providing methods for switching between systems. Other software listed in this section modifies or enhances system-level functions. Such operations as selecting your startup disk, colorizing applications, loading system extensions, editing resources, and managing memory are handled by these programs.

Color Alias

Switches the color depth you require for each program you are using without using the Monitors control panel. The program switches your main monitor to the color depth you have preset, sets the sound volume, and can turn off the Quadra's 68040 cache, all before opening the original application.

Desktop Remover

Removes the System 6 Desktop file from the hard disk. This file is not used by System 7. If you do switch from System 7 to System 6 after removing the Desktop file, your Mac simply rebuilds it.

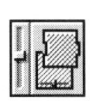

Extension Manager
Selectively turns off or on system extensions, control panels that contain system extensions, and Chooser devices. You can define sets of extensions and enable or disable each set. You can designate the types and creators of items that Extension Manager includes.

Overhead
Measures the overall performance of a Macintosh in terms an engineer or advanced user can understand. It analyzes the raw speed of the microprocessor (a measure of the computer's maximum potential speed), the effect system overhead has on the maximum speed of event processing, and the interference by system overhead on normal application event processing.

SCSI Startup
Enables you to make a SCSI disk the startup disk by dragging that disk's icon to the SCSI Startup icon. Otherwise, you have to open the Startup Disk control panel to change the startup disk.

Shutdown Items
Sets up your Macintosh to open selected items during the shutdown process, just as the Startup Items folder does at startup time. Any item placed in the Shutdown Items folder is opened (played, if it's a sound) during shutdown just as if you double-clicked the item in the Finder. PICT-type graphics are displayed, and QuickTime movies can be played as well.

System Picker
Enables you to pick which System Folder your Mac will use when you next restart it. You can choose among multiple System Folders on a single hard disk, multiple hard disks, or multiple partitions of hard disks.

Too Many Lawyers...
Teaches respect for an important Apple legal requirement.

zapParam™
Zaps (resets to factory settings) the Parameter RAM while using System 7.

Summary of system management software
Table 13-4 summarizes the pertinent data about system management software. (Note that CP is a control panel, EXT is a system extension, and APP is an application program.)

Table 13-4:	System management software				
Software	*Type*	*Size*	*Cost*	*Source*	*Author*
Color Alias	APP	18K	$10	BMUG	Mark Adams
Desktop Remover	APP	6K	Free	BMUG	Adam Stein

(continued)

Table 13-4:	System management software *(continued)*				
Software	**Type**	**Size**	**Cost**	**Source**	**Author**
Extension Manager 1.6	CP	29K	Free	BMUG/BCS•Mac	Ricardo Batista
Overhead	APP	10K	Free	BMUG	Anabolic Systems
SCSI Startup	APP	16K	$2	BMUG	Robert Gibson
Shutdown Items 2.41	APP	69K	Free	BMUG	John Covele
System Picker	APP	30K	Free	BCS•Mac	Kevin Aitken
Too Many Lawyers...	EXT	5K	Free	BMUG	David Koziol
zapParam™ 1.0a1	CP	27K	Free	BMUG/AOL	Reata Software

Windows and dialog boxes

This section of shareware and freeware enhances the performance of the windows and dialog boxes with System 7.

Aurora

Adds color to windows, menus, scroll bars, and buttons throughout your applications. Figure 13-5 displays the dialog boxes used to select colors for windows, title bars, text, and menus with Aurora.

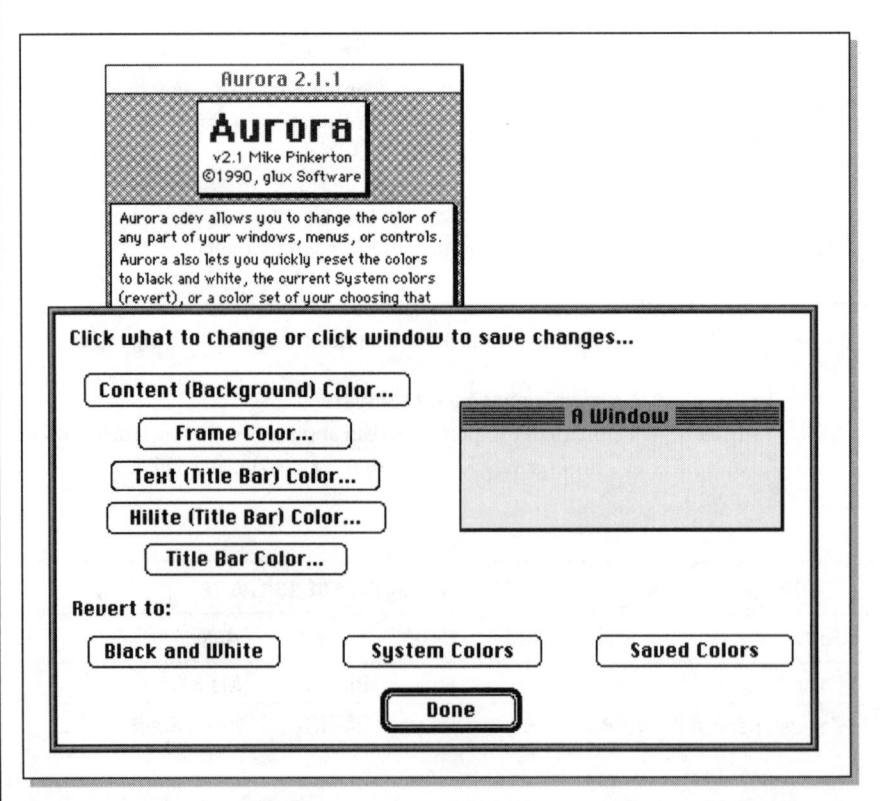

Figure 13-5: Aurora can colorize your menus, dialog boxes, title bars, and buttons via its flexible control panel.

Escapade
Enables you to use the keyboard to operate buttons in dialog boxes, and to select commands from menus without resorting to using the mouse. This control panel can be customized to work with function keys and common Macintosh keyboard equivalents, as well as any other keyboard requirements you may specify.

Kilroy
Makes your Macintosh historic, as in WWII. Install this control panel device (which includes a system extension) and see what pops up on dialog boxes in the least expected places...

PickTURE
Adds a scrollable list of thumbnail previews of your files to every Open dialog box. You can see what is in a file and then open it by double-clicking its thumbnail.

WindowWizard
Displays a menu that lists the currently active application's foreground and background windows. Using this tool enables you to go to other windows within the application without having to resort to the Open command.

ZoomBar
Groups windows together so that they appear either stacked or tiled no matter what size you make any individual window. The utility resizes all of the windows together to maintain the stacking order. This tool enables you to reach all windows you need without worrying about the size of the currently active window.

Summary of windows and dialog box software
Table 13-5 summarizes the pertinent data about window and dialog box software. (Note that CP is a control panel, EXT is a system extension, and APP is an application program.)

Table 13-5: Window and dialog box software

Software	Type	Size	Cost	Source	Author
Aurora 2.11	CP	19K	Free	BCS•Mac	Mike Pinkerton
Escapade 1.3.2	CP	50K	Free	BMUG	Christopher Wysocki
Kilroy	CP	12K	Free	BMUG	Dave Koziol
PickTURE 1.12	EXT	102K	Demo	BMUG	Boris Tsikanovsky
Window Wizard	EXT	26K	$20	BMUG	Eric del la Musse
ZoomBar	CP	72K	$5	BCS•Mac	Brian Westley

Sounds
This section includes sound utilities and a sample of the many shareware and freeware system sounds that have been recorded. Install sounds by dragging their icons to the System Folder icon, and select them with the Sound control panel.

BeepSounds
An assortment of system sounds from the sublime (symphony) to the ridiculous (burps) for placement in your System file.

CARP
Replaces Apple's CD Remote application for use in playing audio compact discs from your Macintosh. CARP stands for Craig's Audio ROM Player.

sndConverter
Converts sounds from other Macintosh system versions to be compliant with System 7 snd (the system sound format) requirements.

SoundExtractor
Extracts sounds from suitcases, applications, and HyperCard stacks and plays them. The program also converts the sounds into System 7-compliant snd files and places them where you specify.

Summary of sounds software
Table 13-6 summarizes the pertinent data about the sounds and sound utilities. (Note that CP is a control panel, EXT is a system extension, and APP is an application program.)

Table 13-6: Sounds Software

Software	Type	Size	Cost	Source	Author
Beep Sounds			Free	BMUG	
CARP 1.0a	APP	73K	$10	BMUG	Craig Marciniak
sndConverter 1.2.1	APP	29K	Free	BMUG/AOL	Joe Zobkiw
SoundExtractor	APP	34K	$5	BMUG	Alberto Ricci

Menus, folders, and icons
This section covers software that enhances menus, folders, and icons. In addition, several little programs have been included in this section because they reside on the Menu bar.

Folders and icons
America Online, CompuServe, Berkeley Macintosh User Group (BMUG), and other Macintosh user groups maintain extensive libraries of color icons, some of them 3-D, for use in replacing standard icons. These icons are stored in Scrapbook files that you place in your System Folder after removing your everyday Scrapbook file. Then you can copy the icons from the special Scrapbook file to the Get Info windows of your old, boring icons. The following list describes examples of these icon libraries.

- ✦ AFC Helmet Icons: a selection of American Football Conference helmets
- ✦ Color Hard Disk Icons: a Scrapbook containing landscapes, arrows, sunsets, comic book characters, and business symbols for use as icons

- ✦ Mo' Better folders: a series of abstract designs and business symbols on colored folders
- ✦ Mo' Fun Icons: a collection of icons that leans toward cute symbols and abstracts
- ✦ New Color Icons for System 7: more folder designs, including application icons attached to color folders

BeHeirarchic
Creates submenus in the Apple for folders (or aliases of folders) in the Apple Menu Items folder.

CClock
Displays an analog clock in a window on the Mac. You can resize and reposition the window anywhere, and the program remembers where you put it every time you open it. You can set up to 50 alarms for any time up to the year 2079, and you can select a chime from among your system sounds to sound on the hour, half-hour, or both. You can also open other applications from this program and create a menu of applications to be opened at any time. Figure 13-6 displays the colored analog clock produced by CClock.

Figure 13-6: CClock provides an analog or digital alarm clock with a versatile interface for scheduling and opening applications.

Custom Killer
Removes custom icons from files, folders, and even disks. You drag an item, or multiple items, to the Custom Killer icon for quicker response than using the Finder's Get Info command.

Dropple Menu
Enables you to drag items to folders in the Apple menu, or to drag documents to programs in the Apple menu.

Helium
Enables viewing and printing help balloons without using the Help menu. Press a magic key (which you can select) to inflate the balloons as needed.

Ikon VII
Provides a MacPaint- or SuperPaint-based toolkit for creating custom colored icons for folders and files on your Macintosh. The application includes sample icons, as well as software to create and install your own icon designs.

Just Click
Enables you to switch to the next open program listed in the Application menu simply by clicking the menu icon. You don't have to choose the program from the menu.

PwrSwitcher
Enables you to switch to the next open program with your keyboard instead of the Application menu. You switch by pressing either Power-On or Esc plus one other key, which you designate in the PwrSwitcher control panel.

Visage™
Installs new, colored icons for your disks without using the Get Info command. The application contains a library of disk shapes and cartoon characters from which to choose, and you can install your own icons into the library for customized use. Figure 13-7 displays the dialog box within Visage you use to select new icons for your disks.Summary of menu, folder, and icon software

Figure 13-7: Visage enables you to liven up your disk drive icons from its library of colored icons.

Table 13-7 summarizes the pertinent data about the menu, folder, and icon software. (Note that CP is a control panel, EXT is a system extension, and APP is an application program.)

Table 13-7: Menu, folder, and icon software

Software	Type	Size	Cost	Source	Author
BeHierarchic	CP	24K	$10	BMUG	Fabien Octave
CClock 2.2	APP	36K	$15	BMUG	Stephen Martin
Custom Killer	APP	20K	$2	BMUG	Robert Gibson
Dropple Menu	EXT	9K	Free	BMUG	Fred Monroe
Helium 2.1.1	CP	52K	$7	BMUG/BCS•Mac	Robert Mathews
Ikon VII	APP	12K	Free	BMUG	Golden Eagle Software
Just Click	EXT	12K	Free	BMUG	Tactic Software
PwrSwitcher 1.0	CP	16K	Free	BMUG	David Lamkins
Visage™	APP	84K	$25	BMUG	Scott Searle

Network enhancements

This section describes shareware and freeware that enhances the performance of System 7's file sharing features. Some software that enhances AppleShare and other network services is also described.

Anchor Stuff

Mounts a network or secondary hard disk without using the Chooser. The application operates as an alias on your startup disk and does not require any other copies on the network or server to perform its function.

DownLine

A drop-box backup program that offers automatic archiving and de-archiving functions in the background while you work with another program. The software can read and write to other archiving formats, such as StuffIt and PackIt.

MailSlot

Creates a small electronic mail system for your network. The software monitors a designated mail folder and informs you when mail has been delivered to that folder from another node on the network.

Mount Alias

Automatically creates aliases for AppleShare volumes when you connect to them.

SpeedMessage

Transmits a message to another Macintosh connected to tiny networks. One copy of SpeedMessage can establish a link with another copy of a SpeedMessage open on another Mac on the network or a copy open on the same computer as the original (or even with itself!), thus establishing a small electronic mail system. The software will also transmit very short segments (five seconds) of voice mail between computers on a network.

Summary of network enhancing software

Table 13-8 summarizes the pertinent data about network enhancement software. (Note that CP is a control panel, EXT is a system extension, and APP is an application program.)

Table 13-8: Network enhancement software

Software	Type	Size	Cost	Source	Author
Anchor Stuff	APP	7K	Free	BMUG	Zerom
DownLine 1.1.1	APP	100K	$25	BMUG	Morpheus Systems
MailSlot 1.0	CP	65K	$10	BMUG	AnalySYS Software
Mount Alias 1.0b1	CP	16K	Free	BMUG/BCS•Mac	Jeff Miller
SpeedMessage 1.12	APP	86K	Free	BMUG	Scott Johnson

PowerBook enhancements

This section describes shareware and freeware that enhances the performance of Macintosh PowerBooks.

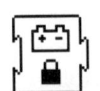

SafeSleep™
Provides enhanced security for PowerBooks. The program blanks the screen and requests a password whenever a sleeping PowerBook is awakened.

Siesta
Puts your PowerBook into sleep mode when you press an FKey. Sleep mode preserves the charge in your battery, enabling you to use the computer longer between recharges.

SpinD™
Spins down the hard disk inside your PowerBook when you press a preset FKey. Spinning down (or putting to sleep) the hard drive saves battery power and enables you to use your PowerBook longer between recharges.

Zync
A file synchronization system that copies files between your PowerBook and your desktop computer (or between any two hard disks).

Summary of PowerBook enhancing software

Table 13-9 summarizes the pertinent data about PowerBook enhancement software. (Note that CP is a control panel, EXT is a system extension, and APP is an application program.)

Table 13-9: PowerBook enhancement software

Software	Type	Size	Cost	Source	Author
Safe Sleep ™ 1.2	EXT	3K	Free	BMUG	Bill Steinberg
Siesta	CP	17K	$5	BMUG	Andrew Welch
SpinD™	FKey	1K	Free	BMUG	Bill Steinberg
Zync	APP	19K	Free	BMUG	Ricardo Batista

Summary

- Independent programmers have written shareware and freeware that enhances the performance of System 7. These small system extensions, control panels, and applications are available from Macintosh user groups and electronic information services such as CompuServe or America Online.

- Alias management shareware includes programs that create and track aliases throughout your system, system extensions that manage alias placement (including within the Apple menu), and control panels that enable you to delete aliases without using the Find command.

- Disk and file management software creates a RAM disk out of application memory, tracks and enables you to edit creator and type information, helps you keep icons up to date, and more.

- Finder management shareware performs such functions as substituting applications to open documents whose application is not on any disk, generating color desktop patterns, locating files better than Finder 7's Find command, switching between applications, creating alternative Application menus, and managing font and desk accessory suitcases.

- System management shareware deletes outmoded Desktop files, selects startup disks, manages the orderly shutdown of your Macintosh, and zaps the parameter RAM.

- Windows and dialog boxes are enhanced under System 7 through such shareware software as Aurora, a program that colorizes windows and dialogs, and PickTURE, a demo package for an application that enables you to look at the contents of a file while in the Open dialog box.

- Additional sounds and color icons add to the creativity of your work on the Macintosh. Menu-related software adds submenus to the Apple menu and gives you more control over balloon help.

- File sharing and AppleShare server access is enhanced by software that mounts volumes, manages small electronic mail services, and transfers messages across networks.

- PowerBooks can run longer on batteries when they use the available battery-saving software.

- Shareware carries some minimal costs, so be sure to read the ReadMe files accompanying the software to find out how to register with the author.

Part III
Customizing System 7

Part IV:
Appendixes

Appendix A **311**
Product Compatibility Table

Appendix B **339**
Glossary

Appendix C **347**
Installing System 7.1

Appendix A
Product Compatibility Table

Moving to System 7 is as much a lifestyle change for your programs as it is for you. Most of the programs you already have will work with System 7. Many will have minor cosmetic flaws that won't affect their operation. Some will lose minor capabilities but still be able to function. A number of programs won't work with 32-Bit Addressing turned on or with virtual memory active. Several important System 7 capabilities — balloon help, publish and subscribe, program linking, and data access — don't work in a program until its developer updates it to take advantage of them. Lesser improvements such as separate large and small icon designs, color icons, and the New Folder button in the Save As dialog box may also require software revision.

To see how compatible with System 7 your programs and hardware products are, see Table A-1. (You can usually find a program's version number in its info window; use the Finder's Get Info command.) If your version number is greater than the version listed in the OK column, you don't have to upgrade before using the product with System 7. The Best column lists the lowest version number that's fully compatible with System 7 (or if none is planned, the best version to use). For more information on any product, contact the company listed in the Source column. The information in this Appendix is based on developer reports and has not been independently verified.

Compatibility Checker

You can also check compatibility using the Compatibility Checker software that comes with System 7. It checks most of your software against its database of compatible software. Besides checking for compatibility, Compatibility Checker removes incompatible system extensions from your System Folder and places them in a separate folder.

The Compatibility Checker software seems to confuse people. Contrary to its goal of aiding in a smooth transition to System 7, its report apparently gives some people the mistaken impression that none of the software they already own will work with System 7. In fact you can use all items that Compatibility Checker identifies as "compatible" or "mostly compatible" without upgrading. You only have to get new versions of items Compatibility Checker classifies as "must upgrade" for System 7. The many programs listed as "not avail." may be compatible or they may not — Compatibility Checker does not know. You can either contact the publisher of each product or simply try each one with System 7.

Compatibility Checker 1.1 (the latest at this writing) completely ignores desk accessories and over 100 other items, as listed in Table A-2. These include installers, software packaged with an application that Compatibility Checker already checks, and some items replaced when you upgrade to System 7.

Compatibility Checker ignores desk accessories because there's no way to positively identify most of them. Compatibility Checker, like the Finder, identifies programs not by name (which anyone can change), but by a four-letter creator code. Under System 6 and earlier systems, desk accessories had to be either installed in the System file or stored in suitcase files and could not have unique creator codes. Under System 7, most desk accessories have the same creator code, that of Font/DA Mover, when you drag them out of their suitcase files. Some desk accessories introduced after System 7 do have unique creator codes, but Compatibility Checker 1.1 does not check for them. Incidentally, all desk accessories with the common creator code have the same icon because the creator code determines the icon.

Table A-1: Product compatibility

Product	Version OK	Version Best	Notes	Source
_DATE	NI	NI		T/Maker Co., 415 962-0195
~Font Porter	NI	NI		Adobe Systems, 415 961-0911
~OracleInit	1.0.1.9	1.0.1.9		Oracle, 800 672-2531
1 Shot Opener	NI	NI		Baseline Publishing
1 Shot Worksheet	NI	NI		Baseline Publishing
3+File	NI	NI		3 COM, 800 NET-3COM
3+Mail CP	NI	NI		3 COM, 800 NET-3COM
3D Life Forms	1.1	1.1		MacroMind, 415 442-0200
3D Works	1.1	1.2		MacroMind, 415 442-0200
4D Calc	NI	NI		Acius, 408 252-4444
4D Compiler	NI	NI		Acius, 408 252-4444
4D SQL Server	NI	NI		Acius, 408 252-4444
4D Write	NI	NI		Acius, 408 252-4444
4TH DIMENSION	NI	NI		Acius, 408 252-4444
800k Eject INIT	NI	NI		Apple Computer, 800 776-2333
800k Eject INIT	NI	NI		Authorized Apple Dealer
911 Utilities	1.1	1.1		Microcom Software, 919 490-1277
A.M.E. INIT	NO	NO		Casady & Greene, 408 484-9228
Aaps DigiVideo	1.3	NI	32	Aaps
Aask	NO	NO	NN	CE Software, 515 224-1953

Legend: NO none available • **NI** no information • **CS** contact source for version info • **32** 32-Bit Addressing problem • **VM** virtual memory problem • **UG** get from user group, info system, or dealer • **$0** free upgrade • **NN** not needed with System 7 • **S7** comes with System 7 • **FS** file sharing problem • **!!** upgrade strongly recommended • **TT** can't set TrueType sizes above 127.

(continued)

Table A-1: Product compatibility (continued)

Product	Version OK	Version Best	Notes	Source
Abaton Scanner Driver	NI	NI		Everex Systems
Accelerator	1.01	1.01	!!	SuperMac Technology, 408 245-0646
Accelerator	NI	NI		Radius, 408 434-1010
Accelerator	NI	NI		RasterOps, 408 562-4200
Access PC	2.0	2.0		Insignia Solutions, 800 876-3872
ActaAdvantage	1.0	1.04		Symmetry, 602 998-9106
ActiveMemory	2.0	2.0		ASD Software 714 624-2594
Address Book Plus	NI	NI		Power Up Software, 415 345-9381
AdminLAT	NI	NI		DEC, 508 467-5111
Adobe Illustrator	NI	NI		Adobe Systems, 415 961-0911
Adobe Photoshop	NI	NI		Adobe Systems, 415 961-0911
Adobe Separator	NI	NI		Adobe Systems, 415 961-0911
Adobe Streamline	NI	NI		Adobe Systems, 415 961-0911
Adobe Type Manager	NI	NI		Adobe Systems, 415 961-0911
Adobe Type Reunion	NI	NI		Adobe Systems, 415 961-0911
Adobe TypeAlign	NI	NI		Adobe Systems, 415 961-0911
AffiniFile	1.1	1.1		Affinity Microsystems, 303 442-4840
AfterDark	2.0V	2.0V		Berkley Systems, 510 540-5535
Alarming Events	1.1	1.1		CE Software, 515 224-1953
AlarmsClock		NI	NI	Now Software, 503 274-2800
Alchemy	2.23	2.6		Passport Design, 415 726-0280
Aldus Freehand	3.0	3.1		Aldus, 206 628-2040
Algebra	1.0	NI		Wings for Learning, 800 321-7551
Algebra Shop	NI	NI		Scholastic, 800 541-5513
AlisaMail				Alisa Systems, 800 992-5472
AlisaTalk				Alisa Systems, 800 992-5472
Amazing Paint	1.0.3	1.0.3		CE Software, 515 224-1953
America Online	NI	NI		America Online Incorporated, 800 827-6364
American Discovery	3.0	3.0		GreatWave Software, 408 438-1990
AntiToxin	2.1	2.1		Mainstay, 818 991-6540
APIDriver	NI	NI		Avatar, 508 435-3000

Legend: NO none available • **NI** no information • **CS** contact source for version info • **32** 32-Bit Addressing problem • **VM** virtual memory problem • **UG** get from user group, info system, or dealer • **$0** free upgrade • **NN** not needed with System 7 • **S7** comes with System 7 • **FS** file sharing problem • **!!** upgrade strongly recommended • **TT** can't set TrueType sizes above 127.

(continued)

Table A-1: Product compatibility *(continued)*

Product	Version OK	Version Best	Notes	Source
APIPrinter	NI	NI		Avatar, 508 435-3000
Apple File Exchange	NI	NI		Apple Computer, 800 776-2333
Apple File Exchange	NI	NI		Authorized Apple Dealer
Apple HD SC Setup	NI	NI		Apple Computer, 800 776-2333
Apple HD SC Setup	NI	NI		Authorized Apple Dealer
Apple-Digital	NI	NI		DEC, 508 467-5111
AppleTalk Tuner	NI	NI		Solana Electronics
Archive	NI	NI		Software Architects, 206 487-0122
Art Importer	2.0	2.0		Altsys, 214 680-2093
ArtWorks	1.0	1.0		Deneba Software, 305 594-6965
Astrix	NI	NI		Microseeds Publishing, 802 879-3365
AT Driver	NI	NI		Pacer Software, 508 898-3300
AtOnce!	NI	NI		PeachTree, 800 346-5317
AudioMedia	NI	NI		Digidesign
AudioTrax	1.0	1.0.1		Passport Design, 415 726-0280
AutoSave II	NI	NI		Magic software
AutoStart	NI	NI		Fifth Generation Systems, 800 873-4384
Avatar Control Panel	NI	NI		Avatar, 508 435-3000
BackBurner	1.0	1.0		Specular International, 413 549-7600
BackFAX	NI	NI		Solutions, 604 731-8648
Backmatic	NI	NI		Magic software
Big Thesaurus	2.0	2.0		Deneba Software, 305 594-6965
Blockers and Finders	1.0	2.0		Wings for Learning, 800 321-7551
C-A-T III	1.0	1.2		Chang Laboratories, 408 727-8096
C-Server	NI	NI		Solana Electroncis
C-Server Manager	NI	NI		Solana Electronics
CA Cricket Presents	2.0.1	2.1		Computer Associates Intl., 800 531-5236
Calendar Creator	NI	NI		Power Up Software, 415 345-9381
CalendarMaker	3.0	3.0.1	32	CE Software, 515 224-1953
CannonMO INIT	NI	NI		Software Architects, 206 487-0122
Canvas	1.0	3.0.4		Deneba Software, 305 594-6965
Capture	4.0	4.0		Mainstay, 818 991-6540

Legend: NO none available • **NI** no information • **CS** contact source for version info • **32** 32-Bit Addressing problem • **VM** virtual memory problem • **UG** get from user group, info system, or dealer • **$0** free upgrade • **NN** not needed with System 7 • **S7** comes with System 7 • **FS** file sharing problem • **!!** upgrade strongly recommended • **TT** can't set TrueType sizes above 127.

(continued)

Table A-1: Product compatibility (continued)

Product	Version OK	Version Best	Notes	Source
Carbon Copy	2.0.3	2.0.4		Microcom Software, 919 490-1277
CEToolBox	1.6.5	1.6.5	$0	CE Software, 515 224-1953
Cheque	NI	NI		Baseline Publishing
Claris CAD	NI	NI		Claris 408 727-8227
Claris CGT	NI	NI		Claris 408 727-8227
Claris Resolve	NI	NI		Claris 408 727-8227
Classic/SE Display	NI	NI		Radius, 408 434-1010
ClearVue/Classic	NI	NI		RasterOps, 408 562-4200
ClearVue/SE	NI	NI		RasterOps, 408 562-4200
ClickChange	1.0.5	1.05.2		Dubl-Click, 818 888-2068
ClickPaste	2.1.2	2.1.2		Mainstay, 818 991-6540
Clicktracks	NI	NI		Passport Design, 415 726-0280
Clinic	NI	NI		Symantec, 800 441-7234
Coach Pro	4.0	4.0		Deneba Software, 305 594-6965
Coax Gateway Server	NI	NI		Avatar, 508 435-3000
Color MacCheese	NI	NI		Baseline Publishing
Color Pivot Resolutions	NI	NI		Radius, 408 434-1010
Color-Space	NI	NI		Mass Microsystems, 408 522-1200
ColorBoard 364 F.G.	NI	NI		RasterOps, 408 562-4200
ColorSnap 32+	1.13	1.2		Computer Friends 503 626-2291
ColorStudio	1.5	1.5		Fractal Design, 408 688-8800
Comic Strip Factory	NI	NI		Foundation Publishing, 612 445-8860
Comment	NI	NI		Deneba Software, 305 594-6965
CommGate	NI	NI		Solutions, 604 731-8648
Complete Undelete	2.0	2.0.1		Microcom Software, 919 490-1277
ConcertWare	4.0.5	4.0.5		GreatWave Software, 408 438-1990
Connect	NI	1.55		Connect, 800 262-2638
Connect	NI	NI		Pixar, 510 236-4000
ConnectivityLoader	NI	NI		Avatar, 508 435-3000
ConnectivityManager	NI	NI		Avatar, 508 435-3000
Control-1	NO	NO	NN	CE Software, 515 224-1953
Cricket Draw 3	1.0.1	1.0.1		Computer Associates Intl., 800 531-5236

Legend: NO none available • **NI** no information • **CS** contact source for version info • **32** 32-Bit Addressing problem • **VM** virtual memory problem • **UG** get from user group, info system, or dealer • **$0** free upgrade • **NN** not needed with System 7 • **S7** comes with System 7 • **FS** file sharing problem • **!!** upgrade strongly recommended • **TT** can't set TrueType sizes above 127.

(continued)

Table A-1: Product compatibility *(continued)*

Product	Version OK	Version Best	Notes	Source
Cricket Graph 3	1.0	1.0		Computer Associates Intl., 800 531-5236
CS-1	NI	NI		Digidesign
Curator	NI	NI		Solutions, 604 731-8648
Customizer		NI	NI	Now Software, 503 274-2800
CUT Driver	NI	NI		Avatar, 508 435-3000
DART	NI	NI		Apple Computer, 800 776-2333
DART	NI	NI		Authorized Apple Dealer
DATa	NI	NI		Digidesign
Data Models	NI	NI		Sunburst, 800 628-8897
DAtabase Builder	NI	NI		Baseline Publishing
DAtabase Converter	NI	NI		Baseline Publishing
DAtabase Personalizer	NI	NI		Baseline Publishing
DAtabase Upgrader	NI	NI		Baseline Publishing
DataPak	NI	NI		Mass Microsystems, 408 522-1200
DataPrism	NI	1.7		Brio, 415 961-4110
DataStream	NO	NO		SuperMac Technology, 408 245-0646
DaynaFile	NI	NI		Dayna Communication
Dbase Mac	NI	NI		New Era Software
Decimal & Fraction Maze	1.2	1.2		GreatWave Software, 408 438-1990
DECNet Control	NI	NI		DEC, 508 467-5111
DECnet with TXXNet	2.4	2.4		Oracle, 800 672-2531
DECNet/Mac	NI	NI		DEC, 508 467-5111
DeltaGraph	NO	NO		Deltapoint, 408 648-4000
DeltaGraph Professional	2.0	2.01		Deltapoint, 408 648-4000
DesignStudio	NI	NI		Manhattan Graphics, 800 572-6533
DeskPicture		NI	NI	Now Software, 503 274-2800
DFT Driver	NI	NI		Avatar, 508 435-3000
DigiSystem INIT	NI	NI		Digidesign
Digital Darkroom	2.01	2.01		Aldus, 206 628-2040
DigiVideo Color App	1.05	NI		Aaps
Direct Mail Application	NI	NI		Baseline Publishing
Disinfectant	NI	NI		Northwestern University

Legend: NO none available • **NI** no information • **CS** contact source for version info • **32** 32-Bit Addressing problem • **VM** virtual memory problem • **UG** get from user group, info system, or dealer • **$0** free upgrade • **NN** not needed with System 7 • **S7** comes with System 7 • **FS** file sharing problem • **!!** upgrade strongly recommended • **TT** can't set TrueType sizes above 127.

(continued)

Table A-1: Product compatibility *(continued)*

Product	Version OK	Version Best	Notes	Source
Disk Copy	NI	NI		Apple Computer, 800 776-2333
Disk Copy	NI	NI		Authorized Apple Dealer
Disk First Aid	NI	NI		Apple Computer, 800 776-2333
Disk First Aid	NI	NI		Authorized Apple Dealer
DiskDoubler AutoStart	NI	NI		Fifth Generation Systems, 800 873-4384
DiskDup+	2.1.2	2.1.2		Roger Bates
DiskDup+	NI	NI		LACie Limited, 503 520-9000
DiskExpress I	NO	NO		Alsoft, 713 353-1510
DiskExpress II	2.07	2.07		Alsoft, 713 353-1510
DiskFit Pro	NI	NI		Dantz Development, 510 849-0293
DiskLockAutoStart	NI	NI		Fifth Generation Systems, 800 873-4384
DiskPaper Reader	NI	NI		Farallon Computing, 510 596-9000
DiskTop	4.02	4.02		CE Software, 515 224-1953
DiskTop.Extras	1.0.1	1.0.1		CE Software, 515 224-1953
Dollars and $ense	5.0	5.0		Software Toolworks, 415 883-5157
DOS Mounter	NI	NI		Dayna Communication
Double Helix	NI	NI		Helix Technology, 708 205-1669
Double Helix Client	NI	NI		Helix Technology, 708 205-1669
Double Helix Engine	NI	NI		Helix Technology, 708 205-1669
Double Helix Server	NI	NI		Helix Technology, 708 205-1669
DoubleTalk	NI	NI		Baseline Publishing
DrawOver	NI	NI		Adobe Systems, 415 961-0911
Dreams	1.0	1.1		Innovative Data Design, 510 680-6818
DRIVEMANAGER	7.0	7.24		GCC, 617 890-0880
Dynodex	NI	NI		Portfolio Systems, 408 252-0420
DynoPage	NI	NI		Portfolio Systems, 408 252-0420
E-Machines	3.0	3.2		E-Machines, 503 646-6699
Easy Color Paint	NI	NI		Creative Software
EasyShare	NI	NI		Symmetry, 602 998-9106
ECK	NI	NI		Digidesign
Empower II	NI	NI		Magna
Encore	2.0	2.5.2r2		Passport Design, 415 726-0280

Legend: NO none available • **NI** no information • **CS** contact source for version info • **32** 32-Bit Addressing problem • **VM** virtual memory problem • **UG** get from user group, info system, or dealer • **$0** free upgrade • **NN** not needed with System 7 • **S7** comes with System 7 • **FS** file sharing problem • **!!** upgrade strongly recommended • **TT** can't set TrueType sizes above 127.

(continued)

Table A-1: Product compatibility *(continued)*

Product	Version OK	Version Best	Notes	Source
EtherPort	NI	NI		Shiva, 617 252-6400
EtherPort II	NI	NI		Shiva, 617 252-6400
EtherPort SE	NI	NI		Shiva, 617 252-6400
Exodus	NI	NI		White Pine Software, 603 886-9050
Explorer	1.0	NI		Wings for Learning, 800 321-7551
Exposure Pro	NI	NI		Baseline Publishing
Exposure Pro Customizer	NI	NI		Baseline Publishing
Exposure Pro Personalizer	NI	NI		Baseline Publishing
Express Tape	NI	NI		Baseline Publishing
Extension Manager	1.0.1	1.0.1	32	CE Software, 515 224-1953
EZ-Menu	1.1	1.1	32	CE Software, 515 224-1953
EZVision	NI	NI		Opcode Systems, 415 856-3333
F2MO	NI	NI		Software Architects, 206 487-0122
F2RC	NI	NI		Software Architects, 206 487-0122
Family Builder	NI	NI		Altsys, 214 680-2093
Fast Forms	NI	NI		Power Up Software, 415 345-9381
Fast Forms Filler	NI	NI		Power Up Software, 415 345-9381
FastBack IIAutoStart	NI	NI		Fifth Generation Systems, 800 873-4384
FastPath Manager II	NI	NI		Shiva, 617 252-6400
FaxGate	NI	NI		Solutions, 604 731-8648
File DirectorAutoStart	NI	NI		Fifth Generation Systems, 800 873-4384
FileDual	1.0	1.0		ASD Software 714 624-2594
FileForce	NI	NI		Acius, 408 252-4444
FileGuard	2.5.3	2.7		ASD Software, 714 624-2594
FileMaker	NI	NI		Claris, 408 727-8227
FileMaker II	NI	NI		Claris, 408 727-8227
FileMaker PLUS	NI	NI		Claris, 408 727-8227
FileMaker PRO	NI	NI		Claris, 408 727-8227
FileSaver	NI	NI		Symantec, 800 441-7234
Finder Sounds	NI	NI		Greg Smith
FinderKeys	NI	NI		Now Software, 503 274-2800
Findswell	NI	NI		Working Software, 408 423-5696

Legend: NO none available • **NI** no information • **CS** contact source for version info • **32** 32-Bit Addressing problem • **VM** virtual memory problem • **UG** get from user group, info system, or dealer • **$0** free upgrade • **NN** not needed with System 7 • **S7** comes with System 7 • **FS** file sharing problem • **!!** upgrade strongly recommended • **TT** can't set TrueType sizes above 127.

(continued)

Table A-1: Product compatibility (continued)

Product	Version OK	Version Best	Notes	Source
FireWorks	1.1	1.2		MacroMind, 415 442-0200
FlashTalk	NI	NI		Sitka, 800 445-8677
FolderBolt	NI	NI		Kent Marsh Ltd.
FolderBolt Admin.	NI	NI		Kent Marsh Ltd.
FolderLockAutoStart	NI	NI		Fifth Generation Systems, 800 873-4384
FolderShare	1.1	1.1	32	CE Software, 515 224-1953
Font HarmonyAutoStart	NI	NI		Fifth Generation Systems, 800 873-4384
Font/DA Juggler	NO	NO		Alsoft, 713 353-1510
Font/DA Mover	NI	NI		Apple Computer, 800 776-2333
Font/DA Mover	NI	NI		Authorized Apple Dealer
Fontographer	3.3	3.5.1		Altsys, 214 680-2093
Fontastic Plus	2.0	2.0.2		Altsys, 214 680-2093
Fontstudio	2.0	2.0		Letraset USA, 201 845-6100
FormatterFive	NI	NI		Software Architects, 206 487-0122
FormatterOne	NI	NI		Software Architects, 206 487-0122
FormatterTwo	NI	NI		Software Architects, 206 487-0122
Forms Designer	NI	NI		SoftView Inc.
Forum	NI	NI		Pacer Software, 508 898-3300
FoxBase+	NI	NI		Fox Software, 419 874-0162
FrameGrabber 324	NI	NI		RasterOps, 408 562-4200
FrameMaker	3.0	3.0.1		Frame Technology, 408 433-3311
FrameReader	3.0	3.0		Frame Technology, 408 433-3311
Galaxy	NI	NI		Opcode Systems, 415 856-3333
Galaxy Plus	NI	NI		Opcode Systems, 415 856-3333
Gallery Effects	1.0	1.5		Aldus, 206 628-2040
Gallery Effects Texture Art	1.0	1.0		Aldus, 206 628-2040
Gallery Effects Volume 2	1.0	1.0		Aldus, 206 628-2040
Gateway Client Driver	NI	NI		Avatar, 508 435-3000
GatorBox TFTP	1.0	1.0		Cayman Systems, 617 494-1999
GatorInstaller	1.0	2.1		Cayman Systems, 617 494-1999
GatorKeeper	1.5.0	2.1		Cayman Systems, 617 494-1999
Genetics Model	1.0	NI		Wings for Learning, 800 321-7551

Legend: **NO** none available • **NI** no information • **CS** contact source for version info • **32** 32-Bit Addressing problem • **VM** virtual memory problem • **UG** get from user group, info system, or dealer • **$0** free upgrade • **NN** not needed with System 7 • **S7** comes with System 7 • **FS** file sharing problem • **!!** upgrade strongly recommended • **TT** can't set TrueType sizes above 127.

(continued)

Table A-1: Product compatibility *(continued)*

Product	Version OK	Version Best	Notes	Source
Geometric Supposer Quad.	NI	NI		Sunburst, 800 628-8897
Geometric Supposer Tria.	NI	NI		Sunburst, 800 628-8897
GOfer	NI	NI		Microlytics, 716 248-9150
Grammatik Mac	NI	NI		Reference Software, 415 541-0222
Graph 3D	NI	NI		Acius, 408 252-4444
Gravity Model	1.0	NI		Wings for Learning, 800 321-7551
GroupWriter	NI	NI		Sunburst, 800 628-8897
GuardCard Configure	1.0	1.0		Innovative Data Design, 510 680-6818
Hammer Install	NI	NI		FWB, 415 474-8055
Hand-Off II	2.2.0	2.2.5		Connectix, 415 571-5100
Hard Disk Deadbolt	NI	NI		FWB, 415 474-8055
Hard Disk Installer	NI	NI		Mitek Systems, 800 367-5660
Hard Disk Toolkit Software	NI	NI		FWB, 415 474-8055
HayesConnect	NI	NI		Hayes Microcomputer, 404 441-1617
HayesConnect Server	NI	NI		Hayes Microcomputer, 404 441-1617
HDBackup	NI	NI		Apple Computer, 800 776-2333
HDBackup	NI	NI		Authorized Apple Dealer
HDP	NI	NI		FWB, 415 474-8055
Heap Fixer	NO	NO	NN	CE Software, 515 224-1953
HeirDA	NI	NI		Now Software, 503 274-2800
HostPrint	NI	NI		IdeaAssociates, 800 257-5027
HPMO	NI	NI		Software Architects, 206 487-0122
HyperCard	NI	NI		Claris, 408 727-8227
HyperSound & Toolkit	NI	NI		Farallon Computing, 510 596-9000
Icon-it!	2.0	2.0		Tactic, 305 665-4665
IconMover	3.0	3.0	32	CE Software, 515 224-1953
IdeaComm Mac	NI	NI		IdeaAssociates, 800 257-5027
IdeaComm Printer	NI	NI		IdeaAssociates, 800 257-5027
IdeaComm Utilities	NI	NI		IdeaAssociates, 800 257-5027
IdeaLink	NI	NI		IdeaAssociates, 800 257-5027
ifXFS	NI	NI		SoftView Inc.
Image Assistant	NI	NI		Caere, 408 395-7000

Legend: NO none available • **NI** no information • **CS** contact source for version info • **32** 32-Bit Addressing problem • **VM** virtual memory problem • **UG** get from user group, info system, or dealer • **$0** free upgrade • **NN** not needed with System 7 • **S7** comes with System 7 • **FS** file sharing problem • **!!** upgrade strongly recommended • **TT** can't set TrueType sizes above 127.

(continued)

Table A-1: Product compatibility (continued)

Product	Version OK	Version Best	Notes	Source
ImageStudio	1.7	1.7a		Fractal Design, 408 688-8800
ImageWorks	NI	NI		MacroMind, 415 442-0200
ImpressIT	NI	NI		Radius, 408 434-1010
In-Box	NI	NI		Sitka, 800 445-8677
In/Out	1.0.2	1.0.2		CE Software, 515 224-1953
In/Out Server	NO	NO		CE Software, 515 224-1953
Infini-D	1.0	2.0		Specular International, 413 549-7600
INIT Analyzer	NI	NI		Baseline Publishing
INIT Manager	NI	NI		Baseline Publishing
INITPicker	2.02	2.02		Microseeds Publishing, 802 879-3365
Installer	NI	NI		Apple Computer, 800 776-2333
Installer	NI	NI		Authorized Apple Dealer
Instant Update	1.0.1	1.0.1		ON Technology, 617 876-5122
IntelliDraw	1.0	1.0		Aldus, 206 628-2040
InterBase	NI	NI		Sitka, 800 445-8677
Interbridge Manager	NI	NI		Hayes Microcomputer, 404 441-1617
InterNet Manager	NI	NI		Shiva, 617 252-6400
JetLink Express	NI	NI		GDT Softworks, 604 291-9121
Jukebox	NI	NI		Farallon Computing, 510 596-9000
KidsMath	1.1	2.0		GreatWave Software, 408 438-1990
KidsTime	1.3	1.3		GreatWave Software, 408 438-1990
Kiwi POWER MENUS	1.0	1.0		Kiwi, 805 685-4031
Kiwi POWER WINDOWS	1.0	1.5.2		Kiwi, 805 685-4031
KiwiEnvelopes	3.1.1	3.1.6		Kiwi, 805 685-4031
KiwiFinder Extender	NO	NO		Kiwi, 805 685-4031
LapLink	NI	NI		Traveling Software, 206 483-8088
Laser Award Maker	NI	NI		Baudville, 616 698-0888
LaserWriter Font Utility	NI	NI		Apple Computer, 800 776-2333
LaserWriter Font Utility	NI	NI		Authorized Apple Dealer
LAT	NI	NI		DEC, 508 467-5111
Layout Mover	NI	NI		Baseline Publishing
LetraStudio	NO	2.0		Letraset USA, 201 845-6100

Legend: **NO** none available • **NI** no information • **CS** contact source for version info • **32** 32-Bit Addressing problem • **VM** virtual memory problem • **UG** get from user group, info system, or dealer • **$0** free upgrade • **NN** not needed with System 7 • **S7** comes with System 7 • **FS** file sharing problem • **!!** upgrade strongly recommended • **TT** can't set TrueType sizes above 127.

(continued)

Table A-1: Product compatibility *(continued)*

Product	Version OK	Version Best	Notes	Source
Lexis/Nexis	NI	NI		Mead Data Central
Live List	NI	NI		Digidesign
Lookup	NI	NI		Working Software, 408 423-5696
LWStatus	NI	NI		Farallon Computing, 510 596-9000
Mac Daisy Link	NO	NO		GDT Softworks, 604 291-9121
Mac II Video Card Utility	NI	NI		Apple Computer, 800 776-2333
Mac II Video Card Utility	NI	NI		Authorized Apple Dealer
Mac-To-Mac	1.1.0	2.0		Caravelle Networks, 613 596-2802
Mac240	NI	NI		White Pine Software, 603 886-9050
MacBanner	1.0	1.0	32	CE Software, 515 224-1953
MacBillboard	4.1	4.1		CE Software, 515 224-1953
MaccessCardReader				ASD Software, 714 624-2594
MacDraft	2.0	2.1		Innovative Data Design, 510 680-6818
MacDraw	NI	NI		Claris, 408 727-8227
MacDraw II	NI	NI		Claris, 408 727-8227
MacDraw Pro	NI	NI		Claris, 408 727-8227
MacFlow	3.5.3	3.7		Mainstay, 818 991-6540
MacInTax	NI	NI		SoftView Inc.
MacInteriors	1.0	1.0	VM	Microspot Ltd., 408 253-2000
Macintosh Common Lisp	NI	NI		APDA, 800 282-2732
Macintosh Workstation	NI	NI		APDA, 800 282-2732
MacIRMA for LC	NI	NI		DCA, 404 740-0300
MacIRMA for NuBus	NI	NI		DCA, 404 740-0300
MacIRMA for SE	NI	NI		DCA, 404 740-0300
MacIRMA for SE/30	NI	NI		DCA, 404 740-0300
MacLink Plus/PC		5.0	7.0	
MacLink Plus/Translators	5.0	7.0		DataViz, 203 268-0030
MacLink Plus/WANG VS	5.0	7.0		DataViz, 203 268-0030
MacMainFrame 3287	NI	NI		Avatar, 508 435-3000
MacMainFrame Checker	NI	NI		Avatar, 508 435-3000
MacMainFrame Client	NI	NI		Avatar, 508 435-3000
MacMainFrame Workstation	NI	NI		Avatar, 508 435-3000

Legend: NO none available • **NI** no information • **CS** contact source for version info • **32** 32-Bit Addressing problem • **VM** virtual memory problem • **UG** get from user group, info system, or dealer • **$0** free upgrade • **NN** not needed with System 7 • **S7** comes with System 7 • **FS** file sharing problem • **!!** upgrade strongly recommended • **TT** can't set TrueType sizes above 127.

(continued)

Table A-1: Product compatibility *(continued)*

Product	Version OK	Version Best	Notes	Source
MacMoney	3.50	4.0		Survivor Software Ltd., 310 410-9527
MacNetway 3270	NI	NI		Avatar, 508 435-3000
MacNetway 3287	NI	NI		Avatar, 508 435-3000
MacPaint	NI	NI		Claris, 408 727-8227
MacPassword	NI	NI		Evergreen Software, 206 483-6576
MacPlot Configure	NI	NI		Microspot Ltd., 408 253-2000
MacPlot Professional	4.0	4.0.1		Microspot Ltd., 408 253-2000
MacProject	NI	NI		Claris, 408 727-8227
MacProject II	NI	NI		Claris, 408 727-8227
MacProteus Batteries	NI	NI		Digidesign
MacProteus Front Panel	NI	NI		Digidesign
MacRecorder Driver	NI	NI		Farallon Computing, 510 596-9000
MacroMaker	NI	NI		Apple Computer, 800 776-2333
MacroMaker	NI	NI		Authorized Apple Dealer
MacroMind Accelerator	3.0	3.1		MacroMind, 415 442-0200
MacroMind Director	3.0	3.1		MacroMind, 415 442-0200
MacroMind Player	3.0	3.1.1		MacroMind, 415 442-0200
MacroModel	1.0	1.0		MacroMind, 415 442-0200
MacSafe	NI	NI		Kent Marsh Ltd.
MacSafe II Admin	NI	NI		Kent Marsh Ltd.
MacsBug	NI	NI		APDA,. 800 282-2732
MacSchedule	2.5.3	3.0		Mainstay, 818 991-6540
MacSchedulePLUS	1.0.3	1.0.5		Mainstay, 818 991-6540
MacSnoop	NI	NI		Evergreen Software, 206 483-6576
MacSpin	NI	NI		Abacus Concepts, 510 540-1949
MacTools Backup	2.0	2.1		Central Point Software, 503 690-8090
MacTools Mirror	2.1.1	NI	CS	Central Point Software, 503 690-8090
MacTools Optimizer	2.0.1	NI	CS	Central Point Software, 503 690-8090
MacTools Partition INIT	1.0	NI	CS	Central Point Software, 503 690-8090
MacTools Rescue	1.1.1	NI	CS	Central Point Software, 503 690-8090
MacTOPS Filing	NI	NI		Sitka, 800 445-8677
MacVision Image Processing	4.1	4.1		Koala Technologies, 408 776-8181

Legend: NO none available • **NI** no information • **CS** contact source for version info • **32** 32-Bit Addressing problem • **VM** virtual memory problem • **UG** get from user group, info system, or dealer • **$0** free upgrade • **NN** not needed with System 7 • **S7** comes with System 7 • **FS** file sharing problem • **!!** upgrade strongly recommended • **TT** can't set TrueType sizes above 127.

(continued)

Table A-1: Product compatibility (continued)

Product	Version OK	Version Best	Notes	Source
MacWrite	NI	NI		Claris, 408 727-8227
MacWrite II	NI	NI		Claris, 408 727-8227
MacWrite Pro	NI	NI		Claris, 408 727-8227
Magic	1.1	1.1		MacroMind, 415 442-0200
Magic Typist	1.2.1	1.2.1		Tactic, 305 665-4665
MailMaker	NI	NI		Solutions, 604 731-8648
MailMate/MM				Alisa Systems, 800 992-5472
MailMate/QM				Alisa Systems, 800 992-5472
Manager 7	1.0	1.0		SuperMac Technology, 408 245-0646
Managing Your Money	NI	NI		MECA Software, 800 288-6322
Marathon Comm	NI	NI		Dove Computer, 919 763-7918
MarcoPolo	1.02	2.0		Mainstay, 818 991-6540
Mariah	1.0	1.0		Symmetry, 602 998-9106
MarkUp	2.0	2.0		Mainstay, 818 991-6540
Master List	NI	NI		Digidesign
Master Tracks Pro 4	NI	NI		Passport Design, 415 726-0280
Master Tracks Pro 5	5.0	5.0.2		Passport Design, 415 726-0280
MasterColor	NI	NI		Baseline Publishing
MasterFinder	2.0	2.1		Tactic, 305 665-4665
MasterJuggler	1.58	1.58		Alsoft, 713 353-1510
MasterPaint	NI	NI		Baseline Publishing
Math Shop	NI	NI		Scholastic, 800 541-5513
Math Shop Jr.	NI	NI		Scholastic, 800 541-5513
Math Shop Spotlight :F&D	NI	NI		Scholastic, 800 541-5513
Math Shop Spotlight :W&M	NI	NI		Scholastic, 800 541-5513
Mathematica	NI	NI		Wolfram Research, 217 398-0700
Mavis Beacon Teaches Typing	1.3	1.3		Software Toolworks, 415 883-5157
Max	NI	NI		Opcode Systems, 415 856-3333
Maxima	2.0.0	2.0.3		Connectix, 415 571-5100
MediaGrabber	NI	NI		RasterOps, 408 562-4200
MediaMaker	1.2	1.2	32	MacroMind, 415 442-0200
MediaTracks	NI	NI		Farallon Computing, 510 596-9000

Legend: NO none available • **NI** no information • **CS** contact source for version info • **32** 32-Bit Addressing problem • **VM** virtual memory problem • **UG** get from user group, info system, or dealer • **$0** free upgrade • **NN** not needed with System 7 • **S7** comes with System 7 • **FS** file sharing problem • **!!** upgrade strongly recommended • **TT** can't set TrueType sizes above 127.

(continued)

Table A-1: Product compatibility *(continued)*

Product	Version OK	Version Best	Notes	Source
Meeting Maker	1.0	1.0.5	ON	Technology, 617 876-5122
Memory Manager INIT	NI	NI		Apple Computer, 800 776-2333
Memory Manager INIT	NI	NI		Authorized Apple Dealer
MenuFonts	4.0	4.04		Dubl-Click, 818 888-2068
Metamorphosis Professional	2.0	2.04		Altsys, 214 680-2093
Metro CD INIT	NI	NI		Everex Systems
Micro PLANNER MANAGER	1.0	1.3		Micro Planning, 303 757-2216
Micro PLANNER X-PERT	2.0	2.3		Micro Planning, 303 757-2216
MicroPhone II	3.0	4.0		Software Ventures, 800 336-6477
Microsoft BASIC	NI	NI		Microsoft, 800 426-9400
Microsoft Excel	NI	4.0		Microsoft, 800 426-9400
Microsoft File	2.0	2.0		Microsoft, 800 426-9400
Microsoft Flight Simulator	4.0	4.0		Microsoft, 800 426-9400
Microsoft Mail	NI	NI		Microsoft, 800 426-9400
Microsoft PowerPoint	NI	NI		Microsoft, 800 426-9400
Microsoft Schedule+	NI	NI		Microsoft, 800 426-9400
Microsoft Word	4.0	5.1		Microsoft, 800 426-9400
Microsoft Works	2.00b	3.0		Microsoft, 800 426-9400
Microsoft Write	NI	NI		Microsoft, 800 426-9400
MIDI Manager	NI	NI		APDA, 800 282-2732
MIDI Port Fix	NI	NI		Digidesign
MindWrite	2.1	2.1a	32, VM	Deltapoint, 408 648-4000
Miracle Piano Teaching System	1.0	1.0		Software Toolworks, 415 883-5157
MitekSQ INIT	NI	NI		Mitek Systems, 800 367-5660
Mobius	4.5	5.01		MOBIUS Technologies, 510 654-0556
Mobius CDEV	1.0	1.0		MOBIUS Technologies, 510 654-0556
MockTerminal Utility	NO	NO		CE Software, 515 224-1953
ModelShop	1.1	1.2		MacroMind, 415 442-0200
Modern Artist	NO	NO		Computer Friends, 503 626-2291
Money Building Blocks	NI	NI		Sunburst, 800 628-8897
MORE	NI	NI		Symantec, 800 441-7234
MPW	NI	NI		APDA, 800 282-2732

(continued)

Legend: NO none available • **NI** no information • **CS** contact source for version info • **32** 32-Bit Addressing problem • **VM** virtual memory problem • **UG** get from user group, info system, or dealer • **$0** free upgrade • **NN** not needed with System 7 • **S7** comes with System 7 • **FS** file sharing problem • **!!** upgrade strongly recommended • **TT** can't set TrueType sizes above 127.

Table A-1: Product compatibility (continued)

Product	Version OK	Version Best	Notes	Source
Multi Clip	2.1.7c	2.1.7c		Olduvai, 305 665-4665
Multi-Driver	1.3.8	1.3.8		Insignia Solutions, 800 876-3872
MultiClip	NI	NI		Olduvai, 305 665-4665
MultiDisk	1.27	1.27		Alsoft, 713 353-1510
MultiMaster	NI	NI		Now Software, 503 274-2800
MusicTime	1.0	1.0v2		Passport Design, 415 726-0280
NameServer	2.5	2.5.1	32	CE Software, 515 224-1953
NetCopy	NI	NI		DEC, 508 467-5111
NetSwitch	NO	NO		3 COM, 800 NET-3COM
Netway 1000	NI	NI		Avatar, 508 435-3000
Netway 3270A	NI	NI		Avatar, 508 435-3000
Netway 3270A/G	NI	NI		Avatar, 508 435-3000
Network DiskFit	NI	NI		SuperMac Software, 408 773-4489
NightWatch Admin.	NI	NI		Kent Marsh Ltd.
NightWatch Professor	NI	NI		Kent Marsh Ltd.
NightWatch ShutDown	NI	NI		Kent Marsh Ltd.
Nisus	3.06	3.06		Paragon Concepts, 619 481-1477
NodeHint	NI	NI		Farallon Computing, 510 596-9000
Norton Utilities	NI	NI		Symantec, 800 441-7234
NoteWriter II	NI	NI		Passport Design, 415 726-0280
Notification Toolbox	1.0.3	1.1	32	CE Software, 515 224-1953
NowMenus	NI	NI		Now Software, 503 274-2800
Number Munchers	NI	NI		MECC
NumberMaze	1.0	1.2		GreatWave Software, 408 438-1990
NumberMaze Decimals & Fractions	1.0	1.0		GreatWave Software, 408 438-1990
ODMS Client	NI	NI		Odesta, 708 498-5615
ODMS Design Station	NI	NI		Odesta, 708 498-5615
ODMS Server	NI	NI		Odesta, 708 498-5615
Okyto	1.0	1.0		The FreeSoft Co., 412 846-2700
OmniPage	3.0	3.0		Caere, 408 395-7000
OmniPage Direct	NI	NI		Caere, 408 395-7000

Legend: **NO** none available • **NI** no information • **CS** contact source for version info • **32** 32-Bit Addressing problem • **VM** virtual memory problem • **UG** get from user group, info system, or dealer • **$0** free upgrade • **NN** not needed with System 7 • **S7** comes with System 7 • **FS** file sharing problem • **!!** upgrade strongly recommended • **TT** can't set TrueType sizes above 127.

(continued)

Table A-1: Product compatibility *(continued)*

Product	Version OK	Version Best	Notes	Source
OmniPage Pro	2.1	2.1		Caere, 408 395-7000
Omnis	7.0v1.0	7.0v1.1		Blythe Software, 415 571-0222
OMS	NI	NI		Opcode Systems, 415 856-3333
On Cue	NI	NI		ICOM Simulations, 708 520-4440
ON Location	1.0.2	2.0.1		ON Technology, 617 876-5122
OnCue 2	2.0	2.0.1		ICOM Simulations, 708 520-4440
OPTIMA/32	NO	NO		Connectix, 415 571-5100
Oracle	2.0	2.0		Oracle, 800 672-2531
Oracle Client Tools	2.0	2.0		Oracle, 800 672-2531
Oracle Server	1.1	1.1		Oracle, 800 672-2531
ORACLE Settings	2.0.1	2.0.1		Oracle, 800 672-2531
Oracle SQL*Net	1.5	1.5		Oracle, 800 672-2531
Oracle*Card	1.1	1.1		Oracle, 800 672-2531
OutNumbered!	NI	NI		Learning Company, 510 792-2101
PacerLink	NI	NI		Pacer Software, 508 898-3300
PackIt III	1.3	1.3		Harry Chesley
PageMaker	4.0	4.2a		Aldus, 206 628-2040
Painter	1.0	1.2		Fractal Design, 408 688-8800
Pantone Color Toolkit	NI	NI		Radius, 408 434-1010
PartnerAutoStart	NI	NI		Fifth Generation Systems, 800 873-4384
PassProof	1.01	1.1		Kensington Microware Ltd., 800 535-4242
PatchBay	NI	NI		APDA, 800 282-2732
Pathworks	1.1	1.1		Oracle, 800 672-2531
Peripheral Vision	NI	NI		Peripheral Vision
Personal Press	1.01	2.0		Aldus, 206 628-2040
Personality!	NI	NI		Baseline Publishing
Persuasion	2.0	2.12		Aldus, 206 628-2040
PhoneNET CheckNET	NI	NI		Farallon Computing, 510 596-9000
PhoneNET Liaison	NI	NI		Farallon Computing, 510 596-9000
PhotoMac	NI	NI		Data Translation, 508 481-3700
PhotoRMan	NI	NI		Pixar, 510 236-4000
PictureBase	1.1	1.2		Symmetry, 602 998-9106

Legend: NO none available • **NI** no information • **CS** contact source for version info • **32** 32-Bit Addressing problem • **VM** virtual memory problem • **UG** get from user group, info system, or dealer • **$0** free upgrade • **NN** not needed with System 7 • **S7** comes with System 7 • **FS** file sharing problem • **!!** upgrade strongly recommended • **TT** can't set TrueType sizes above 127.

(continued)

Table A-1: Product compatibility (continued)

Product	Version OK	Version Best	Notes	Source
PixelPaint	NI	NI		SuperMac Software, 408 773-4489
PixelPaint Professional	NI	NI		SuperMac Software, 408 773-4489
PLICDR	NI	NI		PLI, 510 657-2211
Plus Display	NI	NI		Radius, 408 434-1010
Plus/WANG OIS	5.0	7.0		DataViz, 203 268-0030
Point of View	NI	NI		Scholastic, 800 541-5513
Port Control	NI	NI		Dove Computer, 919 763-7918
PowerBook Utilities	1.0	1.0		Connectix, 415 571-5100
POWERicons	NI	NI		Magic Software
PowerPrint	1.0	2.0		GDT Softworks, 604 291-9121
Precision Color	NI	NI		Radius, 408 434-1010
PrePrint	1.5	1.51		Aldus, 206 628-2040
PressWise	1.0	1.0		Aldus, 206 628-2040
PrintLink Collection	4.0.1	4.1		GDT Softworks, 604 291-9121
Prism	2.3	3.0		Analytical Vision, 919 851-8111
Prodigy	1.0	1.5		SuperMac Technology, 408 245-0646
Profiler	NI	NI		Now Software, 503 274-2800
Programmer's Key	NI	NI		P. Mercer
Public Folder	NI	NI		Claris 408 727-8227
Pyro!AutoStart	NI	NI		Fifth Generation Systems, 800 873-4384
Q-Sheet A/V	NI	NI		Digidesign
QM Administrator	2.5	2.5.1		CE Software, 515 224-1953
QM Forms	2.5	2.5.1	32	CE Software, 515 224-1953
QM Menu	2.5	2.5.1	32	CE Software, 515 224-1953
QM Remote	2.5	2.5.1		CE Software, 515 224-1953
QM Server	2.5	2.5.1		CE Software, 515 224-1953
QUED-M	2.09	2.09	32	Paragon Concepts, 619 481-1477
Quick Mount	NI	NI		Apple Computer, 800 776-2333
Quick Mount	NI	NI		Authorized Apple Dealer
QuickCAD	NI	NI		Radius, 408 434-1010
QuickColor	NI	NI		Radius, 408 434-1010
QuickDex	NI	2.58		Casady & Greene, 408 484-9228

Legend: NO none available • **NI** no information • **CS** contact source for version info • **32** 32-Bit Addressing problem • **VM** virtual memory problem • **UG** get from user group, info system, or dealer • **$0** free upgrade • **NN** not needed with System 7 • **S7** comes with System 7 • **FS** file sharing problem • **!!** upgrade strongly recommended • **TT** can't set TrueType sizes above 127.

(continued)

Table A-1: Product compatibility (continued)

Product	Version OK	Version Best	Notes	Source
Quicken	1.5	3.0		Intuit, 415 858-6040
QuickImage24	NI	NI		Mass Microsystems, 408 522-1200
QuicKeys	2.1	2.1.2a		CE Software, 515 224-1953
Quickletter	NI	NI		Working Software, 408 423-5696
QuickLock	NI	NI		Kent Marsh Ltd.
QuickView Studio	2.0	2.0		E-Machines, 503 646-6699
Radius Grabber	NI	NI		Radius, 408 434-1010
Radius Theatrics	NI	NI		Radius, 408 434-1010
Radius/GX	NI	NI		Radius, 408 434-1010
RadiusMath	NI	NI		Radius, 408 434-1010
RadiusWare	NI	NI		Radius, 408 434-1010
RasterOps Monitors	NI	NI		RasterOps, 408 562-4200
Read-It!	3.0	3.08		Tactic, 305 665-4665
READ-IT! O.C.R.	NI	NI		Oldovai, 305 665-4665
Reading Maze	1.0	1.2		GreatWave Software, 408 438-1990
Ready Set Go!	NI	NI		Manhattan Graphics, 800 572-6533
Ready Set Go! 5	1.0	1.0		Manhattan Graphics, 800 572-6533
RecvInit	NI	NI		PLI, 510 657-2211
Redirector	NI	NI		Pacer Software, 508 898-3300
Redux	1.63	1.63		Microseeds Publishing, 802 879-3365
Reggie	NI	NI		White Pine Software, 603 886-9050
RenderApp	NI	NI		Pixar, 510 236-4000
RenderMan	1.1	1.1		MacroMind, 415 442-0200
RenderWorks	1.1	1.2		MacroMind, 415 442-0200
ResEdit	NI	NI		APDA, 800 282-2732
Retro.SCSI	NI	NI		Dantz Development, 510 849-0293
Retrospect	NI	NI		Dantz Development, 510 849-0293
RetrospectINIT	NI	NI		Dantz Development, 510 849-0293
RicohCart	NI	NI		Software Architects, 206 487-0122
RicohMO	NI	NI		Software Architects, 206 487-0122
Rival	1.1.9	1.1.9		Microseeds Publishing, 802 879-3365
RocketWare	NI	NI		Radius, 408 434-1010

Legend: **NO** none available • **NI** no information • **CS** contact source for version info • **32** 32-Bit Addressing problem • **VM** virtual memory problem • **UG** get from user group, info system, or dealer • **$0** free upgrade • **NN** not needed with System 7 • **S7** comes with System 7 • **FS** file sharing problem • **!!** upgrade strongly recommended • **TT** can't set TrueType sizes above 127.

(continued)

Table A-1: Product compatibility (continued)

Product	Version OK	Version Best	Notes	Source
Runtime Converter	NI	NI		Odesta, 708 498-5615
Sade	NI	NI		APDA, 800 282-2732
SAM Intercept	NI	NI		Symantec, 800 441-7234
SAM Intercept Jr	NI	NI		Symantec, 800 441-7234
SAM Virus Clinic	NI	NI		Symantec, 800 441-7234
SampleCell Editor	NI	NI		Digidesign
Sans Faute	NI	NI		Acius, 408 252-4444
SaveGuard	NI	NI		Now Software, 503 274-2800
Screen Locker	NI	NI		Now Software, 503 274-2800
ScreenGems	1.1	1.1		Microseeds Publishing, 802 879-3365
ScreenRecorder	NI	NI		Farallon Computing, 510 596-9000
Screenshot	NI	NI		Baseline Publishing
SCSIInUse	NI	NI		Sam Barone
SCSIProbe	NI	NI		Robert Polic
SDLC Driver	NI	NI		Avatar, 508 435-3000
SDLC Gateway Server	NI	NI		Avatar, 508 435-3000
SecondSight	2.0	2.0		The FreeSoft Co., 412 846-2700
Sentinel	NI	NI		SuperMac Software, 408 773-4489
Server Control	NI	NI		Avatar, 508 435-3000
Shiva Config	NI	NI		Shiva, 617 252-6400
Shiva Net Manager	NI	NI		Shiva, 617 252-6400
Shortcut	1.6	1.6		Aladdin Systems, 408 761-6200
ShowPlace	NI	NI		Pixar, 510 236-4000
Silhouette	NI	NI		Everex Systems
Silver INIT	NI	NI		LACie Limited, 503 520-9000
Silverlining	NI	NI		LACie Limited, 503 520-9000
SILVERRUN-DFD	1.1.5	2.1.1		CSA Research Ltd., 800 537-4262
SILVERRUN-ERM	NI	NI		CSA Research Ltd., 800 537-4262
SILVERRUN-ERX	2.0.5	2.1.1		CSA Research Ltd., 800 537-4262
SILVERRUN-ERX->RDM	2.0.5	2.1.1		CSA Research Ltd., 800 537-4262
SILVERRUN-LDM	NI	NI		CSA Research Ltd., 800 537-4262
SILVERRUN-RDM	2.0.5	2.1.1		CSA Research Ltd., 800 537-4262

Legend: NO none available • **NI** no information • **CS** contact source for version info • **32** 32-Bit Addressing problem • **VM** virtual memory problem • **UG** get from user group, info system, or dealer • **$0** free upgrade • **NN** not needed with System 7 • **S7** comes with System 7 • **FS** file sharing problem • **!!** upgrade strongly recommended • **TT** can't set TrueType sizes above 127.

(continued)

Table A-1: Product compatibility *(continued)*

Product	Version OK	Version Best	Notes	Source
SILVERRUN-SRL	NI	NI		CSA Research Ltd., 800 537-4262
SILVERRUN-WRM	2.1.0	2.1.1		CSA Research Ltd., 800 537-4262
Silverscan	NI	NI		LACie Limited, 503 520-9000
SimpleShare	1.3	1.3		Symmetry, 602 998-9106
Sketcher	1.0	1.0		Fractal Design, 408 688-8800
Slimline INIT	3.09	3.09		Control Concepts, 703 876-6444
Slimline Installer	3.61	3.61		Control Concepts, 703 876-6444
SmartAlarms	NI	NI		JAM, 203 630-0055
Smartcom	NI	NI		Hayes Microcomputer, 404 441-1617
Smartcom II	NI	NI		Hayes Microcomputer, 404 441-1617
SmartForm Assistant	NI	NI		Claris, 408 727-8227
SmartForm Designer	NI	NI		Claris, 408 727-8227
SmartFormat	NI	NI		MacLand, 800 333-3353
SmartFormat Syquest	NI	NI		MacLand, 800 333-3353
SmartImage	NI	NI		MacLand, 800 333-3353
SmartRestore	NI	NI		MacLand, 800 333-3353
SmartScrap & The Clipper	NI	NI		Solutions, 604 731-8648
SNA.3278	NI	NI		Avatar, 508 435-3000
SnapJot	NI	NI		Wildflower, 708 916-9360
Soft Pivot	NI	NI		Radius, 408 434-1010
SoftNoted	NO	NO		Insignia Solutions, 800 876-3872
SoftPC	CS	2.5		Insignia Solutions, 800 876-3872
SoftPC EGA/AT	CS	2.5		Insignia Solutions, 800 876-3872
SoftTalk	NI	NI		Sitka, 800 445-8677
Sony MO	NI	NI		Software Architects, 206 487-0122
Sound Accelerator	NI	NI		Digidesign
Sound Designer II	NI	NI		Digidesign
Sound Designer II SC	NI	NI		Digidesign
Sound Edit	2.05	2.05		MacroMind, 415 442-0200
Sound Edit Pro	2.05	2.05		MacroMind, 415 442-0200
SoundClips	2.0	2.0		Tactic, 305 665-4665
SoundEdit	NI	NI		Farallon Computing, 510 596-9000

Legend: NO none available • **NI** no information • **CS** contact source for version info • **32** 32-Bit Addressing problem • **VM** virtual memory problem • **UG** get from user group, info system, or dealer • **$0** free upgrade • **NN** not needed with System 7 • **S7** comes with System 7 • **FS** file sharing problem • **!!** upgrade strongly recommended • **TT** can't set TrueType sizes above 127.

(continued)

Table A-1: Product compatibility (continued)

Product	Version OK	Version Best	Notes	Source
SoundMaster	NI	NI		Bruce Tomlin
Speed Beep	NI	NI		L Products
SpeedCard	1.76	1.76	$0	SuperMac Technology, 408 245-0646
Spellswell	NI	NI		Working Software, 408 423-5696
Spool	NI	NI		Sitka, 800 445-8677
SQL*forms	1.0.1	1.0.2		Oracle, 800 672-2531
SQL*Net	1.5	1.5		Oracle, 800 672-2531
StarCommand	NI	NI		Farallon Computing, 510 596-9000
StartUp Manager	NI	NI		Now Software, 503 274-2800
Statistics Workshop	NI	NI		Sunburst, 800 628-8897
Status Mac	3.0	3.0		ON Technology, 617 876-5122
STATUS*Mac	2.0	3.0		Pharos Technologies, 800 548-8871
StatView 4.0	NI	NI		Abacus Concepts, 510 540-1949
StatView II	NI	NI		Abacus Concepts, 510 540-1949
StatViewSE+Graphics	NI	NI		Abacus Concepts, 510 540-1949
Stepping Out II	NI	NI		Berkley Systems, 510 540-5535
StrataClip	1.0	1.0		Strata, 801 628-9751
StrataFlight	NI	NI		Strata, 801 628-9751
StrataType	1.0	1.0		Strata, 801 628-9751
StrataVision 3d	1.0	2.6		Strata, 801 628-9751
Studio Vision	NI	NI		Opcode Systems, 415 856-3333
Studio/1	NI	NI		Electronic Arts, 415 572-2787
Studio/32	NI	NI		Electronic Arts, 415 572-2787
Studio/8	NI	NI		Electronic Arts, 415 572-2787
StuffIt Classic	NO	NO		Aladdin Systems, 408 761-6200
StuffIt Deluxe	3.0	3.0		Aladdin Systems, 408 761-6200
StuffIt Light	3.0	3.0		Aladdin Systems, 408 761-6200
StuffIt SpaceSaver	1.0	1.0		Aladdin Systems, 408 761-6200
StyleMerger	1.0	1.2		Altsys, 214 680-2093
Success With Writing	NI	NI		Scholastic, 800 541-5513
Suitcase IIAutoStart	NI	NI		Fifth Generation Systems, 800 873-4384
SUM Partition	NI	NI		Symantec, 800 441-7234

Legend: NO none available • **NI** no information • **CS** contact source for version info • **32** 32-Bit Addressing problem • **VM** virtual memory problem • **UG** get from user group, info system, or dealer • **$0** free upgrade • **NN** not needed with System 7 • **S7** comes with System 7 • **FS** file sharing problem • **!!** upgrade strongly recommended • **TT** can't set TrueType sizes above 127.

(continued)

Table A-1: Product compatibility *(continued)*

Product	Version OK	Version Best	Notes	Source
SUM Shield	NI	NI		Symantec, 800 441-7234
SUM Tools	NI	NI		Symantec, 800 441-7234
Sumo	NI	NI		Sumo Systems, 408 453-5744
Super Boomerang	NI	NI		Now Software, 503 274-2800
Super3D	2.5	2.5		Aldus, 206 628-2040
SuperANOVA	NI	NI		Abacus Concepts, 510 540-1949
SuperCard	1.5	1.6		Aldus, 206 628-2040
SuperClock!	NI	NI		Steve Christensen
SuperGlue	NI	NI		Solutions, 604 731-8648
SuperLaserSpoolAutoStart	NI	NI		Fifth Generation Systems, 800 873-4384
SuperPaint	3.0	3.0		Aldus, 206 628-2040
SuperVideo	2.2	2.49	$0	SuperMac Technology, 408 245-0646
SuperView	NO	NO		SuperMac Technology, 408 245-0646
SuperView II	NO	NO		SuperMac Technology, 408 245-0646
Swivel 3D	1.2	1.5		MacroMind, 415 442-0200
Swivel 3D Professional	2.11	2.4		MacroMind, 415 442-0200
SyQuest	NI	NI		Software Architects, 206 487-0122
SyQuest INIT	NI	NI		MacLand, 800 333-3353
TAA	NO	2.1		CE Software, 515 224-1953
TahitiMO	NI	NI		Software Architects, 206 487-0122
Talking Moose	NI	NI		Baseline Publishing
Talking Reader Rabbit	NI	NI		Learning Company, 510 792-2101
Tangent.INIT	2.0.1	2.0.1		CE Software, 515 224-1953
TapeDriver	3.0	3.0		SuperMac Technology, 408 245-0646
TCP/IP with MacTCP	1.1	1.1		Oracle, 800 672-2531
TCPort	2.2	2.2		Oracle, 800 672-2531
TCPort	NI	NI		Novell, 800 638-9273
TeachText	NI	NI		Apple Computer, 800 776-2333
TeachText	NI	NI		Authorized Apple Dealer
Teleport	1.6	2.3		Global Village, 800 736-4821
TELNET Driver	NI	NI		Pacer Software, 508 898-3300
Template Printer	2.0	2.0.1	32	CE Software, 515 224-1953

Legend: NO none available • **NI** no information • **CS** contact source for version info • **32** 32-Bit Addressing problem • **VM** virtual memory problem • **UG** get from user group, info system, or dealer • **$0** free upgrade • **NN** not needed with System 7 • **S7** comes with System 7 • **FS** file sharing problem • **!!** upgrade strongly recommended • **TT** can't set TrueType sizes above 127.

(continued)

Table A-1: Product compatibility *(continued)*

Product	Version OK	Version Best	Notes	Source
Tempo II Plus	3.0	3.0		Affinity Microsystems, 303 442-4840
The Bank Street Writer	NI	NI		Scholastic, 800 541-5513
The Connection	NI	NI		Kent Marsh Ltd.
The Namer	NI	NI		Apple Computer, 800 776-2333
The Namer	NI	NI		Authorized Apple Dealer
The Oregon Trail	NI	NI		MECC
THINK C	NI	NI		Symantec, 800 441-7234
THINK Pascal	NI	NI		Symantec, 800 441-7234
ThinkTank	NI	NI		Symantec, 800 441-7234
Thunder 7	NI	NI		Baseline Publishing
Thunder 7 Utility	NI	NI		Baseline Publishing
Timbuktu	NI	NI		Farallon Computing, 510 596-9000
Timbuktu/Remote	NI	NI		Farallon Computing, 510 596-9000
Time Drive	NI	NI		LACie Limited, 503 520-9000
TMON Professional	3.0	3.0.1		ICOM Simulations, 708 520-4440
Token Ring Driver	NI	NI		Avatar, 508 435-3000
Token Ring Gateway Server	NI	NI		Avatar, 508 435-3000
TOPS	NI	NI		Sitka, 800 445-8677
TrafficWatch	NI	NI		Farallon Computing, 510 596-9000
TrafficWatch II	NI	NI		Farallon Computing, 510 596-9000
Trapeze	2.1	2.1	32	Deltapoint, 408 648-4000
TrashGuard	1.0	1.0		ASD Software 714 624-2594
TRAX	2.1	2.2		Passport Design, 415 726-0280
Tri-Data API	NI	NI		Avatar, 508 435-3000
TrueForm Fill Out	NI	NI		Adobe Systems, 415 961-0911
TrueForm Setup	NI	NI		Adobe Systems, 415 961-0911
TrueType INIT	NI	NI		Apple Computer, 800 776-2333
TrueType INIT	NI	NI		Authorized Apple Dealer
TssNet				Alisa Systems, 800 992-5472
TurboMouse	3.0	4.0		Kensington Microware Ltd., 800 535-4242
Turbosynth	NI	NI		Digidesign
Two Page Display	1.3	1.3		SuperMac Technology, 408 245-0646

Legend: NO none available • **NI** no information • **CS** contact source for version info • **32** 32-Bit Addressing problem • **VM** virtual memory problem • **UG** get from user group, info system, or dealer • **$0** free upgrade • **NN** not needed with System 7 • **S7** comes with System 7 • **FS** file sharing problem • **!!** upgrade strongly recommended • **TT** can't set TrueType sizes above 127.

(continued)

Table A-1: Product compatibility (continued)

Product	Version OK	Version Best	Notes	Source
Typist	NI	NI		Caere, 408 395-7000
UltraPaint	1.0	1.0.5		Deneba Software, 305 594-6965
Update Collection	NI	NI		Odesta, 708 498-5615
V.I.P.	2.51	2.5		Mainstay, 818 991-6540
Vaccine	1.0	1.0.1	32	CE Software, 515 224-1953
Vantage External	NI	NI		Baseline Publishing
Vantage Opener	NI	NI		Baseline Publishing
VDISK Driver	NI	NI		Pacer Software, 508 898-3300
VectRMan	NI	NI		Pixar, 510 236-4000
Ventura Publisher	NI	NI		Ventura Software, 800 822-8221
VersaCAD 3D	NI	NI		VersaCAD, 617 275-1800
VersaCAD II	NI	NI		VersaCAD, 617 275-1800
VideoPaint	1.1a	1.1a		Tactic, 305 665-4665
VideoSync	NI	NI		APDA, 800 282-2732
Virex	3.5	3.82		Microcom Software, 919 490-1277
Virtual	3.0.0	3.0.1		Connectix, 415 571-5100
Vision	NI	NI		Opcode Systems, 415 856-3333
VTXpress	NI	NI		White Pine Software, 603 886-9050
Wagon Train 1848	NI	NI		MECC
Watch	1.6	1.7.2		Cayman Systems, 617 494-1999
White Knight	11.0	11.0		The FreeSoft Co., 412 846-2700
Widgets	3.04	3.04	32	CE Software, 515 224-1953
WindowWatch	1.53	1.53		ASD Software, 714 624-2594
Wingz	1.1	1.1		Informix, 800 331-1763
Word Munchers	NI	NI		MECC
WordFinder	NI	NI		Microlytics, 716 248-9150
WordFinder Plus	NI	NI		Microlytics, 716 248-9150
WordPerfect	NI	NI		WordPerfect Corp., 801 225-5000
WriteNow	NI	NI		T/Maker Co., 415 962-0195
WYSIWYG Menus	NI	NI		Now Software, 503 274-2800
XP60+B	NI	NI		SuperMac Software, 408 773-4489

Legend: **NO** none available • **NI** no information • **CS** contact source for version info • **32** 32-Bit Addressing problem • **VM** virtual memory problem • **UG** get from user group, info system, or dealer • **$0** free upgrade • **NN** not needed with System 7 • **S7** comes with System 7 • **FS** file sharing problem • **!!** upgrade strongly recommended • **TT** can't set TrueType sizes above 127.

Table A-2: Some items Compatibility Checker 1.1 ignores

Item name	
4D Customizer	Foreign File Access (Apple CD-ROM)
4D External Mover	Forms Installer for Status Mac
4D Tools	FoxInstall
6.0.7 AppleShare	Gallery (Studio/1, /8, /32)
7.0 Installer	General 6.0.x
A.M.E. Utility	General Controls
A/ROSE	IIfx Serial Switch
ABKey (KidsTime)	ImageWriter
ADSP	INIT Tracker
AGXit! (Persuasion)	INITLoader
Aldus Installer	Installers
AME Tools	Instrument Maker (ConcertWare)
American Discovery	IQShell (before CD-ROM)
AppleTalk ImageWriter	Keyboard
Brightness	KidsMath
Canvas Separator 1.0	KidsNotes (KidsTime)
CD Remote INIT	Labels
CloseView 6.0.7	LaserWriter 1.0 – 5.0
Color	LaserWriter 5.2 – 6.0.1
Cricket Installer	LaserWriter 7.0
Dialog Editor	LaserWriter IISC
Disk Lock Emg. Unlock	Layout Plus (Norton Utilities)
Disk Lock Installer	LQ AppleTalk ImageWriter
DiskLight (Norton Utilities)	LQ ImageWriter
DL Folder Lock	MacApp code
Document readers	MacroMind movie
Dot-To-Dot (KidsTime)	Map
Easy Access	Match-It (KidsTime)
Fax Center	Memory
File Sharing Extension	MITEM modules
File Sharing Monitor	Monitors
FKey Manager	More Graph
Font & Sound Valet	More Library Mover
	MountImage

(continued)

Table A-2: Some items Compatibility Checker 1.1 ignores *(continued)*

Item name	Item name
Mouse	Sharing Setup
MT Player (Media Tracks)	Sound
Music Player (ConcertWare)	Sound-to-Video II
Network	Speed Disk (Norton Utilities)
NumberMaze	Startup 6.0.x
NumberMaze D&F	Startup Disk
Omnis 5	StyleWriter
Personal LaserWriter SC	SUM Backup
Personal LaserWriter LS	SUM Disk Clinic 2.0
Personal LaserWriter LS Prep	SUM Encrypt
Portable cdev 6.0.x	SUM Install
Portable Profiler	SUM QuickCopy
Print Monitor	SUM Recover
Quicken to MacinTax Export	SUM Tune Up
QuickInstall	SuperEdit
Reading Maze	Table Editor (PageMaker 4)
Responder	Tops DA installer
ResponderINIT	TOPs Translators
Retrospect Updater	Users & Groups
SAM Exceptions Copier (SAM 3.0)	Views
Scanner (Apple)	WingzAid for 6.0.5
Self-Extracting Archive (Compact Pro)	°Remote for Retrospect
Self Unstuffing Archive (StuffIt)	- AL Compression

Judge Compatibility Yourself

Software publishers make nebulous claims about how well their products work with System 7. They commonly describe products as *mostly compatible, compatible,* or *savvy.* What do those terms mean? To be considered mostly compatible, a program merely needs to hobble along in System 7. Such a program can have problems ranging from minor ugliness to significant but isolated incompatibilities that you can usually avoid but that may cause crashing, freezing, or unexpected quitting.

To be considered compatible, a program must work as well with System 7 as with earlier system software. A compatible program doesn't crash even when virtual memory and file sharing are turned on. But it does not have to work while other programs are open, unless it did that with MultiFinder active in System 6.

If a compatible program takes advantage of at least some major System 7 capabilities, then Apple and the program's developer consider it System 7 savvy. Unfortunately, this term has no precise meaning so you have to look for specific features and capabilities. Here's a checklist to consider.

- ✔ Cooperates in System 7's multitasking by sharing processor time with other open programs.
- ✔ Works with 32-Bit Addressing turned on.
- ✔ Has balloon help, ideally for all menus, dialog boxes, tool palettes, and special window controls in their various states (active, inactive, and so on).
- ✔ Allows setting any font size and avoids font conflicts by identifying fonts internally by name.
- ✔ Permits incremental font scaling.
- ✔ Allows publishing, subscribing, or both (as appropriate).
- ✔ Provides standard publisher and subscriber options.
- ✔ Shows borders of publishers and subscribers you select.
- ✔ Enables you to show or hide borders of all publishers and subscribers.
- ✔ Allows subscriber adornments (such as changing the font throughout a subscriber).
- ✔ Allows stopping all edition updates.
- ✔ Recognizes the four basic Apple events that the Finder sends — Open Application, Open Document, Print Document, and Quit Application.
- ✔ Recognizes more than the basic four Apple events.
- ✔ Uses special folders as needed — Preferences, Extensions, and Control Panels.
- ✔ Has complete icon families — black-and-white, 16-color, and 256-color icons in standard and small sizes — for the program, all document types, and stationery.
- ✔ Knows how to handle stationery documents.
- ✔ Includes a New Folder button in the Save dialog box.
- ✔ Includes the program name in all documents so the Finder can always tell you which program opens a document.
- ✔ Opens Data Access Manager query documents, which greatly simplify retrieving data from complex databases.

Appendix B
Glossary

32-Bit Addressing A System 7 capability that increases the amount of RAM that some Macintosh models can use.

active window The frontmost (topmost) window on the desktop in which you view, create, or edit a document. Only the active window has visible scroll bars and stripes in its title bar.

alert box A dialog box, often accompanied by the system alert sound, that notifies you of an error message or provides you with a warning.

analog data Sound, video, or other information stored as wave forms (often on magnetic tape).

Apple events Systems 7's language for IAC. Programs can send messages to one another.

Apple File Exchange A utility program for converting documents from one format to another, for example from MS-DOS to Macintosh.

Apple menu Lists the items contained in the Apple Menu Items folder, which is in the System Folder. Choosing an item from the Apple menu opens the item.

AppleShare Apple's file sharing software designed specifically for dedicated file sharing on larger networks. AppleShare is compatible with System 7's file sharing capabilities.

AppleTalk The networking software built into every Macintosh and most Laser-Writers.

Application menu The menu located at the far right end of the menu bar that lists which programs are open and provides commands for hiding them.

application program Software developed for a specific purpose such as word processing or number crunching.

auto scroll To scroll without using the scroll bars by dragging the pointer from inside a window past the window's edge.

background copying The capability of Finder 7 to copy or duplicate items in the background while you work with other programs.

bitmap A graphic image composed of black dots and white dots. *Compare* **pixmap.**

bitmapped font *See* fixed-size font.

cache *See* Disk Cache.

capture To digitize video from videotape, video camera, or other TV-compatible source. Same as **grab.**

cdev Acronym for Control Panel Device; *see* **control panels.**

checkbox A small box that you use to turn an option in a dialog box or window on or off. When an "x" appears in a checkbox, the option is on; when a checkbox is empty, the option is off.

Chooser A desk accessory that lets you choose among different devices, such as printers and shared disks on a network.

Clipboard A storage place for whatever you last cut or copied. Pasting puts a copy of the Clipboard into a document or other area you're editing.

codec A shortened form of "compressor-decompressor;" a technical term for **compressor.**

Component Manager The system software that registers components so application programs can find out what component services are available and use them.

component A software module that provides a service to or extends the capabilities of one or more application programs, for example by compressing and decompressing data or controlling an external device such as a digitizer card, scanner, or VCR.

compression algorithm A method for compressing and decompressing data. Each compression algorithm generally works best with one type of data, such as sound, photographs, video or motion pictures, and computer-generated animation.

compression ratio Indicates the amount of compression and is calculated by dividing the size of an original image by the size of the compressed image. Larger compression ratios mean greater compression and generally mean poorer image quality.

compressor Something that compresses data so that it takes less space to store, and decompresses compressed data back to its original form for playing or changing. A compressor may consist of software, hardware, or both.

control panels Small programs that let you change various Macintosh settings such as mouse options, date and time, and the Finder window format. Control panels are located in the Control Panels folder inside the System Folder.

DAL Acronym for Data Access Language, which is built into System 7 and simplifies retrieving data from a database management system.

DBMS Acronym for database management system. A program which manages large amounts of structured data.

deselect To cancel the currently selected item, usually by selecting something else.

desktop database Information the Finder keeps in an invisible file about items on the desktop, in folders, and in disks. This information includes info window comments, icon graphics, folder locations, and more.

desktop The location of the Trash icon, disk icons, and optionally other icons.

dialog box A window that contains a message, requests information from you, or allows you to change settings.

digital data Sound, video, or other information stored as a sequence of on and off pulses. *Compare* **analog data.**

digitize To convert analog data to digital data.

dimmed Appearing grayed out; indicates an icon, menu item, or other item is unavailable or in use.

directory dialog box The dialog box you get when you use an Open, Save As, or other disk-related command, in which you locate files and change disks from within an application program.

Disk Cache That portion of the Macintosh main memory which is set aside to store frequently used information from disk. You adjust the size of the disk cache using the Memory control panel.

drag select To select text, graphics, icons, or other items by dragging the cursor across them.

driver Software that controls the operation of a peripheral device, such as a printer or disk drive. Some drivers are represented by icons in the Preferences folder, which are inside the System Folder.

Easy Access A control panel that assists people who have difficulty typing on the keyboard or manipulating the mouse.

edition A file that contains a live copy of a publisher. When the publisher changes, the edition is updated. Subscribers contain copies of editions. *See also* **publisher** and **subscriber.**

EtherTalk An AppleTalk network connected by Ethernet cables.

expansion card A removable circuit board that plugs into a slot inside some Macintosh models. An expansion card enables the computer to use a special device or to perform an additional function.

file A document, program, or other named body of information stored on a disk.

file server A computer that contains files shared by other computers on a network.

Finder The part of the Macintosh system software that creates the desktop environment and keeps track of your files, folders, and disks.

fixed-size font A font made up of bitmapped characters. Each fixed-size font looks good in only one size.

Font/DA Mover A utility program for adding and removing fonts and desk accessories from older system software.

format A standard for organizing, storing, and exchanging data.

fps Frames per second; the measure of **frame rate.**

frame differencing An image compression technique that removes from a frame everything that's unchanged from the previous frame. *Compare* **spatial compression.**

frame One still image that is part of a series of still images, which, when shown in sequence, produce the illusion of movement.

frame rate The number of frames displayed in one second. The TV frame rate is 30 fps in the U.S. and other countries that use the NTSC broadcasting standard; 25 fps in countries that use the PAL or SEACAM standard. The standard movie frame rate is 24 fps.

full motion Video displayed at frame rates of 24 to 30 fps. The human eye perceives fairly smooth motion at frame rates of 12 to 18 fps.

generation loss Degradation of a video image and sound track caused by making a copy on analog tape. Copying digital data involves no generation loss.

grab To digitize video from videotape, video camera, or other TV-compatible source. Same as **capture.**

grayscale monitor A video monitor that displays shades of gray (not just black and white).

IAC An acronym for interapplication communication. IAC allows programs to communicate with each other.

Image Compression Manager The system software that compresses and decompresses still and moving images.

INIT An old name for a system extension.

insertion point The place in a document where something will be added; marked in text by a flashing vertical line. You move the insertion point by clicking at another spot with the mouse.

JPEG An international standard specified by the Joint Photographic Experts Group for compressing individual natural images, which vary smoothly and have few edges or other sharp detail.

K An abbreviation for kilobyte.

kilobyte An amount of memory or disk space equal to 1024 bytes.

LocalTalk Apple's cabling system for connecting computers, printers, and other devices to make an AppleTalk network. LocalTalk uses the built-in printer ports of Macintosh computers and the LocalTalk ports of many LaserWriter printers.

lossless A type of compression algorithm that regenerates exactly the same data as the uncompressed original and has a relatively low compression ratio.

lossy A type of compression algorithm that achieves a relatively high compression ratio by losing data when it compresses and regenerating an approximation of the uncompressed original when it decompresses.

MB Abbreviation for megabyte.

media integration *See* **multimedia.**

megabyte An amount of memory or disk space equal to 1024 kilobytes or 1,048,576 bytes.

memory The part of the computer hardware that stores information for fastest retrieval.

MIDI An acronym for Musical Instrument Digital Interface. An international standard that enables a computer to control digital musical instruments and perform music on them.

mouse tracking The relationship between how fast you move the mouse and how fast the pointer moves on the screen.

Movie Controller Apple's standard on-screen, mouse-operated control for playing, stopping, stepping through, browsing, and setting the loudness of movies.

Movie Toolbox System software services that make it easy for application programs to play, cut, copy, and paste QuickTime movies.

movie 1. Any time-related data, such as video, sound, animation, and graphs that change over time. 2. Apple's format for organizing, storing, and exchanging time-related data.

MPEG An international standard still under development by the Motion Picture Experts Group for compressing moving images. In its current incarnation, it has a high compression ratio but does not allow random access to individual frames.

MultiFinder A part of Macintosh system software older than System 7 that lets you open multiple programs simultaneously.

multimedia A presentation combining text or graphics with video, animation, or sound, and presented on a computer.

nested folder A folder you have put inside another folder in the process of organizing your disks.

network A collection of interconnected, individually controlled computers, printers, and other devices together with the hardware and software used to connect them. A network lets users share data and devices such as a printer.

NTSC The broadcast TV standard specified by the National Television Standards Committee and used in the United States, Canada, Mexico, Japan, and Korea. *Compare* **PAL** and **SECAM.**

PAL A broadcast TV standard based on the Phased Alternate Line method and used primarily in Western Europe.

parent folder The folder that contains a nested folder.

PhoneNet An inexpensive cabling system for connecting computers, printers, and other devices to make an AppleTalk network. Uses the built-in printer ports of Macintosh computers and the LocalTalk ports of many LaserWriter printers.

PICT Apple's standard format for individual graphic images.

pixel Short for picture element. The smallest dot that the computer and monitor can display.

pixmap A graphic image composed of color dots. *Compare* **bitmap.**

playback rate The number of frames shown per second in a motion picture.

PMMU Acronym for paged memory management unit. The part of the computer hardware that makes virtual memory possible.

poster A single image that represents a movie. If not explicitly designated for a movie, it is the movie's first frame.

PostScript font A text font designed for use with Adobe System's page description language, PostScript.

preview 1. A short (five seconds or less) excerpt of a movie, with an optional independent sound track. 2. A thumbnail of a PICT image.

printer port The socket on the computer's back panel marked with a printer icon. You can attach a printer or a LocalTalk connector to it.

program An application program, desk accessory, or other software. Consists of a set of instructions that tell the computer how to perform a task.

publisher Part of a document, a copy of which has been saved as an edition for other documents to subscribe to. *See also* **subscriber** and **edition.**

QuickTime A set of system software extensions, formats, image compressors, and user interface guidelines for consistent integration of movies in any application program.

RAM An acronym for random-access memory. Holds open programs, documents, and parts of the system software that have been copied from disk. The contents of RAM are lost when the computer is turned off.

random access The ability to immediately access a specific frame of a movie (more generally a specific unit of data) without going through frame by frame (unit by unit) from the beginning.

real time Happening at the rate at which events actually occur.

ROM Acronym for read-only memory. Holds much of the system software. The contents of ROM are set permanently during manufacturing and are not lost when the computer is turned off.

SECAM A broadcast TV standard (Sequential Couleur à Memoire) used in France, the Soviet Union, and Eastern Europe.

shared item A folder or disk you are using from another computer on your network, or a folder or disk of yours that someone else on the network is using.

SIMM An acronym for Single Inline Memory Module. A circuit board that contains RAM chips and snaps into a socket inside the computer.

spatial compression An image compression technique that removes data from an individual image by analyzing the data within that image. *Compare* **frame differencing.**

start-up disk A disk with the Finder and System files in its System Folder, which allows the computer to begin operation.

stationery A document which acts as a template and has set graphic or text elements which you created. Each time you open a stationery pad the original remains unchanged and you get a copy.

subscriber A copy of an edition that has been placed in a document and can be updated automatically when the edition is updated by its publisher. *See also* **publisher** and **edition.**

System extensions Software that expands the capabilities of system software. System extensions are normally stored in the Extensions folder of the System Folder.

System file A file containing sounds, language scripts, and system software. In System 7.0.1 and earlier, the System file also contains fonts and keyboard layouts. A System file must be in the System Folder for the Macintosh to start up.

System Folder The folder that contains the System file and Finder.

system software Software that supports application programs by managing memory and by communicating with input and output devices. Also known as the operating system.

TeachText A utility program supplied with the system software. It has limited word-processing capabilities, and can display, copy, and print graphics documents saved in the PICT format.

temporal compression Another term for **frame differencing.**

title bar The top part of some Macintosh windows that contains the name of the window. You drag a window by its title bar.

Token-Ring network A type of network commonly used by IBM computers.

TokenTalk Optional software included with System 7 that allows a Macintosh equipped with an extra-cost adapter to connect to a Token-Ring network.

track One channel of a QuickTime movie, containing video, sound, closed-captioned text, MIDI data, time codes, or other time-related data.

TrueType A font technology built into System 7 for displaying and printing text smoothly at any size and any resolution.

utility program Software that handles specialized tasks such as installing software, keeping track of appointments, blanking the screen, and so on.

virtual memory A System 7 capability that allows some Macintosh computers to increase the amount of memory available for opening programs and documents by using hard disk space as if it were RAM.

volume A disk, part of a disk, or other storage device that looks and works like a disk on the computer. Each volume has its own icon on the desktop. Hard disk and file servers are the most often referred to volumes.

Appendix C
Moving To System 7

If you're not already using System 7, should you? If you are already using it, would an older version of system software work better for you? These are the questions this appendix addresses. In addition, this appendix has complete installation instructions.

Equipment Requirements

All Macintosh models except the three oldest can use System 7. Only the original Mac 128K, the Mac 512K, and the Mac XL lack the necessary software in their ROMs (read-only memory). All other models can use System 7 if they have sufficient RAM (random-access memory) and disk space.

Memory requirements

System 7 requires at least 2MB of RAM. You can tell how much RAM your Macintosh has by choosing About the Finder from the Finder's Apple menu. In the dialog box that appears (Figure C-1), the Total Memory is the amount of RAM installed, reported in K instead of MB. To convert to MB, divide the number of K by 1024 (for example, 2048K ÷ 1024 = 2MB).

You'll need more than the minimum 2MB if you use large or complex application programs or if you want to open several programs at once. As a rule of thumb, figure you'll need 1MB more than you need with older system software. You'll enjoy System 7 more if your Macintosh has at least 4MB of RAM.

For advanced graphics, intensive page layout, and the like, go for more than 4MB of RAM. System 7's 32-Bit Addressing capability lets you use more than 8MB of RAM on most Mac models (not on a Classic, SE, Plus, or Portable). Be careful, though, because

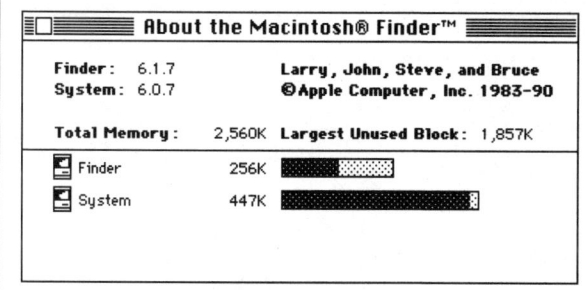

Figure C-1: Checking installed memory.

some software (particularly old versions) crashes if you turn on 32-Bit Addressing, and turning 32-Bit Addressing on and off frequently isn't practical because you must restart your Mac each time you do. For more information on compatibility, see Appendix A, and for more information on 32-Bit-Addressing, see Chapter 5.

Each Macintosh model has specific memory configuration rules. You can only install RAM modules, called SIMMs (single inline memory modules) in certain combinations on each model. Table C-1 has the basic rules; dealers and companies that sell SIMMs have complete details.

Table C-1: Macintosh memory configurations

Model	Permanent RAM (MB)	Expansion slots	Expansion card sizes	Total RAM (MB)
Plus, SE	0	4	256K, 1MB	1, 2, 2.5, 4
Classic	1	1	1MB, 1.5MB, 3MB	1, 2, 2.5, 4
Classic II, Performa 200	2	2	1MB, 4MB	2, 4, 10
LC, LC II, Performa 400	2	2	256K, 512K, 1MB, 2MB, 4MB	2, 3, 4, 6, 10
SE/30, II, IIx, IIcx	0	8	256K, 1MB, 4MB, 8MB, 16MB	1, 2, 3, 4, 5, 6, 8, 9*, 10*, 12*, 16*, 17*, 18*, 20*, 24*, 32*, 64*, 65*, 66*, 68*, 80*, 128*
IIsi	1	4	256K, 512K, 1MB, 2MB, 4MB, 16MB	2, 3, 5, 9, 17, 65
IIci	0	8	256K, 512K, 1MB, 2MB, 4MB, 8MB, 16MB	1, 2, 3, 4, 5, 6, 8, 9, 10, 12, 16, 17, 18, 20, 24, 32, 33, 34, 36, 40, 48, 64, 65, 66, 68, 72, 80, 96, 128
IIfx	0	8	1MB, 4MB, 8MB, 16MB	4, 8, 16, 20, 32, 36, 48, 64, 68, 80, 96, 128
IIvx, Quadra 700, Performa 600	4	4	1MB, 4MB, 8MB, 16MB	4, 8, 20, 36, 68
Quadra 900, 950	4	16	1MB, 4MB, 8MB, 16MB	4, 8, 12, 16, 20, 24, 28, 32, 36, 40, 52, 64, 68, 72, 76, 80, 84, 88, 96, 100, 112, 128, 132, 136, 148, 160, 192, 196, 208, 256
PowerBook 100, 140, 145, 170	2	1	2MB, 4MB, 6MB	2, 4, 6, 8
PowerBook 160, 180	4	1	2MB, 4MB, 12MB	4, 6, 8, 16
PowerBook Duo 210, 230	4	unknown	unknown	4 —24

*The SE/30, II, IIx, and IIcx cannot use 32-Bit Addressing and require the MODE/32 software (free from Apple dealers) to make use of more than 8MB total RAM for opening programs. The Mac II and IIx require special 4MB SIMMs. Specify your Mac model when ordering. The Mac II cannot use SIMMs larger than 1MB in bank A unless it has the SuperDrive upgrade.

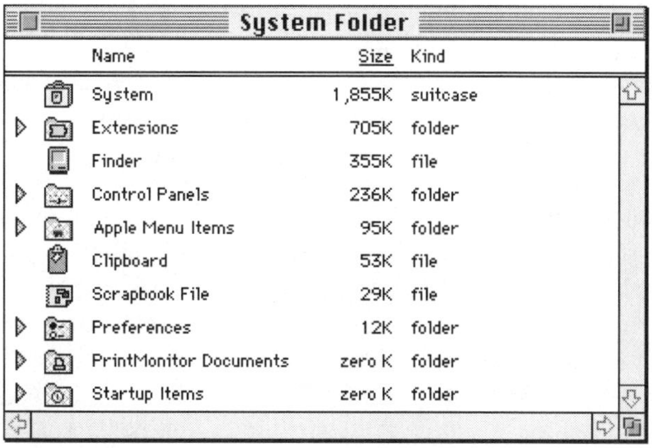

	Name	Size	Kind
	System	1,855K	suitcase
▷	Extensions	705K	folder
	Finder	355K	file
▷	Control Panels	236K	folder
▷	Apple Menu Items	95K	folder
	Clipboard	53K	file
	Scrapbook File	29K	file
▷	Preferences	12K	folder
▷	PrintMonitor Documents	zero K	folder
▷	Startup Items	zero K	folder

Figure C-2: A typical System Folder after installation.

If your Mac needs more RAM, you can have it upgraded by a trained technician or you can upgrade it yourself. Upgrading involves opening the Macintosh (tricky on a Plus, SE, SE/30, Classic, and Classic II), removing some small circuit boards called SIMMs, and snapping in other SIMMs. You must also cut a resistor on a Mac Plus or older SE and move a jumper on a newer SE. Complete instructions come with the SIMMs, which you can order by mail from a plethora of companies who advertise in *Macworld, Mac User,* and *MacWeek* magazines. If you don't want to do the upgrade yourself and you live in a metropolitan area, use the Yellow Pages to shop for the best deal. Memory prices are highly competitive.

Disk requirements

Not only do you need plenty of memory, you also need a hard disk to make practical use of System 7. A standard installation of System 7 with software and fonts for LaserWriter printing takes up 3.2MB of disk space, as shown in Figure C-2. Additional control panels, desk accessories, fonts, sounds, and extensions increase the size.

You can install a stripped-down System 7 on a 1.4MB high-density floppy disk, but you can't do much with it. Worse, System 7 on a floppy disk is pokey.

A hard disk is easy for anyone to plug into the back of a Macintosh. Like memory prices, hard disk prices are competitive. You can buy a good-quality new 40MB hard disk from someone other than Apple for less than the cost of an Apple external floppy disk drive.

Which System Version to Use

Compared to System 6 and earlier versions of system software, System 7 delivers a substantially improved Finder, virtual memory (on most Mac models), file sharing, multiple programs open at once, outline fonts, and other cosmetic improvements. With a growing number of applications, System 7 also delivers 32-Bit Addressing, balloon help, publish and subscribe, program linking, and user scripting. Detracting from these benefits are System 7's cost, memory and disk consumption, here-and-there slowness, and complexity. Any one of these drawbacks may dissuade you from using System 7 for awhile. But as more applications exploit System 7 and as Apple fixes its problems, you'll find saying no harder to do. The Macintosh community is not going back to System 6.

Who should use System 6

However, you should probably stick with System 6.0.7 (without MultiFinder) for its lower memory demands if you have a Mac Plus, SE, Classic, Portable, or PowerBook 100 with 1MB or 2MB of RAM. Moreover, Finder 7 is noticeably slow on those models, particularly on the Plus. (Apple does recommend System 7 for the PowerBook 100, but it works very well with System 6.0.7. All other PowerBooks require System 7.) Of course you can use System 7 on these models if you need its capabilities, for example file sharing on a network, or if you want to use application programs that require System 7.

You can continue using System 6 on a Mac SE/30, LC, II, IIx, IIsi, IIcx, IIci, or IIfx if you have application programs that won't work with System 7. Most of the programs you already have will work with System 7, but there are exceptions (for more compatibility information, see Appendix A).

Who should use System 7

With any Mac except a Plus, SE, Classic, Portable, or PowerBook 100, System 7 should be your first choice. System 7 is your only choice if you have a Mac Classic II, LC II, IIvi, IIvx, any PowerBook except the 100, any Quadra, or any Performa.

If you already have System 7.0 or 7.0.1, you may be interested in upgrading to System 7.1. It offers the special Fonts folder for more easily removing and installing fonts, WorldScript for extended foreign language support, and QuickTime for movies. System 7.1 is also somewhat faster and should be more reliable than Systems 7.0 and 7.0.1, which have proven to be more reliable than System 6. For many current System 7 users, these improvements are tempting but hardly compelling. The upgrade is worth the cost and bother only if you change your font setup frequently, work with foreign languages, or want to see QuickTime movies.

Who should use System 7 Tune-Up

If you use System 7.0 or 7.0.1, by all means install Apple's System 7 Tune-Up version 1.1.1. Do not install earlier versions of the Tune-Up, and do not install the Tune-Up with System 7.1, which includes all of the Tune-Up's benefits. The System 7 Tune-Up makes System 7.0 and 7.0.1 easier to use on Macs with less than 4MB of RAM, increases printing performance, and fixes minor bugs. You install it with Apple's standard, easy-to-use Installer program, which is included. The System 7 Tune-Up is available free or for a small charge from Apple dealers, user groups, and on-line services.

With Tune-Up installed, the system opens an application even if there is less memory available than the application prefers, as long as the memory available meets the application's minimum requirement. For example, Microsoft Excel prefers 1536K but will work (with some limitations) in as little as 512K. Without the Tune-Up in these situations, you see an alert such as "Microsoft Excel prefers 1536K of memory, 900K is available, do you want to open using available memory?"

If you try to open an application that needs more memory than is available, a tuned-up System 7 suggests quitting all programs with no open windows — or the largest open program, if all have open windows. Unfortunately, letting the Finder decide which programs to quit can hasten memory fragmentation (see "Memory Fragmentation" in Chapter 6). To avoid memory fragmentation, you must quit programs in the reverse of the order in which they were opened.

Without the Tune-Up, the system software's memory size (which includes the Finder) creeps steadily upward during a work session. The system software's memory size grows each time you open an application program, desk accessory, or control panel. More system software memory is released when you quit a program with the Tune-Up installed than without. You don't have to restart as often to bring system software's memory size back down.

When there is too little memory to print a document in the background, the tuned-up system asks if you wish to print the document immediately. You decide whether to wait while printing proceeds in the foreground or quit the program to make memory available for background printing.

If you aren't using a networked printer, file sharing, or other network services, you free up 100K to 125K of RAM by turning off AppleTalk in the Chooser and restarting your Mac. If you want to use network services later, you must turn AppleTalk back on and restart again.

The Tune-Up increases LaserWriter performance an average of 40 percent and StyleWriter performance almost 100 percent, especially with text documents. The ImageWriter speed also increases dramatically with a tuned-up System 7. One reason for faster printing on an ImageWriter or StyleWriter is better TrueType management. With Tune-Up the system software doesn't purge TrueType font images from memory as often as without. This improves text display speed on-screen as well as text printing speed.

The System 7 Tune-Up also speeds up file copying in the Finder about 20 percent. The new Chooser 7.1 that you get with Tune-Up is also faster; improvements are most noticeable in big networks with many zones and devices. Incidentally, the Installer program puts Chooser 7.1 into the Apple Menu Items folder, replacing the old Chooser. The Installer will not remove the old Chooser if you previously re-named it or moved it out of the Apple Menu Items folder.

Besides improving performance and memory use, the System 7 Tune-Up fixes several bugs. It eliminates the mysterious disappearance of files and folders from Finder windows (the Finder's Find command can usually locate the missing items). In addition, File Sharing Extension 7.0.2 eliminates bugs that could corrupt a shared file when two or more network users access the file at the same time. Tune-Up makes Print Monitor more reliable and less prone to crashing; allows certain fixed-size fonts to be purged from memory as needed; fixes occasional strange behavior of aliases in the Trash; and eliminates a problem that could hang the computer while using the serial ports during heavy file sharing activity. The System 7 Tune-Up also fixes a problem that sometimes causes the keyboard on a Mac Classic to stay asleep after startup until you move the mouse. System 7.0.1 also includes this fix.

Mixing Systems

Like many Macintosh users, you may have access to more than one Macintosh. Or your Macintosh may be connected to a network with others. In either scenario, some computers may use System 7 while others use older system software, such as System 6.

Mixed networks

All computers on a network must use compatible versions of LaserWriter software. Otherwise the printer must be reinitialized whenever someone uses it with a version of LaserWriter software incompatible with the previous user's version. Prior to System 7, this situation meant all computers on a network had to upgrade to a new version of system software at the same time. Not so with System 7.

System 7 and System 6 can coexist on the same network if all System 6 users install LaserWriter software version 6.1, 7.0, or higher. LaserWriter 6.1 comes with System 6.0.8 (in fact the only difference between System 6.0.7 and 6.0.8 is the version of LaserWriter software), and LaserWriter 7 comes with System 7. The LaserWriter software must be installed using the Installer program on the *Printing* disk (see Figure C-3); dragging the LaserWriter icon from that disk to the System Folder does not work.

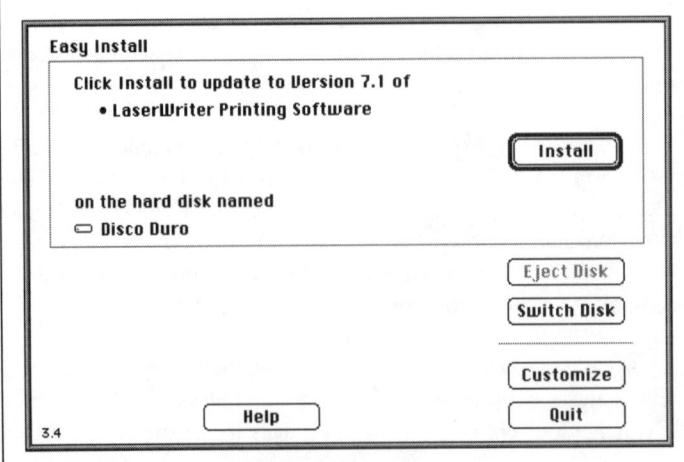

Figure C-3: Installing LaserWriter software.

Extra folders and missing items

When using disks with System 6 after using them with System 7, you may think icons that were on the desktop have mysteriously vanished. But they're only moved to the Desktop Folder. In System 7, the Desktop Folder is always open and its contents are displayed on the desktop, but the folder itself is invisible. In System 6, the Desktop Folder from System 7 becomes visible but its contents are concealed inside it instead of being on the desktop. System 7's Trash folder also becomes visible when you use older system software. It contains items you dragged to the Trash and left there (by virtue of not using the Empty Trash command) in System 7. If you were using System 7's virtual memory and restarted with System 6, a file named *VM Storage* shows up on the hard disk you had designated (with the Memory control panel) for virtual memory storage.

Desk accessories and fonts

Older system software sees individual desk accessories and fonts as meaningless documents with blank icons. To use fonts and desk accessories from System 7 with older system software, they must be in suitcase files. Then you must install the suitcase files using the Font/DA Mover program or utility software such as Suitcase II or Master Juggler.

Automatic rebuilding

When you restart your Macintosh with System 7 after using an earlier version of system software, the Finder may automatically rebuild its desktop database on the startup hard disk. In the process you lose all comments from Get Info windows.

Switching Systems

If you need to you can switch between System 6 and System 7, even if you have only one disk drive. To install a second System Folder on a disk, you must drag the System file out of the existing System Folder and rename that System Folder (perhaps naming it System Folder 6). If you don't remove the System file, the Installer program updates the existing System Folder instead of creating a new System Folder. After installation, move the old System file back to its previous location, either by dragging it there or by selecting it and choosing the Put Away command. Leave the older System Folder renamed. A System Folder can have any name; having a System file and a Finder together in the same folder qualifies that folder as a System Folder regardless of its name.

Apple ordinarily advises against installing two System Folders on the same disk because you can't be sure which will be used during startup, making it the active, or blessed, System Folder. You can use utility software such as System Picker (described in "System Management" in Chapter 13) to designate which System Folder will be the blessed one during the next startup or restart.

Where To Get System 7

If System 7 didn't come with your Macintosh, you once could get it by copying it free from a cooperative dealer or colleague; at low cost from user groups; or for the cost of downloading from on-line information services. As of October 1992 Apple plans to no longer license system software distribution through those means. You cannot legally copy System 7.1 from a friend or co-worker, although it is possible to do so successfully.

Now you must buy System 7 from Apple or a software reseller. The following packages are available:

- System 7.1 Update Kit

  - $34.95 in the U.S. direct from Apple (call 800-769-2775). Availability and pricing vary in other countries.

  - Intended for upgrading one Macintosh to System 7.1 from System 7.0 or 7.0.1. Can also be used with this book to upgrade from System 6 (see "How To Install System 7" later in this chapter).

  - Contains 1.4 MB (or 800K) installation disks, a QuickTime 1.5 disk, and the manual *System 7.1 Update Guide*. Does not include System 7 documentation or Compatability Checker software.

- System 7 Personal Upgrade Kit

  - $99 list price (commonly discounted) in the U.S. from Apple dealers and various software resellers. (Free to anyone who has a proof-of-purchase for version 7.0 of the Personal Upgrade Kit in the U.S. after September 1, 1992; call 800-769-2775). Available outside the U.S. from Apple dealers at prices that vary by country.

  - Intended for upgrading one Macintosh to System 7.1 from System 6.

  - Contains 1.4 MB installation disks, a QuickTime 1.5 disk, the Compatibility Checker software, and the manuals *Desktop Macintosh User's Guide* and *System 7 Upgrade Guide*. Apple's At Ease software is also included for a limited time.

- System 7 MultiPack

  - $499 in the U.S. from Apple dealers and various software resellers beginning November 30, 1992. (Free to anyone who has a proof-of-purchase for the System 7 Group Upgrade Kit in the U.S. after September 1, 1992; call 800-769-2775). Available outside the U.S. from Apple dealers at prices that vary by country.

  - Intended for upgrading up to ten Macs to System 7.1 from System 6.

  - Contains a CD-ROM with the 7.1 system software in several language versions, QuickTime 1.5, t, and the Compatibility Checker software. Also contains the same software on 1.4 MB disks, as well as the manuals *Desktop Macintosh User's Guide*, *System 7 Upgrade Guide*, and *Administrator's Handbook*.

All these packages include one year of toll-free telephone support. If you purchase a System 7 Personal Upgrade Kit or a System 7 MultiPack and do not have a 1.4MB SuperDrive (or equivalent), you can get 800K disks at no charge from Apple (call 800-769-2775).

Apple plans to offer a volume-purchase plan after November 30, 1992. If you need to upgrade a large number of Macs, call 800-769-2775 or your Apple representative.

You can pay for direct phone support from Apple ($2 per minute) even if you didn't buy Apple's official upgrade kit. Call 900-535-2775. In addition, you can listen to prerecorded answers to frequently asked questions by calling 408-257-7700. You pay only for the call.

How To Install System 7

Before installing System 7 or upgrading from System 7.0 or 7.0.1 to 7.1, you need to evaluate how compatible the current version of System 7 is with the software you already have — application programs, desk accessories, control panels, system extensions, hard disk software, and so on. Check your software with Apple's Compatibility Checker program (which comes with System 7) and the compatibility listings in Appendix A. For software not covered in either of those places, use the compatibility checklist in Appendix A. Decide which of your software needs upgrading right away, and spend the money for compatible versions.

System 7.1 consists of a minor rewrite of System 7.0 to add localization modules to the operating system. Localization is the ability to apply a local area's culture to software, especially in the case of the Macintosh operating system the ability to use non-Roman fonts throughout the Macintosh's system. Thus, changes were made to the operating system in those places where fonts make an impact—the Text Manager, the Resource Map, and in Fonts themselves. You must be aware of these changes to properly install System 7.1, since the compatibility of your existing system extensions and control panel devices, as well as some of your applications are affected by Apple's modifications.

The Compatibility Checker that comes with the new operating system enables you to check your system extensions, control panel devices, and application programs for compatibility with System 7.1. The Compatibility Checker is a HyperCard application which removes incompatible system utilities from your system folder and places them in a separate folder. The HyperCard stack checks all of your third-party software against its database of compatible software. Since this list is incomplete, it is only a starting point for the process of upgrading your software to System 7.1.

Before you can work effectively under System 7.1 you must decide which application programs you want to run under System 7.1 (and therefore spend the money to upgrade to System 7-compatible versions).

Note that not all vendors have finished developing 7.1 compatible versions of their software. You will have to contact each vendor and inquire as to the status of their upgrades.

For software not covered in either of those places, use the compatibility checklist in Appendix A. Decide which of your software needs upgrading right away, and spend the money for compatible versions. A good rule of thumb for compatibility is that the program should be compatible with System 7.1 if it was System 7-compatible and does not require the use of downloadable fonts to operate.

Any font management software (such as Adobe Type Manager or Type Reunion) will not be compatible as of yet and should be removed from your system folder.

In addition, check your virus protection software for compatibiity, since most virus checkers check for the system's resource map. Since the Resource Map has been re-designed, the anti-virus software may no longer be compatible. Call the software vendor to confirm compatibility before re-installing the anti-virus application.

Also note that the list of compatible programs supplied by Apple is not accurate and should not be trusted. Call or write each vendor to get up-to-date information on compatibility.

Preparing your Macintosh

After assessing the compatibility of your software, check that you have the proper amount of memory and storage space as described earlier in this Appendix. Reviewing your configuration prior to upgrading will save you time later, should you have problems with the process.

Always perform a full backup of your hard disk before changing systems to ensure the security of your data.

You shouldn't install System 7.1 directly into your current System Folder because you are starting with a fresh slate — a new system. Don't run the risk of carrying over minor damage that might exist in your current System Folder to your new system software. Take this opportunity to install a clean version of the system software. The following steps enable you to save your desk accessories, system extensions, sounds, and control panels, as well as remove fonts from the system that you want to use on the new system.

1. If you are updating from an earlier version of System 7, drag all of your PostScript printer fonts from the Extensions folder to an empty folder. Open your System file and drag all TrueType fonts, fixed-size fonts, and sounds to an empty folder named Resources.

   If you are upgrading from System 6, drag all of your PostScript printer fonts from the System Folder to an empty folder. Use the Font/DA mover to move all fonts and desk accessories from the System file to suitcase files, separating fonts and desk accessories into different suitcases. Put the suitcase files in an empty folder named *Resources*.

2. Drag all nonstandard control panels (called cdevs or control panel devices in System 6), system extensions (called startup documents and INITs in System 6), and preference and setting files and folders from the old System Folder to the Resources folder you used in step 1.

If you are upgrading from an earlier version of System 7, look for items to move in the Control Panels folder, the Extensions folder, the Preferences folder, and the System Folder itself.

If you are upgrading from System 6, everything is in the System Folder.

3. Drag the System file and Finder from your System Folder to the Trash and empty it. The Mac no longer recognizes that folder as a System Folder (that is, a folder containing startup information) despite its name.

4. Rename your System Folder so the new system software won't be installed in it.

Installing System 7

After saving the fonts, desk accessories, control panels, system extensions, preferences, and settings files and folders from your old System Folder, you are ready to upgrade your Macintosh to System 7. The following steps tell you what to do:

1. Insert the *Install 1* disk from the System 7.1 Upgrade Kit into your internal disk drive or open the *Install 1* file on the network. Figure C-4 displays the contents of the disk called *Install 1*.

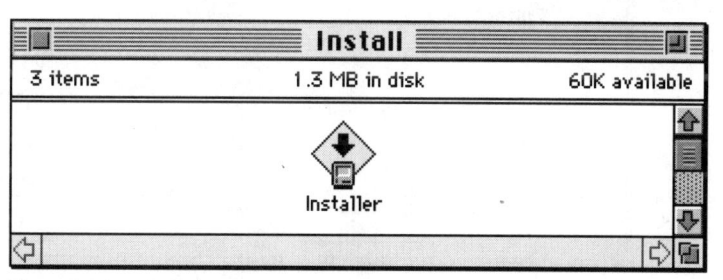

Figure C-4: Install 1 Disk.

2. Start the Installer program by double-clicking its icon in the Install 1 window. After a few seconds, the Welcome to the Installer dialog box appears, as shown in Figure C-5.

3. When the "Welcome to the Installer" notice appears, click the OK button to proceed. The Easy Install dialog box appears, as shown in Figure C-6. This dialog box identifies the disk on which the software will be installed, describes what will be installed, and asks you to decide whether you want to install the complete system or only portions of the system.

Figure C-5: Welcome to the Installer program.

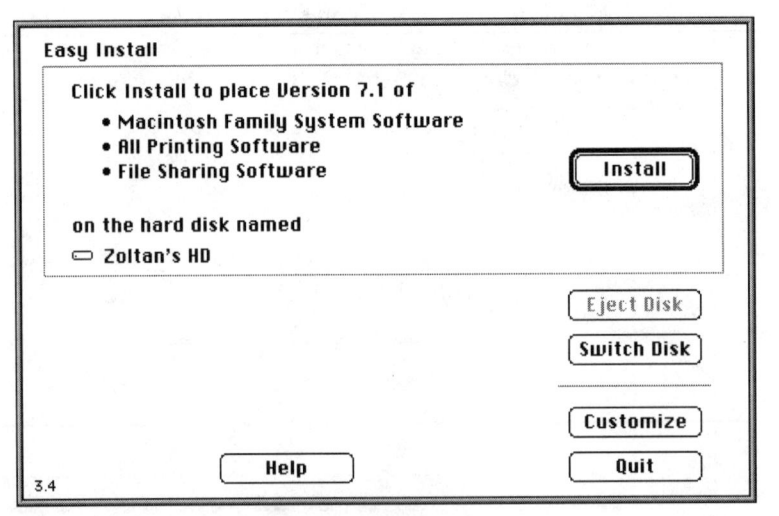

Figure C-6: Easy Install performs a full installation.

4. Make sure the hard disk displayed is the one you want to install the software on. If you have more than one hard disk, you can switch disks by clicking the Switch Disk button.

5. Click the Install button if you wish to install all parts of System 7, or click the Customize button if you want to install only portions of the System.

If you click Install, the Installer installs a version of the system software that works on all Macintosh models, software for all Apple printers, and network software for file sharing.

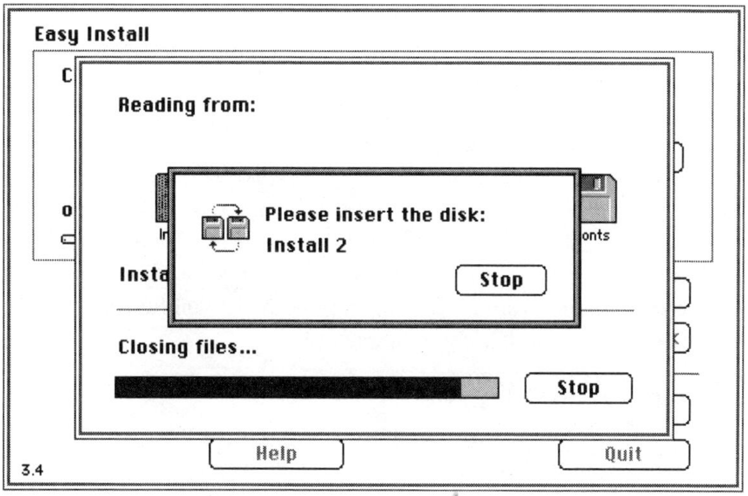

Figure C-7: Insert the requested disk.

If you click Customize, the Custom Installation dialog box appears, listing all available components of the system software. Scroll through the list and select the items you want to install. If you select one item, the Installer displays a detailed description of it. If you select multiple items, the Installer lists the first few by name. To select multiple items, press Shift while clicking each item. Be sure to select software needed for your printer and your network.

6. The Installer commences to instruct you to insert the upgrade kit disks into the Macintosh until the installation is complete, as shown in Figure C-7. You insert all disks except the Disk Tools disk for a full installation. For a customized installation, the system informs you of the disks you need. If you are installing from a network, these disk-insertion requests do not appear.

7. When the Installer finishes, it asks you if you want to quit or restart the Macintosh. Restart to begin using System 7.

8. After restarting with System 7, update the new System Folder with items from your old System Folder, if any.

If you saved the fonts, desk accessories, control panels, system extensions, preferences, and so on from your old System Folder as instructed in the previous section, drag them to the System Folder icon (not the System Folder window). The Finder puts them where they belong. Note, however, that the Finder does not place preferences or settings files in the Preferences folder. You can try dragging them there yourself, but old application programs may not find them there.

If you did not follow the instructions in the previous section, the Installer installs System 7 over your old system software. It puts all your fonts in the Fonts folder, control panels in the Control Panels folder, system extensions and printer software in the Extensions folder, and desk accessories in the Apple Menu Items folder. It leaves all preferences and settings files and folders loose in the System Folder.

If your Macintosh will not restart

If you installed System 7.1 by overwriting your System 6 or 7 System Folder and your Macintosh will not restart, try to restart your Macintosh with all system extensions off by pressing Shift until the Welcome to Macintosh message appears. Then follow the instructions in "Troubleshooting a Conflict" in Chapter 4 to resolve a possible conflict among your system extensions. When you find an incompatible extension, contact its publisher about upgrades.

Recovering disk space

You can recover some disk space after installing System 7 by removing fonts, control panels, and desk accessories. Depending on your needs, you may be able to do without Easy Access (for people who can't type with two hands or who need to move the mouse precisely from the keyboard), CloseView (a magnifying glass for the vision impaired), Map (a longitude/latitude map of the world), and if you work on a solitary Macintosh, Users & Groups, Sharing Setup, and File Sharing Monitor (all used by file sharing). If you choose the Easy Install option, you can also remove printer extensions from the Extensions folder for printers you never use. For example, if you only use a StyleWriter, you do not need the LaserWriter or ImageWriter extensions.

Using desk accessories

You do not have to keep desk accessories on the Apple menu to use them with System 7. You can remove a desk accessory from its suitcase and use it like an application program. Placing items on the Apple menu (by putting their icons in the Apple Menu Items folder) simply makes them easily accessible. For more information, see "Your Own Apple Menu" in Chapter 5.

Some desk accessories, such as spell checkers and art effects, require special installation procedures to work with System 7. Contact the software publisher to get installation instructions or upgrades for System 7.

Index

—A—

About the Finder command, 347
About This Macintosh command, 152
 See also TattleTale (utility program)
access privileges. *See* file sharing; networks
active programs, 27-28, 73
active window, 8, 339
"address error" error message, 78
Adobe Type Manager (ATM), 118, 175
AFC Helmet Icons (icon library), 302
Agfa Compugraphic, 186
AKA (utility program), 291, 292
Alarm Clock, 133
alarms
 with Alarm Clock, 133
 sounding with CClock (utility program), 303, 305
alert box, 339
alert messages
 from background programs, 75
 See also warnings
Alias Assassin (utility program), 291, 292
AliasBOSS (utility program), 291, 292
Alias Director (utility program), 291, 292
aliases
 advantages of, 161-162, 270
 for CD-ROM folders, 170, 260
 changing, 163-164
 changing original items, 164-165
 of control panels, 142
 creating, 162-163
 finding original items, 165-166
 for floppy disks, 260
 for folders, 270

how to use, 11-13, 166-172
on desktop, 167-168, 260
removing, 161, 164, 259-260
of Trash, 260
utilities for enhancing, 291-292
"The alias 'FileName' could not be opened, because the original item could not be found." message, 165
"The alias 'FileName' could not be opened...The problem has now been corrected." message, 162
AliasZoo (utility program), 291, 292
Amsallem, Thierry, 238
analog data, 339
Anchor Stuff (utility program), 305, 306
animation, with QuickTime extension, 229
AppDisk, 292, 294
Apple Animation compressor, 237
Apple events, 243-244, 339
 and program collaboration, 46
Apple File Exchange, 339
Apple Graphics compressor, 237-238
Apple logo, in item names, 139
Apple menu, 339
 alises in, 166
 customizing, 138-141
 for opening items at startup, 24-25
 tips for using, 272-273
Apple Menu Items folder, 120
Apple Photo compressor, 237
Apple Raw compressor, 238
AppleScript, 46
AppleShare, 122, 189, 190, 213, 339
 setup, 34-35

AppleTalk, 193, 201-202, 339
Apple Video compressor, 237
Application menu, 28, 73-75, 339
   desk accessories in, 132
   tips for using, 272-273
application programs, 339
   checking for System 7 compatibility, 311-338
   making aliases for, 162-163
   utilities for accessing, 294, 304
   See also programs; troubleshooting
Applicon (utility program), 294, 298
archiving functions, with DownLine utility, 305
arrow keys, navigating in directory windows, 68
At Ease, 47, 109-113
   for enhancing network security, 216
ATM (Adobe Type Manager), 118, 175
audio compact disks, utility for playing, 302
Aurora (utility program), 300, 301
auto scroll, 339
auxiliary folders, 126

— B —

background copying, 339
background operations, 75
background programs, 28
"bad F-line instruction" error message, 78
"bad SANE opcode" error message, 79
balloon help, 36-37, 70-73
BCS.Mac (Boston Computer Society Macintosh User Group), 290
beeps
   from background programs, 75
   in System file, 116, 117
   See also sounds
BeepSounds (utility program), 302
Before Dark (utility program), 294-295, 298
BeHeirarchic (utility program), 303, 305

Berkeley Macintosh User Group (BMUG), 290
"Binary-Decimal Conversion package not present" error message, 78
"BitEdit not present" error message, 78
bitmapped fonts, 340
bitmaps, 340
Bitstream Inc., 186
blank icons, 279
blank spaces, in item names, 127, 139
Blindfold (utility program), 295, 298
BMUG (Berkeley Macintosh User Group), 290
bomb alert box, 77, 279-280
borders, around Save or Save As dialog boxes, 20
Boston Computer Society Macintosh User Group (BCS.Mac), 290
Brightness control panel, 143
bulletin boards, 210-211
   See also file sharing; networks
BunchTyper (utility program), 293, 294
"bus error" error message, 78

— C —

Calculator, 134
calendar, setting with General Controls control panel, 56, 145
capturing, 340
Carpetbag (utility program), 295, 298
CARP (utility program), 302
Casady & Greene Inc., 186
CClock (utility program), 303, 305
cdevs, 22, 121, 142, 340
CD-ROM
   aliases for folders, 170, 260
   file sharing, 196
   for movies, 229
checkboxes, 340
checkmarks, as used in this book, 7
Chicago font, 283

"CHK error" error message, 78
Chooser, 134, 340
    for AppleTalk, 193
    enhanced, 31-32
    for file sharing, 32-33, 213-214
clipboard functions
    alias for, 166-167
    with Scrapbook, 137-138
clock, displaying with CClock (utility program), 303, 305
clock desk accessory, 133
close box, 8
Close command, on desk accessories' menus, 132-133
CloseView control panel, 143
codec, 340
collapsing folders, 82
Color Alias (utility program), 298, 299
ColorBoard (RasterOps), 238
Color control panel, 8-9
Color Hard Disk Icons (icon library), 302
colors
    advantage of, 55
    Aurora utility for enhancing, 300
    for desktop patterns, 57-58, 271
    for icons, 62-63, 257, 263-266
    for icons with Ikon VII (utility program), 304, 305
    for monitors, 147-148
    on menus, 64-65
    for windows, 8, 50
    for windows components, 60
Command-key combinations, 68-69
CommentKeeper (utility program), 293, 294
comments
    preserving for old icons with Get Info command, 64
    preserving with CommentKeeper (utility program), 293, 294

Compatibility Checker, 311-312, 336-337, 355
compatibility issues
    lists of products with compatibility ratings, 312-335
    and old icons, 64
    testing with Compatibility Checker, 311-312, 355
Component Manager, 232-233, 340
components, 232, 340
compressing, graphics, 48, 234, 236-238
compression algorithm, 236, 340
compression ratios, 236, 340
compressors, 340
control panels, 141-143, 340
    caution on including in Startup Items folder, 121
    making aliases for, 162-163
    tips for using, 271-272
    troubleshooting, 127-129, 280-281
    Brightness, 143
    CloseView, 143
    Date & Time, 143-144
    Easy Access, 144-145
    Extension Manager (utility for activating), 299
    General Controls, 145
    Keyboard, 145
    Map, 145-147
    Monitors, 147-148
    Mouse, 149
    Numbers, 149
    Portable, 149
    PowerBook, 149
    Sound, 149
    Startup Disk, 150
    Text, 150-151
Control Panels folder, 121-122, 141
    improved, 22-23
Control Tower (Simple Software), 251
copy-and-paste operations, 43-44, 270

copying
- aliases, 164
- in background, 41-42
- desk accessories, 24
- between documents, 43-44
- fonts, 261

copyrights
- to publicly distributed software, 289
- and restrictions on file sharing, 198
- and restrictions on video reuse, 238
- symbol, 286

"couldn't find hierarchical menu's parent" error message, 79
"couldn't load CDEF" error message, 79
"couldn't load MBDF" error message, 79
"couldn't load WDEF" error message, 79
Create Publisher command, 219-220
currency symbols, setting with Numbers control panel, 149

customizing
- Apple menu, 138-141
- desktop, 56-58, 283-285
- icons, 10-11, 62-64, 102-104
- with stationery pads, 37-38
- System 7, 359

Custom Killer (utility program), 303, 305

—D—

DAL (Data Access Language), 122, 251, 254, 340
DAL Preferences, 123
DAM (Data Access Manager), 44-46
databases, accessing from System 7, 251-254
Date & Time control panel, 143-144
DBMS (database management systems), 251, 341
dead keys, 134
decimal separators, setting with Numbers control panel, 149
dedicated file servers, 190

deleting
- aliases, 161, 164, 259-260
- custom icons with Custom Killer utility, 303
- files and folders with Obliterate utility, 297
- fonts, 179-181
- items from Apple menu, 25

deselecting, 341

desk accessories
- advantages of, 131-132
- aliases for, 162-163
- caution on including in Startup Items folder, 121
- icons for, 23-24
- opening and exiting, 132-133
- opening with Carpetbag utility, 295
- tips for using, 270-271
- using like application programs, 360
- Alarm Clock, 133
- Calculator, 134
- Chooser, 134
- Key Caps, 134-136
- Note Pad, 136
- Puzzle, 136-127
- Scrapbook, 137-138

desktop, 341
- aliases on, 167-168, 260
- and At Ease restrictions on, 47
- blank icons on, 279
- choosing, 66-67
- customizing, 56-58, 271, 283-285
- organizing with At Ease, 47, 109-113
- switching drives from, 19
- uncluttering, 281
- utilities for handling, 292-294, 298

Desktop button, 19-20
desktop databases, 97-98, 279, 341
Desktop folder, 125
Desktop Remover (utility program), 298, 299
"Device Manager error" error message, 78

diacritics, with Option-key combinations, 134-136
dialog boxes, 341
   shaded, 60
   utilities for enhancing performance, 300-301
diamond symbols, in item names, 127, 139
digital data, 341
digitizing, 341
   with QuickTime extension, 229
dimming, 341
directories, *See also* folders
directory dialog boxes, 65-70, 341
   aliases in, 168
   improved, 19-21
   tips for using, 269-270
Discolour (utility program), 293, 294
Disk Cache, 31, 155-156, 276, 341
"Disk Initialization package not present" error message, 78
disks
   aliases for, 162-163, 169
   Locksmith utility for locking or unlocking, 293
   recovering space on, 360
   start-up, 345
"divide by zero" error message, 78
documents
   aliases for, 11, 162-163
   labeling, 15-17
   opening by dragging icons, 40-41, 69
   sharing by means of aliases, 170-171, 275
   sharing with publish and subscribe operations, 43-44, 217-227, 345
DownLine (utility program), 305, 306
dragging the mouse, improved, 39, 341
drag selecting, 341
Drive7 driver software (Casa Blanca), 159
drivers, 159, 341
drives, switching from desktop, 19
Dropple Menu (utility program), 303, 305
DTPrinter (utility program), 295, 298

—E—

Easy Access control panel, 144-145, 271, 341
Easy Alias (utility program), 292
editions, 217, 221, 341
   updating, 226
   See also publish and subscribe operations
electronic mail system, with MailSlot utility, 305
Empty Trash command, 42-43, 269
error messages, interpreting, 77-80
"error type *n*" error message, 78
Escapade (utility program), 301
Escape key, for canceling directory dialog, 69
EtherTalk, 123, 191, 341
exiting
   desk accessories, 132-133
   interrupting with Shutdown Delay utility, 297
expanding folders, 82
expansion cards, 341
expansion card sizes and slots, by model of Macintosh, 348
Extension Manager (utility program), 128, 299, 300
extensions, troubleshooting, 127-129
Extensions folder, 122-123

—F—

Farallon PhoneNet, 191, 273, 344
files, 342
   sharing. *See* file sharing
   utilities for handling, 292-294, 295, 301
"The file server is closing down in *n* minutes" message, 195
file servers, 342
   accessing with aliases, 13
   advantage of dedicated, 32, 190
file sharing, 32-35, 189-190
   access, 194, 198-203, 212-215
   access control, 204-211, 216

activating, 195-198
with aliases, 171-172
and automatic document updating, 43
and bulletin boards, 210-211
by data access, 251-254
by linking programs, 46-47, 243-250
and cartridge or disk switching restrictions, 278
closing down or disconnecting, 195, 212, 215
monitoring activity, 211-212
optimizing, 198
with publish and subscribe operations, 43-44, 217-227, 345
tips for optimizing, 273-275
See also networks

File Sharing Extension, 122
File Sharing folder, 123
File Sharing Monitor control panel, 34-35, 198, 211-212
"file system map inconsistent" error message, 78
Find Again command, 18
Find command, 85-86
   enhancements, 18-19
   searching by labels, 15, 16
Finder 7 Menus! (utility program), 295, 298
Finder, 342
   and At Ease system extension, 109-113
   background operations, 98-99
   copying from, 41-42, 98-99
   desktop database, 97-98
   folder organization, 81-84, 125-127, 266-268
   icons, 10-11, 62-64, 102-104
   keyboard shortcuts, 40
   out of memory, 276
   renaming from, 92-96
   selecting from, 92, 96-97
   stationery pads, 100-101
   System folder placements, 125, 267
   tips for using, 266-268
   Trash disposal and Clean Up, 105-108
   utilities for enhancing, 293, 294-298
   views, 14, 87-90, 268
   window handling, 17-18, 84, 90-91, 267-268
Finder Help, 123
Finder Palette (utility program), 295-296, 298
Finder Preferences, 123
Finder Shortcuts option, 36
finding, specifying criteria for, 18-19
Find Next command, 268
Find Original button, 165
Find Pro II (utility program), 295, 298
fixed-size fonts, 173-174, 342
"floating point coprocessor not installed" error message, 79
floppy disks
   aliases for, 260
   utility for spotting bad sectors, 293
Folder Bolt (Kent-Marsh), 216
Folder Icon Maker (utility program), 296, 298
folders
   aliases for, 11, 162-163, 169
   auxiliary, 126
   caution on including in Startup Items folder, 121
   collapsing and expanding, 82
   labeling, 15-17
   nested, 38-39, 81, 161, 344
   opening by clicking, 69, 82
   opening with Save button, 21, 68, 69
   parent, 344
   proper contents of, 125-127
   sharing. *See* file sharing
   utilities to enhance, 293, 296, 302-305
   vanishing with mixed System 6 and System 7, 353
   viewing organization of, 13-14, 81-84
   See also directories; System folder

Font/DA Mover, 120, 178, 342
font families, 177
fonts
   adding or removing, 179-181
   aliases for, 162-163
   Carpetbag utility for opening, 295
   changing default (with It's Your Default utility), 296
   choosing, 176-177
   combining types of, 181-182
   duplicating, 261
   fixed-size, 173-174, 342
   installing, 25-26
   PostScript, 118, 175-176
   in suitcase files, 119-120, 179, 261, 297, 353
   TrueType, 174-175, 182-187, 346
   variable-size, 26, 175
   viewing samples of, 177-178
Fonts folder, 118-120, 178
   reorganized, 25
"Fonts need to be stored in the Fonts folder..." message, 179
"Force *program* to quit?" warning, 79, 280
Force Quit button, 79
foreign languages. *See* multiple languages
formats, 342
fps (frames per second), 230, 342
fragmentation of memory, 154-155, 277
frame differencing, 236, 342
frame rates, 342
frames, 342
Freeware, 289-290
   lists of, 291-307
Frontier (Userland), 46, 251
full motion, 342

—G—

games
   Puzzle, 136-127, 270
   with QuickTime, 229
General Controls control panel, 56, 145
generation loss, 342
Get Info command
   for finding alias originals, 165
   preserving comments for old icons, 64
grabbing, 342
graphics, compressing with QuickTime extension, 48
grayscale monitors, 342
grouping
   files by type with Put Away (utility program), 293, 294
   files with Scale (utility program), 293, 294
   users of networks, 202-203
   windows with ZoomBar utility, 301

—H—

HAM (Microseeds), 141
hard disk
   aliases on, 171-172
   required for System 7, 50, 349
   specifying for system startup, 150
Hard Disk Toolkit driver software (FWB), 159
Helium (utility program), 303, 305
help
   with balloon help, 36-37, 70-73
   with Helium (utility program), 303, 305
Help menu, 71
Hide Balloons command, 36, 70
Hide Others command, 75, 76, 267

hiding
  balloons, 36
  borders, 222
  icons, 295
  non-active program windows, 75, 76
  windows, 29, 267, 272
highlighting, of icons, 63, 64
hot spots, 294
"How many minutes until the sharing is disabled?" message, 195
Hypercard
  memory required by, 153-154
  producing sounds, 117
  scripting, 251

— I —

IAC (interapplication communication), 243, 342
icons
  for active program, 27, 28
  for aliases, 164
  blank, 279
  in colors and gray, 9-10, 257, 263-266
  customizing, 10-11, 62-64, 102-104
  for desk accessories, 23-24
  for file sharing privileges, 197, 198, 199, 200, 203, 208
  for folders, 262, 263
  for fonts, 177
  hiding with Blindfold utility, 295
  for network control panels, 192
  on Apple menu, 24
  renaming, 11, 258-259
  for shared files or folders, 214
  shrunken, 10
  for stationery pads, 37
  tips for using, 257-266
  used in this book's margins, 3
  utilities to enhance, 302-305

Ikon VII (utility program), 304, 305
"illegal instruction" error message, 78
Image Compression Manager, 232, 342
ImageWriter system extension, 122
inactive windows, with gray borders, 59
INIT, 342
insertion point, 343
  setting to flash with General Controls control panel, 145
installing
  sound and fonts, 25-26
  System 7, 355-360
"International Utilities not present" error message, 78
Interrupt switch, 79, 280
items
  dragging with Dropple Menu utility, 303
  opening from Apple Menu Items folder, 120
  opening upon system shutdown, 299
  opening upon System 7 startup, 120-121
  selecting in multiples, 17
  See also documents; folders; programs
It's Your Default (utility program), 296, 298

— J —

JPEG standard, 343
Just Click (utility program), 304, 305

— K —

keyboard
  adjusting with Easy Access control panel, 144-145, 341
  changes with System 7, 285-287
  navigating from, 20-21, 67-69
  pushing buttons from (Escapade utility), 301
  See also key combinations

Keyboard control panel, 67, 117, 145
keyboard equivalents
    of copy-and-paste commands, 270
    for directory dialog boxes, 68, 269
    for Finder operations, 108-110
Keyboard menu, 49
keyboard shortcuts, 40
    Finder 7 Menus! utility for changing, 295
    for Finder window, 40
Key Caps, 134-136, 271
Key Repeat Rate setting, 67, 145
kilobytes, 343
Kilroy (utility program), 301
K (kilobytes), 343

— L —

labeling, documents, folders and programs, 15-17
Label menu, 15-16
Labels control panel, 17, 271
Largest Unused Block, 154
LaserWriter system extension, 122, 282
Last Edition Used (alias), 123
latitude and longitude, setting for your Macintosh, 145
Letraset, 186
lines, drawing as separators in Apple menu, 140
linking, programs, 46-47, 243-250
Linotype-Hell Co., 186
"List Manager not present" error message, 78
list views, customizing, 14-15
LocalTalk, 189, 343
    establishing networks, 191
location (latitude and longitude), setting for your Macintosh, 145
Locksmith (utility program), 293, 294
lossless compression algorithm, 236, 343
lossy compression algorithm, 236, 343

— M —

MacDraw Pro, 121
Macintoshes
    as dedicated file servers, 190
    memory configurations by model, 348
    memory usage displays, 152
    movie-capable, 229, 230
    preparing for System 7 installation, 356-357
    restarting, 79
    and settings for Disk Cache, 155-156
    settings for Portables and Powerbooks, 149
    user groups, 290
    using 32-bit addressing, 156-157
    utilities for, 289-290, 291-306, 346
    See also control panels; keyboard; monitors; mouse; speed considerations; System 7
MacProject (Claris), 247, 250
MailSlot (utility program), 305, 306
Maintain Adornment command, 224
Make Alias command, 12, 163
Map control panel, 145-147, 271-271
Massini, Fulvio, 238
mathematical operations
    with Calculator, 134
    copying into Calculator, 270
MAXIMA (Connectix), 157
MB (megabytes), 343
megabytes, 343
memory, 343
    Disk Cache, 31, 155-156
    fragmentation of, 154-155, 277
    freeing by quitting programs, 121, 276-277
    increasing, 29-31
    managing, 151-155
    partitions for each application, 75
    penalties of file sharing, 34
    required for System 7, 50, 347-349
    size of aliases, 162

32-bit addressing, 29
tips for optimizing, 276-277
virtual, 29-31, 157-159, 346
warning of usage of Trash items, 42
Memory control panel, 29, 30
"Memory Manager error" error message, 79
menu, setting to flash with General Controls control panel, 145
"menu purged while in use" error message, 79
menus
    in colors, 64-65
    utilities to enhance, 302-305
messages
    from background programs, 75
    with SpeedMessage (utility program), 305, 306
    See also warnings
MIDI (Musical Instrument Digital Interface), 343
Mo' Better folders (shareware folder designs), 303
Mo' Fun Icons (shareware icon designs), 303
monitor, adjusting with Brightness control panel, 143
monitors, grayscale, 342
Monitors control panel, 147-148
    setting colors from, 61
Monotype Typography Inc., 186
MooV format, 230, 233-234
More Choices button (Find command), 18
Mount Alias (utility program), 305, 306
mouse, adjusting with Easy Access control panel, 144-145, 341
Mouse control panel, 149
Mouse Keys, 144, 271
mouse tracking, 343
Movie Controller, 343
movies, 343
    with QuickTime extension, 48, 229
Movie Toolbox, 231-232, 343

moving
    aliases, 163
    desk accessories, 24
MPEG standard, 343
MultiFinder, 73, 344
multimedia presentations, 344
multiple languages
    choosing, 117, 150
    and WorldScript language script system, 49, 118
multitasking
    with Applications menu for switching, 74-75
    challenges of, 27, 73-74

— N —

naming
    with cut-and-paste operations, 69
    duplicate copies, 41
    icons, 11
    items to affect startup order, 127-128
    labels, 17
    networks and Macs, 31
    See also aliases
nested folders, 38-39, 81, 161, 344
network administrator, 190
Network control panel, 192-193
Network Extension, 122
networks, 344
    AppleTalk, 193, 201-202, 339
    automatic document updating, 43
    identifying your Macintosh, 194
    mixing System 6 and System 7, 352
    publish and subscribe operations, 218
    selecting and connecting, 191-193
    Token-Ring, 346
    TokenTalk, 123, 191, 346
    utilities to enhance, 305-306
    See also file sharing

Network Trash folder, 124
New Color Icons for System 7 (shareware icon designs), 303
New Folder command, 266-267
New User command, 200
Northwest Airlines, 239
Note Pad, 136
Now Utilities, 141
NTSC standard, 230, 344
Numbers control panel, 149
"numeric overflow" error message, 78

— O —

Obliterate (utility program), 297, 298
opening
   desk accessories, 132
   items from Apple Menu Items folder, 120, 138
   items upon System 7 startup, 120-121
   programs by clicking, 69, 295
Open Query command, and DAM (Data Access Manager), 44-46
Option-key combinations, 68-69, 134-136
outline fonts, 174
"out of memory" error message, 78
Overhead (utility program), 299, 300
Owner icon, 199-200
Owner Passwords, for file sharing/network access, 194

— P —

paged memory management units (PMMUs), 30, 157, 344
PageMaker (Aldus), 118, 178
PAL standard, 230, 344
parent folders, 344

passwords
   for file servers, 13
   for file sharing/network access, 13, 194, 200, 201, 213
   security for, 216, 274
patterns, for desktop, 56-58, 145, 283-285, 294
performance. *See* speed considerations
PhoneNet (Farallon), 191, 273, 344
PickTURE (utility program), 301
PICT format, 234, 344
pixels, 344
pixmaps, 237, 344
playback rates, 344
PMMUs (paged memory management units), 30, 157, 344
pointing hand symbol, as used in this book, 7
Portable control panel, 149
ports, printer, 344
posters, 344
PostScript fonts, 26, 118, 175-176, 344
Power Alias (utility program), 292
PowerBooks
   control panel, 149
   utilities to enhance, 306-307
Preferences folder, 123-124
previewing, 344
   files with PickTURE utility, 301
   movies, 235
printer drivers, 122
printer ports, 344
printers, utility for representing with icon, 295
printing
   Key Caps, 136
   See also fonts
PrintMonitor system extension, 122
privileges for file access. *See* file sharing; networks

programs, 345
    activating, 28
    activating by clicking, 69, 295
    activating with Just Click (utility program), 304, 305
    aliases for, 11
    background, 75
    finding authors of, 282-283
    labeling, 15-17
    linking, 46-47, 243-250
    reducing memory used by, 153-154, 276-277
    scripting, 251
    and sudden quits, 279
    See also application programs; compatibility issues; troubleshooting
publish and subscribe operations, 43-44, 217-227, 345
Publisher Options command, 223
publishers, 217, 219-220, 345
Put Away command, 269
Put Away (utility program), 293, 294
Puzzle, 136-127, 270
PwrSwitcher (utility program), 304, 305

— Q —

QuarkXPress, 121
queries, 252
    Open Query command, 44-46
query documents, 253-254
QuicKeys (CE Software), 251
QuickTime extension, 48, 122, 229-240, 345
quick tips, this book's icon for, 3
QuickView Studio (E-Machines), 238
Quit command, on desk accessories' menus, 132-133

— R —

RAM, 345
    by model of Macintosh, 348
    and Disk Cache, 31
    finding how much you have, 347
    for movies, 229, 230
    required for System 7, 50, 347-349
    and 32-bit addressing, 29
RAM disk, AppDisk utility for, 292
random access, 345
real time, 345
register users of networks, 200
remote access. *See* file sharing; networks
Remote Access control panel, 191-192
renaming
    aliases, 164
    icons, 11, 258-259
Rescued Items folder, 124, 269
ResEdit, 257, 283
Resolve, 247-250
restarting your Macintosh, 79
ROM, 345

— S —

SageSleep (utility program), 306, 307
"SANE error" error message, 78
"SANE not present" error message, 78
"SANE transcendental functions" error message, 78
Save-A-BNDL (utility program), 293, 294
Save As command, keyboard use in, 67-68
Save command
    creating new folders with, 21
    keyboard use in, 67-68
Scale (utility program), 293, 294

Scrapbook, 137-138, 271
    non-standard, 272
screen, magnifying with CloseView control panel, 143
scripting, programs, 251
scripts, for program collaboration, 46-47
scroll arrow, 8
scroll box, 8
scrolling
    by dragging items, 17
    in directory windows, 68
SCSI Startup (utility program), 299, 300
searches. *See* finding
SECAM standard, 230, 345
"Segment Loader error" error message, 78
Set Password button, 213
shading, for 3-D effects on window components, 59
shared items, 345
    aliases for, 170
    See also file sharing
Shareware, 289-290
    lists of, 291-307
Sharing command, 198
Sharing Setup control panel, 34-35, 194, 275
Show Balloons command, 36
Show Borders command, 222
Show Clipboard command, alias for, 166-167, 273
Shutdown Delay (utility program), 297, 298
Shutdown Items (utility program), 299, 300
Siesta (utility program), 306, 307
SIMMs (single inline memory modules), 345, 348
size box, 8
Slow Keys, 144, 271
sndConverter (utility program), 302
Sorenson, Don, 239

"Sorry, this item is not an alias (oops!). The problem has now been corrected." message, 162
sorting, list view items, 17
Sound control panel, 117, 149
    advantage of installing sounds in, 25
SoundExtractor (utility program), 302
sounds
    extra system alert, 272
    installing, 25-26
    making aliases for, 162-163
    saving with Scrapbook, 137-138
    utilities to enhance, 295, 301-302
    See also beeps
SparedDisk (utility program), 293, 294
spatial compression, 236, 345
special characters
    with Chicago font, 283
    in items names, 127
    keyboard equivalents, 286-287
speed considerations
    and Calculate Folder Sizes option (Views control panel), 268
    and Disk Cache, 31, 155-156, 276, 341
    and graphics image compression, 236-238
    and hiding windows, 272
    and memory used by programs, 153-154
    with multitasking, 27-28
    penalties of color windows, 62
    penalties of file sharing, 32
    when file sharing, 274
    See also memory; troubleshooting
SpeedMessage (utility program), 305, 306
SpinD (utility program), 306, 307
"stack collision with heap" error message, 78
"Standard File not present" error message, 78

Startup Disk control panel, 150
   SCSI Startup (utility program) for circumventing, 299
start-up disks, 345
Startup Items folder, 120-121
   aliases in, 167
   suppressing activation of, 285
Stationer (utility program), 294
stationery pads, 37-38, 100-101, 261, 345
   creating with Stationer (utility program), 294
Sticky Keys, 144, 271
StyleWriter system extension, 122
submenus, 140-141
   BeHeirarchic utility for creating, 303
Subscriber Options command, 223-224
subscribers, 217, 345
   See also publish and subscribe operations
suitcase files
   for older fonts and desk accessories, 119-120, 179, 261, 353
   utility for creating, 297
Suitcaser (utility program), 297, 298
switching
   cartridges when file sharing, 278
   drives from desktop, 19
symbols
   used in this book's margins, 3
   See also icons; special characters
System 6
   compared to System 7, 349-350
   utility for removing Desktop file, 298
System 7
   advantages of, 1, 50-51
   compared to System 6, 349-350
   customizing, 359
   hard disk required for, 349
   helpful utilities for transitioning from System 6, 298-300
   installing, 355-360
   Macintosh models for, 50
   memory required for, 347-349
   mixing with System 6, 352-353
   switching between System 6, 352-353
   where to find, 353-355
   See also compatibility issues; file sharing; Macintoshes; troubleshooting; utility programs
system extensions, 122-123, 280-281, 345
   Extension Manager utility for activating, 299
System file, 25-26, 116-118, 346
System Folder, 115-116, 346
   adding/deleting items in, 125-126, 127, 267
   aliases in, 168-169
   reorganized, 21-22
   specifying for next startup (System Picker utility), 299
System Picker (utility program), 299, 300
system software, 346
   reducing memory used by, 152-153
System 7 Tune-Up, advantages of, 350-352

—T—

Tab key, for alternating between or on windows, 68, 69
TattleTale (utility program), 297, 298
TeachText, 346
templates, sharing by means of aliases, 170-171
temporal compression, 346
Temporary Items folder, 124
Text control panel, 150-151
"The alias 'FileName' could not be opened, because the original item could not be found" message, 165
"The alias 'FileName' could not be opened...The problem has now been corrected" message, 162
"The file server is closing down in *n* minutes" message, 195

"These items need to be stored in special places inside the System Folder..." message, 125
third-party software. *See* application programs; compatibility issues; utility programs
32-bit addressing, 29, 156-157, 339, 347-348
thousands separators, setting with Numbers control panel, 149
3-D shading, of active window, 8
3-D window components, 58-59
tildes, in item names, 127
tiles, 294
time
   calculating difference betwen locations, 145
   and clock desk accessory, 133
   displaying with CClock (utility program), 303, 305
   setting with Date & Time control panel, 143-144
time zone, setting for your Macintosh, 145
title bar, 8, 346
Token-Ring networks, 346
TokenTalk, 123, 191, 346
Too Many Lawyers... (utility program), 299, 300
tracks, 346
Trash
   aliases of, 260
   emptying, 42-43
   on networks, 197, 275
   tips for handling, 268-269
Trash Chute (utility program), 297, 298
Trash folder, 124
TrashMan (utility program), 297, 298
Trash Selector (utility program), 297, 298
triangles, beside folder icons, 14, 82
troubleshooting
   after System 7 installation, 360
   caution on use of shareware and freeware, 290
   desk accessories, 24
   file sharing, 35, 278

fonts, 26, 278
HyperCard sounds, 26
items in special folders, 127-129
memory extensions, 31
multitasking, 28
old cdevs, 22
old preference files, systems extensions, 21
old screen fonts, 26
stationery pads, 37
System 7, 278-281
system errors, 77-80
undescriptive help balloons, 37
See also speed considerations
troubleshooting tips, this book's icon for, 3
TrueType fonts, 26, 174-175, 182-187, 346
   combining with fixed-size, 181-182
Tune-Up, advantages of, 350-352
24stv (Radius), 238

— U —

undocumented features, this book's icon for, 3
"unimplemented trap" error message, 78
"unserviceable interrupt" error message, 78
"unserviceable slot interrupt" error message, 79
user groups, 290
UserLand Frontier, 46, 251
Users & Groups control panel, 34-35, 198-203
   for linking programs, 246
Users & Groups Data File, 123
utility programs, 289-290, 346
   lists of, 291-306

— V —

variable-size fonts, 26, 175
Veronica Broadcasting, 239
VideoSpigot (SuperMac), 238

viewing
    font samples, 119
    items, 14-15
Views control panel, 14-15
virtual memory, 29-31, 157-159, 346
Virtual utility (Connectix), 157
virus protection
    for network users and file sharers, 216
    software compatibility with System 7, 356
Visage (utility program), 304, 305
VM Storage file, 159
volumes, 346

— W —

warnings
    programming with Alarm Clock, 133
    sounding with CClock (utility program), 303, 305
    this book's icon for, 3
    when discarding Trash, 42-43, 268
    See also alert messages
windows
    active versus inactive, 8
    in colors, gray or black-and-white, 8, 50
    customizing, 58-62
    hiding, 29, 267, 272
    improved in Finder, 17-18
    inactive with gray borders, 59
    utilities for enhancing performance, 300-301
    zooming, 17, 84
WindowWizard (utility program), 301
WorldScript language script system, 49, 118

— X —

Xs, as used in this book, 7

— Z —

zapParam (utility program), 299, 300
ZMakeAlias (utility program), 292
ZoomBar (utility program), 301
zoom box, 8
zooming, windows, 17, 84
Zync (utility program), 306, 307

Notes

Notes

Notes

Notes

Notes

Notes

Notes

Notes

Notes

Macworld Authorized Editions

Macworld Guide to Microsoft Word 5
by Jim Heid
Macworld magazine's "Getting Started" columnist

New from the bestselling author of Macworld Complete Mac Handbook

Learn the new Word the easy way with this *Macworld* Authorized Edition.

Highlights:
- Up-to-date for Word 5 — covers all new features
- With step-by-step instructions for mastering everyday word processing tasks
- FREE Illustrated Quick Reference Card includes keyboard shortcuts and type tips

$22.95 [$29.95 Canada]
ISBN: 1-878058-39-8
448 pages. Available now.

Macworld Authorized Editions

Macworld Networking Handbook
by Dave Kosiur, Ph.D.
Macworld magazine
Contributing Editor
and Nancy E.H. Jones

The *Macworld* Authorized Edition for anyone who manages Mac networks.

Highlights:
- The only practical, hands-on guide that explains Macintosh networking from the ground up
- Design, installation, and management of AppleTalk internets explained simply
- Expert advice on optimizing your network's performance
- Covers Apple-to-IBM, Apple-to-DEC networking

$29.95 [$39.95 Canada]
ISBN: 1-878058-31-2
600 pages. Available June.

Macworld Authorized Editions

Macworld Music & Sound Bible
by Christopher Yavelow

"Invaluable for anyone interested in music and sound on the Mac."
— Alan Kay, Mac Guru

Finally, the definitive guide to music, sound, and multimedia on the Mac.

Highlights:
- Covers the latest hardware, software, and techniques in music and sound
- With interviews and forewords written by industry notables including Herbie Hancock, Craig Anderton, Mark Lacas, Patrick Moraz, Morton Subotnik, and more
- Over 1400 pages crammed with everything you need to know about using music, MIDI, and digital audio in composition, performance, film, video, multimedia, and programming
- Over 500 illustrations and figures

$37.95 [$47.95 Canada]
ISBN: 1-878058-18-5
1400 pages. Available now.

Macworld Authorized Editions

**Macworld Guide To
Microsoft Works 3**
by Barrie A. Sosinsky

Highlights:

- Learn how to use all Works modules: word processing, database, spreadsheet, draw, charting and communications

- Expert tips on using Works in your business: spreadsheet and database publishing, using templates, and running Works on a network

- Special advice on using Works on the road with your PowerBook

$22.95 [$29.95 Canada]
ISBN: 1-878058-42-8
433 pages. Available now.

Other Macintosh Titles from IDG

Macs For Dummies
by David Pogue

Highlights:
- The light-hearted, "Dummies" approach modified specifically for the Mac user
- How to get the basics done without the techno-babble
- Evangelist-free Mac: cuts through the hype and shows you how!

$16.95 [$21.95 Canada]
ISBN: 1-878058-53-3
336 pages. Available now.

Future *Macworld* Titles

Macworld Guide To Microsoft Excel
by David Maguiness

Build spreadsheets quickly with this Macworld Authorized Edition to Excel 4.

Highlights:
- Crunch numbers easily with this quick start guide to Excel — task-by-task instructions make it simple
- Use the straightforward tutorials and start working right away
- FREE Illustrated Quick Reference Card
- Tabbed for easy look-ups

$22.95 [$29.95 Canada]
ISBN: 1-878058-40-1
448 pages. Available November.

Macworld Authorized Editions

Macworld Complete Mac Handbook
by Jim Heid, *Macworld* magazine's "Getting Started" Columnist

The most complete guide to getting started, mastering, and expanding your Mac.

Highlights:

- Loaded with tips and techniques for using the Mac and Mac software better
- For beginners or seasoned veterans
- FREE *Macworld* System 7 Reference Card!

$26.95 [$35.95 Canada]
ISBN: 1-878058-17-7
576 pages. Available now.

Macworld Read Me First Book
Edited by Jerry Borrell, *Macworld* magazine's Editor-in-Chief

Macworld's experts recommend the best hardware and software configurations and offer start-up advice.

Highlights:

- A friendly and authoritative guide for first-time users
- With sections from *Macworld* magazine's most popular experts
- Optimize hardware and software to meet your individual needs

$22.95 [$30.95 Canada]
ISBN: 1-878058-19-3
336 pages. Available now.

BMUG *A Computer User Group*

BMUG is a member supported non-profit organization dedicated to helping Macintosh users. Membership comes with two 400 page BMUG Newsletters (printed semi-annually), access to our FirstClass BBS with e-mail and file library, and the BMUG Helpline for technical advice and assistance. BMUG also makes educational products such as *Zen and the Art of Resource Editing–The BMUG Guide to ResEdit* and *The BMUG Guide to BBSes and Beyond,* a diffinitive source for info about e-mail and the InterNet. BMUG also has a huge library of publically distributable software available on 800K disks or on CD-ROM (The BMUG PD-ROM). A CD-ROM with over 500MB of QuickTime movies called The BMUG TV-ROM is also available.

One year membership $40

A year membership with BMUG gets you two of our semi-annual 400 page newsletters. access to our graphical user interface bulletin board system for an hour a day, and unlimited access by phone to our famous BMUG Helpline so you can get answers to all your technical questions!

System 7 Utilities $15

These 5 disks come with over one hundred System 7 specific utilities to help you use your Mac more effectively. These applications, Extensions and Control Panels will let you use System 7 to its absolute fullest. A must for any savvy Mac user.

Color Icons $15

These 5 disks are jam packed with over 2000 icons for your viewing pleasure, in color and black-and-white. With System 7 you can simply paste them on the items; with System 6 you may need to use ResEdit.

To order membership or disks call:
800-776-BMUG [2684]

FAX to: 510-849-9026 (VISA or MasterCard only)
Mail to: BMUG, 1442A Walnut Street #62, Berkeley, CA 94709-1496

International Data Group (IDG), and IDG Books Worldwide, Inc., an affiliate of IDG based in San Mateo, CA, are committed to directing the power of business and industry toward improving the environment.

▲▼▲

This book was printed on recycled paper, and can be recycled.

IDG BOOKS

Order Form

Order Center: (800) 762-2974 (7 a.m.–5 p.m., PST, weekdays)
or (415) 312-0650
Order Center FAX: (415) 358-1260

Quantity	Title & ISBN	Price	Total

Shipping & Handling Charges

Subtotal	U.S.	Canada & International	International Air Mail
Up to $20.00	Add $3.00	Add $4.00	Add $10.00
$20.01–40.00	$4.00	$5.00	$20.00
$40.01–60.00	$5.00	$6.00	$25.00
$60.01–80.00	$6.00	$8.00	$35.00
Over $80.00	$7.00	$10.00	$50.00

In U.S. and Canada, shipping is UPS ground or equivalent. For Rush shipping call (800) 762-2974.

Subtotal _____
CA residents add applicable sales tax _____
IN residents add 5% sales tax _____
Canadian residents add 7% GST tax _____
Shipping _____
TOTAL _____

Ship to:
Name _____
Company _____
Address _____
City/State/Zip _____
Daytime phone _____

Payment: ☐ Check to IDG Books   ☐ Visa   ☐ MasterCard   ☐ American Express
Card # _____   Expires _____

Please send this order form to: IDG Books, 155 Bovet Road, Suite 610, San Mateo, CA 94402.
Allow up to 3 weeks for delivery. Thank you!

BOB110292

Fold Here

Place
stamp
here

IDG Books Worldwide, Inc.
155 Bovet Road
Suite 610
San Mateo, CA 94402

Attn: Order Center / System 7.1, 2nd Ed.

IDG Books Worldwide Registration Card
Macworld Guide To System 7.1, 2nd Edition

Fill this out — and hear about updates to this book and other IDG Books Worldwide products!

Name _____

Company/Title _____

Address _____

City/State/Zip _____

What is the single most important reason you bought this book? _____
_____

Where did you buy this book?
- ❏ Bookstore (Name: _____)
- ❏ Electronics/Software store (Name: _____)
- ❏ Advertisement (If magazine, which? _____)
- ❏ Mail order (Name of catalog/mail order house: _____)
- ❏ Other: _____

How did you hear about this book?
- ❏ Book review in: _____
- ❏ Advertisement in: _____
- ❏ Catalog
- ❏ Found in store
- ❏ Other: _____

How many computer books do you purchase a year?
- ❏ 1   ❏ 6-10
- ❏ 2-5   ❏ More than 10

What are your primary software applications?
_____
_____
_____

How would you rate the overall content of this book?
- ❏ Very good   ❏ Satisfactory
- ❏ Good   ❏ Poor

Why? _____

What chapters did you find most valuable? _____

What chapters did you find least valuable? _____

What kind of chapter or topic would you add to future editions of this book? _____
_____

Please give us any additional comments. _____
_____

Thank you for your help!

❏ I liked this book! By checking this box, I give you permission to use my name and quote me in future IDG Books Worldwide promotional materials. Daytime phone number _____ .

❏ FREE! Send me a copy of your computer book and book/disk catalog.

Fold Here

Place
stamp
here

IDG Books Worldwide, Inc.
155 Bovet Road
Suite 610
San Mateo, CA 94402

Attn: Reader Response / System 7.1, 2nd Ed.